CCi
CORINTHIAN COLLEGES, INC.

Wordsmith

A Guide to College Writing

Pamela Arlov

Custom Edition

Taken from:

Wordsmith: A Guide to College Writing, Second Edition
by Pamela Arlov

Wordsmith: A Guide to Paragraphs and Short Essays, Second Edition
by Pamela Arlov

PEARSON
Custom Publishing

PEARSON
Prentice Hall

Cover images courtesy of Getty Images, Inc.

Taken from:

Wordsmith: A Guide to College Writing, Second Edition
by Pamela Arlov

Published by Prentice Hall
Upper Saddle River, New Jersey 07458

Wordsmith: A Guide to Paragraphs and Short Essays, Second Edition
by Pamela Arlov

Published by Prentice Hall

This special edition published in cooperation with Pearson Custom Publishing.

Printed in the United States of America

20 19 18 17 16 15 14

ISBN 0-536-85125-5

2004240176

LR/LD

Please visit our web site at *www.pearsoncustom.com*

PEARSON Custom Publishing

PEARSON CUSTOM PUBLISHING
75 Arlington Street, Suite 300, Boston, MA 02116
A Pearson Education Company

Contents

Chapter 30 Words Commonly Confused 505

Chapter 31 Capital Letters 515

Chapter 32 Apostrophes 527

Chapter 33 Quotation Marks, Underlining, and Italics 539

Part 1
Composition

1 The Writing Process

prewrite PLAN draft PLAN REVISE proofread DRAFT plan PREWRITE plan DRAFT revise PROOFREAD prewrite DRAFT revise REVISE plan PREWRITE proofread PLAN REVISE plan REVISE plan PROOFREAD plan PROOFREAD

Writing is not a single act, but a process composed of several steps. As with most processes—swinging a baseball bat, playing the clarinet, or surfing the Internet—it is sometimes easier to do than to analyze. When people try to analyze how they write, their descriptions of the process are uniquely their own. Yet from a sea of individual accounts, the same steps emerge.

One writer, Antonio, describes the process this way:

> Well, first, I need time to think. If I have a while before the paper is due, I never start right away. Some people might call it procrastination, but it works for me. After the ideas have had time to percolate, I sit at the computer and just start writing. I just let my ideas flow, good or bad. If that doesn't work, sometimes I try a more organized approach, jotting down an outline. It's all a part of finding my focus. Then, once I know what I want to say, I just write. I am a slow writer because I try to get it right the first time. But I never do. If I look at it the next day, I see where the holes are—where I've left out details. I'm bad about that. So my second draft is always better than my first. When I'm finished, I check to make sure my commas are in the right place and my grammar is okay. Then I'm ready to turn it in.

The Writing Process

Though everyone approaches writing a little differently, most people follow a process similar to the one just described. The writer in the example above may not be aware of it, but he is following all of the steps in the **writing process:** prewriting, planning, drafting, revising, and proofreading.

Prewriting

| ". . . first, I need time to think."

Prewriting covers a range of activity from casually thinking about your topic to going through a prewriting exercise to get your thoughts on paper. You will probably find yourself doing some form of prewriting throughout the writing process. When you are sitting at a traffic light and the perfect example to illustrate your point pops into your head, you are prewriting. When you realize that your paragraph isn't working the way you wanted and you stop to list ideas or figure out another approach, you are returning to the prewriting stage. Prewriting *is* thinking, and the more thought you put into your paper, the stronger it will be.

Planning

| "It's all a part of finding my focus."

Careful and thoughtful **planning** makes a paragraph easier for you to write and easier for your readers to read. Your plan may include a topic sentence, your statement of the main idea. Because it states the main idea, the topic sentence forms the cornerstone of your paragraph. Besides a topic sentence, your planning will probably include an informal outline. An outline can be as simple as a list of the points you will develop in a paragraph. Don't be afraid that planning will waste your time. Careful planning—or lack of it—always shows in the final draft.

Drafting

| "I just write."

Sometimes **drafting** is a quick process, with ideas flowing faster than you can get them down on paper. At other times, the process is slow and difficult. Your thoughts grind to a standstill and you become frustrated, thinking you have nothing to say. If you get stuck during the drafting process, don't quit in frustration. The creative process is still at work. What is happening to you happens to all writers. *Write through* the problem, or, if necessary, return to the planning or prewriting stage.

As you draft your paper, you should not worry about grammar, spelling, or punctuation. Stopping to look up a comma rule will only distract you. Concentrate on ideas and save the proofreading for later.

Revising

> "I see where the holes are."

In its Latin roots, the word *revising* means "seeing again." **Revising** is difficult because it is hard to see your work with the eyes of a reader. Writers often see what they *meant* to say rather than what they really said. Sometimes they take for granted background knowledge that the reader may not have. Because of these difficulties, it helps to put your draft aside for a day or so before trying to revise it. With twenty-four hours between writing and revising, you will see your paper more clearly. It is also helpful to ask someone else to look at your work—a friend, classmate, or relative. Ask the person to focus on the *content* of your paper rather than on grammar, spelling, or punctuation. Ask which ideas are clear and which ones need more explanation. Ask how well your examples illustrate your points. A reader's comments can help you see your paper in a new light.

One word of advice—if you don't know how to use a computer, learn. Writing multiple drafts is much easier on a computer. Once you learn to write on a computer, the paragraphs, essays, term papers, and reports you will write in college will look much less intimidating.

Proofreading

> "I check to make sure my commas are in the right place and my grammar is okay."

Proofreading is the final polish that you put on your paragraph. When you proofread, consider such things as grammar, spelling, and word choice. Replace vague words with specific words. Take out words that are not carrying their weight. Look at connections, making sure ideas flow smoothly from one sentence to the next. Because the stages of the writing process overlap, you have probably done some minor proofreading along the way. Before the final proofreading, set your paragraph aside for a while. Then proofread it once more to give it the luster of a finished piece.

An Important Point

If you go through the writing process expecting the steps to fall in order, like the steps involved in changing the oil in your car, you may think the process is not working. However, writing a paragraph is not a sequential process. It is a repetitive process, more like driving a car than changing its oil.

If you take a two-hundred-mile trip, the steps you follow might be described as "Turn on the ignition. Put the car in drive. Accelerate. Brake. Put the car in park. Turn off the ignition." Yet it is not that simple. During a two-hundred-mile drive, you repeat each step not once but several times, and you may even stop for rest or fuel.

Writing a paragraph works in the same way. You may list the steps as "prewrite, plan, draft, revise, proofread," but it is not that simple. You may change the order of the sentences as you write the first draft or correct a spelling mistake as you revise. Sometimes you repeat a step several times. You may even stop for rest or fuel, just as you do when you drive. Eventually, both processes will get you where you want to go.

Exercise 1 The Writing Process

Answer the questions below to review your knowledge of the writing process.

1. The five steps in the writing process are ___________, ___________, ___________, ___________, and ___________.
2. The "thinking step" in the writing process is called ___________.
3. The part of the writing process that involves correcting grammar and punctuation is called ___________.
4. Major changes would most likely be made during the ___________ step in the writing process.
5. True or false? The steps in the writing process often overlap. ___________

The Writing Process: Stephanie's Paragraph

The next section follows the development of one writer's paragraph from start to finish. In writing her paragraph, Stephanie went through several forms of prewriting, made two different outlines, conferred with members of her writing group and her instructor, and wrote two rough drafts. (Only the first of the two drafts is shown here because the final draft reflects all of the changes Stephanie made.) Before turning in her final draft, Stephanie also proofread the paragraph once from top to bottom and twice from bottom to top. Then she asked a member of her writing group to look over the final draft for any mistakes she had overlooked.

The steps that Stephanie goes through are steps that you will take as you learn the writing process. You will also share some of her frustrations. But like Stephanie, you will find that what seems difficult at first is attainable, one step at a time.

Stephanie's Assignment

Stephanie's instructor handed out a list of three paragraph topics. Stephanie chose to write on this one: "Write about a piece of music or art that has a message for you. Don't just describe the piece of music or art; tell your reader how it affected you."

Stephanie's instructor suggested that the students prewrite, then make an outline. Earlier, the class had been divided into writing groups of four or five people who would help one another during the term. The instructor suggested that the writing groups meet to discuss each student's outline. Then, students would write a rough draft to bring to individual writing conferences with the instructor.

Stephanie's Prewriting

In class, Stephanie did a form of prewriting called *freewriting*. (For more information on freewriting and other forms of prewriting, see Chapter 2.) In this prewriting, Stephanie did not worry about grammar or spelling, but focused on gathering ideas. Stephanie's prewriting is reproduced here without correction.

> I remember the day my art class went to an exhibit at the museum and I saw a piece of art — I don't know what to call it. Not a painting or a drawing, but something the artist had put together. Built. I was trailing behind the class and something just pulled me over into the corner where it was. It was just me and that piece of art, and when I lifted the curtain — Wow! I was so knocked out. I remember my art teacher used to talk about what art meant, and I never understood until that day. I felt all sorts of emotion. I think I'll go over to the Tubman this weekend and see if it's still there.

Later, Stephanie visited the museum and took the following notes:

> "Beauty Standard" by Ce Scott
>
> Black frame, masks placed at top & bottom. Each side has female figure tied at ankles, wrist, and eyes with golden cord. They have bodies like models — thin & beautiful. Masks are just blank — no real features. Frame has tiny words repeated over

and over "dark brown eyes big full lips flat wide nose." Velvet curtain — very mysterious hangs there. Golden tassels hang down. "Mirror" embroidered on. Card says "Lift the curtain to see the image by which each of us should be judged."

Stephanie's Rough Draft

Ce Scott's artwork Beauty Standard is a piece of art with a message. It hangs in the Tubman African American Museum. It has a black frame decorated with female figures bound at the wrists, ankles, and eyes with golden cord. They have bodies like models, thin and beautiful. At the center of the frame is a black velvet curtain embroidered with the word "Mirror." On the frame, in small writing are the words "dark brown eyes big full lips flat wide nose." A card beside the work invites the viewer to lift the cloth and see "the image by which each of us should be judged." Underneath is a mirror—not the one held up by society, but one that reflects the image of whoever looked into it. The message is that the only beauty standard you need to meet is your own.

Stephanie's Writing Group Meets

Next, Stephanie met with her writing group. A transcript of the portion of the session dealing with Stephanie's outline appears below.

Transcript: Writing Group Session,
Monday, September 7

Eddie: Okay, who's the first victim? Tran?

Tran: I don't want to go first. Stephanie?

Stephanie: I may as well. I think I need major help. (Stephanie passes out copies of her prewriting and rough draft, and the group reads silently.)

Tran: I like it. You have good grammar and spelling.

Stephanie: You're just saying that because I got you off the hook. You didn't have to go first. (Laughter.)

Kelly: I like it, too. But your prewriting is really different from the rough draft.

Stephanie: Yeah, the prewriting doesn't have much detail. I had to go back to the museum to look at the piece again because I had forgotten a lot.

Eddie: Yes, but I like the prewriting. I can tell you were really excited about the painting.

Stephanie: It's not a painting. I'm not sure what you'd call it.

Eddie: Whatever. But in the prewriting, I can tell it really had an effect on you. In the rough draft, the excitement disappears. It's just a description.

Kelly: Eddie is right. I mean, it's a good description, but it needs more of you in it.

Stephanie: Yeah, I see what you mean.

Tran: I chose the same topic, except I'm doing my paragraph on music. Anyway, I remember that the assignment said to tell how the music or art affected you.

Stephanie: That's right! I do need to put more of my reaction in there somehow. But won't that make it too long?

Kelly: Well, you heard what Dr. Pettis said. Plenty of support.

Stephanie: Okay, guys. Thanks. You've been a big help. Anything else?

Tran: Yeah. Will you help me with my grammar? (Laughter.)

Stephanie's Final Draft

Stephanie wrote a second rough draft. Then, she met with her instructor for a conference before writing her final draft. Stephanie's final draft appears below.

Beauty Standard

I always thought of art as something to hang on a wall, never as something that had a message for me. Then last fall, at the Tubman African American

Museum, I saw a piece of art called Beauty Standard by Ce Scott. It had a black frame decorated with female figures bound at the wrists, ankles, and eyes with golden cord. At the center of the frame hung a black velvet curtain embroidered with the word "Mirror." A card beside the work invited the viewer to lift the cloth and see "the image by which each of us should be judged." On the frame, in small writing were the words "dark brown eyes big full lips flat wide nose." The words made me think of the sixties slogan, "Black is beautiful." It was a statement of pride and at the same time a demand to be included. At the time, society's beauty standard was a white one. And even though ideas of beauty now include different races, so many people are still left out—the old, those who are overweight, and even those who are just average. Suddenly, I felt angry and a little afraid to lift the velvet curtain. I looked at the bound female figures and understood that society binds me, too. Hesitantly, I lifted the curtain. My own face, skeptical and a bit defiant, looked back at me. It was a mirror—not the one held up by society, but one that reflected the image of whoever looked into it. As clearly as if she were in the room, the artist was telling me, "The only beauty standard you need to meet is your own."

Stephanie's Approach to Writing—and Yours

Stephanie's final draft is the product of many hours' thought and work, and it is at least partly a result of her willingness to listen to the advice and comments of others.

Writing is a process of trial and error, and sometimes it feels like mostly error. Even experienced writers often find writing difficult, often wonder if they have anything worthwhile to say or the ability to say it. If you fear writing, even if you dislike it, you are not alone. But writing is a skill that improves with practice, and if you give it serious effort, you will amaze yourself. The following list, "Five Quick Takes on Writing," may help you put the task of writing in perspective.

* *Five Quick Takes on Writing*

1. Take it a step at a time. Writing is often a slow process, and it always requires thought.
2. Take it seriously. The ability to write clearly and well will benefit you academically, professionally, and personally throughout your life.
3. Take it easy. Don't expect yourself to be perfect.
4. Take it to the limit. Stretch the limits of your imagination. Refuse to limit yourself by labeling yourself a poor writer.
5. Take it with you. Writing is a vital part of the real world. Make it a part of your life.

Group Exercise 1 The Ideal Conditions for Writing

In a group of three or four, discuss the ideal conditions for writing. Think about questions such as these: What tools do you enjoy working with? Do you write best with music or in absolute silence? Do you like having others around or do you prefer to be alone? Do you need coffee or snacks when you write? Do you need room to pace or do you think best seated in front of a desk or computer? After each group member has contributed, see what differences and similarities exist among members of your group. Have a spokesperson report your group's findings to the rest of the class.

Writing for Right-Brained Writers

This section is for those of you who rebel at the idea of a step-by-step approach like the one described in this chapter and outlined in the writing assignment at the chapter's end. Although prewriting, planning, drafting, revising, and proofreading are identifiable steps in the writing process, there's no law that says everyone has to approach them in exactly the same way.

For some people, a step-by-step approach does not come naturally. These people have a thinking style that is most often called "right-brained" or "holistic." The human brain is divided into two halves, or hemispheres, and most people are wired to rely heavily on the left hemisphere—the half responsible for logical, sequential, step-by-step thinking. Some people, however, rely more heavily on the right half of the brain, the part responsible for seeing the whole, for thinking in images, and for flashes of insight.

The following questions may help you decide if you are a right-brained thinker.

1. If you were asked to analyze how you write, would your answer be "I don't know. I just do it"?
2. When you are required to turn in an outline, do you usually complete it *after* you have written the paper?
3. If you were asked to describe your usual prewriting technique, would you say, "I never prewrite"?
4. Do you often arrive at the right answer to math problems without following the steps?
5. Do you have a hard time getting detail into your writing?
6. Are you a "big-picture person" rather than a "detail person"?

If you answered "yes" to three or more of the questions above, you may have been seen as a rebel because you don't always follow a step-by step, conventional approach to your work. But the chances are that whatever other characteristics you possess, you are also a right-brained writer.

Right-brained people are often intuitive, seeing the big picture before others do. They have a strong creative streak. They sometimes grasp ideas easily without knowing why or understanding how. But unlike their persistent, list-making, left-brained brothers and sisters, right-brained people often have trouble with the details. Planning isn't in their natures, and they tend not to have systems or specific steps to rely on. Whatever the task is, they "just do it."

If you are right-brained, does that mean that the methods in this text won't work for you? No. They *will* work. But you may have to work at them a bit harder. Give them a chance. Don't count them out until you have had enough experience with them to determine whether they work for you or not.

There are other strategies you can use, too. Unlike more conventional methods, the following tips were crafted with you in mind. These ideas may give you the extra boost you need to harness your creativity and let your right-brained way of thinking work for you, not against you. If your thinking style is left-brained, read on anyway. There may be something here that you can use along with the logical, step-by-step approach that works so well for you.

Tips for Right-Brained Writers

Find your most creative time and use it for writing. Some people find that they are at their best in the mornings. Others find that their creative juices begin to flow around 9:00 or 10:00 P.M. Writing will be easier if you schedule it during your natural period of creativity.

Use your rough draft as your prewriting. Since you think in terms of the whole, you may find it easier to do a rough draft than to prewrite. Consider your rough draft a form of prewriting, to be extensively revised before you turn it in.

Give your brain an assignment. When you have writing to do, let your right brain work on it while you are doing other things. At the beginning of the day, for instance, look over the assignment for a few minutes. Then come back to it in the evening and reap the benefits of having worked on the topic subconsciously. Or think about your topic before you go to sleep at night, then write in the morning. This technique can work not only in prewriting but also in revising.

Realize that doing the grunt work is a necessary evil. Right-brained people are less likely to put in the time it takes to master the basics because doing so may be tedious and boring to them. They are also less likely to plan. But even the most brilliantly creative people need self-discipline. It's a hard lesson to learn, but mastering the basics is essential to creative work. Singers spend endless time on breath control and scales. Artists learn anatomy and basic drawing. It is those efforts that set them free to do their best work. The payoff in mastering the basics is that once you learn them, you can forget about them. They will be second nature. The same goes for planning. Once you have made a plan, you are free to do the creative work. Doing the grunt work now always pays off in more freedom later.

Make a commitment to writing. Many professional writers are right-brained and face the same resistance that you do. Invariably, they say that the only way they can maintain the extended effort it takes to write books, plays, or novels is to have a routine and to write every day.

Writing Assignment 1 Writing and You

Write a paragraph describing your attitudes toward writing. Use the following steps.

Step 1: Prewrite. Jot down a few of the words that come to mind when you think of writing. Think of any significant experiences you have had that have shaped your attitude toward writing. Consider your writing habits. Are you organized? Do you procrastinate?

Step 2: Plan. Look over your prewriting. Try to sum up your attitude toward writing in a single word or phrase, and then construct an opening sentence for your paragraph using that word or phrase. Use one of the sentences below, filling in the blank with your word or phrase, or construct your own sentence.

My attitude toward writing is ______________________________

______________________________.

When I think about writing, I feel ______________________________

______________________________.

My feelings about writing have always been ______________________________

______________________________.

Once you have constructed an opening sentence, decide how to organize your paragraph. A couple of possibilities are listed below.

1. Take a historical approach, describing the influences that have shaped your writing. Use chronological (time) order.
2. Try a step-by-step approach, describing what you do and how you feel as you go through a writing assignment.

Complete the planning stage by making an outline that briefly lists the points you plan to make in support of your opening sentence.

Step 3: Draft. Write out a rough draft of your paragraph. Focus on expressing your ideas rather than on grammar and punctuation.

Step 4: Revise. Read over your rough draft. Have you left out anything important? Is each idea clearly expressed? Does the paragraph flow smoothly? Is the sequence of ideas logical and effective? If possible, ask a classmate to look over your rough draft with the same questions in mind. Then revise your paragraph, incorporating any necessary changes.

Step 5: Proofread. Check your paragraph for mistakes in spelling, grammar, or punctuation. Look at each sentence individually. Then proofread once more. You have now completed all the steps in the writing process.

2

Preparing to Write

Q: What do spiders, heights, and enclosed spaces have in common with the ordinary item pictured below?

A blank sheet of paper

A: They sometimes inspire fear. Many people suffer from arachnophobia (fear of spiders), acrophobia (fear of heights), or claustrophobia (fear of enclosed spaces). Some people also develop a fear called "writer's block" when they are confronted with a blank sheet of paper or a blank computer screen. They fear that they will not be able to think of anything to say, or that if they do find something to say, it will be wrong. Writer's block happens to almost everyone at one time or another. It is not an indication of poor writing ability. In fact, writers who get writer's block are usually those who care about how they present themselves.

One of the best defenses against this kind of fear is prewriting. Prewriting is a playful "safety zone" that you can enter without fear. In prewriting, your purpose is to generate ideas, not to judge them, so you can't go wrong. Even if you don't have writer's block, prewriting can give your writing a jump-start.

Prewriting

Prewriting is the first step in the writing process. It is the act of sorting out your thoughts on a topic and finding out what you have to say about it. Depending on the assignment you are given, prewriting may also include narrowing your topic to a manageable size. Prewriting begins the moment you receive an assignment. Quietly, in the background, part of your mind begins to gather information. However, it usually takes a bit of effort to bring that information to the surface. The prewriting methods in this chapter can jump-start the writing process by helping you collect your thoughts on a topic and get them on paper.

Prewriting Methods

The aim of all **prewriting methods** is the same: to help you get ideas on paper. At this point in the writing process, it is not the quality of ideas that counts, but the quantity.

When you are ready to prewrite, sit at the computer or in a comfortable spot with pen and paper. Relax your mind and body, and remind yourself that prewriting is a playful exercise of the imagination and that it is okay to write down anything that comes to mind. As for the part of your mind that automatically jumps in to criticize what you think and say, give it some time off. Your purpose in prewriting is to put down every thought on your topic, no matter how ridiculous it seems. Later, you can discard what is not usable.

Some of the methods may feel awkward at first. But try them all. One will be right for you.

Brainstorming

Brainstorming, a listing technique, is one of the easiest prewriting techniques. To brainstorm, take a few minutes to list whatever comes to mind on your topic. Your purpose is not to censor or come up with the "right" items for your list, but to generate ideas.

Example

Here's how one writer, James, approached a brainstorming exercise on the topic "Describe a favorite holiday memory."

Last 4th of July — family reunion
Lake Sinclair
plenty of food
Aunt Mil's fried chicken
baked beans
over 100 relatives
Mo's girlfriend!
saw Grandaddy Bennett for the last time
paper checkered tablecloths
ants
kids running and screaming
fireworks over lake — color and noise
Jim stretched out in back seat asleep on the way home

When James looked at his prewriting, he was not sure he could use it all, but he knew he had captured some of the vivid images and important memories from his Fourth of July family reunion.

EXERCISE 1 BRAINSTORMING

Brainstorm on one of the following topics; then see if you have an idea for a possible paragraph.

1. the importance of money
2. a holiday memory
3. an unexpected kindness
4. being an outsider
5. a bad habit

Freewriting

Freewriting is nonstop writing on a topic for a set time. The point of freewriting is that your flow of words never ceases; your pen never stops moving. If you have nothing to say, repeat your last thought again and again until a new thought replaces it. Do not worry about spelling, about clarity, or about whether your thoughts are logically connected. Just write.

Example

Emily did the following freewriting when her instructor asked the class to write on the topic "Discuss one of your pet peeves and why it annoys you."

Let's see. Right now I am peeved about having to write about a pet peeve. Ha, ha! Seriously, I am an easy going person and do not get too upset over anything. I don't like telephone salespeople. I don't like loud commercials. I don't like my ex-boyfriend. I don't like people who are late. I don't like it when a class or meeting is held up because some people are late. Yesterday, in Freshman Orientation, we had a quiz and when it was time for class to start, the instructor said, "we'll just wait a minute or two in case someone else comes in." Excuse ME, but I made it to class on time. Why should I wait for someone who is late? I can think of plenty of other examples. Is my ten minutes up yet? No. The minister at our church always starts services on time and it doesn't matter how many people come in late but when my cousin got married the ceremony was supposed to be at 7 P.M and it did not start until 7:30. People just keep coming in, right up until about 7:25. I think spending a lot of money on a wedding is a waste — they should just buy furniture or something.

EXERCISE 2 FREEWRITING

Freewrite on one of the following topics; then see if you have a focus for a possible paragraph.

1. What is your pet peeve?
2. What is your favorite time of day?
3. Is honesty always the best policy?
4. What is your biggest complaint about college professors?
5. What can you tell about a person from the way he or she dresses?

Invisible Writing: A Computer Technique

Invisible writing is a freewriting technique especially for writing on a computer. Turn on your computer, and once you have a blank screen in front of you, type the words "Invisible Writing" at the top of the page. Then turn your monitor off or adjust the contrast button at the bottom of your screen until the words are no longer visible and your screen is completely dark.

Freewrite for five to ten minutes. It is especially important not to worry about spelling errors. With this method, you can hardly avoid them. At first, you may feel strange, even anxious, pouring your words into the dark computer screen. Soon, though, your fingers and your thoughts will fly.

EXERCISE 3 INVISIBLE WRITING

Do an invisible writing on one of the following topics.

1. taking chances
2. superstitions

3. television or radio commercials
4. driving habits
5. ending a friendship

Clustering

Clustering is a technique designed to boost your creativity by stimulating both hemispheres of the brain. The left hemisphere, or "left brain," is used in logical tasks that move in 1-2-3 order. When you count to ten, write a sentence, or make an outline, you use your left brain. Your right brain, on the other hand, specializes in tasks involving visual images and intuition. Since clustering involves both listing (a left-brain task) and drawing (a right-brain task), it allows you to tap both your logical side and your creative side.

To cluster, begin with a circled word—your topic. From there, map out associations. Some people branch ideas from the central word like quills on a porcupine. Others group ideas when they cluster, with smaller clusters branching out from larger ones. When this type of cluster is finished, it resembles a biology textbook's diagram of a molecule.

What your diagram looks like does not matter. In clustering, what matters is that you get your thoughts on paper using both images and words.

Look at the following examples of clustering.

Example

Brandon did his "porcupine" cluster on the topic "your chosen career."

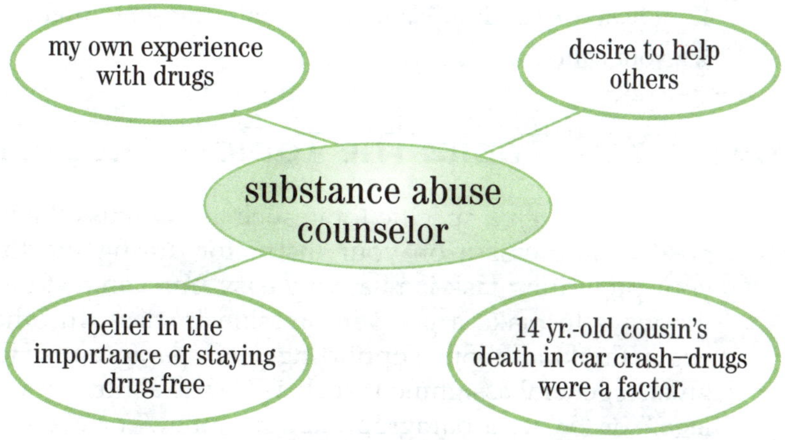

Example

Here is Kara's "molecule" cluster on the topic "Internet shopping."

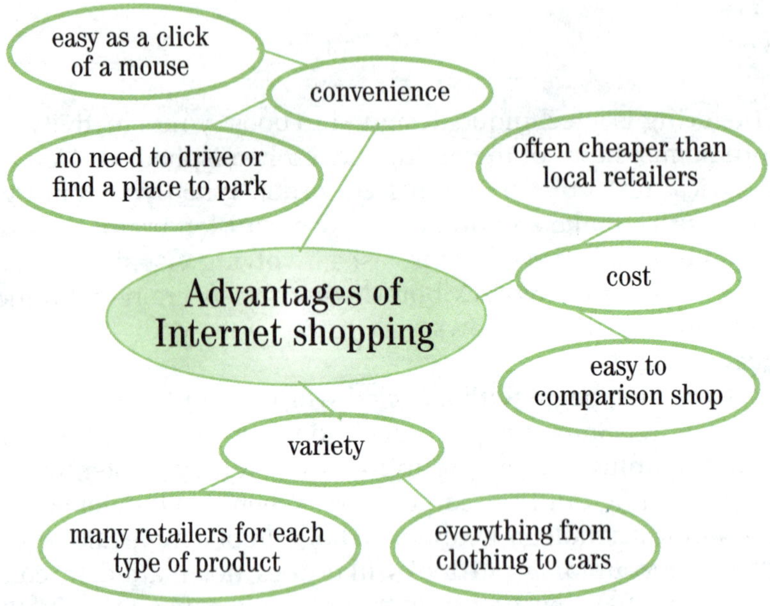

EXERCISE 4 CLUSTERING

Draw a cluster diagram using one of the following topics.

1. credit cards
2. your favorite sport
3. your best or worst date
4. advantages or disadvantages of public transportation
5. your eating habits

Narrowing Your Topic: The Topic-Subtopic Method

If you are given a specific topic such as "Discuss the best way to make a positive impression on your instructor during the first week of class," your prewriting task is relatively easy. You can just begin thinking about the ways to make a good impression in class. In other words, you can begin thinking about supporting your paragraph. However, if you are given a general assignment such as "Write about something related to college," or "Write a paragraph about money," or even "Write a paragraph about a topic of your own choosing," then your task is a much larger one. Entire books have been written about college, and the books and magazines about money take up considerable shelf space in any bookstore. Therefore, you need to narrow and focus the topic so that it is manageable in a single paragraph.

For some writers, narrowing a topic becomes a natural part of the prewriting process. Other prefer to narrow their topic in a separate step or series of steps.

One way to narrow a topic is with a simple method called the **topic-subtopic method.**

Steps in the Topic-Subtopic Method

Step 1: Write down the topic.

Step 2: List possible subtopics.

Step 3: Look over the list of subtopics and pick the one you are most interested in. This subtopic now becomes your topic.

Step 4: Repeat the process until you have narrowed your topic to an appropriate size for a paragraph.

In the example below, the writer has taken a general topic, "animals," through three narrowings. In the first narrowing, she has made a list of subtopics. From that list, she has chosen the subtopic "pets." From there, she will repeat the process until she has narrowed the topic to the right size for the paragraph she wants to write.

General topic	Subtopics	
animals	wild animals	
	endangered species	
	pets	← (new topic)
	farm animals	
	animals raised for food	
	working animals (seeing-eye dogs, police dogs)	

"Pets" is narrower than "animals," but it is still a very broad topic. The writer does a second narrowing, this time with "pets" as the general topic.

General topic	Subtopics	
pets	dogs	← (new topic)
	cats	
	how to bathe a pet	

Subtopics, continued

pampered pets
mistreated pets
exotic pets (snakes, hedgehogs, etc.)

Once the writer has decided on the topic "dogs," she decides to do a third narrowing of the topic:

Topic	*Subtopic*	
dogs	training	← (new topic)
	breeds	
	working dogs (drug-sniffing dogs, assistance dogs for blind)	
	feeding	

The writer decides to take the subtopic "training" and make it the subject of a paragraph. She is through with the narrowing process. Now, to flesh out the details of her paragraph, she does a brainstorming exercise. Her brainstorming follows.

Basic Training for Dogs

based on kindness and reward
no yelling or hitting
use food rewards
one trick or skill at a time
the basics — "down," "sit," "stay"
persistence and repetition
be consistent — don't say "down" one time and "get down" the next

Exercise 5 Narrowing a Topic

Take one of the following broad topics and narrow it to paragraph size, following the topic-subtopic method shown above. Take your topic through as many narrowings as are needed to bring it down to paragraph size.

1. the environment
2. alcohol
3. education
4. money
5. transportation

Outlining

Outlining is often the last step in the prewriting process. Once you have used one of the other prewriting methods, making an outline will take you one step further in the writing process. Forget about the formal outline with its Roman numerals, ABCs, and 123s. A short paragraph calls for a short outline. Your outline may be just a few words jotted on a page, or it may include a topic sentence and a brief listing of support. Below is Emily's outline of her paragraph describing her pet peeve.

```
Topic Sentence: I am an easygoing person, but it
annoys me when a meeting, class, or other event
does not begin on time because some people are
late.
   Freshman orientation class—quiz delayed because
     of people who were late
   Meeting with friends in restaurant—waited fifteen
     minutes to order until Kylie came.
   Cousin's wedding—delayed a half hour because of
     late arrivals.
   Summary sentence: Classes, meetings, and other
gatherings should not be arranged for the con-
venience of latecomers, but for those who care
enough to arrive on time.
```

Exercise 6 Outlining

Take one of the topics you have done a practice prewriting on and make an outline for a paragraph.

Journal Writing

Journals are "daily writings"—the word *journal* comes from *jour,* the French word for *day.* Journals are usually composed of informal writings on a variety of subjects. **Journal writing** allows you to experiment with the techniques you are learning in your writing class. In a journal, the only form of writing you should avoid is "diary mode." An "I-got-up-I-fed-the-dog-I-went-to-school" format makes for dull writing and even duller reading. Write about issues that matter to you. Tell your dreams.

Describe your grandfather's tool shed. Work toward detailed writing that follows a logical pattern.

Whether or not you receive credit for it in class, make journal writing a habit. Practice is the only thing that is guaranteed to make you a better writer. Courses and texts are of limited value without time spent alone with a word processor or pen and paper. If you think, "It won't matter. I'll never be a good writer," ask yourself this: How good a driver would you be if the only driving you had done was in a driver education course? You can be a better writer. Journal writing will start you on your way.

Journal Topics

1. What are some reasons for keeping a journal or diary?
2. If you had one day of your life to live over, which one would it be?
3. If you were cleaning out your mental closet, what would you most want to throw away?
4. Who is your role model? Why?
5. Is it better to have an assertive, in-your-face personality or to be laid-back and slow to show anger?
6. Other than food, water, and sleep, what *must* you have every day? Why?
7. If every job or career paid the exact same salary, what kind of work would you choose?
8. Discuss one item that fits this description: "It plugs into the wall, and I couldn't live without it."
9. If people had fur, what changes would take place in society?
10. If you had to live without television, how would you spend your extra time?
11. If you could have one talent that you do not now possess, what would it be?
12. If you could bring one fictional character to life (for whatever reason—to be your friend, to benefit humanity, or to solve a problem), who would it be?
13. If you could travel to any place in the world, where would you go?
14. Describe one effective method you use to reduce stress.
15. Describe the one place that, for you, is "heaven on earth."
16. What can you tell about people from the way they carry themselves—that is, the way they stand, sit, or move?
17. Is it better to have a wide circle of friends or just a few close friends?

18. Describe your general style of dealing with problems. Do you meet problems head-on, or do you hide your head in the sand and hope they will go away? Do you enlist the help of others, or try to solve your problems alone? Illustrate your journal entry with at least one example.
19. Which is more important, independence or security?
20. By the end of the twenty-first century, what change, development, or discovery would you most like to see? Why?

The Progressive Writing Assignment

How It Works

Begin by choosing one of the topics below; it will serve as the basis your first paragraph. In this chapter, you will complete prewriting for the paragraph. Throughout the next four chapters, each Progressive Writing Assignment will take you a step further toward a paragraph. By the time you have finished the final assignment, you will have completed all the steps in the writing process and will have a complete paragraph.

Progressive Writing Assignment: Prewriting

In this chapter, your Progressive Writing Assignment is a prewriting assignment. Choose one of the topics below—one you would like to write a paragraph about—and follow the instructions.

Topic 1: Discuss the results of taking a specific piece of advice from a friend or family member.

Tips for Prewriting

Prewrite on the topic, using one or several of the methods outlined in this chapter. As you prewrite, consider the different types of advice you have been offered: bad advice, good advice, advice that got you in trouble, or advice that cost you money. Consider the different people who have offered you advice. Taking a broad approach allows you to consider many different possibilities.

What Now?

After you have completed your prewriting, you should have more material than you will be able to use. To prepare for the next step in the Progressive Writing Assignment, choose piece of advice that you want to focus on in your paragraph.

Topic 2: Discuss your decision to attend college.

Tips for Prewriting

Prewrite on the topic, using one or several of the methods outlined in this chapter. As you prewrite, consider all factors that surround your decision. What are they? Some people are motivated to attend college by the expectations of family or friends. Some are trying to put the past behind them, while others are trying to fulfill lifelong ambitions. Some people arrive certain of success; other fear failure. Consider everything surrounding your decision to attend college: your reasons, your expectations, the reaction of friends and family, and your own hopes and fears.

What Now?

After you have completed your prewriting, you should have more material than you will be able to use. To prepare for the next step in the Progressive Writing Assignment, decide which ideas you want to focus on.

Topic 3: Discuss your greatest fear.

Tips for Prewriting

Prewrite on the topic, using one or several of the methods outlined in this chapter. Consider that fears sometimes have a strong basis in reality: A person whose parents and grandparents died young may have a fear of not living long enough to see her children grow up. Just as often, though, fears seem irrational. A person with a steady job and a comfortable home may fear being homeless. Write down your fears, rational and irrational, and try to decide what lies behind them. Consider also how you deal with your fears. Do you have a specific method for coping with them, or do you just live with them?

What Now?

After you have completed your prewriting, you should have more material than you will be able to use. To prepare for the next step in the Progressive Writing Assignment, decide which ideas you want to focus on in your paragraph.

Topic 4: Discuss types of stress experienced by college students.

Tips for Prewriting

Prewrite on the topic, using one or several of the methods outlined in this chapter. Everyone experiences stress from many sources, such as overwork, family problems, or even boredom. However, there are some kinds of stress that may be specifically associated with college. In this paragraph, you will write about some of the types of stress experienced by college students. Thinking about your own stress is a good starting point, but imagine the kinds of stress experienced by students who may not be like you: older students, working students, students who have children. What kinds of stress are common to all college students, and which are particular to certain groups?

What Now?

After you have completed your prewriting, you should have more material than you will be able to use. To prepare for the next step in the Progressive Writing Assignment, decide which types of stress you want to focus on in your paragraph.

3

Writing Paragraphs: Topic Sentences

A Silly Riddle

How is a topic sentence like a compass?

a. It always points to magnetic north.
b. It's useful on a hiking expedition.
c. It shows exactly where you are headed.

The riddle in the box above may be silly, but the comparison it makes is valid. A topic sentence *is* like a compass. It shows your reader exactly where your paragraph is headed, and it also helps to keep you on track as you write your paragraph. It gives **direction** to your paragraph.

Direction is one of four characteristics of effective writing that you will read about in this text and learn to develop in your own writing. Before exploring the topic sentence further, look at the four characteristics of effective writing introduced below.

Characteristics of an Effective Paragraph

1. **Direction** means that the paragraph has a strong topic sentence that states the main idea and sets the course that the paragraph will follow.
2. **Unity** means that the paragraph makes one main point and sticks to that point.

3. **Coherence** means that the ideas in the paragraph are logically connected and easy to follow.
4. **Support** means that the paragraph contains specific and detailed discussion of the idea stated in the topic sentence.

Direction: Shaping the Topic Sentence of a Paragraph

A topic sentence provides direction by stating the main idea of a paragraph and answering the reader's unspoken question, "What is your point?"

Functions of a Topic Sentence

A topic sentence does two things. First of all, it tells the *general topic* of the paragraph. Second, it makes a *specific point about the topic.*

Example

topic / specific point about the topic

✔ Carrying a homemade lunch instead of eating out has had unexpected benefits.

topic / specific point about the topic

✔ Knowing how to research using a computer is an essential skill in college.

specific point / topic

✔ There are many creative ways to hide thinning hair.

EXERCISE 1 ANALYZING TOPIC SENTENCES

In each of the topic sentences below, underline the topic and double-underline the specific point the writer is making about the topic.

1. Praise can be a powerful motivator.
2. Saying "no" is a skill that my brother Brian has never developed.
3. Talk shows on television are often offensive.
4. My willpower unravels at the sight of chocolate.

5. Some of my coworkers have little patience with machines.
6. Stromboli's Italian Grill is my favorite restaurant.
7. A successful letter of complaint has three essential elements.
8. My brother's fondness for loud music irritates the rest of the family.
9. The woman who lives next door is incurably nosy.
10. Poor organization can make studying difficult.

EXERCISE 2 ANALYZING TOPIC SENTENCES

In each of the topic sentences below, underline the topic and double-underline the specific point the writer is making about the topic.

1. Gossip can be hurtful.
2. Listening is difficult for some people.
3. Watching television is often a waste of time.
4. Finding time to exercise is difficult for me.
5. Peer pressure can weaken even the strongest will.
6. My experience working at the Burger Basket convinced me to avoid fast-food places.
7. Trying to find information on the Internet can be frustrating.
8. During the past year, my cola habit has gotten out of hand.
9. Gas prices vary in different parts of town.
10. My vacation will give me a chance to do some work around the house.

EXERCISE 3 COMPLETING TOPIC SENTENCES

Complete the topic sentences below. Underline the topic once. Then double-underline the point about the topic.

1. Taking an aerobics class ______________________________.
2. ______________________________ is something no home should be without.
3. In the morning, ______________________ helps me prepare to face the day.
4. ______________________________ is my favorite piece of furniture.
5. To avoid last-minute cramming for tests, ______________________.

EXERCISE 4 WRITING TOPIC SENTENCES

Write five topic sentences. Underline the topic once. Then double-underline your point about the topic.

1. ____
____

2. ____
____

3. ____
____

4. ____
____

5. ____
____

Writing Topic Sentences That Fit

A topic sentence also provides direction by precisely outlining the territory the paragraph will cover. A topic sentence that is *too broad* outlines more territory than a paragraph can comfortably cover. A topic sentence that is *too narrow* draws the boundaries of the paragraph uncomfortably small, usually by focusing on some fact that would make a good supporting detail but that does not lend itself to development.

Look at the following sample topic sentences on the subject "computers."

✗ Computers have changed modern society.

This topic sentence is too broad. It promises more than one paragraph can deliver. Think of all the ways computers have changed modern life: they have changed the way stores keep track of inventories, the way banks work, and the way groceries are checked out. They have created new jobs and made others obsolete. They have altered our ideas about what skills are essential and have raised new concerns about privacy and access to information. The topic "how computers have changed society" could easily be the subject of a book.

✘ My computer has a floppy drive and a CD drive.

This topic is too narrow. It tells the reader that the writer will discuss a specific computer, her own, and that the focus will be the computer's CD and floppy drives. While the sentence might work as a supporting point in a paragraph, it is too narrow to be a topic sentence. A topic sentence that is too narrow is a dead-end statement, a fact that does not invite exploration. A good topic sentence opens a door to discussion.

✔ A computer can link a person who is disabled or homebound to the outside world.

This topic sentence is neither too broad nor too narrow. Within this paragraph, the writer can discuss how a computer helps a disabled person to bank or shop online. She can tell how a computer links a homebound person to people and information sources around the world. The sentence opens a door to an area of discussion and exploration that is neither too narrow nor too broad to develop in one paragraph.

Exercise 5 Analyzing Topic Sentences

Each set of sentences below contains one topic sentence that is too broad, one that is too narrow, and one that would make a good topic sentence for a paragraph. In the blank to the left of each sentence, label it TB (too broad), TN (too narrow), or TS (topic sentence).

Set 1

_____ **a.** The functions of a bank are many and varied.

_____ **b.** Fees that banks charge seem to target lower-income customers.

_____ **c.** My checking account is with First National Bank.

Set 2

_____ **a.** My brother Simon often stays awake until 2:00 or 3:00 A.M.

_____ **b.** My brother Simon is a night owl.

_____ **c.** My brother Simon has different levels of energy at different times of the day, week, month, and year.

Set 3

_____ **a.** Ordering merchandise by mail has several advantages.

_____ **b.** I received a Land's End catalog in today's mail.

_____ **c.** Mail-order firms have been a vital part of American business for many decades.

Set 4

_____ **a.** Coping with my father's illness has been difficult for my family.

_____ **b.** Life has its ups and downs.

_____ **c.** Last year, my father had major surgery.

Set 5

_____ **a.** The commercials for Mercedes project a classy image.

_____ **b.** CNN and MSNBC are news channels.

_____ **c.** Television exerts a positive influence on American society.

EXERCISE 6 ANALYZING TOPIC SENTENCES

Each set of sentences below contains one topic sentence that is too broad, one that is too narrow, and one that would make a good topic sentence for a paragraph. In the blank to the left of each sentence, label it TB (too broad), TN (too narrow), or TS (topic sentence).

Set 1

_____ **a.** My cat has a marking on her back that looks like the number three.

_____ **b.** Training a dog to sit on command is a simple process.

_____ **c.** Pets are wonderful.

Set 2

_____ **a.** Housing costs vary widely across the United States.

_____ **b.** A one-bedroom apartment in the Aspen Forest apartment complex costs $570 per month.

_____ **c.** A first time homebuyer should consider several factors when searching for a home.

Set 3

_____ **a.** Gasoline stations have been a part of the American landscape for almost a century.

_____ **b.** In my grandfather's time, gasoline cost fifty cents per gallon.

_____ **c.** The gasoline station of my grandfather's time offered services that are unheard of today.

Set 4

_____ **a.** Requiring fingerprints of citizens who obtain drivers' licenses is a bad idea.

_____ **b.** Many laws are unjust and should be repealed.

_____ **c.** In some states, a driver's license must bear the driver's fingerprint.

Set 5

_____ **a.** Fish are fascinating creatures.

_____ **b.** My sister's angelfish is named Gabriel.

_____ **c.** An aquarium is like a small entertainment center for the home.

Group Exercise 1 Writing a Topic Sentence Exercise Confident? Go solo!

Have you had enough test *taking*? Form a test *making* team with two or three of your classmates and write an exercise similar to the one above. Choose three to five of the topics below, and for each topic, write a topic sentence that is too broad, one that is too narrow, and one that would fit a paragraph. Then trade tests with another group and see how your group's performance—as test makers and as test takers—stacks up to theirs.

Topics

1. books
2. garbage
3. beverages
4. music
5. schools
6. furniture
7. nature
8. people
9. food
10. television

Where Should a Topic Sentence Go?

If you look carefully at the paragraphs in textbooks, essays, and news stories, you will see that a topic sentence may appear anywhere in a paragraph. However, the most common position for a topic sentence is at or near the beginning of a paragraph. Placing the topic sentence at the beginning of a paragraph lets your reader know exactly where the paragraph is going and gives the impression that you have thought about the organization of your paragraph. And you *will* have thought about it. The very act of constructing a topic sentence places your focus on the main idea of your paragraph and helps keep you on track in supporting that idea.

Topic Sentence First

Placing the topic sentence first is often your best choice. A topic sentence conveys your main idea and provides a strong, clear opening for your paragraph.

Example

Since I began carrying a homemade lunch to my part-time job at the mall, I have discovered the benefits of brown-bagging. The most obvious benefit is that bringing a lunch from home saves money. At the mall's food court, the price of a sandwich and chips or a slice of pizza and a soft drink can easily approach five dollars. But for less than ten dollars, I can buy a six-pack of soft drinks, a loaf of bread, and enough pimento cheese and peanut butter to make lunches for a week or more. Another benefit of brown-bagging—an unexpected one—is that I feel less rushed. Before I started bringing a lunch, my thirty-minute lunch break was consumed by a mad dash to the food court to stand in line, find a table, gulp down my food, and rush back to work. Now, I take a leisurely lunch in the employee break room, reading a magazine as I eat. Usually, I have an extra fifteen minutes to read and relax or take a stroll around the mall's upper level. I also benefit from the improved nutrition of my homemade lunches. Turkey on whole wheat or even peanut butter and jelly from home is lower in fat and calories than a hamburger or slice of pizza from the food court. For me, brown-bagging means that a healthier wallet, a more relaxed lunch break, and improved nutrition are "in the bag."

Topic Sentence after an Introductory Sentence

Sometimes, you may wish to include background material before you state the main point of your paragraph. In these instances, condense the background material to one introductory sentence. After your introductory sentence, state the topic sentence.

Example

Baldness runs in my family, and at thirty-five, I have come to accept my hair loss. **But as my hairline receded over the years, I discovered several creative ways to hide thinning hair.** My first solution to baldness was to wear a hat. Baseball caps in summer and knit caps in winter were only the beginning. During an "arty" phase in my mid-twenties, I wore a beret, and in the back of a closet somewhere, I still have a dashing Indiana-Jones-style hat. Another method I used to hide my thinning hair was the "comb-over"—combing hair over a bald spot. In the earliest stages of baldness, the method worked well for me. But as my hairline receded further, I stopped using the comb-over. I had seen too many men who looked ridiculous with just a few strands of foot-long hair covering a completely bald dome. The best method I have found to hide thinning hair is the one I use now. I have shaved my head completely. Now, no one can tell whether I am bald by nature or by choice. Shaving my head has helped me to get over my embarrassment at being bald. I have finally come to realize that bald is beautiful.

Exercise 7 Finding Topic Sentences

One of the following paragraphs begins with an introductory sentence, while the other starts with the topic sentence. Underline the topic sentence in each paragraph.

Paragraph A

The glamour of Tyra Banks, Cindy Crawford, or Kate Moss may appeal to some, but my favorite models are not the ones who strut the runways for six figures a year. I like the real people who model the clothes in the Wal-Mart ads. In this week's Wal-Mart flyer, "Nellie, Associate" is modeling a red sweatshirt and matching sweatpants. She is not as thin or regal-looking as Tyra Banks, but I can tell her smile is real. She is looking up at Tequila, her daughter, who is modeling a powder-blue sweat outfit and reaching for her mother as she perches on the shoulders of "Calvin, Brother in Law of Nellie, Associate." On another page is "Brent, Tire and Lube Manager Trainee," a young man with a goatee and a shaved head. He wears a corduroy vest and a plaid shirt that looks ready to have its sleeves rolled up for some real work. In another section of the flyer, "Wendy, Customer Service Manager" models a cranberry-colored mock turtleneck. With her flying red hair, scrubbed, natural-looking skin, and ample frame, she doesn't look like a model. But a size-eighteen woman could look at the picture and have no doubt that she, like Wendy, would look really good in that top. The models in the Wal-Mart ads, real people who look good in real clothes, are much more appealing to me than the highly paid models whose only business is beauty.

Paragraph B

My brothers, Brad and Roy, are very different in their attitudes about money. Brad and his wife Lexie believe in living for today. They have a new house on the north side of town, a new sport utility vehicle, and a two-year-old Volvo. Their clothes are always designer labels in the latest fashions, and their home is a showplace of fine furniture. But they seldom have time to enjoy these things because they both work two jobs to pay off the massive debt they have accumulated. It is as though their possessions own them. My brother Roy goes a bit too far in the opposite direction. He puts every spare penny away for the future. Though he has a good job, he drives a thirteen-year-old car that rattles as if only habit is holding it together. He argues constantly with his wife, who simply wants decent clothes for herself and their children. Worse yet, he insists on buying nothing but practical gifts. I thought Andrea would divorce him when he gave her a hand-held vacuum for her birthday so that she could vacuum the inside of her car at home instead of taking it to the car wash. My two brothers agree on politics, football, and religion, but they will never agree about money.

Progressive Writing Assignment

Progressive Writing Assignment: Topic Sentence

If your instructor has assigned the Progressive Writing Assignment, you have already completed your prewriting for one of the topics below. In this chapter, you will complete your topic sentence.

Topics and Tips for Writing a Topic Sentence

The Topics

Topic 1: Discuss the results of taking a specific piece of advice from a friend or family member.

Topic 2: Discuss your decision to attend college.

Topic 3: Discuss your greatest fear.

Topic 4: Discuss types of stress experienced by college students.

Tips for Writing a Topic Sentence

- Decide on the points you will cover in your paragraph and the order in which you will present them. Then write a tentative topic sentence.
- Make sure that the topic sentence presents a specific topic and makes a point about that topic.
- Check to make sure that your topic sentence is not too broad. For example, for Topic 4, "Discuss types of stress experienced by college students," the following topic sentence would be too broad:

  ✗ Everybody experiences stress at one time or another.

  The sentence is too broad because the paragraph is not about "everybody"; it is about college students. Two better topic sentences are shown below:

  ✔ College students are prone to certain kinds of stress.

  ✔ College students most often experience stress related to academic performance and lack of time.

- Check to make sure that your topic sentence is not too narrow. For example, for Topic 2, "Discuss your decision to attend college," the following topic sentence would be too narrow:

  ✗ I began college just two months ago.

  The sentence is too narrow because it does not address the idea of a decision to attend college. While the sentence might be appropriate as a supporting detail, it is too narrow to be a topics sentence. Two better topics sentences are shown below:

  ✔ Stuck in a dead-end job, I decided to attend college so that I could do something that will make a difference.

  ✔ Attending college will help me realize my lifelong dream of being a nurse.

4

Writing Paragraphs: Support

Which party sounds more appealing?

You are invited to hang out with Andrew on the third or fourth Saturday of this month. We will get the party started whenever everyone gets there, and we will all have a great time. Call me and I'll let you know where the party will be held.

You are invited to an end-of-summer bash at Michael's place on Saturday, August 24. We will start at 7:30 P.M. with party games and volleyball. Then we will have grilled chicken, seafood and drinks. Later, we'll dance to some great music. Dress is casual—shorts or jeans are fine.

In the box above, the second invitation would be the clear winner for most people. It's not just the appeal of games, food, and music that make the invitation interesting. The invitation's appeal lies at least partly in its specific detail. On the other hand, the first invitation gives no time, no place, and no idea of what activities to expect or how to dress. In planning a party or in writing a paragraph, the key is in the details. Specific support is one of the keys to good writing. Before looking at paragraph support, review the four principles of effective writing below. The highlighted principle, support, is the focus of this chapter.

Characteristics of an Effective Paragraph

1. **Direction** means that the paragraph has a strong topic sentence that states the main idea and sets the course that the paragraph will follow.
2. **Unity** means that the paragraph makes one main point and sticks to that point.
3. **Coherence** means that the ideas in the paragraph are logically connected and easy to follow.
4. **Support** means that the paragraph contains specific and detailed discussion of the idea stated in the topic sentence.

Support: Using Specific Detail

A strong topic sentence, unity, and smooth transitions give a paragraph structure and style. Only **support** can give it life. Without specific details, a paragraph remains on a broad, general level. What is it like to read a paragraph without specific details? Imagine watching a movie, television show, or video that never shows a closeup but instead maintains a camera distance of ten feet from every character. You would probably feel detached and uninvolved. Readers feel the same way when a writer never gets close enough to the subject to describe it in detail.

The Difference Between Topic Sentences and Supporting Sentences

A topic sentence provides direction—the road map for a paragraph—but supporting sentences supply the scenery. While topic sentences are broad and general, large enough to encompass the entire paragraph, supporting sentences are specific, giving details and examples. The following exercise provides practice in distinguishing topic sentences from supporting details.

EXERCISE 1 DISTINGUISHING TOPIC SENTENCES FROM SUPPORTING DETAILS

Each numbered item contains three supporting details and one topic sentence. Write *SD* beside each of the three details and *TS* beside the topic sentence.

1. a. _____ Finally, he began throwing a tennis ball for his dog, who barked loudly in appreciation.

   b. _____ Then he put on a CD by a group called the Funk Brigade and turned the volume up.

c. _____ First, he turned on the television to provide background noise.

d. _____ It was too quiet in the room, so Marcus decided to make some noise.

2. a. _____ In the second book, Harry meets Dobby, a house-elf who nearly kills Harry in an effort to help him.

b. _____ J. K. Rowling's popular *Harry Potter* books follow the adventures of a young wizard as he learns his craft.

c. _____ In the first book, Harry, who has always felt like the odd one out, finds out that he is a wizard and begins to discover his powers.

d. _____ The third book introduces Harry to a mysterious character named Sirius Black and to the soul-sucking guardians of Azkaban Prison.

3. a. _____ Being late is a harmful habit to acquire.

b. _____ People who are late to classes or meetings often miss important information.

c. _____ People who arrive late for appointments or meetings often anger those who have to wait.

d. _____ Although the impression may be inaccurate, people who are late are often perceived as rude or selfish.

4. a. _____ Tires that are not properly inflated can pose a danger to both driver and passengers.

b. _____ Windshield wipers that are excessively worn can pose a danger in rainy weather.

c. _____ Bald tires, worn tires, and tread that is unevenly worn can cause a car to lose traction on the road.

d. _____ Failure to take care of small details of car maintenance can make driving dangerous.

5. a. _____ The close companionship that arises between the adopted animal and its owner can benefit both animal and human.

b. _____ Shelter animals are euthanized if they are not adopted, so adopting a pet from the pound saves a life.

c. _____ Adopting a pet from the animal shelter can benefit both animal and owner.

d. _____ Pound puppies and kittens are usually spayed or neutered before adoption, saving the owner veterinary fees.

Recognizing Specific Detail

One of the most difficult tasks a writer faces is providing strong, specific supporting details. If a writer provides only vague, sketchy details, the picture presented to the reader will be fuzzy and out of focus. As details become sharper and more specific, the picture becomes clear. The following exercise will give you practice in recognizing sharp, clear detail.

EXERCISE 2 RECOGNIZING SPECIFIC DETAILS

Each of the following topic sentences is supported by three details. Place a check (✔) beside the two details that are sharp and specific. Place an ✘ beside the detail that needs to be more specific. Then, in the space provided, rewrite the vague sentence to make the supporting detail more specific.

1. All day long, Nicole was haunted by the number 8.

_____ **a.** At the driver's license bureau, she pulled the number 8 out of a machine marked "Take a number."

_____ **b.** At lunchtime, the first potato chip she pulled out of her bag was shaped like the number 8.

_____ **c.** On her way home, yet another incident occurred involving the number 8.

____

____

2. Rodrigo's search for an apartment was long and difficult.

_____ **a.** He looked at several apartments that were not suitable in terms of his financial situation.

_____ **b.** Many of the apartments he could afford were too far away from work and school.

_____ **c.** Finally, he found a small, affordable attic apartment close to his work and within walking distance of the college.

____

____

3. For several reasons, majoring in the health sciences is a good idea.

_____ **a.** An aging population ensures that health-care professionals will be in demand for decades to come.

_____ **b.** A variety of fields from respiratory therapy to x-ray technology gives a student a wide range of choice.

_____ **c.** A nursing shortage means that anyone with a nursing degree has it made.

____

____

4. The small, crowded office was messy.

_____ **a.** In the corner, a trash can overflowed with paper and discarded soft-drink cans.

_____ **b.** The desk was also in disarray.

_____ c. Papers were spread in piles across the floor and around the desk, leaving little room for walking.

____

____

5. Elena worried that her memory was getting worse.

_____ a. She forgot an important appointment last week.

_____ b. She was constantly losing her glasses, her keys, and her wallet.

_____ c. She could no longer remember the items she needed at the grocery store without making a list, and she often forgot to bring the list.

____

____

Using Specific Words

Sometimes, a simple change in word choice makes all the difference. You paint a clearer picture for your reader when you use specific words and phrases: *four hours of research in the library* instead of *a lot of work, Ella's Soul Food Café* instead of *a restaurant, glared* instead of *looked*, or *a map of Florida, deck of cards, and two dollars in change* instead of *things.*

Making Nouns Specific

Consider the following sentence.

✘ Richard put *a heavy item* in his trunk, then drove away from the *building.*

Different readers will put different interpretations on this sentence. What did Richard put in his trunk? What kind of building did he leave? Specific detail would serve a twofold purpose: it would clearly convey the writer's meaning, and it would capture the reader's interest. Consider the revisions below.

✔ Richard put *a bulging briefcase* in his trunk, then drove away from *the law office.*

✔ Richard put *his ex-wife's body* in his trunk, then drove away from the *small white house where they had spent so many years together.*

✔ Richard put *a case of hymnals* in his trunk, then drove away from the *Harvest Religious Bookstore.*

Notice how the detail not only provides more specific information but also helps to characterize Richard. How does your impression of him change with each example?

EXERCISE 3 USING SPECIFIC WORDS

Create a new impression of Richard by varying what he puts in the trunk and the location described in the sentence.

1. Richard put ____________________ in his trunk, then drove away from the ____________________.

2. Richard put ____________________ in his trunk, then drove away from the ____________________.

3. Richard put ____________________ in his trunk, then drove away from the ____________________.

4. Richard put ____________________ in his trunk, then drove away from the ____________________.

5. Richard put ____________________ in his trunk, then drove away from the ____________________.

Practice in Making Vague Nouns Specific

Look at the following list. The nouns in the left-hand column provide little information, while those in the right-hand column are specific. Notice, too, that the more specific term is often not simply a noun, but a phrase.

Vague Term	Specific Term
✘ course	✔ Introduction to Social Problems
✘ clothing	✔ man's herringbone jacket, size 42
✘ student	✔ Gloria Hollinger, first-year nursing student
✘ car	✔ 1965 Ford Mustang
✘ sandwich	✔ turkey on five-grain bread with mayonnaise

EXERCISE 4 CHOOSING SPECIFIC TERMS

From the three choices for each of the sentences below, circle the most specific choice to fill in the blank.

1. Carlos ate ________ at noon.
   - a. a nutritious meal
   - b. a tomato sandwich
   - c. delicious food
2. When Larry took ________, he felt better.
   - a. a pill
   - b. two Excedrin tablets
   - c. the advice of a respected physician
3. Ana said the ________ was breathtaking.
   - a. spectacular view of the surrounding scenery
   - b. works of some nineteenth-century poets
   - c. ride on the Scream Machine
4. The vendor sold ________ from the back of a pickup truck.
   - a. ripe peaches and black velvet art
   - b. various wares in a wide range of colors
   - c. electronic devices that may have been stolen
5. Melanie's mother said, "Would you help me ________?"
   - a. complete a few simple household chores
   - b. chop these onions
   - c. do some errands
6. The little girl sat beside her mother in the veterinarian's waiting room, carefully holding ________.
   - a. her animal companion
   - b. a scrawny black kitten
   - c. a cute, cuddly pet
7. On the refrigerator were ________.
   - a. a child's drawing of a house, a grocery list, and a dentist's appointment card, held in place by colorful magnets
   - b. photographs, papers, children's art, and reminders
   - c. twelve magnets, along with the usual odds and ends that tend to accumulate under refrigerator magnets

8. Gerald's parents thought Kim was weird because ________.
   a. her appearance was unusual
   b. she had a pierced tongue and two-tone hair
   c. she did not look the way they thought a normal teenager should look
9. Because Harold did not believe in banks, he kept his money ________.
   a. in a place he thought was safe
   b. hidden away where no one who might want to steal it could find it
   c. in a waterproof plastic pouch buried under a rock
10. Pat believes she was straightforward and open, but other people saw her as ________.
   a. rude and tactless
   b. something else
   c. a person with an attitude that was often perceived negatively by those who had to be around her

EXERCISE 5 CHOOSING SPECIFIC TERMS

Three possible replacements follow each general term. One of the possible replacements is vague, while the other two are specific and thus would be acceptable substitutes. Circle the two specific terms in each of the following items.

1. tool
   a. hammer
   b. instrument
   c. spatula
2. test
   a. examination
   b. SAT
   c. math final
3. restaurant
   a. Vernon's Veggie Bar
   b. a hot dog stand on the corner
   c. an eatery
4. shoes
   a. sandals
   b. loafers
   c. footwear

5. noise
   a. sound
   b. earsplitting rock music
   c. click
6. pet
   a. animal companion
   b. Fluffy
   c. white hamster
7. home
   a. doublewide mobile home
   b. living space
   c. mansion
8. book
   a. telephone directory
   b. *War and Peace*
   c. published volume
9. ice cream
   a. delicious dessert
   b. pint of Rocky Road
   c. Ben and Jerry's Cherry Garcia
10. illness
   a. mumps
   b. disease
   c. food poisoning

Making Pronouns Specific

> "I wanted to register today, but they wouldn't let me."
>
> "Everybody says Ms. Torres is a tough teacher."
>
> "The candidate says he will not increase taxes, but nobody believes him."

Sentences like this are common in conversation and usually go unchallenged. In writing, though, precision is necessary. Readers usually do not have access to the writers of the books, stories, and essays they read, and so they cannot ask questions like "Who are *they?*" or "What do you mean by *everybody?*" Look at the revised versions of the statements you just read:

I wanted to register today, but the clerks in the Registrar's Office wouldn't let me.

Two of the students in my sociology class say Ms. Torres is a tough teacher.

The candidate says he will not increase taxes, but few voters believe him.

Forcing yourself to be more specific may also force you to be more accurate. The "everybody" who tells you to enroll in a certain teacher's class may turn out to be two fellow students. And if you truly wanted to prove that "nobody" believes what a candidate says, you'd have to ask every voter—an impossible task.

EXERCISE 6 REPLACING VAGUE PRONOUNS

Replace the italicized pronouns with more specific expressions.

1. *Things* were only getting worse, so Curtis decided to move out of his parents' house.

   ____

2. Sheila followed several leads from the help wanted ads and attended an interview arranged by her school's career counselor, hoping to find *something* before graduation.

   ____

3. Dr. Madison did a brain scan on the patient but didn't find *anything.*

   ____

4. My trash container sat by the curb all day, but *they* didn't pick it up.

   ____

5. The family walked into the dining room where the table was set for Thanksgiving. *Everything* looked delicious.

   ____

Making Verbs Specific

Verbs bring life and movement to writing. Vague, poorly chosen verbs add nothing to your writing, or worse yet, drag it down. Well-chosen verbs leap off the page, adding power and energy to your writing.

Choosing effective verbs means rejecting the easy choice and looking for powerful verbs that express your meaning exactly.

A *thesaurus,* or dictionary of synonyms, helps you choose the best word for the situation. But shades of meaning vary, so don't just choose a synonym at random. If you are not sure of a word's exact meaning, check your dictionary.

Examples

✘ Exhausted after studying for the exam, I *went* to bed at midnight.

✔ Exhausted after studying for the exam, I *stumbled* to bed at midnight.

✘ At 3:00 P.M. on the last day of school, the doors *were opened* and students *came* from the building, yelling and shouting.

✔ At 3:00 P.M. on the last day of school, the doors *burst* open and students *streamed* from the building, yelling and shouting.

EXERCISE 7 USING SPECIFIC VERBS

Cross out the italicized verb in each sentence and replace it with a verb that more effectively conveys the sense of the sentence.

1. Angrily, Beatrice *retrieved* the envelope from the table.

____

2. Smoothly, the sailboat *moved* across the water.

____

3. When the cable snapped, the elevator *descended* fifteen stories.

____

4. Albright's glove *contacted* his opponent's jaw, sending the man reeling toward the edge of the ring.

____

5. A small bird *was* on the highest branch of the cherry tree.

____

6. The garbage truck *moved* down the street, spewing noxious fumes.

____

7. The crowd *reacted* as fireworks appeared in the inky night sky.

____

8. When asked if he wanted to speak before he was sentenced, the defendant *commented*, "Please believe me! I do not know who committed this horrible crime, but I swear that I am innocent."

____

9. Five thousand fans *filled* the small concert hall, screaming and shouting their approval.

____

10. The angry customer said that a loose shopping cart had *harmed* her new car.

____

Exercise 8 Making Verbs Specific

Cross out the italicized verb in each sentence and replace it with a verb that more effectively conveys the sense of the sentence.

1. The ball seemed to take flight, *going* over the outfield and into the stands.

____

2. The squirrel grabbed the acorn and quickly *went* up the tree trunk.

____

3. The roller coaster made a slow ascent, then *moved* toward the ground as its passengers screamed delightedly.

____

4. Suddenly, Tom *came* into the room, yelling, "Quick! Somebody call an ambulance!"

____

5. As Andrea flipped the light switch, dozens of cockroaches *moved* across the wall and into the cracks near the baseboard.

____

6. Lightning *was seen* and thunder rolled.

____

7. The basketball *went* into the street just as a garbage truck rattled around the corner.

____

8. As he stormed out of his boss's office, Phil *commented*, "And you know what you can do with your lousy job!"

____

9. Annoyed at the interruption from a young fan, the athlete hastily *signed* his name on the program and abruptly turned away.

____

10. When the phone rang at 3:00 A.M., Channing sleepily *reached* for the receiver.

____

Making Sentences Specific

Sentences with specific language are sentences with power. As you write, strive for forceful verbs and vivid phrases. As you revise, look for opportunities to make vague language more specific. Look at the following examples to see how much stronger a sentence becomes when specific words replace vague words.

Examples

Vague Word Choice

✘ Eager shoppers *entered the toy store* when the *popular toy* came in.

Specific Word Choice

✔ Eager shoppers *mobbed Toy World* when the *Avengers of Doom action figures* came in.

Vague Word Choice

✘ When my mother comes to visit, she brings *all kinds of stuff* with her.

Specific Word Choice

✔ When my mother comes to visit, she brings *four suitcases, a shopping bag filled with homemade goodies, and her miniature poodle, Pierre.*

Vague Word Choice

✘ When Martin looked in his refrigerator, he found *there was not much to eat.*

Specific Word Choice

✔ When Martin looked in his refrigerator, he found *only a half-empty jar of pickles and the two-week-old remains of a takeout dinner from Junior's Barbecue.*

Vague Word Choice

✘ Sylvester could not concentrate on the test. *The noise around him* grated on his nerves.

Specific Word Choice

✔ Sylvester could not concentrate on the test. *The popping of gum in the back of the room, a burst of laughter from outside the building, and even the breathing of the student beside him* grated on his nerves.

Exercise 9 Making Sentences Specific

Rewrite the sentences so that they contain more specific detail. Feel free to use more than one sentence if you wish.

1. The newscaster reported that *a terrible thing* had happened in *a large city.*

   ____

2. The clock was shaped like *an animal* and painted *in bright colors.*

   ____

3. Lynn put a package from *a store* in the back seat because her trunk had *something* in it.

   ____

4. On their way to *their destination,* Asha and her husband stopped at *a little place by the roadside.*

   ____

5. *Bad weather* kept Mark from *doing what he had planned.*

   ____

6. When Percy saw *what had happened to his car* he *reacted strongly.*

   ____

7. *A noise* startled the *animal.*

   ____

8. The mailbox held *several unimportant pieces of mail* and *one important piece of mail.*

   ____

9. On our street, *they* have organized a neighborhood watch because of *various crimes that have taken place.*

   ____

10. *In certain situations,* Jack gets *a bad feeling.*

    ____

EXERCISE 10 MAKING SENTENCES SPECIFC

Rewrite the following paragraph, replacing the underlined vague terms with specific details.

When I decided to clean out the small storage closet in our garage, I was amazed at how much junk it contained. First, I cleared and sorted items I had meant to recycle later. Then, I tackled a pile of various garden tools that were dirty. After dealing with the gardening tools, I worked on the shelves. The top shelf was filled with items I had used when I painted the interior of the house last spring. I threw some stuff into a trash bag and kept the rest. Beneath the assorted junk I was clearing away, the middle shelf contained a surprise. A sizeable insect suddenly came out, startling me into dropping and breaking something fragile. When I had swept away what had broken, I rearranged the tools and things on the bottom shelf. Then I threw away one broken item and three empty containers. When I was finally through, I wondered how one small storage closet could have contained so much junk.

EXERCISE 11 ANALYZING PARAGRAPHS FOR SUPPORT

One of the following paragraphs is well supported with specific details and examples, while the other is poorly supported with vague, general sentences. Read each paragraph, then answer the questions at the end of the exercise.

Paragraph A

In my experience, college professors are the worst-dressed people in the world. If there were an award for "worst-dressed professor," my history professor, Dr. Bloom, would be a leading candidate. He is the ultimate fashion victim. When I saw him walk into the classroom on the first day, I could not believe the clothes he was wearing. I thought that maybe he had just been in a hurry that morning, but on the second day of class, his clothing was just as bad. I cannot imagine where he finds that awful clothing. Then there is Professor Hunter, who teaches art. She wears the strangest clothes, even for an art teacher, who might be expected to have unusual taste. It is as if she is living in a different decade. It's a sure thing she hasn't looked at a fashion magazine lately. But I think my personal choice for the worst-dressed professor award is Mr. Nelson, my English teacher. Like clockwork, the same loud pants, jackets, and shirts appear in strict rotation, each for a different day of the week. When I go into his classroom, I make sure I sit in the back. I am not sure I could stand all those bright colors if I were sitting in the front row. I have great respect for my professors' knowledge, but most of them deserve an "F" in fashion.

Paragraph B

In my experience, college professors are the worst-dressed people in the world. If there were an award for "worst-dressed professor," my history professor, Dr. Bloom, would be a leading candidate. When I saw him walk into the classroom on the first day in a green checked shirt, red bow tie and shapeless brown sweater vest, I thought perhaps he was just having a bad day. But each day in Dr. Bloom's class is a parade of mismatched rag-bag fashions: rumpled jackets, baggy pants, and shirts in checks, plaids, and polka dots. Professor Hunter, who teaches art, looks like a folk singer from the seventies with her straight hair and ankle-length dresses. She likes delicate rainbow colors and long strands of beads, an odd combination with her heavy white athletic shoes. But I think my personal choice for the worst-dressed professor award is Mr. Nelson, my English teacher, whose taste is not just bad, but annoyingly predictable. On Mondays, he wears a yellow and green checked polyester jacket with lime-green pants. On Tuesday, it's a polyester jacket in robin's-egg blue with a pair of mustard-colored pants. The polyester parade continues through Friday, when he wakes the class up with a pair of bright red pants worn with a pink shirt. I have great respect for my professors' knowledge, but most of them deserve an "F" in fashion.

■ Questions

Fill in the blanks of each question below.

1. Paragraph _____ is less specific.
2. Paragraph _____ is more specific. Three specific details from the paragraph are ________________________, ______________________________ ______________, and ___________________.

Progressive Writing Assignment

Progressive Writing Assignment: Providing Supporting Details and Examples

If your instructor has assigned the Progressive Writing Assignment, you have already completed your prewriting and your topic sentence. In this chapter, you will provide support for your paragraph.

Topics and Tips for Providing Supporting Details and Examples

The Topics

Topic 1: Discuss the results of taking a specific piece of advice from a friend or family member.

Topic 2: Discuss your decision to attend college.

Topic 3: Discuss your greatest fear.

Topic 4: Discuss types of stress experienced by college students.

Tips for Providing Supporting Details and Examples

- Make sure that your language is specific. Have you used words that create pictures by appealing to the reader's sense of sight, hearing, touch, taste and smell? The following sentences illustrate how specific language might be used to support Topic 3, "Discuss your greatest fear."
  - ✔ If I were homeless, I would have no shelter from the hot sun or the cold rain. On chilly nights, I would lie awake, listening to my stomach growl and feeling the damp chill creep into my bones.
- Check to see that you have supported your paragraphs with specific examples. If you are writing on Topic 1, "Discuss the results of taking a specific piece of advice from a friend or family member," an example might be a *specific example* that describes what happened on a particular occasion.
  - ✔ Thinking of my father's advice, I walked right into my boss's office and said, "Ms. Carmichael, the mix-up with the order yesterday was my fault." She looked at me and said, "Yes, I know that, but I really appreciate hearing it from you."

5

Writing Paragraphs: Unity and Coherence

Not the Real Thing

Modern color copiers have made the counterfeiting of money more widespread. Experts say there are ways to tell if the bill you are holding is counterfeit. Most people say they have too many of the kind of bill they have to pay and not enough of the kind they can spend. Many things can be faked--art, for instance. Just putting a few splashes of paint on a canvas doesn't make it a Picasso. Paint is not just a way to make a house look good; it also protects the surface against weather. It's always a good idea to make sure that you have the real thing--not an imitation.

When you look at the sentences in the box above, you may notice that although they are written in paragraph form, they do not seem to connect with one another. They have no unity because each sentence discusses a different idea. They have no coherence because the sentences do not flow logically into one another. You may suspect, in fact, that the "paragraph" you are reading is not the real thing. A genuine, effective paragraph has four characteristics: direction, unity, coherence, and support.

Characteristics of an Effective Paragraph

Review the characteristics of an effective paragraph below. You have already learned how to give your paragraph direction with an effective topic sentence and how to support that topic sentence with details and examples. This chapter looks at the two final characteristics of an effective paragraph, unity and coherence.

1. **Direction** means that the paragraph has a strong topic sentence that states the main idea and sets the course that the paragraph will follow.
2. **Support** means that the paragraph contains specific and detailed discussion of the idea stated in the topic sentence.
3. **Unity** means that the paragraph makes one main point and sticks to that point.
4. **Coherence** means that the ideas in the paragraph are logically connected and easy to follow.

Unity: Sticking to the Point

Every topic sentence offers a promise of **unity** to the reader, a promise that you will discuss the point advanced in that sentence and no other. If your topic sentence is "My friend Ellen is the messiest person I have ever known," then you will discuss the specific ways in which she is messy. You will not mention the few times you have known her to be neat; you will not discuss the other qualities that make her so good to have as a friend. You will discuss only the piles of clothes stacked on every piece of furniture in her bedroom, the assortment of books, bills, and banana peels on her desk, and the mounds of fast-food wrappers in the back seat of her car. Your paragraph will have unity because it sticks to its topic and to the specific point you make about that topic.

Exercise 1 Finding Problems in Unity

A list of possible supporting points follows each of the topic sentences in the exercise. In each group, circle the letter of the point that interferes with the unity of the paragraph.

1. Topic sentence: Some restaurant customers make trivial complaints in the hope of getting a free meal.

a. Some customers gripe when service is a bit slow.

b. Many complain if they have to make a trip to the emergency room because of food poisoning.

c. Other customers grumble if the coffee is not piping hot or the iced tea is not cold enough.

2. Topic sentence: Fear of serious injury makes many parents hesitate to encourage their children to play football.

 a. Many parents fear that the child may break a bone in a football game.

 b. They fear their child might sustain head injuries during a game.

 c. Some parents fear their child will start to do poorly in academics.

3. Topic sentence: One way that I try to keep in shape is through a proper diet.

 a. I get plenty of exercise.

 b. I eat very few sweets or sugary treats.

 c. I stay away from too many fats.

4. Topic sentence: If I had to give up one modern convenience, I would get rid of my telephone.

 a. Getting rid of my phone would eliminate interruptions from salespeople.

 b. My telephone is a vital link to emergency services.

 c. Without a phone, I would waste less time chatting.

5. Topic sentence: My neighbor's yard is an eyesore.

 a. In his front yard, he has an old Chevrolet up on blocks.

 b. At the side of his house is a beautiful old oak tree.

 c. Because he never mows his lawn, tall grass and weeds surround his house.

EXERCISE 2 FINDING PROBLEMS IN UNITY

A list of possible supporting points follows each of the topic sentences below. In each group, circle the letter of the point that interferes with the unity of the paragraph.

1. Topic sentence: Some crimes go unreported because crime victims believe they are not worth reporting.

 a. petty theft

 b. kidnapping

 c. graffiti

2. Topic sentence: Fear that they will do poorly in the classroom makes many adults hesitant to return to school.

 a. anxiety about taking tests

 b. fear of not understanding the ideas presented

 c. fear that their families will not accept their decision to return to school

3. Topic sentence: One way that I try to keep in shape is through exercise.
   a. lift weights
   b. eat nutritious foods
   c. attend aerobics classes
4. Topic sentence: Writing on a computer has helped me improve my papers.
   a. modern computer lab
   b. ease of revising on computer
   c. spelling check
5. Topic sentence: My neighbor's dog is an annoyance.
   a. "Heinz 57" mutt
   b. barks at night
   c. jumps fence and digs up my flowers

Reinforcing Unity: The Summary Sentence

One way to reinforce paragraph unity is to end the paragraph with a **summary sentence** that echoes the topic sentence. The summary sentence does not repeat the topic sentence; rather, it reinforces it. If the function of a topic sentence is to tell the reader where the paragraph is going, the function of a summary sentence is to tell where the paragraph has been, thus reinforcing the unity of the paragraph. A summary sentence also signals the end of the paragraph and provides a sense of closure.

Example

Topic Sentence

✔ The most valuable lesson I have learned from my parents is to be independent.

Summary Sentence

✔ I will always be grateful that my parents taught me to rely on myself and not on others.

Example

Topic Sentence

✔ A few minor changes could make our campus more welcoming to students with disabilities.

Summary Sentence

✔ These easy and inexpensive changes would ensure that all students feel safe and welcome on our campus.

Exercise 3 Analyzing Paragraph Unity

In each of the following paragraphs, underline the topic and double-underline the specific point that is made about that topic. Then find the two sentences that interfere with the unity of the paragraph. If you have trouble, go back and look at the topic sentence to see the specific point that is made about the topic. Then read again to see which sentences do not support that specific point. Finally, underline the summary sentence of each paragraph.

Paragraph 1

[1]I enjoy spring because it is a season when nature comes alive. [2]Each tree sports a halo of tiny, delicate leaf buds of the palest green. [3]Soon the leaves mature and unfurl, trumpeting a brilliant green message to the world. [4]Flowers nudge their way through a new growth of grass, pushing up to find the sun. [5]Then they open into a rainbow of springtime colors. [6]Each evening, a symphony of sound serenades the listener from shallow ponds where frogs call solemn invitations to prospective mates. [7]Toward morning, as the frogs subside, birds begin their racket, their chatter reverberating from tree to tree. [8]In the ballparks, the crack of the bat and the umpire's cry of "Yer out!" echo again as baseball season opens. [9]Lights blaze, the stands fill, and the odors of hotdogs, popcorn, and beer blend on the evening breeze. [10]It is spring, and nature awakens the world to new possibilities.

Numbers of the sentences that interfere with the unity of the paragraph:___, ___

Paragraph 2

[1]The graduation ceremony at our college is dignified but dull. [2]In a large hall filled with well-dressed parents, relatives, and friends of the graduates, faculty and students file in, dressed in hot, heavy academic robes. [3]The ceremony follows a prescribed routine. [4]First, prospective graduates sing the alma mater, desperately searching their programs for the unfamiliar words. [5]The dean of the college, clad in a flowing robe, welcomes the assembled crowd with appropriate decorum. [6]The graduation speaker, usually a state legislator or

a distinguished graduate, delivers a lengthy discourse as members of the audience yawn, read their programs, or pretend to listen. [7]Then, the anticipated moment arrives and the graduates begin to stir excitedly, waving at parents, who quickly ready cameras and video equipment. [8]In spite of the dean's plea to hold applause until all diplomas have been distributed, whoops and cheers ring out from the audience as eager graduates file across the stage. [9]Finally, the majestic notes of "Pomp and Circumstance" rise in the air and the graduates march out, heads high with the dignity of their newly conferred degrees. [10]The ceremony, with its air of dull formality, is over for another year.

Numbers of the sentences that interfere with the unity of the paragraph: ___, ___

Exercise 4 Analyzing Paragraph Unity

In each of the following paragraphs, underline the topic and double-underline the specific point that is made about that topic. Then find the two sentences that hurt the unity of the paragraph. If you have trouble, go back and look at the topic sentence to see the specific point that is made about the topic. Then read again to see which sentences do not support that specific point. Finally, underline the summary sentence of each paragraph.

Paragraph 1

[1]I enjoy autumn because it is nature's season of color and movement. [2]The temperature falls and the wind picks up, sweeping across country roads and city streets and serving notice that nature's show is about to begin. [3]The summer green of the trees gives way to a fall tapestry of red, orange, gold, and brown. [4]People flock to the mountains to see the autumn splendor before the winter comes. [5]Many people, however, have already taken a summer vacation at the beach before the children head back to school. [6]Finally, as the grasses turn yellow and fields shade into brown, the leaves begin to fall. [7]They float to the ground, where the wind tosses them, forming a multicolored carpet that crunches underfoot as the leaves turn brown. [8]Almost as fast as parents can rake the leaves into big piles,

children are ready to leap into the middle of them and scatter them into a colorful carpet once again. [9]Fall is also a season for Halloween, when children go door to door in scary costumes to collect treats. [10]In fall, nature puts on a spectacular show before the bleakness of winter comes on.

Numbers of the sentences that hurt the unity of the paragraph: ____, ____

Paragraph 2

[1]Last night, the women's softball game at our college was attended by a small but enthusiastic group of supporters. [2]Below me, in the first row of the bleachers, two small boys yelled loudly and waved signs saying "Go, Mom!" whenever their mother came up to bat. [3]Four young men sitting together to my left shouted encouraging comments to the players and stood and clapped whenever the team scored. [4]More interested in gossip than in softball, three women sitting to the far left in the stands ignored the game completely. [5]When Number 34 came up to bat, a woman sitting in a wheelchair beside the bleachers turned to bystanders and said proudly, "That's my daughter." [6]A cluster of students seated near the field clapped rhythmically and cheered, "Go, team, go!" [7]It is a shame that our men's athletic teams have cheerleaders, but our women's teams do not. [8]Entering the ninth inning, our team was winning by five runs, but the fans stayed and cheered as enthusiastically as if the score were tied. [9]As the team left the field, the enthusiastic cheers of the small crowd told the players that their winning efforts had been appreciated.

Numbers of the sentences that hurt the unity of the paragraph: ____, ____

Coherence: Holding the Paragraph Together

If your writing does not have **coherence,** then the sentences in your paragraph are like a pile of loose bricks: there is little connection between them. Coherence is the mortar you use to make your paragraph a brick wall, with solid and strong connections between ideas. To achieve coherence, first make sure your ideas are logically related and well thought out. Then use **coherence tools** to cement the connections between those ideas in the most effective way possible. Two common and easy-to-use coherence tools are *transitional expressions* and *repetition.*

Transitional Expressions

As a writer, you must not only express an idea clearly, you must keep your reader oriented in time and space and aware of relationships between ideas. *Transitional expressions* help you juggle these multiple tasks without detracting from the ideas you express. Ideally, these words and phrases do their job in the background, as guideposts that show the path of your logic and the movement of your ideas through time and space. Below is a list of transitional words and expressions, organized by their function within the sentence.

Some Common Transitional Words and Expressions

** Transitions of Time*

after	during	later	now	suddenly	when
as	first	meanwhile	often	temporarily	while
before	immediately	next	previously	then	yet

** Transitions of Space*

above	beside	down	next to	toward
around	between	in	on	under
behind	by	near	over	

** Transitions of Addition*

also	finally	furthermore	in addition	next
another	first			

* Transitions of Importance

as important	essential	major	primary
equally important	just as important	most important	significant

* Transitions of Contrast

although	even though	in contrast	instead	on the other hand
but	however	in spite of	nevertheless	yet

* Transitions of Cause and Effect

a consequence of	because	since	therefore	for
as a result	consequently	so	thus	

* Transitions of Illustration or Example

for example	for instance	including	such as

EXERCISE 5 USING TRANSITIONAL EXPRESSIONS

In the following paragraph, provide the indicated type of transition in each blank.

[1]Nothing had gone right lately, so _____ (time signal) the doorbell rang, Sam had a feeling it was not the Prize Patrol with a million-dollar check. [2]_____ (contrast signal), he did not expect quite as much trouble as he got. [3]Two police officers were standing _____ (space signal) his porch. [4]"Mr. Williams, we have information that your dog may have bitten a child who lives _____ (space signal) the street," said the tall officer. "It couldn't

have been Killer," said Sam, [5]"_____ (cause-effect signal) he never goes outside except on a leash." [6]"Please bring the dog out _____ (time signal)," said the officer. "I'm afraid we'll have to take him to the pound." Sam knew that his dog had not bitten anyone, [7]_____ (contrast signal) he saw no alternative but to hand over his dog. Would he ever see Killer again? [8]_____ (time signal) he brought Killer out on a leash, the officers had their hands near their guns, as if fearful of being attacked. [9]_____ (contrast signal), when they saw Killer, the officers began to laugh. "That's not the dog we're looking for," said the tall officer, bending to pet the tiny, trembling Chihuahua on the head. "We are looking for a large, fierce dog." [10]_____ (time signal), to Sam's relief, the two officers apologized for bothering him and left.

1. __________ 6. __________
2. __________ 7. __________
3. __________ 8. __________
4. __________ 9. __________
5. __________ 10. __________

Exercise 6 Using Transitional Expressions

In the following paragraph, provide the indicated type of transition in each blank.

[1]_____ (time) the Fresh-Food Supermart was robbed, Shawna had the bad luck to be the only cashier on duty. The robber came in about 7:00 A.M., [2]_____ (time) the store opened. She noticed him right away [3]_____ (cause-effect) his ball cap was pulled low over his eyes and he wore a jacket [4]_____ (contrast) the morning was warm. He loitered for a while [5]_____ (space) the door; [6]_____ (time) he walked up to her register. She must have suspected him [7]_____ (cause-effect) she suddenly remembered

Mr. Monroe, the store manager, saying: "If you are ever robbed, remember that your life is worth more than whatever is in that cash drawer. Stay cool and hand over the money." [8]_____ (time) the robber leaned [9]_____ (space) her and mumbled, "I have a gun. Put the money in a bag." Remembering Mr. Monroe's words, Shawna quickly withdrew the money from the register. [10]_____ (time) she reached for a bag, she was surprised at the words that automatically fell from her lips: "Paper or plastic?" Much [11]_____ (time) Mr. Monroe teased that not only had she remembered his instructions, she had [12]_____ (addition) remembered to offer her unwelcome "customer" a choice.

1.	____________	**7.**	____________
2.	____________	**8.**	____________
3.	____________	**9.**	____________
4.	____________	**10.**	____________
5.	____________	**11.**	____________
6.	____________	**12.**	____________

Using Transitions Effectively

Used skillfully, transitional expressions bring coherence to your writing, but moderation is the key. Using these words unnecessarily or artificially is worse than not using them at all.

Hints for Using Transitional Expressions

- Less is more. Skillfully weaving a few transitional expressions into a paragraph is better than forcing in as many as possible.
- For variety, place transitions somewhere other than the beginning of a sentence. Instead of "However, Arturo refused to place the pink plastic flamingo on his lawn," try "Arturo, however, refused to place the pink plastic flamingo on his lawn."
- Examples are sometimes more effective when they are not preceded by *for example* or *for instance.* If you feel uncomfortable putting an

example in without announcement, try using *for example* in your rough draft and editing it out later.

- When you feel that a particular example needs to be announced, try placing the announcement somewhere other than at the beginning of a sentence. Instead of, "For instance, pasta is filling and low in calories," try "Pasta, for instance, is filling and low in calories."

Exercise 7 Analyzing Use of Transitions

Look at the two paragraphs that follow. Underline the transitional expressions in each. In which paragraph are transitional expressions used more skillfully? Can you pinpoint some of the reasons?

Paragraph 1

The third week of a student's first year in college is often a dangerous one. Like the "seven-year itch" that supposedly makes people give up on romantic relationships, the "three-week shock syndrome" sometimes signals the end of a student's academic career. After the excitement of the first week or two of classes begins to wear off, reality starts to set in. There is more than just the excitement of meeting new people and buying textbooks in a well-stocked bookstore. Those books, with their crisp pages and new smell, must be opened and read, marked and highlighted. The smiling professors who leaned on their lecterns and cracked jokes on the first day of class have turned into serious-faced people who talk faster than their students can write and whose lectures are sometimes boring. Worst of all is the work. Reading assignments, writing assignments, library assignments, and computer lab assignments pile up, waiting to be completed. Who has time to remember it all, much less do it all? Students who make it past the third week of classes usually find that they can adjust, that they can keep up. But some, faced with the shock that college means work, never stay long enough to find out whether they can succeed or not.

Paragraph 2

First of all, the third week of a student's first year in college is often a dangerous one. For example, the "seven-year itch" supposedly makes people give up on romantic relationships, and the "three-week shock syndrome" often signals the end of a student's academic career. In addition, the excitement of the first week or two of classes begins to wear off, and reality starts to set in. More importantly, there is more than just the excitement of meeting new people and buying textbooks in a well-stocked bookstore. In contrast, those books, with their crisp pages and new smell, must be opened and read, marked and highlighted. Furthermore, the smiling professors who leaned on their lecterns and cracked jokes on the first day of class have turned into serious-faced people who talk faster than their students can write and whose lectures are sometimes boring. Just as important, worst of all is the work. To enumerate, there are reading assignments, writing assignments, library assignments, and computer lab assignments. Further, who has time to remember it all, much less do it all? Nevertheless, students who make it past the third week of classes usually find that they can adjust, that they can keep up. In conclusion, some, faced with the shock that college means work, never stay long enough to find out whether they can succeed or not.

The paragraph in which transitions are used more successfully is paragraph ____.

Some reasons are ____

____

____

Exercise 8 Analyzing Use of Transitions

Look at the two paragraphs that follow. Underline the transitional expressions in each. In which paragraph are transitional expressions used more skillfully? Can you pinpoint some of the reasons?

Paragraph 1

One characteristic of successful students is that they know how to study. They know, for instance, that the time to begin studying is not the night before the test but much earlier. The first time they read a section of the textbook, successful students begin their study. They highlight or underline important sections and jot down key terms. When taking notes in class, they use a similar technique, jotting down the most important ideas and later transcribing their notes into a format that will be easy to study. Unsuccessful students, on the other hand, often postpone highlighting the text and organizing their notes until the night before the test, when time is short. Successful study, then, partly depends on beginning well before the date of the test.

Paragraph 2

First, successful students know how to study. First of all, they know that the time to begin studying is not the night before the test but much earlier. For example, successful students usually begin their study the first time they read a section of the textbook. In addition, they highlight or underline important sections and jot down key terms. Next, when taking notes in class, they jot down the most important ideas. Furthermore, they transcribe their notes into a format that will be easy to study from later. However, unsuccessful students postpone highlighting the text and organizing their notes until the night before the test. Therefore, successful study partly depends on beginning well before the date of the test.

The paragraph in which transitions are used more successfully is paragraph ____.

Some reasons are ____

____

____

Repetition

Repetition of Key Words and Phrases

Often, repetition is seen as a negative quality in writing. However, *repetition of key words and phrases* is a method of tying your ideas together and achieving coherence. While no one would advise endless hammering of unimportant words or ideas, repetition of key words and ideas helps to bring your point home strongly.

EXERCISE 9 EXAMINING REPETITION OF IMPORTANT TERMS

The following paragraph is about business telephone manners. Underline the repetitions of the key words *business, telephone* (or *phone*), and *manners.*

At a time when voice mail, answering machines, and computerized telephone answering systems have all but replaced the business telephone call, good telephone manners remain essential. Because the caller on the other end of the phone cannot read lips or minds, it is important for anyone who answers a business telephone to speak clearly, giving his name and the name of the department or company. If it is necessary to ask the caller to hold, it is never good manners to say "Hold, please" and leave the person wondering when, if ever, the phone will be picked up again. Good telephone manners require an explanation, such as "Ms. Smith, our manager, will be happy to help you with that. Would you mind holding for a minute while I get her?" Above all, business telephone manners require giving the caller the idea that her business is appreciated and that the phone call has been a pleasure, not a chore. For example, if the caller says, "Thank you," then the proper reply is not "Yeah, right, no problem." A reply such as "Thank you, Ms. Crabtree. We appreciate your business," demonstrates good telephone manners and excellent business sense. In an impersonal age, adding a personal touch to business telephone calls is not just good manners. It's good business.

Repetition through Pronouns

Pronouns aid coherence by allowing you to refer to someone or something without tedious repetition. Below is a partial list of pronouns often used to substitute for nouns.

Common Pronouns

Subject pronouns:	I, we, you, he, she, it, they, who
Object pronouns:	me, us, you, him, her, it, them, whom
Possessive pronouns:	my, mine, our, ours, your, yours, his, her, hers, its, their, theirs, whose
Indefinite pronouns:	one, anyone, everyone, nobody, some, somebody

In the following sentences, it's easy to see how much more smoothly the words seem to flow when pronouns link sentences and ideas together.

Example

✗ *The dog* woke up, stretched out *the dog's* legs and yawned hugely. Then, as if realizing that *the dog* was supposed to be guarding *the dog's* yard, *the dog* shambled over to the gate and gave a halfhearted bark.

Revision

✔ *The dog* woke up, stretched out *his* legs and yawned hugely. Then, as if realizing that *he* was supposed to be guarding *his* yard, *he* shambled over to the gate and gave a halfhearted bark.

Exercise 10 Using Pronouns to Aid Coherence

Use pronouns to replace the underlined words. Choose from the list of common pronouns above or use any appropriate pronoun.

1. Whenever Lindsay left <u>Lindsay's</u> new bicycle in the driveway, her mother worried that <u>Lindsay's new bicycle</u> would be stolen.

   ______________ ______________

2. When Michael tried to hand the toll booth attendant a dollar, the wind whipped <u>the dollar</u> out of his hand and sent <u>the dollar</u> sailing into the oncoming lanes of traffic.

   ______________ ______________

3. When personal computers first came out, Mr. Willett said that personal computers were just another fad, but now he has decided that he needs a personal computer.

_______________ _______________

4. Because the pizza arrived cold and late, the delivery person did not charge us for the pizza. We decided that a cold, free pizza tasted even better than a hot, fifteen-dollar pizza.

_______________ _______________

5. Timothy looked at the huge parking lot and wondered how he would ever find Timothy's car. He walked down aisle after aisle before he found Timothy's car.

_______________ _______________

Progressive Writing Assignment

Progressive Writing Assignment: Unity and Coherence

If your instructor has assigned the Progressive Writing Assignment, you have already completed your prewriting, a topic sentence, and supporting details. In this chapter, you will make sure your paragraph has unity and coherence.

Topics and Tips

The Topics

Topic 1: Discuss the results of taking a specific piece of advice from a friend or family member.

Topic 2: Discuss your decision to attend college.

Topic 3: Discuss your greatest fear.

Topic 4: Discuss types of stress experienced by college students.

Tips for Unity and Coherence

Staying on Track: Tips for Unity

- Check each paragraph to make sure that every sentence supports the topic sentence.
- Include a summary sentence at the end of the paragraph to reinforce the topic sentence.
  - ✔ No matter what else they learn on campus, most college students also learn to live with stress.
  - ✔ Becoming a nurse will be the fulfillment of a lifelong dream and the beginning of a long and rewarding career.

Transitions: Tips for Coherence

- Read your paragraph aloud to make sure it flows logically.
- Check to make sure transitions between supporting ideas are smooth and that transitional expressions are used where needed.
  - ✔ Academic stress *also* affects most college students.
  - ✔ *However,* I have found ways of coping with my fear of public speaking.

6

Revising, Proofreading, and Formatting

~~making changes~~	*revising*
~~proffreading~~	*proofreading*
~~fORmatTing~~	*formatting*

To many writers, revising, proofreading, and formatting are the Rodney Dangerfield of the writing process: they get no respect. But these final steps in the writing process help you present your ideas in the best possible way. Revising helps you capture your ideas more clearly and accurately, and proofreading and formatting help give them the polish they need before they are ready for an audience.

Revising

If you have ever watched your golden ideas clatter onto the page like a load of rough gravel, you understand the need for revision. **Revising** helps you do justice to your ideas, to give them some of their original polish.

There are also more practical reasons for revision, reasons that have their roots in the difference between writing and conversation. Conversation is constantly under revision. When your listener says, "What do you mean?" and you explain, you are revising. When your listener disagrees and you reinforce your argument or concede a point, you are revising. In a conversation, revision is a response to the listener. But writing does not offer the same opportunity for response. Your reader cannot ask questions. So you have to *anticipate* a reader's objections and meet them before they arise. That means that you need to spot possible misunderstandings and clarify them before the reader sees the finished work. Revising is a process of stepping back and looking at your work with the eyes of a reader.

The word *revise* combines the Latin root meaning *to see* with the prefix meaning *again.* In its most literal sense, *to revise* means *to see again.* "Seeing again" is the essence of good revision. The difficult part is distancing yourself far enough from the work to see it with new eyes. When the work is fresh from your pen or word processor, you often see what you *meant* to say rather than what is actually on the page.

To see your work again, you need to create a space, a mental distance, between yourself and the work. Time is your best ally. Lay the writing aside for at least a twenty-four-hour period. When you return to it, words that aren't precise, sentences that aren't clear, and explanations that don't explain enough are easier to spot.

If you do not have twenty-four hours to lay the work aside, it may help to have someone else look at it. Ask your reader to focus on content and to ask questions about any point that does not seem clear. The written word carries no facial expression, no gesture, and no tone of voice, so it is more open to misinterpretation than is face-to-face communication. Discussing work with a reader can help close the gap between what you *think* you said and what your reader actually sees.

In addition to letting a work "cool" before revising and enlisting the help of a reader, you can also check your paragraph point by point to make sure that it fulfills the purpose you had in mind. There is nothing mysterious about this procedure. It works like the diagnostic test a mechanic might perform to evaluate a car, checking all major systems to make sure they are working as they should. The following revision checklist helps you to go through a paragraph, part by part, to make sure each part is doing the job you intend it to do.

Checklist for Revision

The Topic Sentence

✔ Does the paragraph have a topic sentence that clearly states the main idea of the entire paragraph?

✔ Is the topic sentence the first or second sentence in the paragraph?

The Supporting Sentences

- ✔ Does each sentence of the paragraph support the topic sentence?
- ✔ Do your examples and explanations provide specific detail to support the topic sentence?
- ✔ Is each point you raise adequately explained and supported?

The Ending

- ✔ Is the last sentence satisfying and final-sounding?
- ✔ Does the last sentence serve as a summary or closing sentence for the entire paragraph?

Checking Coherence

- ✔ Is the order of ideas clear and logical?
- ✔ Are transitional words used effectively?

EXERCISE 1 ANALYZING TWO VERSIONS OF AN ESSAY

Read the two versions of the paragraph, "Some Purposes of Urban Legends." Using the above Checklist for Revision as your guide, decide which version is the revision and which is the rough draft.

Version 1

Some Purposes of Urban Legends

[1]Some urban legends, such as the story of a man caught speeding by a high-tech surveillance system, are meant to amuse. [2]The man was mailed a photo of his car's license plate, a radar reading of his speed, and a ticket for $120. [3]He mailed back a photo of a check. [4]The police responded with a photo of a pair of handcuffs. [5]The motorist quickly relented and sent a check. [6]Urban legends are meant to sound a warning. [7]Urban legends that tell of escaped murderers haunting lovers' lane, of babies left alone for "just a moment" with tragic consequences, or of predators stalking women down lonely roads fit this category. [8]I myself cannot imagine a parent being careless with his or her child. [9]There is so

much that can happen to a defenseless baby in seconds. [10]These legends remind us, as we go about our lives, to be careful. [11]A final type of urban legend, the "David and Goliath" story, shows how an average person can fight big business or government and win. [12]One example is the story of a woman who asked a waitress in a department store's tearoom for the store's chocolate chip cookie recipe. [13]She was told she would be charged "two-fifty," and she agreed to what she thought was a $2.50 charge on her credit card. [14]Later, she received a charge card bill for $250. [15]This legend, which still haunts the Internet, reminds its readers that even ordinary people have some measure of power. [16]Urban legends, although mostly untrue, serve a purpose as they tell of funny incidents, tragedy, or an ordinary person's revenge.

Version 2

Some Purposes of Urban Legends

[1]Urban legends, the modern equivalent of ancient folktales, serve a variety of purposes. [2]Some urban legends, such as the story of a man caught speeding by a high-tech surveillance system, are meant to amuse. [3]The man was mailed a photo of his car's license plate, a radar reading of his speed, and a ticket for $120. [4]He mailed back a photo of a check. [5]When the police responded with a photo of a pair of handcuffs, the motorist quickly relented and sent a check. [6]Another type of urban legend is meant to sound a warning. [7]In one story of warning, a couple goes to lover's lane in spite of a news broadcast telling of an escaped murderer called "Hook Hand." [8]When they hear a noise outside the car, they become frightened and start to leave. [9]The car seems to be stuck, but finally they pull away and drive home. [10]As they get out of the car in the young woman's driveway they notice something caught on the bumper: a hook hand. [11]A final type of urban legend, the "David and Goliath" story, shows how an average person can fight big business or government and

win. [12]An example is the story of a woman who asked a waitress in a department store's tearoom for the store's chocolate chip cookie recipe. [13]She was told she would be charged "two-fifty" and she agreed to what she thought was a $2.50 charge on her credit card. [12]Later, she received a charge card bill for $250. [14]When the department store refused to remove the charge, the woman's revenge was swift. [15]She posted the recipe on the Internet for the world to enjoy, along with a letter of explanation. [16]This legend, which still haunts the Internet, reminds its readers that even ordinary people have some measure of power. [17]Urban legends, although mostly untrue, serve a purpose as they tell of funny incidents, tragedy, or an ordinary person's revenge.

The revised version of the paragraph is version _____.

EXERCISE 2 ANALYZING AN UNREVISED ESSAY

Go back to the unrevised version of "Some Purposes of Urban Legends" and fill in the blanks to answer the following questions.

1. A topic sentence should appear before sentence _____ in the unrevised version.
2. A transitional word or expression is needed as the writer moves to a new point in sentence _____.
3. Two sentences that do not support the topic sentences are sentence _____ and sentence _____.
4. More support is needed to fully make the writer's point after sentence _____.

Proofreading

Think about the last time you saw a misspelling in a newspaper. The minute you saw it, your thoughts moved away from the story itself and focused on the error. Similarly, errors in your writing take a reader's focus away from your ideas and put emphasis on grammar, spelling, or punctuation. Naturally, you want the ideas to stand in the foreground while grammar, spelling, and punctuation remain in the background. Proofreading, then, is an essential last step in your writing. Though proofreading is usually a chore, it is a necessary chore.

After you have completed the final revision of your work, proofread it at least twice, once from the top down and once from the bottom up. If you have a special problem area, such as comma splices or subject-verb agreement, you should do at least one extra proofreading focusing on those skills.

Proofreading is the job that is never done. No matter how thorough you are, some little error always escapes your notice. Then, just as you are turning in your beautifully written or word-processed manuscript, the error pops out at you as if it were written in neon. Therefore, the more thorough your approach to proofreading, the better.

The Top-Down Technique

On the first proofreading, scan from the top of the page down. Check to make sure the connections between ideas are smooth and solid and that sentences and paragraphs flow smoothly into one another. Check for parallel structure, clear pronoun reference, and appropriate transitional expressions. After correcting any problems you find in the top-down proofreading, move to the second type of proofreading, the bottom-up proofreading.

The Bottom-Up Technique

The bottom-up proofreading technique is more labor-intensive and more focused than top-down proofreading. When you read from the bottom up, you are no longer reading your essay as a single piece of writing but as disconnected sentences that do *not* flow into one another. Since your focus is on a single sentence, you can look at it closely, as if it is a sentence in a grammar exercise. Read it carefully, correct any errors you find, and then move back to the next sentence.

The Targeting Technique

If you have a "favorite error"—one that seems to plague you more than any other—try an additional proofreading to target that error. Below are some common errors and shortcuts to finding those errors. As you become more experienced, you will find yourself devising your own strategies to target your problem areas.

Subject-verb agreement. Check each subject-verb sequence. Look for present-tense verb forms and make sure they agree with their subjects.

Comma splices and run-ons. Target long sentences; they are more likely to be run-ons. Target commas and see if there is a sentence on both sides of the comma; if so, you have a comma splice.

Other comma errors. Target each comma and question its reason for being there. If you aren't sure why it is there, maybe it doesn't belong.

Pronoun agreement. Look for the plural pronouns *they* and *their,* and make sure that they have a plural, not a singular, antecedent.

Sentence fragments. Using the bottom-up technique, read each sentence to see if it could stand on its own.

Proofreading the Word-Processed Paragraph

Spelling and grammar checkers can be helpful in proofreading, but they are no substitute for knowledge and judgment. A spelling or grammar checker can find possible errors and suggest possible solutions. However, it is up to you to decide what, if anything, is wrong and how to fix it.

Even when you use spelling and grammar checkers, you should do at least two separate proofreadings. The following sentence, in which all words are spelled correctly, may illustrate the need:

> Weather or knot ewe use a spelling checker, you knead too proofread.

Whether to proofread onscreen or print out a hard copy to proofread is a personal choice. Some writers find it easier to scroll up and down on the computer screen, viewing the paragraph in small segments. Others swear that they cannot see their errors until they hold the printed copy in their hands. Find out what works best for you and proceed accordingly.

Group Exercise 1 Proofreading a Paragraph Confident? Go solo!

Each of the twenty sentences in the paragraph below contains an error. Form a small proofreading team with two or three of your classmates. Pooling your knowledge, see how many errors you can identify and correct.

An Urban Legend

[1]Urban legends are stories that are often told but is seldom true. [2]One urban legend involves a young college woman traveling home for the Thanksgiving holiday's. [3]As she leaves, the dorm's custodian warned her to take precautions against the Road Killer, who is known to prey on women driving alone. [4]On the road, she stops before dark to get gas, however; she can't get the pump to work. [5]She drives off, planing to stop somewhere else. [6]But as she drive's, she begins to feel more and more apprehensive. [7]It is now fully dark, so she decide to stop at a full-service station. [8]So that she won't have to get out of the car again. [9]It seems like hrs. before she finds a station with a sign that says, "We Pump." [10]She hands the attendant her credit card, she notices he is looking at her and at her car with a strange expression. [11]As he walks toward his booth to check her credit, she feels majorly creeped out. [12]The attendant comes back and said a representative of the credit card company wants to talk to her on the phone. [13]She fears a trick but, the attendant is insistent. [14]she gets out of the car. [15]And walks toward the attendant's booth. [16]He follows closely, goes in behind her slams the door, and locks it. [17]Just as she is about to scream, he says, "I've called the police, and they're on there way. There is a man crouched in the back seat of your car." [18]Urban legends like this one are all most never true. [19]People, find them interesting. [20]Because they represent events that could happen.

Corrections

1. ____________________
2. ____________________
3. ____________________
4. ____________________
5. ____________________
6. ____________________
7. ____________________
8. ____________________
9. ____________________
10. ____________________

11. ____________	**16.** ____________
12. ____________	**17.** ____________
13. ____________	**18.** ____________
14. ____________	**19.** ____________
15. ____________	**20.** ____________

Formatting

You have heard it all your life: first impressions count. The document you hand to your instructor, the resumé you hand to a prospective employer, or the letter you send to the editor of a newspaper has the ability to present a positive first impression or a negative one. When an instructor sees a carefully formatted paper with no smudges, crossovers, or dog-eared edges, the instructor expects that paper to be a good one, written as carefully as it was prepared. On the other hand, a hastily scrawled document smudged with eraser marks or heavily laden with White-Out suggests that the writer did not take the time to create a good impression—or to write a good paper.

Manuscript format is so important that entire books have been written about it. An instructor who asks you to use MLA style, APA style, or Chicago style is referring to styles outlined in books published by the Modern Language Association, the American Psychological Association, and the University of Chicago.

If you are given instructions for formatting a document, follow those instructions carefully. If you have no specific instructions, use the guidelines in the following section. They will help you to format a document effectively, whether that document is written in class or out of class, by hand or on a word processor.

Handwritten Documents

Paragraphs and Essays

For handwritten paragraphs and essays, use lined white 8½ × 11-inch paper and blue or black ink. Write on one side of the paper only, and leave wide margins.

In the upper right-hand corner of the page, put your name and the date. If you wish, include your instructor's name and the name of the class for which you are preparing the assignment. Center your title, if any, on the first line of the paper, but do not underline the title or put it in quotation marks. Indent each paragraph five spaces, or about three-quarters of an inch. In a handwritten document, do not skip lines unless your instructor specifically requests it. If you make an error, draw a single line through the error and rewrite your correction above the crossed-out error. Put a single paper clip, not a staple, in the upper left corner to join the pages.

Essay Tests

When you take an essay test, you may be required to use a "blue book" or to write on the test itself. If you are allowed to use your own paper, use lined paper and write on one side only.

Answers to questions on essay tests should be written in blue or black ink. Since time is too limited for a rough draft, take a moment to organize your thoughts, and then answer the question. Indent each paragraph five spaces (three-quarters of an inch to one inch). State your main idea first; then add specific supporting details and examples.

If you misspell a word or make a mistake, cross through it with a single line. Be sure to write clearly and legibly, and if your handwriting is difficult to read, try printing instead.

Word-Processed Documents

Setting up the Word-Processing Software

Choose a font and a font size that are easily readable, such as Times New Roman in a 12-point size. Do not use a bold or italic font.

Margins should be one inch all around. One-inch margins are the default on most word processors, so you probably will not have to set margins. Set the word processor to double-space the text. Leave the right edge ragged rather than justifying it. (To justify means to line up in a straight edge, like a newspaper column. Most word processors have settings that allow you to justify, but these settings are not commonly used for academic work.)

Formatting the Document

Put your name and the date in the upper right corner of the page. Other information, such as the name of your instructor or the class for which you are preparing the assignment, is optional. Center the title and indent each paragraph as shown in the sample that follows. A title page is not necessary unless your instructor asks for one.

Derek Smith

April 1, 2004

Format Reform

I am ashamed to say that I used to be a format abuser. I used strange fonts such as Adolescence and Space Toaster. I tried to make my papers look longer by using two-inch margins with 14-point font. At my lowest point, I turned in a report on lime-green paper printed in 15-point Star Trek font. A caring instructor saw that I had a problem, and helped me to turn my formatting around. Now, I know how to format a document perfectly.

The first step in formatting a document is setting up the word processor. Margins should be set at one inch all around—left, right, top, and

Printing and Presenting Your Document

When the document has been revised and proofread, print it on good quality 8½ × 11 white paper. To hold the pages together, place a single paper clip in the upper left corner. Do not staple your document or put it in a report cover.

Progressive Writing Assignment

Progressive Writing Assignment: Revising, Proofreading, and Formatting

If your instructor has assigned the Progressive Writing Assignment, you are almost finished. All that remains is to revise the paragraph, proofread it carefully, and put it in the proper format.

Topics and Tips

The Topics

Topic 1: Discuss the results of taking a specific piece of advice from a friend or family member.

Topic 2: Discuss your decision to attend college.

Topic 3: Discuss your greatest fear.

Topic 4: Discuss types of stress experienced by college students.

Tips for Revising, Proofreading, and Formatting

- Ask someone else to look at your paragraph and tell you if any point is not clear or if any idea needs further explanation.
- Evaluate your paragraph using the "Checklist for Revision" in this chapter.
- Use your word processor's spelling and grammar checkers, but don't forget to proofread the document at least three times yourself.
- Check the formatting of your paragraph against your instructor's instructions or against the guidelines in this chapter. Improper formatting can be distracting to a reader, but proper formatting allows your paragraph to shine.

7

Showing and Telling: Description, Narration, and Example

Sir, could you describe the thief who stole your car?
—She was kind of average. You know, medium.

What happened when you went for your job interview?
—It went okay.

What kinds of tests does Professor Madden give?
—Oh, you know, the usual.

The answers to the questions above would be more vivid—and more satisfactory—if the people answering had used description, narration, and example. You will find these techniques useful when you need to provide specific details. With description, you can show your reader what you see, hear, smell, touch, or taste. With narration, you can tell a reader a story that makes a point. With example, you can provide specific illustrations. Your writing comes alive when you describe, tell a story, or give a specific example.

Description

Effective descriptive writing paints a picture for the reader. Just as an artist uses canvas, brush, and paints, the successful painter of word pictures also employs tools of the trade to create a more effective picture.

Your tools as a writer of descriptive paragraphs and essays include sense impressions, spatial order, and use of a dominant impression.

Sense Impressions

Every scrap of information you collect about the world around you comes through your five senses: sight, hearing, smell, taste, and touch. It is logical, then, that descriptions using **sense impressions** present a more real and vivid picture to your reader.

Sight

Visual impressions are strong and lasting. People are not fooled by a clerk's "Thank you" if his facial expression says, "I hate my job." In fact, psychological studies confirm that people are more likely to rely on facial expressions and gestures than spoken words. If it really is true that "seeing is believing," then creating a visual picture for the reader is particularly important in descriptive writing.

Hearing

Our sense of hearing also gives us information about the world around us. We are warned by the blast of a horn, energized by the beat of rock music, or soothed by the thunder of the ocean. Imagery that appeals to a reader's sense of hearing is an essential dimension of descriptive writing.

Smell

The sense of smell has a powerful connection to memory. The smell of freshly popped popcorn may summon the claustrophobic feel of a dark, crowded movie theater. A whiff of furniture polish can bring back an elderly aunt's stately dining room. Using imagery related to smell helps to complete the picture you are creating for your reader.

Taste

Taste imagery will probably play a small role in your writing, unless you are writing about food. However, used sparingly, references to taste can add a touch of spice to your descriptive writing.

Touch

The sense of touch is a backdrop for all experience. As you sit reading this, you may feel beneath you the hard surface of a wooden chair or the softness of sofa cushions. You may be aware of the chill of air conditioning or the warmth of sunlight, the scratch of a wool sweater or the cottony caress of an old pair of jeans. Imagery that brings out textures and temperatures adds the stamp of reality to the picture you are drawing for your reader.

EXERCISE 1 RECOGNIZING WORDS OF THE SENSES

In the following paragraph, underline words and phrases that convey sense impressions.

Water Aerobics

Although I am not athletic, I enjoy my water aerobics class. I feel comfortable around the other women in my class because, like me, they are not athletes. They are not picture perfect models with smoothly muscled arms and concave stomachs, but real women with pudgy stomachs, wide hips, or skinny, toothpick calves. Around them, I feel less self-conscious about the extra twenty pounds I am carrying. I also enjoy the music that accompanies our exercise. The music system is just a small portable CD player, but if it is turned up loudly enough the energizing beat of disco music echoes throughout the pool area. It is impossible to hear "Shake Your Groove Thing" or "Ring My Bell" without wanting to dance. Once the music starts, we move from the hot concrete at the side of the pool into the shock of the cool blue water. The exercise itself may be my favorite part of the experience. The water buoys me up so that the laws of gravity no longer fully apply. Each bounce sends me a foot into the air, and I land lightly and easily. When the class is over, the crisp smell of chlorine stays with me, reminding me of the laughter of classmates, the blare of music, and the temporary freedom from gravity that I experience in my water aerobics class.

EXERCISE 2 WRITING SENSORY DESCRIPTIONS

Write a phrase that describes each of the following words in sensory terms. Then note whether you describe the word through sight, hearing, smell, taste, or touch. The first one is done for you.

1. cup
   a smooth, heavy ceramic cup (touch)
2. chair
   ______
3. grass
   ______
4. hat
   ______
5. moonlight
   ______
6. air freshener
   ______
7. french fries
   ______
8. tire
   ______
9. cloud
   ______
10. dirt
   ______

Spatial Order

Spatial order shows the layout of anything that takes up space. Use spatial order to present physical objects in a way that makes sense: bottom to top, left to right, background to foreground, outside to inside—in short, in any organized fashion. Below is a partial list of words commonly used when referring to space.

above	beyond	near	right
ahead	by	next to	south
around	down	north	toward
behind	east	on	under
beside	in	over	underfoot
between	left	overhead	west

EXERCISE 3 RECOGNIZING EFFECTIVE USE OF SPATIAL ORDER

Look at the following short paragraphs. In which paragraph is spatial order used in a more organized and coherent way?

Paragraph 1

The top drawer of my desk was a mess. The tape I was looking for was all the way in the back. A deck of playing cards secured with a rubber band sat beside a flashlight that had no batteries. The first thing I saw when I opened the drawer was a jumble of papers. Near the front of the drawer were a crumpled yellow sheet with an e-mail address written on it, several grocery store and gas receipts, and an envelope that had once contained a bank statement. Pencils without points, paper clips, and assorted change were scattered in the tray at the front of the drawer. It was difficult to explain why some of the items near the back of the drawer had been saved at all: a catnip mouse without a tail, an empty tape dispenser, and an unfolded gum wrapper on which someone had written "23cd" seemed to have no use. I took the roll of tape, then closed the drawer, resolving to clean it out the moment I had time.

Paragraph 2

The top drawer of my desk was a mess. The first thing I saw when I opened the drawer was a jumble of papers. Near the front of the drawer were a crumpled yellow sheet with an e-mail address written on it, several grocery store and gas receipts, and an envelope that had once contained a bank statement. Pencils without points, paper clips, and assorted change were scattered in the tray at the front of the drawer. A deck of playing cards secured with a rubber band sat beside a flashlight that had no batteries. It was difficult to explain why some of the items near the back of the drawer had been saved at all: a catnip mouse without a tail, an empty tape dispenser, and an unfolded gum wrapper on which someone had written "23cd" seemed to have no use. The tape I was looking for was all the way in the back. I took the roll of tape, then closed the drawer, resolving to clean it out the moment I had time.

The paragraph that uses spatial order more effectively is paragraph _____.

Establishing a Dominant Impression

Description is more than a tangle of unrelated details. In descriptive writing, every detail should join in conveying a single **dominant impression.** Imagine that your job is to describe a house that you pass every day. If your description is to stick in your reader's memory, it must be more than simply a jumble of shutters, bricks, and roofing tiles. A dominant impression not only makes your description more memorable, but it also adds to the unity of the description. What is your overall impression of that house? Is it cheerful? Eerie? Prim? Dignified? The word that you choose to describe the house conveys your dominant impression. As you describe the house, each detail should contribute to the dominant impression.

If you are describing a house that is eerie, include details designed to send chills up the reader's spine: the loose, creaking shutters and the blankly staring windows. If cheerful dandelions bloom in the yard, let them bloom unseen. Details that do not reinforce the dominant impression do not belong in your description.

Exercise 4 Supporting the Dominant Impression

In each list below, circle the letter of the detail that would *not* support the dominant impression of the topic sentence.

1. The bank building looks *dignified.*

a. Black marble covers the front of the building.

b. The tinted glass doors look heavy and substantial.

c. Graffiti is spray-painted on the sidewalk that leads up to the door.

d. Gold letters spell out the bank's name.

2. The bathroom is *messy.*

a. Toothpaste is spattered on the sink and mirror.

b. Damp towels have been thrown on the floor.

c. Children's tub toys are scattered on the sink and in the tub.

d. Clean towels are folded and stored on a shelf.

3. My brother is *studious.*

a. He finishes his homework as soon as he comes home from school.

b. He likes to play video games.

c. He researches subjects like astronomy and geology in the Internet.

d. He hates to see school let out for the summer.

4. The basement is *a fire hazard.*

a. Newspapers dating back to 1972 are stacked beside the furnace.

b. Boxes of firecrackers sit near an open can of charcoal starter.

c. A black widow spider has made her nest on a box of broken glass and rusty nails.

d. A rusty chainsaw with a frayed cord is plugged into the wall.

5. The man seemed *prosperous.*

a. He drove a new Mercedes.

b. He lived in a large, expensive brick house on the north side of town.

c. His battered wallet held two dollars and a picture of his family.

d. His designer suit was tailored to perfection.

Wordsmith's Corner: Sample Descriptive Paragraphs

Below are two examples of descriptive writing. Read each paragraph and answer the questions that follow.

Descriptive Paragraph 1

In this paragraph, the writer draws a portrait of a homeless man.

Interstate Sam

Interstate Sam is a figure of weary dignity. His tired face is an ebony mask, ancient and unreadable. His shoulders bend as if under a heavy load. Sometimes he stands slumped onto his shopping cart as if he has fallen asleep. In winter, a battered green coat shrouds the many layers of clothing that sag from his thin frame like tattered robes. In rain, his cape is a yellow plastic banner, positioned so that the word SALE stretches from shoulder to shoulder across his stooped back. He leans on his rusty cart, shifting the weight from his overburdened feet, but he carries no sign reading "Stranded" or "Will Work for Food." He asks for nothing, and people say he accepts nothing that is offered. He scrounges through dumpsters for food or, less likely, buys it with the thick sheaf of bills he is rumored to carry. Interstate Sam lives his life in the street, yet holds the world at arm's length with his stoic solitude.

Questions

1. Underline the topic sentence of the paragraph. Does it state the dominant impression?

   ____

2. What is the dominant impression in this paragraph? List three details that reinforce it.

   ____

   ____

   ____

   ____

3. Is the sensory imagery in the paragraph mainly sight, hearing, smell, taste, or touch? List three details expressed in sensory terms.

   ____

   ____

   ____

   ____

Descriptive Paragraph 2

Luis writes about a subway station as seen through a child's eyes.

The Subway Station

When I was a child, the subway station seemed like a strange and frightening place. Going down the steep steps into the dark subway, with its smell of dirt, shoes, and sweat, I felt like I was descending into a sinister underground world. In the station, standing with my father on a cement floor that was lumpy with ingrained chewing gum, I looked around at the people. They leaned against pillars, read newspapers, or sat on benches, appearing ordinary enough. But I had been warned against strangers, and here they were, loitering in close proximity. The woman in the striped dress could be a kidnapper, or the thin man's briefcase might hold a gun. I watched the strangers warily, occasionally getting an annoyed glare in return. Then my attention would turn to the steep drop at the edge of the platform. There was always one daredevil standing right at the edge, peering into the dark tunnel as if to make the train arrive faster. I hung well back. If I approached the edge, some unseen force might propel me over the steep drop and onto the third rail. Even if I survived the fall, contact with the third rail would mean instant electrocution. As I watched the person at the edge of the platform, wondering when he would fall, my ears caught the distant rumble of an approaching train. As the strangers folded their papers and rose from their benches, I covered my ears in dread. The rumble became a huge, echoing roar, and the roar became a piercing screech of brakes as the subway came to a stop. On board the train, my fears subsided as clacking, noisy wheels carried us through the dark tunnel and toward the light.

Questions

1. Underline the topic sentence of the paragraph. Does it state the dominant impression?

___

2. What is the dominant impression in this paragraph? List three details that reinforce it.

___

___

___

___

___

___

3. Give examples from the paragraph of imagery expressed in terms of smell, touch, and hearing.

___

___

___

Topics for Practicing Descriptive Writing

Descriptive Assignment 1: Fish Story

Paragraph or Journal Entry

You are a striped bass, living in the depths of a cool blue lake. Your days are peaceful and food is plentiful. You spend most of your time half hidden among the rocks and weeds, but sometimes you swim quickly, darting through the cool water. At other times, you are so filled with the joy of life that you leap high out of the water, your iridescent scales shining in the sun. Today, as you venture from among the weeds, you see a quick flash near the surface of the lake. Maybe it's food.

Describe what happens, focusing on your five senses.

Descriptive Assignment 2: A Beautiful Place

Paragraph

In a single-paragraph composition, describe the most beautiful place you have ever visited. Your dominant impression will be one of beauty, so focus on those details that contributed most to the beauty of the place you are describing.

Descriptive Assignment 3: A Place

Paragraph

In one paragraph, describe a place. It can be a store, an office, a nightclub, a park, a church sanctuary, or any place of your choosing. In your topic sentence, state the dominant impression in one word, choosing a word from the list below or thinking up your own word. Make sure all details of your description reinforce that dominant impression. *Hint:* Your topic sentence will follow this pattern:

The ________ was/is ____________________.

bleak	crowded	filthy	noisy
chaotic	depressing	gloomy	orderly
cheerful	dull	impersonal	serene
colorful	eerie	lonely	shabby
cozy	elegant	messy	spotless

Descriptive Assignment 4: A Person

Paragraph or Essay

Write a paragraph or essay describing a person. You may describe someone you know well, such as a friend or relative, or someone you see often but don't really know, such as a library worker or a fellow student. Be sure that you state a dominant impression in your topic sentence. A few possibilities are listed below. Make sure that all the details in your paragraph support the dominant impression. Focus on details that can be expressed through sight, hearing, smell, taste, and touch.

arrogant	easygoing	graceful	neat
dignified	elegant	gruff	unhappy
disorganized	forbidding	messy	upbeat

Narration

Narration is the art of storytelling. A good story pulls your readers in, captures their imaginations and keeps them wondering what will happen next. What is the difference between a narrative that succeeds and one that fails? To make your narrative a success, try some of the techniques outlined below.

Steps to Writing a Successful Narrative

Select Detail Carefully

A good narrative is not burdened by endless details. Provide details that move the story forward, but leave out anything that might slow its progress. In a successful narrative, every detail is significant. Suppose you are telling about the time you locked yourself out of your house and had to convince a passing police officer that you were not a burglar. Details about what you ate for breakfast, the decor of your house, or how you spent the hours or days leading up to the event do not matter. Focus instead on the incident itself.

Use Chronological Order

Most stories are best told in the order in which they happen, with background details near the beginning of the narrative.

Keep the Timespan Short

In a short, paragraph- or essay-length narrative, you can't tell your whole life's story. Your narrative packs more punch if you keep the timespan short—preferably less than an hour and certainly less than twenty-four hours.

Center on Conflict

Most successful narratives center around conflict. It may be inner conflict, conflict with another person, or conflict with an outside force—a tornado, an economic recession, or something else beyond the individual's control. When the conflict ends, the story ends, too.

Use Dialogue

Use dialogue for dramatic moments when you want to show your reader exactly what was said and done or when you want readers to draw their own conclusions about the events that took place. For the strongest effect, use dialogue sparingly.

Know Your Purpose

The purpose of the story is its reason for existence, the reason that you find it worth telling. If no change takes place, if no lesson is learned, if nothing happens, your reader will ask impatiently, "What is the *point?*" Before you tell a story, know your reasons for telling it.

> **Building Connections**
>
> Descriptive writing skills can also be incorporated into narrative writing. Your narrative becomes even stronger when you present it in terms of sight, sound, touch, taste, and smell.

Exercise 5 Choosing Relevant Details

Imagine that you are writing a narrative about being stranded on a lonely highway. You have brainstormed to gather every available detail about the incident without trying to judge the importance of each detail. Now it is time to choose the details you will include in your paragraph. Place a checkmark beside those details that you would include in the finished paragraph and an X beside those that you would leave out. If there are details you are unsure about, mark them with an "M" for "maybe." Then compare your answers with those of your classmates and discuss the items on which you do not agree.

Topic Sentence: A few months ago, I had a frightening experience on a lonely highway.

_____ a. It was dark.

_____ b. There were few other cars on the road.

_____ c. The temperature outside was a comfortable 72 degrees.

_____ d. The radio was turned up loud, and I was singing with it.

_____ e. I heard a loud pop.

_____ f. Suddenly, my car became hard to steer.

_____ g. I get an oil change every 3,000 miles.

_____ h. My car is red.

_____ i. I realized my tire was going flat.

_____ j. I pulled over on the shoulder of the road.

_____ k. I found a flashlight in the glove compartment.

_____ l. I found a pack of spearmint gum in the glove compartment.

_____ m. I really prefer cinnamon gum.

_____ n. My dentist has told me that I should chew only sugarless gum.

_____ o. The batteries in the flashlight were dead.

_____ p. I wished I had a cell phone.

_____ q. Not a single car had driven by.

_____ r. I found the jack and the spare tire in the trunk.

_____ s. I saw a single headlight in the distance.

_____ t. I remembered a story on last night's news about the world economy.

_____ u. I remembered a story on last night's news about the "Motorcycle Murderer" who preys on stranded motorists.

_____ v. I have never had dandruff.

_____ w. My heart was pounding.

_____ x. A motorcycle pulled up and a tall, helmeted figure got off.

_____ y. When he said "Hello," I recognized his voice and realized that it was my friend Jack.

_____ z. He helped me change the tire, and I drove safely home.

Wordsmith's Corner: Sample Narrative Paragraphs

In the paragraphs below, look at the way two writers approach narrative writing. Then answer the questions that follow each narrative.

Narrative Paragraph 1

Melanie, the writer of this narrative paragraph, tells how a crab supper became less than appetizing.

A Painful Meal

A few years ago, I was invited for a "catch your own" crab supper at my uncle's rented beach house.

It was not the pleasant experience I expected. It started enjoyably enough as we lowered baited traps from the dock and pulled them up, sometimes with two or three crabs in each of them. Then we went back to the beach house and Uncle Ed began preparations, using tongs to place the twitching crabs in a large pot, then adding vinegar and water. "Wait a minute," I said. "You aren't going to boil them alive, are you?" Uncle Ed looked at me in surprise, but patiently explained, "That's the way they're cooked. They can't feel anything—crabs are just one step above insects." I watched as he turned on the heat. As the water became warmer, I could hear the crabs scrabbling against the sides of the metal pot. Uncle Ed looked at me and laughed at my horrified expression. "It's just a reflex," he said. But as the water became warmer, the noise from the pot grew more desperate. Finally, there was silence. Uncle Ed took the crabs from the pot and dumped them on newspapers spread on the kitchen table. Uncle Ed looked at me and said, "Mel, you're not still worried about these crabs, are you?" My mother was giving me a warning glance, so I said, "No, it's fine." I felt my stomach do a flip as my uncle put three large crabs in front of me. The crabs' white flesh was tender, but for me, it might as well have been Styrofoam. Since that day, I have not eaten crab. No one can tell me they don't suffer.

Questions

1. Underline the topic sentence of the paragraph.
2. About how much time does the narrative cover?

   ____

3. What is the main point of the narrative, the writer's reason for writing it?

   ____

   ____

Narrative Paragraph 2

In this paragraph, André writes about the night that changed his life.

My Last Night at the Kwik-Stop #7

Just a few months ago, as I worked the night shift at the Kwik-Stop #7, my entire life changed direction. It was about 11:00 P.M., and the store was deserted. A man came in, a baseball cap pulled low over his eyes and his jacket collar turned up to cover his face. In a flash, he was standing in front of me, pointing the metallic nose of a revolver at my head. "Give me all the money in that register. Don't pull any tricks or I'll kill you," he said. I could hear his voice trembling, and I realized he was scared. All I could think of was that a scared robber was more likely to pull the trigger. Time seemed to slow down. I could hear the robber yelling at me to hurry, but the words barely registered. Beneath the counter, I saw the red "panic button" that would silently summon the police if only I would press it. I could not. I opened the drawer and placed each stack of bills on the counter, twenties, tens, fives, and ones. The robber scooped them off the counter, jabbed the gun at me, and said "Don't call the police for at least an hour." I don't know how many minutes passed before I grabbed the keys with trembling hands, locked the door, walked back behind the counter and pushed the red button. The next day, when I took stock of the life I had almost lost, I realized I had lived twenty-three years and had done absolutely nothing I could be proud of. That day, I quit my job at the Kwik-Stop and filled out a college application. I had always said I would go to college someday, but I never thought someone would have to hold a gun to my head to make me do it.

Questions

1. Underline the topic sentence of the paragraph.

2. About how much time does the narrative cover?

____

____

3. What is the main point of the narrative, the writer's reason for writing it?

____

____

Topics for Practicing Narrative Writing

Narrative Assignment 1: Wake-Up Call

Journal Entry

You wake with the sun in your eyes, wondering why your bed seems to be rocking underneath you. Then you realize that you are not in your bed, but in a small boat on a vast ocean. In the distance, you see what looks like a small island.

Tell the story in a journal entry.

Narrative Assignment 2: Treat or Mistreat?

Paragraph

Write about a time when someone treated you in one of the following ways. Make sure your one-paragraph story has a purpose by focusing on the way the incident made you feel. Were you sad? Surprised? Angry?

Someone misjudged you.

Someone gave you praise or credit you did not deserve.

Someone encouraged you.

Someone ridiculed you.

Someone treated you with unexpected kindness.

Someone treated you unfairly.

Narrative Assignment 3: Transformation

Paragraph

Write a narrative paragraph describing a life-changing event that took place in less than an hour.

Narrative Assignment 4: A Significant Goodbye

Paragraph or Essay

Write a narrative paragraph or essay about a significant ending in your life. Some possibilities include your last day of high school or high school graduation, a time when you said goodbye to a person who was important in your life, or your last day on the job. Alternatively, you might focus on a symbolic ending when you realized that the end of something was at hand: the end of your childhood, the end of a relationship, or the end of a grudge or other feeling that you had held for some time. Make sure that the incident you choose is one that will fit into a paragraph or essay. It would be hard, for instance, to write a narrative that fully discussed your first marriage or first job—unless it lasted only an hour or two.

Examples

Examples are one of the best ways to get a point across because they provide a concrete illustration of your point. If you say your father is sentimental, your reader gets the general idea. If you say he gets teary-eyed over Hallmark commercials, you give specific support to the general idea. Examples are specific illustrations, exact instances. They may range in length from a single word to a single sentence to an entire paragraph.

The Short Example

A **short example** may be a word or a phrase, but it must be a specific, concrete example. It cannot simply be a synonym. The word *canine,* for instance, is a synonym for *dog,* not an example of a dog. An example illustrating the word *dog* might be *Dalmatian, Chihuahua, Raffles, my two-year-old terrier,* or *that mangy mutt across the street.*

EXERCISE 6 ADDING YOUR OWN EXAMPLES

For each of the words or phrases below, an example is given. Add your own example in a word or phrase.

1. song

  a. "Take Me Out to the Ball Game"

  b. ______________________________

2. sport

  a. soccer

  b. ______________________________

3. a proverb or familiar saying
   a. "A stitch in time saves nine."
   b. ______________________________
4. an uncomfortable sensation
   a. walking barefoot across hot sand
   b. ______________________________
5. an uncomfortable social situation
   a. Going on a date for the first time since your breakup and running into your ex's parents.
   b. ______________________________

The Sentence-Length Example

Sometimes you need more than just a word or phrase to illustrate an idea. In such cases, try using a **sentence-length example.** Again, the example needs to be a specific, detailed illustration of the general idea you are discussing. It should not simply be a vague restatement. Look at the following examples to see the difference between a vague restatement and a specific example.

Examples

✘ *Idea + vague restatement:* The new disk jockey on the morning show is really obnoxious. He has an unpleasant attitude that makes listening to his show a bad experience.

✔ *Idea + specific example:* The new disk jockey on the morning show is really obnoxious. He tries to humiliate listeners who call in, and his jokes border on the offensive.

✘ *Idea + vague restatement:* The new grocery store has added whimsical touches to some of its departments. It's enjoyable to shop in a store that is entertaining.

✔ *Idea + specific example:* The new grocery store had added whimsical touches to some of its departments. In the produce department, "thunder" rolls and "lightning" flashes above the vegetable bins before the automatic sprinkler turns on. On the dairy aisle, recordings of mooing cows and clucking hens amuse passing shoppers.

EXERCISE 7 ELIMINATING VAGUE EXAMPLES

Circle the letter of the sentence that is not a specific example.

1. The car was dirty.
   a. The entire vehicle had a filthy appearance.
   b. Brown streaks of mud covered the bumpers and doors.
   c. The windows were specked with the tiny, squashed bodies of dead insects.
2. The man seemed angry.
   a. He spoke loudly and used vulgar language.
   b. He seemed to be in a state of fury.
   c. As he left, he slammed the door behind him.
3. I have spent money carelessly this weekend.
   a. At the mall, I bought two CDs that I could not afford.
   b. Money seemed to run through my fingers like water.
   c. I spent twenty dollars on dinner at the Steak-Out, an expenditure I had not planned.
4. Alfred spent an hour cleaning his apartment.
   a. He picked up magazines, clothes, and papers that cluttered his bedroom.
   b. He vacuumed the carpet and mopped the kitchen floor.
   c. He took the time to get the place looking good.
5. The plant had obviously been neglected.
   a. Someone had ignored the poor philodendron.
   b. Its leaves were dusty and limp.
   c. Its soil was dry.

EXERCISE 8 PROVIDING SPECIFIC EXAMPLES

For each of the following general ideas, provide a specific example in a sentence or two.

1. The garage was a mess.

   ____

   ____

2. After two cups of coffee, I started to come awake.

   ____

   ____

3. In the hallway, Leon complained about his professor.

____

____

4. The evidence indicated that the accused burglar was guilty.

____

____

5. The mailbox contained nothing but junk mail.

____

____

The Extended Example

Sometimes you may wish to develop an idea with an **extended, paragraph-length** example. In this case, your topic sentence states the general idea and the rest of the paragraph provides a detailed example. This sort of paragraph usually ends with a summary sentence that connects the specific example back to the general idea, as in the following short paragraph.

Example

topic sentence

Not long ago, I found myself caught in an uncomfortable social situation. I was out on my first date since the breakup of my three-year marriage. As my date and I entered the restaurant where we were going to eat, we met my ex-wife's parents. When I saw them, I half hoped that they would not speak to me, but they called out, "Andy! Hello!" I had to introduce them to my date, and, to make matters worse, they insisted on filling me in about how well my ex-wife is doing without me. I tried to handle the situation gracefully, but I felt uncomfortable, and I am sure my date did, too.

Extended example

summary sentence

EXERCISE 9 WRITING AN EXTENDEND EXAMPLE

Write an extended example (four sentences or more) to support one of the following topic sentences. Then write a summary sentence to end the paragraph.

1. Not long ago, I found myself caught in an uncomfortable social situation.
2. I can remember how nervous I was on my first day at college.
3. Some of my classmates can be annoying.
4. Some professors can be a real pain.
5. I remember one of the proudest moments of my life.

Wordsmith's Corner: Paragraphs Developed by Example

In the paragraphs below, the writers develop their topics by using examples. Read each paragraph and answer the questions that follow.

Example Paragraph 1

In this paragraph, Justin gives examples of the excuses his friend Leo is constantly making.

No More Excuses

My friend Leo makes up lame excuses whenever there is something he doesn't want to do. Just two weeks ago, he was at my house when he decided he did not want to go in to work. He called his boss and said he had to get a new set of tires put on his truck. Then he sat down and watched TV with me. Not only had he lied, but his excuse was not a very convincing one. Another time, he canceled a date with his girlfriend at the last minute, telling her he had to get a new battery for his truck. She was angry and refused to go out with him again until he apologized. Last weekend, Leo offered the lamest excuse yet. He had promised he would help me move my furniture from my parents' house to my new apartment. He was supposed to bring his truck over about eight o'clock Saturday morning. I waited, then called and left a message on his machine. About 11:30 he called and said he was sorry, but he had been getting a new set of tires put on his truck. I guess he had forgotten he used the same excuse when he called his boss from my house. I think I need a new set of friends—I am beginning to tire of Leo's excuses.

Questions

1. Underline the topic sentence of the paragraph.
2. List three examples given in the paragraph.

 ____

 ____

 ____

 ____

3. Underline the paragraph's summary sentence.

Example Paragraph 2

Olivia's paragraph shows the ways her college's wellness center benefits students.

Athletics for Everyone

Many students at the college I attend complain about paying an athletic fee along with tuition. However, I don't complain because I know that the athletic fee supports a wellness program that benefits all students. The athletic fee funds a health club equipped with weight machines, treadmills, stationary bikes, and free weights. The fee also helps pay the salary of a director who runs the club and teaches classes like stretch and tone, step aerobics, and water aerobics. Fees at private health clubs run hundreds of dollars per year, but the college's athletic fee is only thirty dollars per term. Another benefit of the wellness

```
program is its medical services. A nurse-practitioner
offers advice on diet and nutrition, dispenses
remedies for colds and allergies, and schedules
private consultations on health-related matters. The
athletic fee also subsidizes tetanus immunizations
and flu shots. For commuter students, many of whom
are not covered by health insurance, the service is
essential. At some colleges, only athletic teams
benefit from student athletic fees, but at our
college, the athletic program benefits everyone.
```

Questions

1. Underline the topic sentence of the paragraph.
2. List three examples given in the paragraph.

____

____

____

____

____

3. Underline the paragraph's summary sentence.

Topics for Practicing Writing with Examples

Example Assignment 1: No Accounting for Taste

Paragraph or Journal Entry

Modify the following topic sentence to your liking and write a paragraph or journal entry. Provide specific and detailed examples.

When I go to __________, I notice some people with __________ taste in clothing.

Example Assignment 2: Quotations and Illustrations

Paragraph

Choose one of the following quotations and write a paragraph agreeing or disagreeing with it. Your support should take the form of specific examples that help to prove or disprove the quotation. Your topic sentence will look something like this: "I agree/disagree with Juvenal's statement, 'Luxury is more deadly than any foe.'"

Quotations

Luxury is more deadly than any foe.
—Juvenal

The impossible is often the untried.
—James Goodwin

It is impossible for a man to be cheated by anyone but himself.
—Ralph Waldo Emerson

Success is never final.
—Winston Churchill

How glorious it is—and also how painful—to be an exception.
—Alfred de Musset

In poverty and other misfortunes of life, true friends are a sure refuge.
—Aristotle

There is nothing so easy but that it becomes difficult when you do it reluctantly.
—Terence

Example Assignment 3: Saving and Spending

Paragraph

Are you a person who likes to save money or a person who likes to spend it? In one paragraph, support your answer with specific examples.

Example Assignment 4: People

Paragraph or Essay

Choose one topic from the following list and write a paragraph or essay that illustrates the topic with examples.

a loyal friend
a jealous person
a good or bad boss
a good or bad teacher
a giving person
a thrifty person
an inefficient person
a productive person
an optimist
a pessimist
a self-sufficient person
a bad influence

Topics for Combining Methods of Development

Description, narration, and example are methods of showing or telling a reader exactly what you mean. Combining the methods adds even more power to your writing. The assignments that follow ask you to combine two or more of the methods of development in this chapter.

Building Connections

Methods of development are tools of a writer's trade. Like a carpenter's hammer, saw, and sander, they each do a specific job. Which one should you use? It depends on the job you have to do. Some pieces of writing will require just one method, but most will require you use more than one of your tools of the trade.

Mixed Methods Assignment 1: Brief Encounter

Narration and Description

Narrate a brief encounter that you have had with someone. That person may be a stranger, a relative, a coworker, or a friend. The meeting you describe may be your first meeting with that person or your last, it may be a friendly encounter or an unfriendly one, but it should be significant in some way. As you narrate the encounter, weave in a description of the other person—his appearance, her voice. Try to narrate and describe the encounter so vividly that your reader feels as though he is there with you.

Mixed Methods Assignment 2: The Joy of Life

Description and Example

Runners sometimes experience a rush of endorphins that has been described as a "runner's high." An old song by John Denver describes the feeling of being in the mountains as a "Colorado Rocky Mountain high." Both terms describe special and rare feeling of self-awareness and joy that some might call a "high" and others might simply call the joy of life. What places or activities bring you joy? Describe those place or activities and give specific examples.

Mixed Methods Assignment 3: Childhood Unhappiness

Narration and Description

Write a paragraph narrating an event that upset you when you were a child but that does not seem so serious now. It could be an argument with a childhood friend, trouble with a teacher at school, or a lost game or competition. Make sure that you narrate an even that takes place in a very short span of time—fifteen minutes or less is suggested. As you narrate the event, make sure to weave in relevant details so that your reader sees the fall leaves or the dust that you kick up as you walk across the playground; hears the musical sounds of the ice cream truck or the angry tone in your teacher's voice; or feels the cold rain that soaked you to the skin.

8 Process

When you write a **process** paragraph or essay, you describe how to do something or how it works. Process writing surrounds you. Recipes, instruction manuals, and any of the many self-help books that offer advice on how to become fit, lose weight, save money, or lead a more satisfying life are all examples of process writing. A chapter in your American government text that tells you how a bill becomes a law, the page in your biology text on the life cycle of the fruit fly, and the fine print on the back of your credit card statement that explains how interest is applied are also examples of process writing.

Process essays typically answer questions like the ones that follow.

- What is the best way to handle a broken relationship?
- What is your recipe for an enjoyable vacation?
- Describe an effective process for setting and reaching goals.

Organizing the Process Essay

Some processes are **fixed** processes—that is, ones in which the order of the steps cannot vary. If you tell someone how to change the oil in a car, for instance, you can't place the step "add new oil" before the step "drain old oil." If you explain how a bill becomes a law, you can't place "goes to president for signing or veto" before "approved by both houses of Congress." If you are describing a fixed process, list the steps in chronological order or step-by-step order.

Other processes are **loose** processes. They have no fixed, predetermined order. Loose processes include such things as handling money wisely or becoming physically fit. In describing these processes, it is up to the writer to choose the most logical order.

Imagine that you are writing a paper on handling money wisely. You decide that the steps involved include paying down debt, developing a spending plan, and saving for the future. Developing a spending plan seems logical as a first point, but you can't decide whether to place "saving" or "paying down debt" next in the order. You may say, "It's impossible to save any meaningful amount until debts are paid. Therefore, paying debt before saving is logical." Or you may reason like this: "Most people stay in debt for most of their lives. If it's not a credit card, it's a car loan or a mortgage. The important thing is to pay yourself first, no matter what." Either order is logical. What is important is that you have thought about it and chosen the order that best suits your own philosophy.

One important point to remember when organizing the "how-to" process paper is that many processes require tools or must be done under certain conditions. Ideally, a "how-to" paper should be written so clearly and logically that the reader could carry out the process on the first read-through. Usually, then, step one of your process will direct the reader to gather tools and make preparations. Whether you're telling how to make a pastry or how to defuse a bomb, your reader won't appreciate being led to a crucial point and then being instructed to use a tool that isn't handy.

Building Connections

As you analyze the process you plan to write about, you will find yourself breaking the process into pieces in a way that feels a lot like classification. Process and classification have a lot in common and can often be combined. An essay called "The Road to Alcoholism," for instance, might mainly describe the process by which someone became an alcoholic. However, it would probably also break the process into definite stages—a form of classification.

Introducing the Process Essay

If you are explaining a process with wide appeal to readers, almost any of the types of introduction discussed in Chapter 4 will serve your purpose. However, if you are writing about a process of more limited interest, you may find it useful to motivate a specific audience and explain the value of or reason for the process.

When you motivate a specific audience, you think about who might find your process useful. If you are writing about study strategies, your target audience would be students. If your topic is "choosing a day-care center," your target audience would be parents of young children. Once you have identified your audience, think about how the process will benefit that audience. Readers are more likely to be motivated to read your essay if you can show them that the process has value for them.

Example

Introduction to motivate

Choosing the right day care for your child can mean the difference between a happy child who looks forward to the fun and friends at day care and a child who hangs back in the mornings, reluctant to leave the house. A child's attitude toward day care is often a precursor to his or her attitude about school. Because the choice of day care is so vital, it pays to know what to look for in a day-care center.

Concluding the Process Essay

The conclusion of a process paper should answer the question, *What is the value of the process?* If your paper is a "how-to" process paper, the answer to the question may motivate the reader to carry out the process. If the paper is an explanation of how something works, the conclusion serves as a reminder of the value of or reason for the process.

Examples

Conclusion to motivate

Getting your finances in order is hard work. But consider the rewards. You will no longer be feeding money into the black hole of credit card debt to pay for long-forgotten purchases. And when you get mail from the bank, it will be your savings statement, not an overdraft notice.

Conclusion to explain the value of the process

As the hatchlings make their way instinctively toward the sea, some are plucked from the sand and eaten by hungry gulls. Turtles that survive that crucial journey to the sea may one day return to this very beach to deposit their eggs and begin the cycle of life anew.

Wordsmith's Corner: Examples of Process Writing

Below are two student process essays. Read each and answer the questions that follow.

Process Essay 1

This essay describes a process of self-discovery as the writer confronts a learning disability.

Discovering My Abilities

On my report cards, my teachers used to write, "Erica doesn't apply herself" or "Erica lacks motivation." When I decided to go to college, I thought I had the motivation I needed. But I still had trouble finishing what I started, and I always felt frustrated, disorganized, and ten steps behind the rest of the class. In desperation, I visited the college's counseling center and began a process of self-discovery that turned my life around.

My journey to self-discovery began the day I walked into the counseling center. I came in shyly, just planning to pick up a few brochures. But the counselor, Dr. Fordham, invited me into her office and asked me about my study problems. I told her that I would start writing an essay and find myself playing Solitaire on the computer. I would get most of the work done on a term paper, and then resistance would set in and I would find excuses not to finish. I habitually lost assignment sheets, syllabi, and library books. I was my own worst enemy. After we had talked a bit longer, Dr. Fordham said that some of the habits I mentioned could be symptoms of attention deficit disorder, or ADD. I told her I did not have a learning disability; I was just lazy and disorganized. Dr. Fordham did not press, but along with the study skills brochures she gave me an information sheet on ADD.

The next step in my process of self-discovery involved overcoming denial. When I read the brochure, I recognized myself immediately. However, I was not about to be labeled "learning disabled" at my age. But I reasoned that getting more information could not hurt, so I searched the Internet. Along with other information about ADD, I found an adult ADD checklist. The checklist said that experiencing twenty or more of the symptoms could indicate a tendency toward ADD. I had checked forty-six of them. It was becoming harder for me to deny that I had a problem.

The most difficult step in the process was getting up the courage to be tested. I finally talked to my parents. "So what if you have a learning disability?" my practical mother said. "It's not going to change who you are." My father did some research, and told me that Einstein had a learning disability. Finally, I overcame my reluctance and went to an ADD center that Dr. Fordham recommended. The tests confirmed that I had ADD. Somehow, knowing the truth lifted a weight from my shoulders. Now I was ready to do something about my problem. When a doctor at the center suggested Ritalin, I was doubtful. I had always thought it was some sort of tranquilizer for unruly kids. Dr. Sims told me it was actually a stimulant that helped many people with ADD to focus. After talking with Dr. Sims, I agreed to try it. I also scheduled a visit with a counselor to learn coping techniques. Accepting my learning disability and finding ways of coping was the last step in my process of self-discovery.

Now, dealing with school is much easier. Last term, for the first time, I made the dean's list. It is as if I have discovered my abilities, not my disability. I know that I am not lazy and unmotivated, but a smart and determined person. Now, though, I'm able to show it.

Questions

1. In the space below, write the thesis statement of the essay.

    ____

    ____

2. In the space below, write the topic sentence of each body paragraph.

    ____

    ____

    ____

    ____

    ____

    ____

3. What were the steps the writer followed in accepting her disability?

    ____

    ____

    ____

Process Essay 2

A job in a bakery, an ambition to start a business, and a bit of observation helped the writer of this essay to learn about the process of pleasing a customer.

A Lesson in Customer Service

As a full-time college student majoring in business administration, I have hopes of owning my own business someday. As a part-time worker in a bakery, I see what a hassle owning a business can be. Business owners have to worry about making a profit and keeping employees happy and productive. Most of all, they have to worry about keeping customers, even when they can't always deliver what the customer wants. The other day, I watched Herschel, our bakery manager, deal with a difficult customer. Herschel's behavior showed me how to handle a customer complaint.

The first thing that Herschel did was to accept full responsibility. The customer had been told that there were no angel food cakes. The last two had been thrown out that morning because they were out of date. She was upset. Why hadn't they been marked down? My answer would have been, "Sorry, it's company policy." Herschel took responsibility. He said, "When you buy a cake, I want you to have the freshest one available. If I sell merchandise that is out of date, I know I'm not giving you my best." The woman was still not happy. "Other stores sell out-of-date products at a reduced price," she said. "If I get it for a reduced price, I don't expect it to be as fresh."

As I watched, I was getting a little irritated with the woman, but Herschel explained his position patiently. He spoke of his pride in his products and his belief that every customer was entitled to quality. He spoke calmly and casually, as if the customer were a friend. He leaned forward, his body language saying that their conversation was of great interest. "If you take home a cake or a loaf of bread and you don't eat any for four days," he said, "it should still be good when you open it." The customer said, "Okay, I understand," and started to leave.

I would have probably shrugged and let her walk away, but Herschel took a little extra time to make her feel important. He walked with the woman around the bakery, squeezing loaves of bread and chatting. He pointed out fat free muffins and raisin bread, and told her how much he liked the carrot cake. It was trivial conversation, but the point was not what he said. The point was that his willingness to take time with her suggested that she was a

```
valuable customer. When she left, she was smiling
and carrying a loaf of raisin bread with her.
   Instead of taking the easy way out, Herschel
accepted responsibility for company policies, took
the time to explain, and made the woman feel like
a valued customer. I believe he won a customer for
life. As for me, I received a lesson in customer
service that I will remember when I am running my
own business.
```

Questions

1. In the space below, write the thesis statement of the essay.

   ____

   ____

2. In the space below, write the topic sentence of each body paragraph.

   ____

   ____

   ____

   ____

   ____

3. What are the steps involved in handling a customer complaint, according to the writer?

   ____

   ____

Topics for Process Writing

Process Assignment 1: An Everyday Task

Journal Entry

Write a process journal entry telling your reader how to do a simple, everyday task. Describe it so well and so completely that a reader could complete the process based on your directions alone. Be sure to include at the beginning of the paper any tools that the reader will need. A few suggestions follow.

tying a shoe	starting a car	reading a newspaper
brushing your teeth	feeding a pet	putting on and buttoning a shirt
making toast	putting on makeup	
making coffee	shaving	

Process Assignment 2: The Way You Do the Things You Do

Essay

Write an essay telling your reader how to do something that you do well. It might be a physical skill, like pitching a baseball, driving a car, or doing an aerobic exercise routine. It might be a social skill, like making people feel comfortable or mediating an argument. Or it might be a practical skill or a craft, like getting the most for your money at the grocery store or making a stained-glass window.

Process Assignment 3: The Process of Change

Essay

Change can be difficult, and the process of coping with it is not always easy. Think of a change or transition that was difficult for you and describe in a five-paragraph essay your process of coping with it.

Process Assignment 4: The Right Start

Essay

Write an essay directed at someone who is just getting started in one of the following processes.

starting a physical fitness program
beginning college
setting up a budget
trying to lose or gain weight

Topics for Combining Methods of Development

Definition, classification, and process are methods of showing the limits of a topic—the borders that define it—and of ordering it into steps, stages, or types. The following assignments ask you to combine one or more methods of development.

Mixed Methods Assignment 1: Stress

Essay: Definition and Classification

In this essay, your job is to define the term *stress* and to divide it into types. Your definition must be broad enough to cover all the types of stress that you explore in your essay. As a suggestion for organizing your essay, try defining the broad term *stress* in the introduction. Then, list and define each type of stress in a topic sentence. Since classification essays often incorporate examples, you may wish to support your body paragraphs with examples that give the reader a clear picture of each type of stress.

Mixed Methods Assignment 2: Problems and Solutions

Consultant's Report: Definition, Classification, and Process

You are a consultant. A large organization—it could be a school, a mall, a grocery store, a church, or some other organization that serves many people—has hired you to look at its problems and determine how the organization can fix those problems. It is up to you to choose the organization and define and classify its problems. Just to give some examples, a mall might find that many people with handicaps have trouble moving freely about the mall. They can't climb the stairs, the aisles in some of the stores are too narrow to navigate in a wheelchair, and the food court tables are too close together for them to navigate the food court. You might classify these as "mobility problems." That same mall might find that teenagers, who traditionally have high disposable incomes, are not spending their money. Instead of making the mall stores profitable by buying clothing, CDs, or video games, they are hanging out in the food court with friends or flirting with other teenagers. How can the mall lure these teenagers into the stores to spend money? These problems might be classified as "profitability problems." Or perhaps existing parking is not adequate and there is no land available adjacent to the mall to create more parking—a parking problem. Your first task, then, is to decide on the organization you want to write about and to define and classify its problems.

Once you have listed the problems and classified them into groups, your job is to come up with a process by which the organization can solve its problems.

This report can easily be organized like a traditional essay. The thesis will state the problems faced by the organization, and each body paragraph will define and classify a problem and suggest a process for solving it.

Mixed Methods Assignment 3: What It Is, How It Works

Essay: Definition and Process

Everyone develops ways of doing things—of completing everyday processes—that work for them. Some people even name their systems—Andrea's Clothing Coordination System, Raoul's Never-Fail Approach to Getting a Date, Betty's Efficient Grocery Shopping Method. What's your system? In this essay, your job is to define a process that works well for you, pointing out its advantages over conventional methods. Then, describe the process, step by step, so that a reader could easily follow your directions and use your process.

9

Writing an Essay

T	This ticket entitles those who have
I	mastered the essay to move freely
C	within the academic world, to express
K	themselves in a way that professors will
E	respect, and to modify the essay format
T	to fit any type of academic writing.

You are about to meet a form of writing that offers a ticket to just about anywhere in the academic world. When you master the fundamentals of the essay, you master a form of writing that can be used to express an opinion, analyze a poem, or compare two methods of government. Shrunk down a bit, it can be used to answer a question on an essay test or an employment application. Expanded a bit, it can be used to write a research paper, a term paper, or even a master's thesis. Even this textbook is, in many ways, an expansion of the essay format.

Parts of an Essay

Once you learn to write an essay, you can modify the essay form and length to suit your purpose for writing. Here's how an essay looks: First comes an introduction that catches the reader's attention, provides background, introduces the subject, and states the **thesis,** or the main idea of the essay.

Then come the **body paragraphs.** Each one discusses one aspect of your thesis. The topic sentence of each paragraph tells which thesis point the paragraph will develop.

The essay ends with a **conclusion** that sums up the points you have made and lets your reader know that you have ended the essay.

A diagram of a five-paragraph essay appears below. Study it to get a mental map of the essay, then use it for planning and checking your own essays.

Essay Diagram

Introduction
- The first sentence attracts the reader's attention.
- The introduction provides background and introduces the subject.
- The last sentence states the thesis (main idea) and may list the points of development.

First Body Paragraph
- The topic sentence states the first thesis point that you will develop.
- Support sentences give specific examples, information, and explanation of the topic sentence.
- A summary sentence (optional) sums up the entire paragraph.

Second Body Paragraph
- The topic sentence states the next thesis point that you will develop.
- Support sentences give specific examples, information, and explanation of the topic sentence.
- A summary sentence (optional) sums up the entire paragraph.

Third Body Paragraph
- The topic sentence states the third thesis point that you will develop.
- Support sentences give specific examples, information, and explanation of the topic sentence.
- A summary sentence (optional) sums up the entire paragraph.

Conclusion
- The first sentence of the conclusion is a broad, thesis-level statement. It may restate the thesis.
- The last sentence of the conclusion is satisfying and final-sounding.

Sample Essay

Like Father, Like Son

attention-getting opening

"Like father, like son," my aunt always said. Then her eyes would slide over to my mother in a secretive way, and I knew even as a child that it was not a compliment. Now that I have a child of my own, it is important to me to prove my aunt's words wrong. As a parent, I plan to be different from my own father in all of the ways that count.

thesis statement

topic sentence 1

The first difference that my aunt—and my child—will see in me is that I will lead a more sober life than my father did. During all my growing-up years, my father abused alcohol and drugs. Since he and my mother were not together, I never saw the worst of it. But even on our rare visitation days, he could not take me to a ball game or a mall without stopping by a convenience store for a six-pack. Maybe because of that example—or maybe because I was young and stupid—I followed in my father's footsteps for a while. But now that I am older and have a son, my wild days are over. I realize the importance of setting a good example and of being a role model to him. Drugs and alcohol will never be a part of the image of me that my son Brandon carries through life.

support

summary sentence

topic sentence 2

Another difference will be in my financial support of my child. My father drifted from job to job and had periods of unemployment, so his financial support was undependable. To make ends meet, my mother had to work two jobs, one in the mornings on a hotel janitorial staff and the other waiting tables on a part-time basis. Even then, times were often tough. Financial support is part of being a father. It is the reason that I work, and the reason I am enrolled in school. Brandon's mother will never have to work an extra job because I am not meeting my obligations.

support

summary sentence

(continued)

topic sentence 3 — Unlike my father, I am going to be there for my child. My father's visits were as unpredictable as support — his support checks. He was not there when I was six and had my tonsils taken out, and he was not there for my high school graduation. I will be there for Brandon. Brandon's mother and I have chosen to live separately, but both of us agree that I should have an active role in his life. When he was a baby, I held him and fed him and changed his diapers. Now, I am the one who takes him to t-ball practice and attends all his games. summary sentence — He can count on me to be there during the important moments in his life.

I have never been a perfect person, and I won't thesis restatement — be a perfect father. But I am determined to do better than my father did. I will be a good role model and support my son financially and emotionally. Closing thought — One day, someone may look at us and say, "Like father, like son." When that happens, I want Brandon to feel proud.

Meeting the Challenge of Essay Writing

How do you get from an idea or assignment to a polished, fully developed essay? It is sometimes difficult to make the transition from paragraph-length compositions to essays. The length and the format of your assignments have changed. But the basic principles you have been following have not changed. The writing process is still the same: you still prewrite, plan, draft, revise, and proofread.

Similarly, the characteristics of an effective paragraph also apply to the essay. **Direction, unity, coherence,** and **support** are part of the makeup of effective paragraphs *and* essays. Review those characteristics below, and see how these qualities of effective writing apply to the essay.

Characteristics of an Effective Essay

1. **Direction** means that the essay has a strong thesis sentence that states the main idea and sets the course that the essay will follow.

2. **Unity** means that the essay makes one main point and sticks to that point. Each body paragraph may discuss a different thesis point, but the essay never strays from the idea expressed in the thesis.
3. **Coherence** means that the essay is logically connected and easy to follow.
4. **Support** means that the essay contains specific and detailed discussion of the idea stated in the topic sentence.

Writing the Essay

Because the essay is so much longer than the paragraphs you have been writing, it may appear to be not so much a writing exercise as a major construction project. Like any major project, the construction of an essay is accomplished word by word, sentence by sentence, paragraph by paragraph. The next few sections of the chapter deal with the major parts of the essay and with how those parts fit together to form a coherent whole.

Providing Direction: Writing the Thesis Statement

Your **thesis statement** is the most important sentence in your essay. It states the main idea of your essay, often states or implies your attitude or opinion about the subject, and gives your essay **direction.** In an essay, the thesis statement is the controlling force behind every sentence and every word. It is a promise to your reader that you will discuss the idea mentioned in the thesis statement and no other.

Types of Thesis Statements

When constructing your thesis statement, you have a choice. You may write a **thesis with points** that lists the points the essay will cover or a **thesis without points** that does not list the points of development.

The Thesis with Points

A thesis with points presents the main idea and the points of development, listed in the order in which you will discuss them in the essay. The thesis with points has a long tradition in college writing. Listing your thesis points provides a road map that lets the reader see where the essay is headed.

Examples of a Thesis with Points

Playing with (point 1) my children, shopping with my (point 2) mother and sister, and spending time with my husband (point 3) are my weekend pleasures.

Older students may attend college to prepare for (point 1) a new career, to advance in their (point 2) present career, or to satisfy a hunger (point 3) for learning.

Action (point 1), an exciting plot (point 2), and strong characters (point 3) are essential ingredients for any movie.

Exercise 1 Completing Thesis Statements

Complete the following thesis statements.

1. Our camping trip was a disaster. We were pelted by rain, bitten by __________, and ________ by _______.
2. Writing an essay requires good ideas, __________________, and ____________ _____________________.
3. __________, __________, and _______________ are my mother's best qualities.
4. These days, the best candidate for the job is usually the one _______________ ______, ___________________________, and ___________________.
5. Some of the things people fear about getting old are _________, ________, and ___________.

The Thesis without Points Listed

A thesis without points listed presents the central idea of the essay without enumerating the points of development. Without the "road map" that listing your points provides, it is even more important that your essay flow logically and smoothly. Therefore, topic sentences require careful planning so that they are clearly connected to the thesis. When you plan a thesis without points, plan each topic sentence, too, to ensure that you stay on track. Not listing thesis points does not mean that you do not plan them; it simply means that you do not list them.

Examples of a Thesis without Points Listed

Thesis: My weekend pleasures revolve around my family.

Topic sentence 1: On Friday evenings, my husband and I often enjoy a movie.

Topic sentence 2: On Saturdays, I take the children shopping or swimming.

Topic sentence 3: Every Sunday, we visit my parents or my husband's parents.

Thesis: Starting an exercise program has made me a healthier person

Topic sentence 1: For one thing, exercise has improved my aerobic capacity.

Topic sentence 2: I also feel stronger since I began exercising.

Topic sentence 3: Thanks to my exercise program, I have also dropped a few unwanted pounds.

Thesis: Losing my parents at the age of eighteen was the hardest thing I have ever gone through.

Topic sentence 1: The accident was so sudden and my parents were gone so quickly that I was numb for weeks.

Topic sentence 2: My parents' death left me with a tremendous amount of responsibility.

Topic sentence 3: It is still difficult seeing the milestones ahead that my parents will never share with me.

EXERCISE 2 WRITING THESIS STATEMENTS

For each of the following topics, write a thesis statement without points.

1. What was the best (or worst) day of your life?

____

2. Should drivers and their passengers be required to wear seat belts?

____

3. Is there ever any justification for cheating?

____

4. If you could spend a week visiting any place in the world, where would you go?

____

5. What popular activity do you consider overrated? Why?

____

Getting Started: Introducing the Essay

It is said that you will never have a second chance to make a first impression. Because first impressions are so important, it pays to put extra effort into your introduction. However, an introduction is more than just a way to make a good impression. It does several jobs that no other part of the essay could do quite so effectively.

Purposes of an Introduction

1. **An introduction draws your reader into the essay.** The first sentence of your introduction should be irresistible. It won't always turn out that way, but aim high anyway.
2. **An introduction presents the general topic of your essay.** When you ease into the thesis by bringing up your general topic first, your reader has time to turn her thoughts away from whatever is on her mind—the price of gas or what to eat for lunch—and to get in the mood to listen to what you have to say.
3. **An introduction provides necessary background.** Background information is not always necessary. But if it is, the introduction is a good place for it. Background information tucked into the introduction gives the necessary details to set up the rest of the essay.
4. **The introduction presents your essay's thesis.** The most important job of an introductory paragraph is to present your essay's thesis. Every sentence in the introduction should follow a path of logic that leads directly to your thesis, which will be the last sentence of your introduction. Once you have stated the thesis, stop. Your body paragraphs will flow naturally from a thesis that comes at the end of the introduction.

Writing the Introductory Paragraph

Introductions that draw a reader in don't just happen; they are carefully crafted. Three common types of introduction appear below. Try them all, using the examples as models.

The Broad-to-Narrow Introduction

The *broad-to-narrow introduction* is a classic style of introduction. Sometimes called the *inverted triangle introduction,* it funnels your reader from a statement of your topic to the narrowest point in the introduction: your thesis.

Example

Driving is a great American pastime. Roads and highways swarm with drivers going back and forth from work, school, shopping, or recreation. And with so many drivers on the road, there are bound to be a few who should never have been trusted with that little plastic card called a license. The worst drivers on the road are those who tailgate, those who weave in and out of traffic, and those who drive drunk.

The Narrow-to-Broad Introduction

Instead of beginning with a statement of your general topic, the *narrow-to-broad introduction* begins at a point that is smaller than your thesis—often just a detail—and expands toward that thesis. With this method, you can create an unusual and intriguing opening.

Example

I see the tires first, grimed with the dirt of a long journey. Then I catch a glimpse of a face in the window of the long, boxy vehicle. The RV passes, giving me a last look at the bikes hooked to the back and "The Wanderer" painted above the rear window. I just don't get it. Why would anyone want an RV? An RV is a poor choice for vacationing because of its cost, size, and the chores that come along with it.

The Contrast Introduction

Gold placed on black velvet in a jeweler's window takes on extra luster against the contrasting background. In a *contrast introduction,* your ideas can shine through the drama of contrast. Starting with a contrasting idea is an easy and effective technique to use. Make sure that your introduction contains a change-of-direction signal such as *but* or *however* so that the two contrasting elements are clearly set apart.

Example

Modern life often means that people work long hours to buy possessions that they don't have time to enjoy. Sometimes, it means that children have too many toys and not enough of their parents' time.

But many people have decided to leave the rat race. Instead of striving for more, these families live on less in exchange for working fewer hours or sometimes quitting their jobs entirely and working for themselves. A simpler lifestyle can reduce stress, teach self-reliance, and encourage family unity.

The Body Paragraphs: Unity

Once you begin writing the body of your essay, you are in familiar territory once again. You already know how to write a topic sentence and support a paragraph. In writing the three body paragraphs of a five-paragraph essay, you are simply doing that familiar task three times. In an essay, however, each of the three body paragraphs is directly related to the thesis statement. Specifically, each body paragraph discusses one aspect of the thesis statement. This arrangement gives an essay **unity.** Look at the thesis from an earlier sample essay:

Thesis: As a parent, I plan to be different from my own father in all of the ways that count.

From reading the thesis, it is clear that the writer plans to discuss *ways his parenting style will be different from his father's.* Each body paragraph, then, will discuss one way in which the writer will be different from his own father.

Now look at the topic sentences from the sample essay and notice how each relates directly to the thesis (*being different from his father*) while at the same time discussing a distinct and separate point of that thesis:

Topic Sentence 1: The first difference that my aunt—and my child—will see in me is that I will lead a more sober life than my father did.

Topic Sentence 2: Another difference will be in my financial support of my child.

Topic Sentence 3: Unlike my father, I am going to be there for my child.

A thesis statement gives your essay direction. The topic sentences must follow that direction or the unity of the essay will be compromised.

EXERCISE 3 ELIMINATING FAULTY TOPIC SENTENCES

Each of the following thesis statements is followed by three topic sentences. Circle the letter of the topic sentence that does *not* support the thesis statement.

1. Football is my favorite sport.
   a. When I was in high school, I was on the football team three out of four years.
   b. During football season, I am glued to my television set to watch the games.
   c. Attendance at professional football games has risen in recent years, demonstrating the sport's popularity.
2. Like dogs themselves, there are several kinds of dog owners.
   a. Like the wolves they are descended from, dogs are pack animals and need to be part of a social structure.
   b. Some dog owners simply want a companion around the house or apartment.
   c. Another type of dog owner wants the protection that a dog can provide.
3. The city's new indoor skating park will have several positive effects.
   a. Skaters and skateboarders will have a place to call their own.
   b. Pedestrians will no longer be endangered by fast-moving skaters on downtown streets.
   c. Skating can be dangerous, so skaters and skateboarders should always wear safety equipment.
4. Our college should consider scheduling classes around a "Wonderful Wednesday" or a "Fabulous Friday," a day during the week when no classes meet.
   a. A weekly day off would give students time to go to the library and work on class projects.
   b. The idea has been rejected by the school's administration because students might not use the day productively.
   c. The day would also give professors a chance to catch up on grading and have conferences with students.
5. Looking at movies of the 1950s and movies of today, it is easy to see how their differences reflect social changes over the years.
   a. Romantic comedies of the 1950s almost always ended on marriage, but today's movies reflect a different social trend.
   b. Special effects in 1950s movies were unsophisticated, but today's advanced techniques produce impressive effects.
   c. Minorities and women were often stereotyped in 1950s movies, but today's films have fewer stereotyped characters.

The Body Paragraphs: Support

Once you have written the thesis and topic sentences, you have an outline composed of the main idea and major subpoints of the essay. All that remains is to flesh out the body paragraphs with strong, vivid, detailed support, just as you would in any paragraph. Review the principles of support by completing the exercise below.

EXERCISE 4 RECOGNIZING SPECIFIC SUPPORT

The introduction on recreational vehicles is extended here with three sets of body paragraphs. In the blank to the left of each paragraph, mark *S* if the paragraph contains specific support and *V* if the paragraph contains vague support.

Body Paragraph 1a

_____ First of all, an RV is extremely expensive. As anyone who has ever visited an RV dealer or an RV show can testify, the initial outlay for a new RV is considerable. In addition, there are numerous other expenses associated with RV ownership. Some of those expenses relate to traveling, while others relate to maintenance. For the cost involved in owning and maintaining an RV, a person might be able to enjoy a luxury vacation at the finest hotel.

Body Paragraph 1b

_____ First of all, an RV is extremely expensive. A new RV can cost $100,000 or more, as much as some houses. Add to that the cost of gas, maintenance, hookup at RV parks, storage, and repairs, and an RV becomes even more expensive. If a person put $100,000 in the bank at 5 percent interest instead of buying an RV, he would get $5,000 in interest each year, enough to take a vacation or two every year and still keep his $100,000.

Body Paragraph 2a

_____ Second, an RV is just too large. Its size makes it difficult to maneuver and gives it a greater stopping distance, thus requiring greater driving skill. It can't be parked just anywhere, nor can its driver just whip into a drive-through for a hamburger when the travelers get hungry. Its size also makes storage a problem during the months when it is not being used. My neighbors' RV is too large to fit into their garage, so they had to build a separate storage barn in their backyard just to keep their RV out of the weather. That's fine for people who have the money and the space to build a storage facility, but people who live in condominiums or who have small lots have to make other arrangements. An RV's size makes it more of a liability than an asset.

Body Paragraph 2b

_____ Second, an RV is just too large. The size of an RV is enormous, dwarfing every car on the road. Size has several disadvantages. Many of the maneuvers that drivers of smaller vehicles take for granted cannot be performed by an RV because of its size. Further, there is the consideration of RV storage, which must take size into account. An RV's size makes it more of a liability than an asset.

Body Paragraph 3a

_____ Finally, an RV is just too much work. People who travel in RVs have to clean, cook, make beds, and empty toilets. If they run out of food, they have to shop. If I have to take all that work on vacation with me, I might as well stay at home. When I go on vacation, I want to eat in restaurants and have my food brought to me perfectly prepared. I do not want to stand over a hot stove and know that I have to wash dishes after I eat. In the morning, I want to leave my bed unmade and my towels in the tub, walk on the beach, and come back to my room to find everything in perfect order. In an RV, I would have to do all the work myself.

Body Paragraph 3b

_____ Finally, an RV is just too much work. People who travel in RVs have to do all the work normally associated with a maintaining a house. In many

```
cases, there are other associated tasks that relate
to travel. Why would a person take all of those
household chores on vacation? It seems to me that
the purpose of a vacation is to leave everyday
chores behind. In a hotel these tasks are
accomplished by the hotel staff, so that the
traveler has little to do. That seems like the
ideal situation for any traveler. That way, when
the traveler returns home, he is rested and
refreshed, not worn out from trying to accomplish
all the tasks associated with traveling in an RV.
```

The Body Paragraphs: Coherence

An essay requires not only coherence *within* paragraphs, but coherence *between* paragraphs. That is, movement from one paragraph to the next should seem graceful, natural, and seamless.

Coherence within paragraphs is provided by transitional words, use of pronouns, and use of repetition. (To review these principles, glance back at the section on coherence in Chapter 5.) Look below for tips for making graceful transitions between paragraphs.

Tips for Smooth Transitions

1. In the first body paragraph, you do not necessarily need a transitional word. If you want to use one to indicate that this paragraph is making the first of several points, the choices are easy: *first of all, one reason* (*factor, cause,* or similar term), or *first.*
2. The second body paragraph gives you more choices. You can use a phrase like *a second reason* or a word such as *next, another,* or *also.* For variety, try slipping the word or phrase in the middle of your topic sentence instead of using it at the beginning: "Job security is *another* reason I have chosen a career in the medical field."
3. The third body paragraph gives you all of the transitional options of the second body paragraph and a few others as well. Since the third body paragraph is your last, you can use expressions like *finally* or *the last reason.* If you are using emphatic order (order of importance), you might want to try *most important, the major factor, best,* or *worst.*
4. Transitions of time and place are preferable in narrative or descriptive essays and can be used in any essay organized around time or place. Transitions of time might include phrases such as *after I had finished my*

classes for the day, the next morning, or *a few weeks later.* Transitions of place might include phrases such as *just down the hall, across the room,* or *on the other side of town.* (A more complete listing is found in Chapter 5.)

5. Avoid anything that would confuse your reader or make it seem as though you are just mechanically plugging in transitions instead of trying to write an artful essay. A reader would be confused, for instance, if you used a phrase such as *in conclusion* to begin your last body paragraph. The last body paragraph contains your last major point, but it is not your conclusion. (In fact, *in conclusion* is not even a recommended opening for conclusions.)

   Any transitional sequence that uses counting throughout—*first, second, third; my first reason, my second reason, my third reason*—gives your reader the impression that you are using transitions mechanically and unthinkingly rather than choosing them for best effect. If you use numbers, combine them with other transitional expressions for best effect: *the first reason, another factor,* and *the final cause.*

A Graceful Exit: The Conclusion

The etiquette of concluding an essay, like that of ending a telephone conversation, is simple: keep the goodbye short and don't introduce any new information that keeps the other person hanging on too long.

After the specific and detailed support of the body paragraphs, the first sentence or two of your conclusion takes the reader back to a broad, thesis-level view of the topic. Often, this takes the form of a thesis restatement.

Then comes the closing statement, harder to write but vital because it is the last impression your reader takes away from the essay. The key requirement of a closing statement is that it should *sound* like a closing statement. It should sound as final as the slam of a door.

Sample Conclusion 1: A Summary Conclusion

The summary conclusion sums up the main points and ends with a sentence that provides a ring of finality.

Example

Recreational vehicles are too costly, too big, and too labor intensive. When I go on vacation, I'll drive my own car, stay at a reasonably priced motel, and let someone else do all the work.

Sample Conclusion 2: A Recommendation

A recommendation conclusion suggests a solution to a problem raised in the essay. A logical way to end an essay that discusses a problem is to offer a solution or suggest that one is on the horizon.

Example

In spite of a few problems, our school library is a valuable resource for all students. Extending weekend and evening hours, keeping the computer room open whenever the library is open, and setting aside a special group study area for students who need to converse will go a long way toward easing the frustrations many students experience when they visit the library.

Sample Conclusion 3: A Prediction

A look toward the future is another good way of ending an essay. The example below ends an essay discussing the advantages of online music stores with a summary and a prediction.

Example

Online music stores have a wide selection of merchandise, offer convenience, and allow customers to listen before they buy. With all of those advantages, it won't be long before a majority of people begin turning away from conventional music shops and taking their business online.

Wordsmith's Corner: Sample Essays

Below are two essays. One explores "inner space"—the writer's search for who she is—while the other discusses exploration of outer space. Read each essay and answer the questions that follow.

Essay 1

In the essay, Autumn discusses her lifelong search for her heritage.

A Mixed-up Kid

I opened the wedding invitation and read, "As we form a new union, we draw on the strength of our heritage and the unity of our family. Celebrate with us." A wave of longing and downright envy swept over me. I do not envy Kim her marriage. I envy her strong sense of who she is and where she comes from. It is a feeling I have never known. All my life, I have been searching for who I am.

When I look at the two people who adopted me twenty years ago, I feel lucky, secure, and loved, but I see nothing of where I came from. My mom's red hair and freckles tell of her Irish heritage, but say nothing of mine. She sets our Thanksgiving table with her great-grandmother's crystal and linen, and tells me to look forward, not back. She just doesn't understand. My dad, who has Scottish and Cherokee ancestry, understands a bit more. When I was younger, he would stretch his arm out, comparing his fawn-colored skin to mine. "That's a pretty close match," he'd say. "You might have a little Cherokee in you somewhere." Hearing him say that always made me feel connected and secure.

When I look in the mirror, I see no clear clues to my heritage. I see light caramel skin, coarse, wavy hair, and brown eyes. My face is wide, with a small, flat nose and delicate lips. I am short—just 5′2″—with a sturdy build. When I was in the sixth grade, a new girl at school asked me what race I was. I told her that my parents had told me my background was mixed, but I was adopted and not sure what the mixture was. "I'm a mixed-up kid, too," she said. I thought that was the perfect way of expressing how I felt—a mixed-up kid.

When I look to society to find out who I am, I get no answers. My adoption records are sealed, and my mom and dad know nothing about my birth parents. Was I given up by a teenage mother who loved me but couldn't keep me? Was I thrown in a dumpster by an uncaring parent or left on a doorstep by a desperate one? I may never know. Because I know so little about my background, I have tried to seek a mirror in many different social groups, and I have friends of all races. Yet there is still a part of me that feels like an outsider in any group because I am not sure where I come from.

For the most part, I am a happy person who feels fortunate in her family and friends. Mostly, I follow my mother's advice to look forward and not back. But when I look around me, hoping to see a reflection of who I am, all I see is a mixed-up kid.

Questions

1. Underline the thesis statement. Is it a thesis with points listed or without points listed?

   ____

2. Underline the topic sentence of each paragraph.

Essay 2

Harley, the writer of this essay, discusses the value of the U.S. space program.

The Final Frontier

On the day that I was born, Neil Armstrong, the first person on the moon, took "one small step for man, one giant leap for mankind." I guess that is why I have always taken an interest in our space program. The space program, unlike many government programs, has something to give to every American.

The space program links every American to the mysteries that lie beyond Earth's atmosphere. Human beings have always looked to the heavens with a sense of wonder. Only in the last century have we actually been able to explore our moon and other planets. The Mars *Pathfinder* mission in 1997 gave us a closer look at the red planet with a mobile rover that took soil samples and pictures from all angles, even showing us a Martian sunset. The *Voyager* traveled outward among the planets, taking photographs of red Mars, ringed Saturn, and blue Neptune. In photographing the planet Jupiter and its moons, *Voyager* discovered ice on one of the moons, and where there is water or ice, there is the possibility of some form of life. What could be more exciting than the discovery of life beyond Earth's boundaries?

Another important contribution of the space program is that it gives us heroes in a time when heroes are few. Alan Shepherd, the first American in space, had the courage to go "where no one had gone before" as Americans sat mesmerized in front of black-and-white TV sets. Neil Armstrong, the first to set foot on the moon, was my hero for many years. Sally Ride, the first woman in space, inspired people all over the United States to cheer her on with the words "Ride, Sally Ride!" And who can forget Christa McAuliffe, the first teacher in space, who died tragically in the explosion of the space shuttle Challenger? John Glenn, a veteran space traveler, was the first senior citizen to test the effects of space travel on an aging body. All of these people are heroes because they are pioneers, among the first to travel where our descendants may one day live.

The most important contribution of the space program is the hope it gives for the future. All around us, the earth's resources are being depleted. If we don't replenish the forests, repair the ozone layer, and repopulate endangered species, life on Earth will be in danger. The growth of the human population also raises the possibility that one day, the earth may no longer have room for everyone. The vast, cold reaches of space may hold a solution to these problems. Human beings have lived for months on the Mir space station, and that is just the beginning. Self-sustaining space colonies could eventually provide room for a spreading human population. People may one day find a way to populate the planets in the solar system or even to reach other solar systems through interstellar travel. In the future, space may hold the key to human survival.

Space travel has fascinated me since I was old enough to know that on my birthday, the first human set foot on the moon. I believe that the space

```
program returns value for every penny that is spent
on it. It links us to the ancient mysteries of the
universe, it provides us with heroes, and it brings
hope for a brighter future for every human being.
```

Questions

1. Underline the thesis statement. Is it a thesis with points listed or without points listed?

   ____

2. Underline the topic sentence of each paragraph.

Topics for Writing Essays

Essay Assignment 1: Reflections of You

In Sample Essay 1, "A Mixed-up Kid," the writer speaks of searching for her reflection in her parents, in her own mirror, and in society. Write an essay discussing who you are in your own eyes and in the eyes of two other groups or individuals. Possibilities include your parents, friends, teachers, members of your church, and children. Or you might move in a widening circle, first discussing how you see yourself, how your close friends see you, and how casual acquaintances see you. Another possibility, particularly if your view of yourself has changed radically over the years, is an essay explaining how you saw yourself in the past, how you see yourself now, and how you hope to see yourself in the future.

Constructing Your Essay

Step 1: Prewrite using one of the methods in Chapter 2. Prewriting is even more important in longer compositions, which usually require more thought. Try **freewriting** for ten minutes about the image that you have of yourself and that various other people or groups have of you. Or try a cluster diagram, with each branch of the cluster showing a different view of the person you are. Next, review your prewriting and choose the three viewpoints you want to include in your essay. Make sure that they are separate and distinct viewpoints. If all three viewpoints show you as the same exact person, your three body paragraphs will be nearly identical in content.

Step 2: Plan, making a brief outline of the essay you plan to write. Here's where you'll decide on the order in which to present your paragraphs and get some idea of the supporting examples you want to use. After you've done a scratch outline, write out your thesis statement and your three topic sentences. You may want to change the wording later, but completing a thesis statement and topic sentences prepares you for the next step.

Step 3: Draft your essay as completely as you can. If you have trouble with the introduction, start with your thesis and proceed from there. You can always come back and write your introduction later. Complete each paragraph as if it were an individual paragraph like the ones you have been writing in class, including plenty of specific support for each topic sentence. When you have completed your draft, including the introduction and conclusion, lay it aside for a while before proceeding to the next step.

Step 4: Revise your essay. First, do a visual check. Does your essay look balanced, with the three body paragraphs approximately equal in length? Are the body paragraphs framed by an introduction and conclusion that are shorter than the body paragraphs?

Next, check your word count. If you are writing on a computer, your word processor can check the count for you. If you have written in longhand, pick three lines at random. Count the number of words in each line, add them together, and then divide by three. The result is your average number of words per line. Count the number of lines, then multiply by the average number of words per line. The result is your approximate word count. If your word count is between 400 and 550, you are in the ballpark. If the count is over 600, check to make sure that everything you are saying supports your thesis and that you are not repeating yourself. If your word count is under 400, you probably need to add more support.

Finally, check the specific parts of your essay, using the Checklist for Revision at the end of this chapter.

Once you have completed the Checklist for Revision, you might want to show your essay to a classmate. Ask your classmate to focus on content and clarity. Does he or she understand everything you say? Are examples plentiful and specific?

Once you have looked at your essay, completed the revision checklist, and perhaps gotten a second opinion, rewrite the essay.

Step 5: Proofread after you have revised your essay and are satisfied that it is the essay you want to turn in. Correct any errors in grammar or spelling.

Essay Assignment 2: What Interests You?

In Sample Essay 2, "The Final Frontier," the writer discusses a lifelong interest in the space program. What interests you, either as an onlooker or a participant? Are you a movie buff, a music lover, or a follower of a particular sport? Do you read every book and watch every TV special about a particular historical period? Are you into collecting teacups, playing the alto sax, riding motorcycles, attending garage sales, or singing in a choir or chorus?

Whatever your interest, write about it, following the steps of the writing process as outlined in Essay Assignment 1. To get started, think of the following questions:

How long have you been pursuing your interest?

Who got you started?

What is it that inspires and fascinates you about it?

Are there people associated with it that you admire?

What activities do you participate in that involve your interest?

Checklist for Revision

The Introduction

✔ Does the introduction draw the reader in?

✔ Does the introduction provide background information, if needed?

The Thesis

✔ Is the thesis the last sentence of the introduction?

✔ If the thesis does not include points of development, does it state the main idea broadly enough to include all the points you raise in your body paragraphs?

✔ If the thesis lists points, does it list three separate and distinct points?

Topic Sentences

✔ Does each topic sentence raise one separate and distinct thesis point?

✔ If the thesis lists points, are body paragraphs arranged in the same order as thesis points?

The Body

✔ Does each body paragraph provide specific detail and examples for each thesis point?

✔ Have you provided enough specific support for each thesis point?

✔ Does each sentence of each body paragraph support the topic sentence?

The Conclusion

✔ Is the first sentence of the conclusion a broad, thesis-level statement?

✔ Is the conclusion short, with no new information introduced?

✔ Is the last sentence satisfying and final-sounding?

Checking Coherence

10

Building a Framework:
Thesis and Organization

Your bones
A house's beams
A car's chassis
An egg's shell
A tree's trunk
Your essay's thesis

The items listed above may seem to have little in common, but they are alike in one important way: they all provide a framework. Without the framework of bones, your body would be weak and shapeless. Without a chassis, a car would go nowhere. Without a shell, an egg would run in all directions. Similarly, without the framework of a thesis and organization, your essay might be weak and shapeless, go nowhere, or run in all directions.

When you are ready to begin writing an essay, you are ready to think about the thesis and organization. You know the subject of your essay, and you have decided, through prewriting, what points your essay will cover. Perhaps you have even made a scratch outline. Now, you are ready to write a thesis statement. Several ways of writing a thesis are presented in this chapter, but at heart, a thesis is a very simple: it is the main idea of your essay. Once you have stated the main idea clearly and effectively, you are ready to organize your essay to best advantage.

Structure of an Essay

Title
- Concisely conveys the topic of the essay

Introduction
- Begins with an interesting opening sentence
- Introduces the topic
- Ends with a thesis that presents the main idea and that may list the points that will be covered

First Body Paragraph
- Begins with a topic sentence that introduces the first point of discussion
- Presents examples and details that develop the first point
- May close with a summary sentence that restates the first point

Second Body Paragraph
- Begins with a topic sentence that introduces the second point of discussion
- Presents examples and details that develop the second point
- May close with a summary sentence that restates the second point

Third Body Paragraph
- Begins with a topic sentence that introduces the third point of discussion
- Presents examples and details that develop the third point
- May close with a summary sentence that restates the third point

Conclusion
- Provides a two- to four-sentence ending for the essay
- May sum up the points made in the essay
- Ends on a note of finality

The Structure of an Essay

Before constructing a thesis, study the diagram of a typical essay on the facing page. Then read the essay below, noticing how it corresponds to the diagram. A well-planned thesis statement is an important step in writing a well-structured essay.

A Model Essay

The Advantages of Internet Shopping

Standing in a line at a huge discount store on the Saturday before Christmas, I felt grumpy and impatient. The line had been at a standstill for five minutes, and the toddler behind me in his mother's shopping cart had started to wail loudly. Hunger was beginning to gnaw at the edges of my stomach. When had shopping become such a pain? Recently, however, I have discovered Internet shopping. Convenience, choice, and savings are the reasons I now prefer to do my shopping online.

Convenience is the main advantage of shopping over the Internet. If I want to, I can shop at the same large discount store where I shopped on that miserable Saturday afternoon, with no long lines and no squalling babies. On the Internet, I do not have to circle a huge parking lot searching for a space. I can shop in the quiet and convenience of my own home, with jazz playing softly on the CD player and a cup of hot chocolate in my hand. "No shirt, no shoes, no service" does not apply on the Internet. My flannel pajamas and fuzzy bunny slippers are well within the dress code. And if it's midnight, I can still shop. The Internet is open all night.

A second advantage to Internet shopping is choice. Living in a medium-sized city, I don't have access to the full range of shops that a large metropolitan area would offer. However, the Internet connects me in minutes with a full range of retailers. Since the online environment offers a wide range of stores, from Wal-Mart to Tiffany's, I am sure to find something within my price range. In addition, a wide variety of merchandise is available. I can shop for CDs and listen to samples of music at online music stores. I can buy gifts, flowers, candy and personalized t-shirts for Christmas, birthdays, or Mother's Day. I can even buy textbooks for my classes at an online textbook outlet. With the variety of merchandise offered on the Internet, I can almost always find what I need.

Finally, shopping on the Internet saves both money and time. I don't have to buy gas for my car before I shop online, nor do I buy lunch as I would have if I were at a mall. In addition, since online retailers don't need a brick-and-mortar store, they have lower overhead and often, lower prices. I recently saved $200 on a laser printer by purchasing it online, and shipping was free. Shopping online also takes less time than shopping in a store. Driving around and shopping at malls or discount stores can easily take the better part of a Saturday. Shopping online usually takes less than an hour, even if I visit multiple sites to compare prices. Saving money and time is a big advantage of online shopping.

Internet shopping has many advantages, including convenience, choice, and savings. Next Christmas, I will not drive to a crowded discount store and wear out my feet and my patience looking for a gift; I will turn on my computer instead. I hear that even Santa surfs the Net these days.

Constructing the Thesis Statement

A **thesis statement,** usually placed at the end of your introductory paragraph, states the main idea of your essay, often states or implies your attitude or opinion about the subject, and gives your essay **direction.**

Direction means that the thesis sets the course that the essay will follow. In an essay, the thesis statement is the controlling force behind every sentence and every word. It is a promise to your reader that you will discuss the idea mentioned in the thesis statement and no other.

Types of Thesis Statements

A thesis statement presents the main idea of an essay. Sometimes, it also presents the points that will be covered in the essay. When you construct your thesis statement, you will decide whether to write a thesis that lists points of developments or one that does not.

As you write, you will find that some topics lend themselves to listing points while others do not. Your writing habits can also help you decide which type of thesis to use. Careful, organized writers can usually work with either type. Writers who tend to skip steps, however, find that listing points forces them to be more thorough and organized.

The Thesis with Points Listed

A *thesis with points listed* presents the main idea along with the points of development. These points are listed in the order in which they will be discussed in the essay. The thesis listing points of development has a long tradition in college writing. Listing thesis points provides a road map that lets the reader see where the essay is headed.

Examples

My formula for a successful lawn care business includes *clever advertising*, *competitive prices*, and *reliable service*.

Price, *performance*, and *fit* are factors to consider when shopping for athletic shoes.

Advantages of a Thesis with Points Listed

1. Listing thesis points forces you to plan your essay carefully. If you habitually skim over the prewriting and planning stages, then listing points forces you to think through your topic before you write the essay.

2. Listing thesis points conveys an impression of careful organization. Your reader sees concrete evidence that you have planned before writing.
3. Listing thesis points aids clarity by giving the reader a road map to the development of your essay.
4. Listing thesis points keeps you on track. Your thesis serves as a mini-outline for you to follow as you write.

Three Ways to Write a Thesis Listing Points

When you write a thesis listing points, you may list the points at the end of the thesis statement, at the beginning of the thesis statement, or in a separate sentence.

Points listed at the end of the thesis statement. One way of writing a thesis statement is to present the main idea first and then list the points of development.

Example

I enjoy fishing [thesis] because it relaxes me [point 1], it challenges me [point 2], and it occasionally feeds me [point 3].

The writer's thesis, or main idea, is that fishing relaxes him, challenges him, and occasionally feeds him. Notice that the thesis also conveys the writer's attitude toward his subject: he enjoys fishing. Even without the word *enjoys,* the positive nature of the points conveys the writer's attitude. Also notice the parallel structure of the thesis points. Each point follows the same pattern.

it relaxes me
it challenges me
it (occasionally) feeds me

Although perfect parallel structure will not be possible in every thesis, try to make thesis points as parallel as possible. For more information on parallel structure, see Chapter 25, "Parallel Structure."

Points listed at the beginning of the thesis statement. Listing points first is a bit out of the ordinary. With this technique, you can create a thesis that will not look like everyone else's.

Example

point 1 point 2 point 3

Too little time, a shortage of money, and a lack of belief in my abilities

thesis

made me postpone my college education.

Points listed in a separate sentence. Listing points separately works well for longer thesis statements. If you find your thesis statement becoming long and cumbersome, try listing the points separately.

Example

thesis

AIDS is changing the dating habits of American men and women.

point 1 point 2

People are becoming reluctant to engage in casual sex, choosy about

point 3

the men or women they date, and more likely to remain monogamous.

Exercise 1 Analyzing Thesis Statements

Analyze the three thesis statements below by answering the questions that follow.

1. Good students are likely to attend class regularly, participate enthusiastically, and study often.

a. What is the topic of the essay? ________________________________

b. Are the points of development listed first, last, or separately? __________

____

c. List the points in the order of presentation. Notice the parallel structure.

____

____

____

2. Pride in my accomplishment, the opportunity to help others, and the ability to support my family will be the rewards of earning my nursing degree.

   a. What is the topic of the essay? ______________________

   b. Are the points of development listed first, last, or separately? __________

   ____

   c. List the points in the order of presentation. Notice the parallel structure.

   ____

   ____

   ____

3. Singing with a jazz band gives me an outlet for my creativity, a source of extra income, and a more active social life.

   a. What is the topic of the essay? ______________________

   b. Are the points of development listed first, last, or separately? __________

   ____

   c. List the points in the order of presentation. Notice the parallel structure.

   ____

   ____

   ____

EXERCISE 2 COMPLETING THESIS STATEMENTS

Complete the following thesis statements, making sure to list the points in parallel structure.

1. The convenient parking, the ______________, and the ______________ are advantages of shopping in a mall.
2. Classmates who talk in class, ______________, and ______________ are annoying.
3. ______________, ______________, and ______________ are the main ingredients for a party.
4. Any employer would be fortunate to hire me. I would bring enthusiasm, ______________, and ______________ to my job.

5. I would like living in a small town. Small towns are ____________, ____________, and ______________.

EXERCISE 3 WRITING A THESIS STATEMENT LISTING POINTS

Write a thesis listing points on three of the following topics. Include one thesis with points listed first, at least one with points listed last, and at least one with points listed separately. Remember to use parallel structure.

1. What are the keys to maintaining good health?

____

____

2. If you could possess any one talent or ability, what would you choose? Why?

____

____

3. What are some differences between high school and college classes?

____

____

4. Do you prefer working alone or in a group?

____

____

5. Do you enjoy being outdoors? Why or why not?

____

____

The Thesis without Points Listed

The **thesis without points listed** presents the central idea of the essay without listing the points of development. A thesis that does not list points requires you to plan carefully to keep yourself and your reader on track. Without the road map that listing your points provides, it is even more important that your essay flow logically and smoothly. Thus topic sentences require careful planning so that they are clearly connected to the thesis. When you plan a thesis without points, it is a good idea to plan each topic sentence, too, to ensure that you stay on track. Remember, not listing points does not mean that you do not plan them; it simply means you do not list them.

Examples

Working in a chicken processing plant was a sickening experience.

When I look back ten years from now, I will see that my choice to attend college was the best decision I ever made.

Advantages of a Thesis without Points Listed

1. A thesis without points allows you to state your main idea simply and concisely.
2. A thesis without points works well when the points are long and cumbersome or difficult to write in parallel structure.
3. A thesis without points eliminates the worry that your topic sentences will echo the wording of your thesis too closely.
4. The thesis without points is considered a more advanced technique and is more often the choice of professional essayists.

Below are examples of thesis statements that do not list points, along with possible topic sentences for each body paragraph.

Example 1

Thesis: On the college level, the proper punishment for those caught cheating is expulsion.

Topic sentences:

Body paragraph 1: Expulsion is a severe penalty that will make potential cheaters think twice before being dishonest.

Body paragraph 2: Expelling cheaters will reassure responsible students that honesty really is the best policy.

Body paragraph 3: Most important, a college's refusal to tolerate cheating ensures that a college degree will retain its value.

Example 2

Thesis: Year-round attendance at public schools is a good idea.

Topic sentences:

Body paragraph 1: For working parents, a longer school year would ease summer child-care problems.

Body paragraph 2: Year-round school attendance would prevent "brain drain" during summer vacation.

Body paragraph 3: A longer school year would lead to higher student achievement.

EXERCISE 4 WRITING A THESIS STATEMENT WITHOUT POINTS LISTED

Write a thesis that does not list points on three of the following topics.

1. Do you prefer to write on a computer or with pen and paper?

   ____

   ____

2. Some are promoting the day after Thanksgiving, traditionally a big day for retailers, as "Buy Nothing Day," a day of awareness about consumer habits. Would you participate in "Buy Nothing Day"?

   ____

   ____

3. If you could have an all-expenses-paid trip to anywhere for two weeks, where would you go? Why?

   ____

   ____

4. If you were building a house and had enough in your budget for just one porch, would you choose to build a front porch or a back porch? Why?

   ____

   ____

5. Is it better to grow up in a small family or a large family? Why?

   ____

   ____

Evaluating Your Thesis Points

After you construct your thesis, the next step is to evaluate your thesis points. Specifically, your thesis points should not overlap, should not be too broad, and should not be too narrow.

Avoiding Overlap

When two or more of your points overlap, you risk making the same point more than once. Evaluating the thesis for overlap means making sure that your points of development are distinct, separate points that do not cover the same territory. The following examples show thesis statements with overlapping points.

Example: Thesis with Overlap

Taking out an auto loan has helped me [thesis] to be responsible in making payments [point 1], to handle money wisely [point 2], and to obtain reliable transportation that I could not otherwise afford [point 3].

Analysis: Points 1 and 2 overlap since making payments is a part of handling money wisely. The writer needs to evaluate the support she plans to use for each point and modify the thesis accordingly.

Revision

Taking out an auto loan has helped me to handle my finances responsibly, to establish a good credit rating, and to obtain reliable transportation that I could not otherwise afford.

Analysis: The writer has eliminated the overlap by combining the overlapping points and adding a new point: establishing a credit rating.

Exercise 5 Eliminating Overlap

Each of the following thesis statements contains one point that overlaps with another point. Cross out that point and write in one that does not overlap with any other point.

1. Although I enjoy my job, I sometimes tire of the long hours, the stress, and the pressure.

____

2. Our college's snack bar is a place to meet friends, a place to study, and a place to gather.

____

3. Trustworthiness, honesty, and a sense of humor are qualities I look for in a friend.

____

4. I broke off my engagement because I needed to finish college before marrying, the timing was not right, and I was not ready for a long-term commitment.

____

5. People on public assistance should work for the money they receive. Such work would prepare them for the job market, make them feel good about themselves, and give them experience that might help them find future employment.

____

Avoiding Ideas That Are Too Broad

Ideas that are too broad are too large to develop in a single paragraph. Often, they are also vague because the writer has not taken the time to consider exactly what the paragraph will be about.

Example

A nursing degree will give me a chance to work at a challenging career, to support my family well, and to make the world a better place.

Analysis: The third point, "to make the world a better place," is too broad. Narrowing the idea to cover only the writer's community and relating the idea to the writer's field of study makes the point narrower, more realistic, and easier to support.

Revision

A nursing degree will give me a chance to work at a challenging career, to support my family well, and to educate my community on health issues.

Exercise 6 Eliminating Points That Are Too Broad

Each of the following thesis statements contains one point that is too broad. Cross out that point and write in a point that can be developed within one paragraph.

1. Spending a year or two on a job before going to college can provide a student the opportunity to earn money toward a college education, to see what the real world is like, and to learn responsible work habits.

   ____

2. I like Ms. Brennan, my supervisor, because of her fairness, her sense of humor, and her good qualities.

   ____

3. For me, the ideal job provides on-site child care, up-to-date equipment, and great working conditions.

   ____

4. Losing weight, controlling my temper, and improving myself are some New Year's resolutions I am trying to keep this year.

   ____

5. I dislike driving at night because of poor night vision, fear of something happening to me, and the possibility of a breakdown.

   ____

Avoiding Ideas That Are Too Narrow

Ideas that are too narrow may not produce a paragraph's worth of support. Often, these ideas are better used as supporting detail. When an idea is too narrow, see if it is related to a larger idea that could be used as a topic sentence. If the idea cannot be broadened, discard it and look for another.

Example

My grandmother, the owner of Sally's Frame Shop, has all the characteristics of a good businesswoman. She works hard, says "hello" to customers, and provides quality service.

Analysis: The second point, "says 'hello' to customers," is too narrow to develop as a paragraph. However, saying "hello" is part of a larger issue: treating customers with courtesy.

Revision

My grandmother, the owner of Sally's Frame Shop, has all the characteristics of a good businesswoman. She works hard, treats customers courteously, and provides quality service.

EXERCISE 7 ELIMINATING POINTS THAT ARE TOO NARROW

Each of the following thesis statements contains one point that is too narrow. Cross out that point and write in a point that is large enough to develop within a paragraph.

1. Growing up with three sisters has taught me to stand up for myself, to share my hair dryer, and to cherish my family ties.

   ____

2. I enjoy my job at First National Bank because the working conditions are pleasant, I make $12.80 per hour, and my coworkers are helpful.

   ____

3. The latest safety devices, a medium blue color, and reliability are features I look for in a car.

   ____

4. My dog is playful, protective, and named Butch.

   ____

5. We enjoyed the lake because of its eighty-degree water temperature, its long, sandy beach, and its abundant plant and animal life.

   ____

Organizing Your Essay

As you construct your thesis statement, think about the order of the supporting paragraphs within your essay. Four possible ways of organizing your essay are emphatic order, reverse emphatic order, sandwich order, and chronological order. Above all, choose a method of organization that is logical to you and to your readers.

Emphatic Order

One logical way to present your ideas is in **emphatic order,** or **order of importance.** Leading up to a strong idea with emphatic order gives your essay a "snowball effect": the essay becomes more convincing as it goes along.

You may also wish to experiment with **reverse emphatic order,** beginning with your most important idea and leading to the less important ideas. This type of organization suggests that your strongest idea carries such weight that it demands to be heard first. Your lesser points shore that idea up and lend your thesis further support.

Whether you choose emphatic order or reverse emphatic order, your technique will be sound. The first and last body paragraphs are always strong points of emphasis because readers are more likely to remember points that come first or last.

Example: Emphatic Order

Thesis: Both parents should share equally in raising their children.

Topic sentence 1: Since economic necessity usually forces both parents to work, sharing child-care duties is a matter of fairness.

Topic sentence 2: Sharing responsibility allows fathers to enjoy a closer relationship with their children.

Topic sentence 3: Most important, shared responsibility gives children the active support of both parents.

Example: Reverse Emphatic Order

Thesis: When I bought a new car recently, I looked for cars with the features that were most important to me.

Topic sentence 1: When I began my search for a new car, the most important factor was cost.

Topic sentence 2: After finding cars in my price range, I looked at crash test data to find the cars that were safest.

Topic sentence 3: Finally, I checked *Consumer Reports* to see which cars were most reliable.

Exercise 8 Using Emphatic Order

Develop a thesis statement and topic sentences on two of the following five topics. Use emphatic order for one of your chosen topics and reverse emphatic order for the other.

1. Why are people afraid of aging?
2. What do you hope to accomplish within the next five years?
3. What skills—academic or nonacademic—should everyone have?
4. People usually regard anger as destructive and unproductive. Is anger ever useful?

Your Answers:

Emphatic Order

Thesis ____

____

Topic sentence 1 (least important idea) ______________________

____

Topic sentence 2 (second most important idea) __________________

____

Topic sentence 3 (most important idea) ______________________

____

Reverse Emphatic Order

Thesis ____

____

Topic sentence 1 (most important idea) ______________________

____

Topic sentence 2 (second most important idea) __________________

____

Topic sentence 3 (least important idea) ______________________

____

Sandwich Order

The points you develop within an essay are not always equally strong. When one of your points is weaker than the others, try **sandwich order,** placing your weaker point between the two stronger ones. This method employs the same psychology that is at work when you use emphatic order. If ideas are presented in a sequence, people remember the first and last ideas more strongly than those presented in the middle. Thus the first and last body paragraphs become the "showcase positions" in the essay, the positions to place the material that you want readers to remember.

Example

Thesis: Children benefit from attending day-care centers.

Topic sentence 1: At day-care centers, children benefit from interaction with peers.

Topic sentence 2: Children who attend day-care centers learn rules of behavior and basic skills.

Topic sentence 3: Perhaps most important, day care helps a child to become self-reliant.

Analysis: Point 2 is the weakest point because skills and knowledge children will need in school could also be acquired at home. Point 1 is strong because exposure to many other children is more likely at a day-care center than at home. Point 3 is strong because at a day-care center, without parents to cling to, children are more likely to become independent.

EXERCISE 9 USING SANDWICH ORDER

Develop a thesis and topic sentences for two of the following topics. Decide which point is weakest and sandwich it in the middle of your thesis. Be prepared to explain the logic you used to your instructor and classmates.

1. What can parents do to prepare their children for school?
2. What do people reveal about themselves by the way they speak?
3. Is there any college course you would refuse to take? Why?
4. If you controlled pay scales, what job would pay the highest salary? Why?

Your Answers

1. Thesis ____

____

Topic sentence 1 (strong point) ______________________________

____

Topic sentence 2 (weak point) ______________________________

____

Topic sentence 3 (strong point) ______________________________

____

2. Thesis ____

____

Topic sentence 1 (strong point) ______________________________

____

Topic sentence 2 (weak point) ______________________________

____

Topic sentence 3 (strong point) ______________________________

____

Chronological Order

Chronological order, also called *time order* or *order of occurrence,* is most often used in narratives and storytelling. But chronological order is also useful in essays. In writing about the hassles of being a first-year student, you would probably discuss problems with registration before discussing the first day of class, since registration occurred first. If you were discussing your lifelong love of music, you would probably begin with your childhood piano lessons and end with your participation in your college's community chorus. Chronological order fulfills your reader's expectation to have events described in the order in which they occur.

Example

Thesis: My first day of classes was difficult.

Topic sentence 1: Finding a parking place on the first day of class was more difficult than I expected.

Topic sentence 2: Finding my way around an unfamiliar campus was frustrating.

Topic sentence 3: After dashing into class late, I was embarrassed to realize that I was in the wrong room.

Exercise 10 Using Chronological Order

Using chronological order, develop a thesis and three topic sentences for two of the following topics.

1. What should a job candidate do to make a good impression in an interview?
2. What three people have had the greatest influence on your life?
3. Discuss how you became involved in a hobby that you enjoy.
4. If you had an entire day to spend any way you wanted, what would you do?

Your Answers:

1. Thesis ____

   ____

   Topic sentence 1 ____

   ____

   Topic sentence 2 ____

   ____

   Topic sentence 3 ____

   ____

2. Thesis ____

   ____

   Topic sentence 1 ____

   ____

   Topic sentence 2 ____

   ____

   Topic sentence 3 ____

   ____

Progressive Writing Assignment

Progressive Writing Assignment: Thesis and Outline

If your instructor has assigned the Progressive Writing Assignment, you have already completed your prewriting for one of the topics below. In this chapter, you will complete your thesis and outline. Recall that each assignment takes you a step further toward an essay, and by the end of Chapter 7, you will have a complete essay.

Topics and Tips for Writing a Thesis and Outline

The Topics

Topic 1: Discuss three obstacles to your education.

Topic 2: Discuss your short-term goals, long-term goals, or both.

Topic 3: Discuss the values you have learned by observing members of your family.

Topic 4: Discuss your methods of coping with stress.

Tips for Writing a Thesis and Outline

- Develop a thesis and outline from your prewriting, but don't be afraid to add new material if you have new ideas.
- Decide on the points you will cover in your essay and the order in which you will present them. Then write a tentative thesis.
- If you have listed your thesis points, check to make sure they are parallel and do not overlap.
- Finally, make an outline by writing a topic sentence for each body paragraph and, if you wish, briefly jotting a couple of the major points you will discuss in the essay.

11 Introducing the Essay

Hello! Greetings. Hey, YOU! **Good morning!** *So pleased to meet you.* **Yo, man! How do you do? Hi!** What's your name? **Who the heck do you think you are, buddy? Welcome! Hola.** *It's so nice to meet you.* **I've heard so much about you, I feel like I know you.** So you're the jerk who's been parking in my spot! **Wassup?** *How are you?* **Hey there!** Good to see you. **Do you come here often?** How's it going? *How ya doin'?* **Hiya!**

It is said that you never have a second chance to make a first impression. Because first impressions are so important, it pays to put extra effort into your introduction. However, an introduction is more than just a way to make a good impression. It does several jobs that no other part of the essay could do quite so effectively.

Purposes of an Introduction

1. An introduction draws your reader into the essay.

The first sentence of your introduction should be as irresistible as fresh-baked bread. True, it won't always turn out that way. Aim high anyway. A reader who is drawn in by the first sentence is more likely to read the second and the third.

2. An introduction advances the general topic of your essay.

Have you ever noticed how people approach a topic of conversation? They don't just walk up and say, "The colonization of space may become an increasingly important goal as the world's population increases," or "May I borrow twenty dollars?" Instead, they ease into the conversation, giving their listeners time to make a mental shift to the topic before bringing up the main point.

Your reader needs to make a similar mental shift. When you ease into the thesis by bringing up your general topic first, your reader has time to turn her thoughts away from whatever is on her mind—the price of gas or what to eat for lunch—and to get in the mood to listen to what you have to say.

3. An introduction provides necessary background.

Background information is not always necessary. But if it is, the introduction is a good place for it. Background information tucked into the introduction gives the necessary details without intruding on the rest of the essay. In an essay about your job, for instance, the introduction should include where you work and what you do. Then you won't have to include the information as an afterthought. In an essay about a short story or novel, your introduction should include the title and author's name. If you are writing about an event in your life, use the introduction to establish background details such as your age at the time, where it happened, and who else was involved.

4. An introduction presents your essay's thesis.

The most important job of an introductory paragraph is to present your essay's thesis. Every sentence in the introduction should follow a path of logic that leads directly to your thesis, which will be the last sentence of your introduction. Once you have stated the thesis, stop. Your body paragraphs will flow naturally from a thesis that comes at the end of the introduction.

Types of Introduction

Introductions that draw a reader in don't just happen; they are carefully crafted. Several types of introduction appear below. Try them all, using the examples as models.

Broad to Narrow

The **broad-to-narrow introduction** is a classic style of introduction. Sometimes called the *inverted triangle introduction,* it funnels your reader from a broad statement of your topic to the narrowest point in the introduction: your thesis.

Example

During registration week, tables offering Master Card or Visa applications litter college campuses like autumn leaves. Gifts are offered just for completing an application, and the promise of easy credit is tempting. Once that shiny piece of plastic is in hand, the way it is used can mean the difference between starting out after graduation with a good credit record and starting out under a mound of debt. Establishing a set of simple rules can help to make a credit card an asset instead of a liability.

EXERCISE 1 A BROAD-TO-NARROW INTRODUCTION

Arrange the following numbered sentences into a broad-to-narrow introduction, ending with the thesis.

1. Among the skillet meals, frozen dishes, boxed dinners, and canned cuisine, one convenience food stands out.
2. Manufacturers have developed a variety of convenience foods for people who do not have the time or the desire to prepare food from scratch.
3. Microwaveable frozen meals offer superior variety, nutrition, and ease of preparation.
4. Most people enjoy eating, but not everyone enjoys cooking.

The sentences should be arranged in the following order ____________, ____________, ____________, ____________.

Narrow to Broad

The **narrow-to-broad introduction** is just the opposite of the broad-to-narrow introduction. Instead of beginning with a statement of your general topic, the narrow-to-broad introduction begins at a point that is smaller than your thesis and expands toward that thesis. With this method, you can create an unusual and intriguing opening.

Example

```
   Thousands of feet above the earth, a small
crystal traces a zigzag path to the bleak landscape
below. It is the first snowflake of the season,
soon to be followed by many more that will blanket
the earth in a layer of white. Winter is my
favorite of all the seasons. I love its beauty,
I enjoy the opportunity to ski, and, like a kid,
I can never wait for Christmas to arrive.
```

EXERCISE 2 A NARROW-TO-BROAD INTRODUCTION

Arrange the following numbered sentences so that they form a narrow-to-broad introduction, ending with the thesis.

1. Seeing my father dying without dignity only reinforces my belief that physicians should be allowed to assist the suicides of terminally ill patients.
2. His eyes show no sign of recognition as I enter the room and say, "Hello, Dad."
3. As I stand in the doorway, I see my father, his hand curled like a fallen leaf and tied to the bed's metal safety bar with a Velcro wrist cuff.
4. When he became terminally ill, my father begged for enough pills to kill himself, but Dr. Abercrombie refused to prescribe them.

The sentences should be arranged in the following order __________,

__________, __________, __________.

Quotation

A **quotation** adds sparkle to your introduction and spares you the work of crafting just the right words for your opening—someone else has already done it for you. You do not necessarily have to quote a book, a play, or a famous person. You may quote your best friend, your mother, or your great-aunt Sally. You may quote a commercial, a bumper sticker, or a popular song. You may quote an expert on your subject to lend authority to your words. For a ready-made source of quotations, consult the reference section of your college library for collections of quotations, such as *Bartlett's Familiar Quotations*.

When opening with a quotation, you need to know how to use quotation marks and how to paraphrase a quotation. (See Chapter 33 for more information on quotations.) It is also important to give credit to the author or, if you do not know who originally said it, to acknowledge that the quotation is not your own. In addition, a quotation cannot just hang in space, unconnected to your essay. You need a transition that shows your reader the connection between the quotation and your thesis.

Examples

Quotation Opening—Known Author:

Mark Twain wrote, "Few things are harder to put up with than the annoyance of a good example." *[transition to thesis]* He must have had a brother just like mine. All my life I have tried to live up to the example of a brother who is more athletic, more studious, and more at ease socially than I am.

Quotation Opening—Unknown Author:

A habit *[acknowledgement of outside source]* has been defined as "a shackle for the free." *[transition to thesis]* This statement seems particularly relevant to the habit of smoking. A person who smokes is no longer free but is chained to a habit that is expensive, socially unacceptable, and dangerous.

Paraphrased Quotation—Author and Exact Words Unknown:

[acknowledgement of outside source] I once heard someone say that *[paraphrased quotation]* we get old too soon and smart too late. *[transition to thesis]* That statement is certainly true in my case. I have just begun to understand that my parents were right when they told me I should go to college. At seventeen, I disregarded their advice. Now, at thirty-two, I realize that I need a college education to make a comfortable

```
living, to reach my career goals, and to set the
right example for my children.
```

Exercise 3 Opening with a Quotation

Choosing from the list of quotations below, follow the directions for each numbered part of the exercise.

Quotations

The only way to have a friend is to be one.
—Ralph Waldo Emerson, *Essays, First Series: Friendship*

The real problem is not whether machines think but whether men do.
—B. F. Skinner, *Contingencies of Reinforcement*

In spite of everything, I still believe that people are really good at heart.
—Anne Frank, *Anne Frank: The Diary of a Young Girl*

Everyone is a moon and has a dark side which he never shows to anybody.
—Mark Twain, *Following the Equator*, Vol. 1

Wisdom is not bought.
—African Proverb

Show me someone not full of herself, and I'll show you a hungry person.
—Nikki Giovanni, "Poem for a Lady Whose Voice I Like"

Beware of all enterprises that require new clothes.
—Henry David Thoreau, *Walden*

1. Write an opening sentence using an exact quotation and the author's name.

____

____

2. Write an opening sentence using an exact quotation but pretending you do not know the author's name.

____

____

3. Write an opening sentence paraphrasing one of the quotations and pretending you do not know the author's name.

____

____

4. Write a transitional sentence connecting the quotation to the thesis in the following introduction.

   "The brain is like a muscle," Carl Sagan said. "When we use it, we feel good." (Transitional sentence) ______________________________

   My experiences in a college classroom have made me more self-reliant, more certain of my abilities, and less fearful of being wrong.

5. Write an introduction that opens with a quotation and leads with a transitional sentence into one of the following thesis statements (or one of your own).

   a. People reveal a lot about themselves by the way they dress.

   b. Every first-year student needs to know how to form new relationships during the first term at a new college.

   c. The aspects of my personality that I like least are my impatience, my stubbornness, and my tendency to procrastinate.

   ____

   ____

   ____

   ____

Anecdote

An **anecdote** is a brief story that illustrates a point. Brief is the key word. Introductions should be short, so keep your story to a few sentences and be sure to include a transition that connects the anecdote to the thesis.

Example

When she saw her front door standing open, the woman knew there had been another break-in. She took her five-year-old daughter next door and returned with a neighbor and a borrowed baseball bat. Hesitantly, she entered. Vulgar graffiti covered the walls, and the sofa had been slashed. In neighborhoods like this one where crime is out of hand, residents often feel powerless. But

transition to thesis

community involvement in the form of neighborhood watches, neighbor patrols, and insistence on strong police presence can help residents of high-crime neighborhoods reclaim their streets.

Exercise 4 An Anecdotal Introduction

Read the following anecdotal introduction, then answer the questions that follow.

[1]Last night, my sister Karen picked at her dinner, eating only her salad and her green beans. [2]Before bed, she did fifty stomach crunches, then stood at the mirror critically eyeing her waist, which is approximately the same size as her hips. [3]When I asked what she was doing, she said she was too fat and had to lose weight. [4]Karen is only nine years old, but she is already in pursuit of a goal that is impossible and unhealthy. [5]The modern obsession with having a reed-thin body is encouraged by the fashion industry, the media, and even the manufacturers of food.

1. How many sentences does the anecdote contain? ____________
2. Which sentence contains the transition to the thesis? ____________

Contrasting Idea

Gold placed on black velvet in a jeweler's window takes on extra luster against the contrasting background. Through the drama of contrast, your ideas, too, can shine. Starting with a **contrasting idea** is an easy and effective technique to use, but there are two elements that must not be left out. The first is a change-of-direction signal. When switching from one idea to its opposite, you need a word such as *but* or *however* to signal the change. The second required element is a clear, strong contrast.

Example

When I hit a home run in the bottom of the ninth to win the game for the McDuffie's Auto Parts Tigers, my dad was not there. He missed many family activities because he believed his first duty was to his job. After I graduate from college, I will have a career, but it will not be my only priority. I hope to have a well-rounded life with time for career, time for family, and time for activities that interest me.

EXERCISE 5 OPENING WITH CONTRASTING IDEAS

In the blank below each introduction, write the word that serves as a change-of-direction signal.

1. One of my professors says that students who see college simply as preparation for a career are in the wrong place. College, she says, is for those who want to become well-rounded and educated. I hate to tell her, but if all this place had to offer were wisdom, there would be an abundance of empty seats in the lecture halls. Colleges should replace classes in art appreciation and French with career skills courses, additional courses in the student's major field, and internships in various career fields.

____

2. I used to believe in accepting coworkers as they were. I did my job and minded my own business. If my coworkers goofed off, that was their business. Lately, however, I am becoming increasingly intolerant of people who arrive late, gossip, or don't carry their share of the load.

____

Historical

The **historical introduction** gives the reader background information—the "history" behind your essay. Historical introductions have two functions—to **establish authority** or expertise on a subject or to **set the stage** for your discussion.

Historical Introduction to Establish Authority

Background material can help you establish your authority or expertise on a particular subject. If you are giving advice on car maintenance, for instance, it might help your reader to know that you've worked summers and weekends at Ace's Auto Repair for the last four years, or that your own car is nearing the 200,000 mile mark on the odometer. Readers are more likely to accept advice from those who have some experience or expertise in a particular area.

Example

Through my parents' divorces and subsequent remarriages, I have acquired one stepfather, two stepmothers, three sets of step-grandparents, three stepsisters, two stepbrothers and assorted step-aunts, uncles, and cousins. I speak with the voice of experience when I say that getting along with stepfamilies requires compromise, respect of others' privacy, and willingness to share.

Historical Introduction to Set the Stage

Another reason to use a historical introduction is to give the background that sets the stage for your essay. Information that the reader needs to understand the rest of the essay should be placed in the introduction. If you write about neighbors who donated food, clothing, and money to your family, don't wait until the last paragraph to tell about the house fire that prompted their generosity. Establish those details in the introduction.

Example

My dad was a car enthusiast, and almost from the time I could walk, I followed him around on Saturdays, carrying things and being "helpful." He encouraged my love of cars, and when I was fourteen, he bought me an old junker to rebuild. Restoring cars and working on engines has brought enjoyment, won the respect of other car enthusiasts, and helped me to earn extra income.

Exercise 6 Historical Introductions

Look at each of the following thesis statements and decide whether the writer needs to use a historical introduction (1) to establish authority or (2) to set the stage. Write your choice in the blank beneath each question and be prepared to give reasons for your answer.

1. If you are not satisfied with a product or service, complain immediately, complain to the right person, and suggest a solution to the problem.

____

2. Moving away from home has made me more independent, more confident in my abilities, and more appreciative of my parents.

____

3. Helpful coworkers, a pleasant workplace, and an understanding boss make my job enjoyable.

____

4. Setting up your computer and printer is easier than you think.

____

5. To get a good bargain in a used car, you must do the proper research, have the car checked by a professional, and know how to negotiate with the dealer.

____

Progressive Writing Assignment

Progressive Writing Assignment: Introducing the Essay

If your instructor has assigned the Progressive Writing Assignment, you have already completed your prewriting and written a thesis and outline. In this chapter, you will write your introduction. Recall that each assignment takes you a step further toward an essay, and that you are now one chapter closer to a complete essay.

Topics and Tips

The Topics

Topic 1: Discuss three obstacles to your education.

Topic 2: Discuss your short-term goals, long-term goals, or both.

Topic 3: Discuss the values you have learned by observing members of your family.

Topic 4: Discuss your methods of coping with stress.

Tips for Introducing Your Essay

- Carefully consider which type of introduction would be most effective for your topic. Ask yourself if there is a quotation or anecdote that might be particularly effective with your topic. See if there is a contrasting idea that you could use or a way to lead into your thesis with a broad-to-narrow introduction. Once you have thought through each method of introduction, ask which one would work best with your topic and be most appealing to a reader.
- Place your thesis at the end of your introduction. Then make sure that the sentence that leads into the thesis does its job smoothly, providing a smooth, logical transition from your lead-in to your main idea.

12 Developing Body Paragraphs

> Sparkle
>
> A jeweler judges the quality of a diamond by "The Four C's"—color, cut, clarity, and carat weight. Evaluating by these four standards, the jeweler can determine the value of the gem.
>
> Wouldn't it be nice if there were similar standards we could apply to writing? Direction, unity, coherence, and support are the standards that measure paragraph and essay writing. Check your essays against these standards to see if you have written a real gem—or at least a diamond in the rough.

A paragraph is the smallest multiple-sentence unit of communication in our language. But simply lumping sentences together does not make them a paragraph. A **body paragraph** is a paragraph that supports a larger idea: the thesis statement of an essay. An effective body paragraph has four characteristics: direction, unity, coherence, and support.

Characteristics of an Effective Body Paragraph

1. **Direction** means that the body paragraph has a strong topic sentence that states the main idea and sets the course that the paragraph will follow.
2. **Unity** means that the paragraph makes one main point and sticks to that point.

3. **Coherence** means that the ideas in the paragraph are logically connected and easy to follow.
4. **Support** means that the paragraph contains specific and detailed discussion of the idea stated in the topic sentence.

Direction: Shaping the Topic Sentences of Body Paragraphs

A **thesis statement** gives an essay its overall direction and sometimes provides a road map for the reader by listing points. The **topic sentences** extend that function by charting each leg of the journey as the essay moves through each body paragraph. Each topic sentence outlines one thesis point, thus providing direction for each body paragraph.

The following list outlines the functions of the topic sentences of body paragraphs.

Functions of the Topic Sentence of a Body Paragraph

1. The topic sentence of a body paragraph provides a **thesis link** by mentioning the **general subject** of the essay.
2. The topic sentence of a body paragraph mentions the **specific thesis point** that will be developed within the paragraph.
3. The topic sentence may also provide **transitions** from one paragraph to the next.

Look at the following thesis statements and their topic sentences. Notice that the topic sentences provide a thesis link by mentioning the general subject of the essay. The topic sentences also present the specific thesis points. Notice that if supporting points are listed in the thesis, topic sentences follow the same order.

Example 1

general subject ... point 1
Thesis: A commuter college is a good choice for students with children, students on a budget, and students with full-time jobs.
point 2 ... point 3

point 1
Topic sentence 1: Students who have children find that a commuter college allows them to be students and parents, too.
general subject (thesis link)

general subject (thesis link) (transition)
Topic sentence 2: A commuter college also helps students fit the costs of college into a tight budget.
point 2

point 3
Topic sentence 3: Students who work during the day often prefer to attend night school at a commuter college.
general subject (thesis link)

Example 2

general subject no points listed
Thesis: Making a daily schedule helps me use my time efficiently.

general subject (thesis link) point 1
Topic sentence 1: A daily schedule helps me to set priorities.

general subject (thesis link) point 2
Topic sentence 2: By using a daily schedule I can avoid committing myself to too many activities.

(transition) general subject (thesis link) point 3
Topic sentence 3: Finally, my daily schedule helps to keep my day organized.

Exercise 1 Completing Topic Sentences

A list of incomplete topic sentences follows each of the thesis statements below. Fill in the blanks in each topic sentence. Topic sentences should follow the same order suggested in the thesis.

1. For me, an ideal vacation spot will offer me the opportunity to lie in the sun, to exercise, and to eat a variety of food.

a. When I am on vacation, I enjoy ______________________________.

b. Vacation also gives me the opportunity to ________________________.

c. One of the activities I enjoy most on vacation is ____________________ ____.

2. My favorite piece of furniture is my grandfather's desk. I love it for its beauty, usefulness, and sense of family history.

a. I admire the desk for its __________________________________.

b. Not only is the desk attractive, it is also ______________________.

c. The link to my __________, however, is the main reason the desk is important to me.

3. I am attending college so that I can become an accountant, support my children, and make my family proud.

a. With a college education, I can ______________________.

b. A degree will also help ensure ______________________.

c. As a first-generation college student, I ______________________.

4. At my favorite hangout, the Sand Crab, I enjoy the casual atmosphere, the unique blend of music, and the company of friends.

a. The Sand Crab has a/an __________ that I enjoy.

b. The combination of old and new _______ makes the Sand Crab unique.

c. Best of all, __________ also enjoy gathering at the Sand Crab.

5. When parents go through a divorce, children may be plagued by guilt, divided loyalty, and insecurity.

a. When parents divorce, children may ______________________.

b. Especially if the parents' divorce is a bitter one, children may ________ ______________________.

c. Children of divorce may also experience ______________________.

The Thesis Link

A **thesis link** is a word or phrase that links the topic sentence directly to the central idea of the essay. It is not always enough for the topic sentence to state a thesis point. Linking the topic sentence to the general subject of the essay or to your attitude about that subject reminds your reader that the paragraph is part of a larger whole. At the same time, a thesis link aids coherence by relating the specific point to the thesis. Notice in the examples that each topic sentence contains a word or phrase that links the paragraph to the thesis.

Example 1

Thesis statement: I have achieved higher grades this term [thesis] by improving my study habits [point 1], organizing my time [point 2], and cutting back my work hours [point 3].

point 1 thesis link
Topic sentence 1: Better study habits have been a key to my improved grades.

point 2 thesis link
Topic sentence 2: Planning has also helped me improve my grades.

thesis link
Topic sentence 3: The step that has most affected my GPA was
point 3
reducing my work hours.

Example 2

point 1 point 2
Thesis: An unreasonable boss, inconvenient work hours, and
point 3 thesis
unpleasant duties make me dislike my job at Sadie's Donut Heaven.

point 1 thesis link
Topic sentence 1: Sadie, my boss, makes my job so unbearable at times that I'm sure her name must be short for "Sadist."

thesis link
Topic sentence 2: Another unpleasant part of my job is
point 2
my work schedule.

point 3 thesis link
Topic sentence 3: The work itself makes Donut Heaven anything but heavenly.

Example 3

thesis
Thesis: I have benefited from subscribing to an online computer service.

Although the points are not listed in the thesis, the writer presents them in the topic sentences. The thesis link in each topic sentence will be a reference to the idea of *the benefits of an online computer service*. Points 1, 2, and 3 will be *those specific benefits*.

thesis link point 1
Topic sentence 1: My computer service brings me the news before it appears in the newspaper.

thesis link point 2

Topic sentence 2: Through my link to the Internet, I can visit an art museum without moving from my chair.

thesis link

Topic sentence 3: Another benefit of an online service is the opportunity to "meet" people from all over the country through computer chat rooms and bulletin boards.

point 3

Exercise 2 Providing Thesis Links

Following are five thesis statements and topic sentences that relate to them. Circle the letter of the topic sentence that does not have a thesis link, that is, the sentence that does not mention the general subject of the essay. Then rewrite the sentence, linking it to the thesis.

1. *Thesis:* The size, the location, and the design of my house make it an ideal place to live.
   a. My house is easy to enjoy because it's small enough to take care of easily.
   b. Out in the country, my nearest neighbor is five miles away.
   c. The convenient layout and many windows in my home suit my casual lifestyle.

   ____

   ____

2. *Thesis:* Many people over twenty-five hesitate to return to school because of the demands of their jobs, their commitment to their children, or their fear of returning to the classroom.
   a. Many jobs require special skills or further education.
   b. The demands of parenthood often keep older students from continuing their education.
   c. Perhaps the number one reason older students postpone a return to school is fear.

   ____

   ____

3. *Thesis:* Dieting is difficult for me because I usually eat substantial meals, snack in the evenings, and nibble when I am nervous.
   a. My lifelong habit of eating "three squares a day" defeats any diet I start.
   b. Snacks usually accompany my evening reading or television viewing.

c. Even if a diet is going well, stress often sends me running to the refrigerator.

____

____

4. *Thesis:* Some students are a pain to have as classmates. These include students who never come prepared, those who are noisy, and those who monopolize the class discussion.

   a. Coming to class unprepared is a common occurrence.

   b. Even worse than the unprepared student is the student who distracts the class with unnecessary noise.

   c. Most tiresome of all is the student who monopolizes the class discussion.

   ____

   ____

5. *Thesis:* In recent years, the public has become increasingly unwilling to report crimes.

   a. Many people fear that reporting a crime will provoke retaliation from the criminal.

   b. Some citizens don't want to get involved.

   c. Other crimes go unreported because crime victims believe the police can do nothing to help.

   ____

   ____

Unity: Sticking to the Point of the Essay

An essay with **unity** is like a completed jigsaw puzzle. Every piece is necessary, and each does its part to contribute to the big picture. Each paragraph, each sentence, fits perfectly to support the thesis. When one piece does not fit, the essay lacks unity. Lack of unity occurs within a paragraph when one or more sentences do not support the paragraph's topic sentence. Likewise, when an entire paragraph does not support the thesis of the essay, the essay lacks unity.

Read the paragraph in the example below and see if you can spot the three sentences that interfere with the unity of the paragraph.

Example

[1]I have heard that inside every fat person, there is a thin person waiting to get out, but I believe that just the opposite is true. [2]Inside every thin

person, a fat person is waiting to take control. [3]For most people, maintaining thinness requires self-control at mealtime. [4]A thin person may say "no" to the extra helping of cottage cheese and measure the fat-free salad dressing carefully because it too contains calories. [5]But somewhere inside, an inner, fat self is craving ice cream with chocolate sauce for dessert. [6]Staying thin also requires exercise. [7]The thin person may have plans to attend evening aerobics after work, but the fat person inside would rather curl in front of a fire with a book and a cup of hot cocoa. [8]The thin person who gets up at 5:30 A.M. to jog has to silence the fat self's inner voice, which is whining for just an extra half-hour's sleep. [9]Of course, thin people are better off staying thin. [10]Studies have shown that in general, people who eat less live longer. [11]In addition, people who exercise are healthier and more likely to maintain flexibility and mobility well into old age. [12]All it would take is a moment of weakness for the fat person inside to burst forth, no longer held in by the tight cocoon of thinness.

Were you able to spot the sentences that did not fit? The paragraph lacks unity because sentences 9, 10, and 11 do not support the topic sentence of the paragraph.

Exercise 3 Spotting Problems with Unity

Read the following essay. Find and identify

a. the body paragraph that does not support the thesis statement, and
b. the body paragraph that contains two sentences that do not support its topic sentence.

Choosing a Veterinarian

That squirming, tail-wagging furball that you bring home from the pound or pet store needs more than just love and kibble. Good veterinary care is also essential. If you know what to look for, finding the right veterinarian for your pet can be a simple process.

[1]The first step is to evaluate the veterinarian's office. First, consider its location. It should be close enough to your home to be convenient. In an emergency, you should be able to get there in a few minutes. Next, look at the physical facility itself. Cleanliness is a must. The waiting room should be clean and pleasant, and it should be standard practice for the staff to disinfect the tables in the exam rooms before each use. Next, make sure that the facility's services meet your needs. Some veterinary clinics provide boarding, grooming, and bathing. Some clinics require appointments, while others provide service on a first come, first serve basis. The clinic you choose should be convenient, clean, and provide the services that you need.

[2]Once you have found a clinic you like, the next step is to evaluate the veterinarian and the staff. They should be kind to you and to your pet. Watch the way your pet is handled. Is he handled gently yet confidently, called by name, and spoken to in a kind tone? The vet's approach to your pet should make you smile. If your pet is treated roughly, find another vet. Your vet's treatment of you should pass muster, too. Good veterinarians do not simply treat animals; they also educate owners. They tell you why and how an illness can occur, signs to look for as the pet gets better, and signs that indicate you should bring the pet back. Caring for a sick pet can be difficult because a pet cannot talk to you like a human can. The pet cannot tell you where it hurts or what is wrong.

[3]Even with good veterinary facilities and a competent, caring vet, chances are that the veterinary clinic will not be your pet's favorite place to visit. Many pet owners report that their pets have an uncanny sixth sense about visits to vet. When it's time to go to the vet, these apparently psychic pets disappear under beds, into closets, or

```
behind refrigerators. Repeated calling does not
bring them out, and they must finally be hunted
down and dragged out of hiding. In the car, cats
yowl and dogs whine, and some fearful pets even
have "accidents" on the way, losing control of
their bowel or bladder functions. At the vet's
office most become quiet and docile as the
veterinarian handles them. Rarely, animals become
aggressive, growling or snapping. But though the
visits may be traumatic, they are necessary to a
pet's good health.
   Ensuring good veterinary care is easier if you
know how to pick the right vet for your dog or
cat. Good veterinary care is one way you can repay
the love, loyalty, and companionship your pet
provides.
```

The paragraph that is entirely off the topic is body paragraph _______.

The paragraph that contains two sentences that do not support the topic sentence is body paragraph ________.

Coherence: Holding the Essay Together

An essay with **coherence** is an essay with solid and strong connections between paragraphs and ideas. To achieve coherence, you must first make sure that the ideas you set down are logically related and well thought out. Coherence between ideas can also be aided by transitional words and expressions.

Below is a list of transitional words and expressions, organized by their function within the sentence.

Some Common Transitional Words and Expressions

*** *Transitions of Time***

after	during	later	now	suddenly	when
as	first	meanwhile	often	temporarily	while
before	immediately	next	previously	then	yet

* *Transitions of Space*

above	beside	down	next to	toward
around	between	in	on	under
behind	by	near	over	

* *Transitions of Addition*

also	finally	furthermore	in addition	next
another	first			

* *Transitions of Importance*

as important	essential	major	primary
equally important	just as important	most important	significant

* *Transitions of Contrast*

although	even though	in contrast	instead	on the other hand
but	however	in spite of	nevertheless	yet

* *Transitions of Cause and Effect*

a consequence of	because	since	therefore
as a result	consequently	so	thus

* *Transitions of Illustration or Example*

for example	for instance	including	such as

Making Transitions between Body Paragraphs

When you move from one body paragraph to the next, **transitional words** act as signposts. In the first body paragraph, often no transition is needed. If you use a transitional word or expression, a simple "first of all," or "one reason . . ." usually works well. But avoid a mechanical "first, second, third" approach. Instead, vary your transitional techniques. In the second and third body paragraphs, transitional words create a bridge between paragraphs that suggests that you have discussed a related idea in the preceding paragraph. Because you are adding an idea to the ones you have already discussed, the transitional words you use will be transitions of addition: *also, another, next, an additional (reason, factor, way)*.

Examples

Doing something for someone else is *another* way to shake a bad mood.

Some teenagers' unwillingness to use birth control *also* contributes to the high rate of teen pregnancy.

The *first* step in resolving a conflict is to define the issues involved.

Exercise 4 Using Transitional Expressions

Rewrite the following topic sentences using a transition of addition. The word or phrase you choose will depend on whether you see each sentence as the topic sentence for the first body paragraph, the second body paragraph, or the last body paragraph. The choice is yours.

1. Newspapers are a better source of news than television because the stories go into more detail.

   ____

   ____

2. It is important to find a family doctor after moving to a new town.

   ____

   ____

3. The tailgater is a type of bad driver.

   ____

   ____

4. Using public transportation is cheaper than owning a vehicle.

____

____

5. Good communication skills are essential in a job interview.

____

____

The Transitional Topic Sentence

The **transitional topic sentence** takes a backward glance at the topic of the preceding paragraph before moving on to the topic of the paragraph it leads into. Since the first body paragraph presents the first point of discussion, transitional topic sentences are not used there. Transitional topic sentences can be used only in the second and third body paragraphs of a five-paragraph essay. They are an effective way of moving between paragraphs, but like any other technique, they should not be overdone. One per essay is probably enough. Some examples of transitional topic sentences follow.

Example 1

Not only do illegal drugs pose a health risk, they can also land the user in jail.

Discussion: The writer has discussed the health risks posed by illegal drugs in the preceding paragraph and is now going to discuss the possibility that the user may spend time in jail.

Example 2

A lifetime sentence to the prison of addiction is often the worst consequence of drug use.

Discussion: This variation of the first example merely hints at the topic of the preceding paragraph (the possibility of serving time in jail). The hint provides a connection between paragraphs.

Example 3

Although rock music suits my happy, energetic moods, I turn to the sound of blues when I am depressed.

Discussion: This transition outlines a movement from a paragraph about rock music to a paragraph about blues.

EXERCISE 5 WRITING TRANSITIONAL TOPIC SENTENCES

The following outlines show a thesis and three topic sentences. For each outline, rewrite topic sentences 2 and 3 as transitional topic sentences. The first one is done for you.

1. *Thesis:* I prefer renting videos to going to a movie theater. When I rent a movie, I watch it when I want to, avoid crowds, and spend less money.

Topic sentence 1: One advantage of renting a video is that I can watch it whenever I want to, not when the theater schedules it.

Topic sentence 2: I also like being able to avoid crowds at the theater.

Rewritten transitional topic sentence 2: ______________________________

____

Topic sentence 3: Saving money is another important advantage of renting a video.

Rewritten transitional topic sentence 3: ______________________________

____

2. *Thesis:* Automated answering systems, telephone sales pitches, and repeated wrong numbers have made me hate the telephone.

Topic sentence 1: When Alexander Graham Bell invented the telephone, he never foresaw the horror of automated answering systems.

Topic sentence 2: Telephone sales pitches are another reason I hate the telephone.

____

____

Topic sentence 3: Answering wrong numbers at all hours is an inconvenience of having a telephone.

____

____

3. *Thesis:* In my spare time, I enjoy tennis, woodworking, and reading.

Topic sentence 1: Tennis is one of my favorite spare-time activities.

Topic sentence 2: Another of my hobbies is woodworking.

____

____

Topic sentence 3: Reading is one of my favorite leisure activities.

____

____

Support: Using Specific Detail

Support is the heart of any piece of writing. Even a grammatically perfect essay falls flat without strong, specific support. If a thesis or topic sentence is a promise to the reader to discuss a specific topic, then an essay without solid support makes that thesis an empty promise. No matter how good it sounds, there is nothing behind it.

Although few writers deliberately set out to make empty promises, many do so because providing strong support is one of the most difficult dimensions of writing body paragraphs. It takes practice, thought, and the ability to recognize and to construct specific examples and details.

Why It's Hard to Be Specific

Quick, what did you eat for lunch yesterday?

If you are like most people, you answered with a broad term—*fast food, a sandwich, a microwaveable dinner*—rather than with a specific description, such as *a tuna-salad sandwich on rye toast.*

Being specific does not come naturally because the human brain is programmed to think in categories. This ability to lump things together by function saves you time. It also gives your brain an orderly way to store the information it receives every day. Without the ability to categorize, a football and a baseball would seem to have as little in common as a dandelion and a Phillips screwdriver. Bits of information would be scattered throughout your brain like confetti, impossible to retrieve.

But the ability to categorize can work against you when you write. Most people would complete the sentence "Harold drove to work in his

________" with the word car or truck. Few would fill in *beat-up Chevrolet Caprice that had seen its best days fifteen years ago* or *ten-year-old Volvo without a single scratch or dent*. Such specific examples do not come to mind easily because the human brain, programmed to categorize, looks first at the big picture.

To write rich, detail-packed paragraphs, train yourself to move beyond general categories and to look for the details. This skill is similar to the one that police officers develop when they learn to observe sharply and to remember detail. Police officers, however, receive special training on developing observational skills. Writers are on their own. The exercises in this section are designed to help you move beyond general categories. When you can do that, you will be able to provide examples and details and become a writer who delivers on your promises.

Essay Development Technique 1: Supporting with Specific Examples

Examples are one of the best ways to get a point across because they provide a concrete illustration of your point. If you say your father is sentimental, your reader will get the general idea. If you say he gets teary-eyed over Hallmark commercials, you are giving specific support to the general idea. Examples, then, are specific illustrations, exact instances. Using an example is like making a word or phrase more specific, but on a larger scale since examples range in length from a single word to multiple paragraphs. With an example, you are usually giving your reader both the general idea and a specific example of that idea.

An Example in a Word or Phrase

Examples expressed in a word or phrase are usually used when the author wants to illustrate an idea briefly and then move on. Look at the use of short examples in the following process paragraph.

Example

Cleaning the grout in a ceramic tile floor is a laborious process. Begin by diluting a liquid cleaner with bleach, such as Clorox Clean-up or Comet Gel, to half strength. Then, using the squeeze bottle that the cleaner came in, squeeze cleaner directly into the grout line. After doing a small patch, about a three-foot by six-foot square, allow the cleaner to penetrate for five to ten minutes. Then, using a wire scrub brush, toothbrush, or another small, stiff-bristled brush, scrub the grout clean. Be sure to keep the area properly ventilated and to walk outside the room from time to time for air, especially if you are cleaning a small area such as a bathroom. After the entire floor is complete and the area is completely dry, you are ready to seal the grout.

EXERCISE 6 PROVIDING EXAMPLES

Provide an example of each of the following ideas in a word or a phrase.

1. music
____

2. game
____

3. book
____

4. luxuries
____

5. food
____

6. problems at school
____

7. metals
____

8. injury
____

9. entertainment
____

10. bad habit
____

The Sentence-Length Example

Sometimes, you need more than just a word or phrase to illustrate an idea. In such cases, try giving an example in a sentence or two. The example needs to be a specific, detailed illustration of the general idea you are discussing, not just a vague restatement.

Example 1

✘ *Idea + vague restatement:* The new disk jockey on the morning show is really obnoxious. He has an unpleasant attitude that makes listening to his show a bad experience.

✔ *Idea + specific example:* The new disk jockey on the morning show is really obnoxious. He tries to humiliate listeners who call in, and his jokes border on the offensive.

Example 2

✘ *Idea + vague restatement:* The new grocery store has added whimsical touches to some of its departments. It's enjoyable to shop in a store that is entertaining.

✔ *Idea + specific example:* The new grocery store has added whimsical touches to some of its departments. In the produce department, thunder rolls and "lightning" flashes above the vegetable bins before the automatic vegetable sprinkler turns on. On the dairy aisle, recordings of mooing cows and clucking hens amuse passing shoppers.

Exercise 7 Weeding Out Vague Examples

Circle the letter of the sentence that is a general restatement of the idea, *not* a specific example.

1. We needed a break, so we decided to stop and have something to drink.

- **a.** I ordered coffee, and Marcie had iced tea.
- **b.** We chose from the restaurant's wide selection of refreshing beverages.
- **c.** I went to the kitchen and fixed hot herbal tea with honey and lemon.

2. A conflict broke out.

- **a.** Fists and plates flew as restaurant patrons scuffled over the last yeast roll.
- **b.** Apparently, some sort of disagreement caused an altercation to take place.

   c. John accused Myra of taking his parking place, and the two began to argue.

3. My friends are all trying to be thriftier.
   a. Emily tries to save wherever she can. She knows the value of a dollar.
   b. Tom has decided to bring his lunch instead of eating out every day.
   c. Khara clips coupons and checks grocery store specials before shopping.

4. Kay worked hard sprucing up her yard this weekend.
   a. Wearing heavy gloves, she pulled weeds from the flowerbed in front of the house.
   b. She toiled laboriously on the lawn.
   c. Soaked with sweat, she pushed the mower through tall grass for more than an hour.

5. Researchers have found that many of our grandmothers' home remedies really work.
   a. Chicken soup, the all-time favorite home remedy, eases congestion and aids breathing.
   b. Warm milk really does induce sleep.
   c. It seems that Grandma may have known what she was talking about after all.

Exercise 8 Finding Specific Support

For each of the following general ideas, provide a sentence or two of specific support.

1. The kitchen was a mess.

   ____

   ____

2. Without my glasses, I find it difficult to see.

   ____

   ____

3. In the hallway, two students complained about their English assignment.

   ____

   ____

4. The police found plenty of evidence that the accident had been Darren's fault.

____

____

5. When I met Fern, I knew immediately that she was a heavy smoker.

____

____

6. The two brands of orange juice are quite different in taste and appearance.

____

____

7. The package was damaged when it arrived in the mail.

____

____

8. One look at the teacher's face told the students he was angry.

____

____

9. The mailbox contained nothing but junk mail.

____

____

10. Litter is becoming a problem on Sanford Road.

____

____

The Extended Example

Sometimes you may wish to develop an entire paragraph with an extended, paragraph-length example. In this case, your topic sentence will state the general idea, and the rest of the paragraph will provide a detailed example. In this sort of paragraph, it is important to end with a summary sentence that connects the specific example back to the general idea, as in the following paragraph.

Example

topic sentence

One of the most annoying and time-consuming technological advances is the automated telephone system. Recently, I called a government agency to ask a simple question, but instead of being greeted by a human voice, I reached a recorded menu. "Press 1 if you need directions on filling out forms," the voice began. After listening to the menu and finding no information that I needed, I pressed a number at random. Once I reached a human being, I reasoned, I could find out what I needed to know. Instead, I was connected to yet another recording, which reeled off information, then hung up. I dialed again. Finally, I reached a part of the menu that said, "For permission to speak to an agent, press 4." I pressed the key, astounded that a taxpaying citizen would need permission to speak to someone at a government office. At last I heard the ringing of a phone that I hoped would connect me to a human voice. But it was another recording, saying "For permission to speak to an agent, please hold." Soothing music played in the background as my blood pressure reached new heights. After fifteen minutes on hold, I hung up. I had decided that writing a letter might be the easiest way to bypass the technological obstacles that stood between me and the answer to my question.

extended example

summary sentence

Although the example in the preceding paragraph is a personal example, examples do not necessarily have to be from direct personal experience. Look at the next paragraph for a different kind of extended example, one that is not based on personal experience but on the writer's knowledge of how test anxiety works.

Example

topic sentence

Sometimes, factors totally unrelated to study can interfere with performance on a test. Test anxiety is an excellent illustration. It often strikes students who have prepared adequately and who set high standards for themselves. Test anxiety goes beyond the mild jitters that plague almost every student the night before a test. It holds its victims in a paralyzing grip. Typically, the student with test anxiety looks at the first question on the test, and all the carefully studied material seems to evaporate in a haze of panic. The student knows the material before entering the examination room and may recall both questions and answers after the test has ended, but in the pressure cooker of the test environment, the answers do not come. As the example of test anxiety shows, poor test performance is not always an indication that no studying took place.

extended example

summary sentence

Exercise 9 Writing Extended Examples

Write an extended example to support one of the three topic sentences below. Don't forget to write a summary sentence connecting the example back to the idea in the topic sentence.

Topic sentence 1: Instead of hoping that a problem will go away, the best way to deal with it is to confront it head-on.

Topic sentence 2: Sometimes an opportunity comes along at exactly the right time.

Topic sentence 3: Telephone salespersons can be an annoyance.

____

____

____

____

____

____

____

____

____

____

Essay Development Technique 2: Adding Detail through Comparisons

One way to express ideas is by comparing the familiar with the unfamiliar. If your doctor tells you that a centrifuge separates the liquid parts of your blood sample from the solid by centrifugal force, you may not understand. If she says that a centrifuge separates plasma from solid blood components like a washer on the spin cycle separates water from clothes, then you will understand more readily.

Like an example, a comparison may be brief or extended. Although entire essays are developed using comparison, you may use comparison techniques in any essay to make your writing more specific.

Comparisons Using *Like* or *As*

When you make brief comparisons, you may find the words *like* and *as* useful. A comparison using *like* or *as* is called a *simile.*

Examples

- ✔ Nina moved across the dance floor like a skater on ice.
- ✔ The car was crumpled like a used tissue.
- ✔ Nina moved across the dance floor as gracefully as a skater on ice.
- ✔ The car was as crumpled as a used tissue.

When you make comparison, it is usually more useful to compare unlike things than like things. If you say, for instance, "When Billy opened the presents at his eighth birthday party, he looked like a kid at Christmas," the comparison is not very useful. After all, Billy *is* a child and he *is* opening presents, just as he might at Christmas. However, look at what happens if you compare two unlike things: "When Smitty dealt the hand, Jack picked his cards up one by one and arranged them carefully, looking like a kid at Christmas." The comparison reveals two things about Jack that a reader would not know from the rest of the sentence: he has been dealt a good hand, and he is probably not a very good card player—his face reveals too much.

Examples

✘ Bill's old Ford truck runs like a Chevrolet pickup.

✔ Bill's old Ford truck runs like a Maytag washer.

✘ The car was dented only slightly, but Sam reacted like a typical car enthusiast.

✔ The car was dented only slightly, but Sam squawked like a bird whose baby had fallen from the nest.

Exercise 10 Matching Comparisons

Match each phrase below with one of the sentences to form a logical comparison.

a. seats in a stadium
b. socks left too long at the bottom of a gym bag
c. gravestones in an old cemetery
d. spilled candy
e. needles
f. the sound of computer keys
g. a job interview
h. the rising tide engulfing the shore
i. cats' eyes in the dark
j. hot dogs browning on a grill

_____ 1. His car smelled unpleasant, like _________.

_____ 2. Next to the pool, the sunbathers lay side by side, like _________.

_____ 3. With her dentures, the old woman made a muted clicking noise, like _________.

_____ 4. Calvin's meeting with a date's parents was more like _________ than a social occasion because they asked so many questions.

_____ 5. His eyes were as piercing as ________.

_____ 6. Pebbles of all colors were scattered at the shoreline as carelessly as ________.

_____ 7. On the side of the road, beer cans glinted like ________.

_____ 8. Sleep came over her gradually, like ________.

_____ 9. The new shelf organizers that Tina bought are tiered like ________.

_____ 10. Scarred desks lined the empty classroom in orderly, silent rows like ________.

EXERCISE 11 MAKING COMPARISONS

Use your own comparisons to complete each sentence.

1. Throughout the ceremony, the groom looked bored, like a ______________ ____________________.
2. The small, gray-haired grandmother marched into the mayor's office like ________________________.
3. When the tired-looking server brought my sandwich, it was as tasteless as ________.
4. Marcia's old car was as reliable as ___________.
5. Emerging from the dark theater, Brian felt disoriented, like ______________ ____________________________.
6. After Elton's wife left him, he drifted from job to job and from town to town like ________.
7. I hoped the class would have a relaxed atmosphere, but it was as formal as ____________________.
8. Just before final exams, students burst into a frenzy of activity, like ________.
9. "When I came into this business, I had visions of limos, champagne, and adoring fans," said the actor. "Instead, I'm working as hard as __________ ____________."
10. Looking at the test in front of him, the student sat like ________________.

Progressive Writing Assignment

Progressive Writing Assignment: Writing Body Paragraphs

If your instructor has assigned the Progressive Writing Assignment, you have already completed your prewriting, your thesis and outline, and your introduction. In this chapter, you will complete your body paragraphs.

Topics and Tips for Writing Body Paragraphs

The Topics

Topic 1: Discuss three obstacles to your education.

Topic 2: Discuss your short-term goals, long-term goals, or both.

Topic 3: Discuss the values you have learned by observing members of your family.

Topic 4: Discuss your methods of coping with stress.

Tips for Writing Body Paragraphs

The Topic Sentence: Tips for Direction

- Make sure that each topic sentence mentions the subject of the paragraph and that each topic sentence links back clearly to the thesis with key words. For example, if you chose Topic 1, "Discuss three obstacles to your education," the key words *education* and *obstacles* (or a synonym such as *barriers*) should appear in each topic sentence. A typical topic sentence might read "One of the obstacles to my education is my financial situation."

Transitions: Tips for Coherence

- Use a transitional word such as *also* or *another* in the topic sentences of body paragraphs two and three. (*Another* of my long-term goals is to start my own business.)
- Make one of the topic sentences a transitional topic sentence. (*After I start my accounting business,* my next long-term goal is to start a family.)
- Check each paragraph to make sure it flows logically and has transitional expressions where needed.

Staying on Track: Tips for Unity

- Check each paragraph to make sure that every sentence supports the topic sentence.

Examples and Details: Tips for Support

- Make sure that your language is specific. Have you used words that create pictures by appealing to the reader's sense of sight, hearing, touch, taste and smell?
- Check to see that you have supported your paragraphs with specific examples. If you are writing on Topic 4, "Discuss your methods of coping with stress," you might use a *specific example* that describes what happened on a particular occasion (Last Tuesday, when I was nervous and worried about a job interview the next day . . .). However, you might also decide to use a *typical example* that describes something that customarily occurs (Every evening when I come home from work, I put on my exercise clothing . . .).

13

Concluding the Essay

The ~~conclusion~~
~~culmination~~
~~finish~~ end.

Endings are difficult. Courses end with the pressure of exams. Weekends end with Monday mornings. And for many writers, the ending of an essay is the hardest part to write. However, the etiquette of concluding an essay, like that of ending a telephone conversation, is simple: keep the goodbye short and don't introduce any new information that keeps the other person hanging on too long.

After the specific and detailed support of the body paragraphs, the first sentence or two of the conclusion should take your reader once again to a broad, thesis-level view of the topic. This broader statement may take the form of a summary, a recommendation, or a prediction.

Then comes the closing statement, harder to write but vital because it is the last impression your reader takes away from the essay. The key requirement of a closing statement is that it should *sound* like a closing statement. It should sound as final as the slam of a door.

Methods of Conclusion

To bring your essay to a solid, satisfying close, try one of the following methods of conclusion.

Summary

A **summary conclusion** is the simplest and easiest type of conclusion to write. In the first sentence or two, recap the main points of your essay, making sure to use different wording than you used in your thesis and topic sentences. Your final sentence brings the essay to a close.

In the following example, the writer recaps the major points, then ends with a strong, final-sounding statement.

Example

During my tour of duty with the Air Force, I received hands-on experience in electronics, furthered my education, and developed confidence in my ability to handle my own life. I never piloted a plane while I was in the Air Force, but in many ways, I learned to soar.

EXERCISE 1 ANALYZING A SUMMARY CONCLUSION

1. From the above summary conclusion, try to determine the major points of the essay it concludes. In what order were they most likely presented?

   ____

   ____

   ____

2. Consider the following possible versions of the ending sentence. Which do you think is strongest? Which is weakest? Why?
   a. I never piloted a plane while I was in the Air Force, but in many ways, I learned to soar. (original version)
   b. I learned to soar in many ways although I never piloted a plane while I was in the Air Force.

c. I never piloted a plane, and while I was in the Air Force, I learned to soar in many ways.

____

____

Recommendation

A **recommendation conclusion** suggests a solution to a problem raised in the essay. A logical way to end an essay that discusses a problem is to offer a solution or suggest that one is on the horizon.

Example

> It does not matter whether the shot is fired in the commission of a robbery, in the heat of an argument, or by accident. The result is the same: a life is lost. The logical solution is the one already implemented by more enlightened countries—to outlaw handguns. Outlawing handguns is a major step toward a safer, saner, less fearful society.

Exercise 2 Writing a Recommendation Conclusion

Imagine that you have written an essay discussing the causes of one of the following social problems. Write a brief conclusion (two to four sentences) making general recommendations about working toward a solution.

teenage suicide
violence in the schools
poverty among the elderly

____

____

____

____

____

____

____

____

Prediction

A **prediction conclusion**—look toward the future—is another good way of ending an essay. In the example below, the writer has discussed society's growing dependence on providers of personal service. The ending is a simple yet effective prediction.

Example

A society of graying baby boomers, working parents, and two-income families is becoming increasingly dependent on service providers. In the 21st century, hiring help with housecleaning, lawn maintenance, and child care will no longer be a luxury for many Americans, but a necessity.

EXERCISE 3 WRITING A PREDICTION CONCLUSION

You have written an essay suggesting that the solution to reducing the unwanted pet population is to require that every cat and dog be spayed or neutered within five years. Financial help is available for those who cannot afford the procedure, and exemptions are available for pets too old or ill to withstand the operation. Those who wish to breed their animals may purchase a special breeding license at a cost of $500 per animal.

Write a conclusion of two to four sentences predicting the changes that will occur over the next five years as your plan goes into effect.

Full Circle

A **full circle conclusion** incorporates a word or image from the introduction as a theme in the conclusion, thus bringing the essay full circle to end where it began. This type of conclusion is surprisingly powerful and satisfying.

Example

Below, an introduction is paired with a conclusion that comes full circle, ending with an image from the introduction.

Introduction

The photograph in the magazine showed a laboratory rat with a human ear growing out of its back. The strange-looking creature was part of an experiment in the regrowth of human cartilage through genetic engineering. I immediately thought of my neighbor Otis Needham, who lost an ear to cancer. Genetic engineering is a relatively new field, but it promises quantum leaps in organ and tissue replacement, cure of disease, and prevention of birth defects.

Conclusion

In a laboratory somewhere, a little white rat, burdened with an ear he cannot use, heralds a brighter future for the Otis Needhams of the world. Thanks in part to this little rat and others like him, human beings will live longer and healthier lives through the promise of genetic engineering.

EXERCISE 4 COMPLETING A FULL CIRCLE CONCLUSION

Step 1: Read the following introduction.

I stood in the bookstore line, staring glumly at a green book entitled *Understanding Psychology*. I could not believe my bad luck. Not only was Psychology 101 the only social science elective left, but I had to take it with Nortenson, the toughest psychology professor on campus. Before the quarter was over, however, I was thankful for the luck that led me to Dr. Nortenson's psychology class.

Step 2: Complete the conclusion by writing a first sentence that brings in the image of the book. Notice that the second sentence, beginning "Every time I look at it . . ." makes a transition that suggests that the book is someplace where you see it often. Perhaps the sentence you write could tell where it is.

Conclusion

____

_____________________________. Every time I look at it, I think of what I might have missed if I had been able to get the courses I really wanted last fall. Thanks to my bad luck, I discovered an inspiring teacher, a fascinating field of study, and my future career.

Quotation

A **quotation conclusion** can help you bring your point home solidly and effectively. For the strongest effect, make the quotation your closing statement.

Example

I had always planned to go to college "someday." But it took a loaded gun to make me realize how much of my life I had squandered behind the counter of the Kwik-Stop #7. The day after the robbery, I gave my notice and filled out a college application. At the time, I had never heard of Cervantes, but his words express a truth I realized that day: "By the streets of someday, one arrives at the house of never."

Exercise 5 Ending with a Quotation

Write a conclusion that ends in a quotation. Use a topic and quotation of your own choosing or choose from the lists below.

Quotations

When poverty comes in at the door, love flies out the window.

—Seventeenth-century saying

Our life is frittered away by detail. . . . Simplify, simplify.

—Henry David Thoreau, *Walden*

Lost time is never found again.

—Ben Franklin, *Poor Richard's Almanac*

It is not the man who has too little, but the man who craves more, who is poor.

—Lucius Annaeus Seneca, *Epistles*

Turn your face to the sun, and the shadows fall behind you.

—Maori proverb

Life sucks—and then you die.

—Bumper sticker, circa 1990

A place for everything, and everything in its place.

—Isabella Mary Beeton, *The Book of Household Management*

Have a place for everything and keep the thing somewhere else. This is not advice, it is merely custom.

—Mark Twain, *Notebooks*

The cat in gloves catches no mice.

—Ben Franklin, *Poor Richard's Almanac*

I have often regretted my speech, but never my silence.

—Publius Syrus, *Maxim*

Topics

- In what situations is it most important to be assertive?

- An optimist has been defined as a person who sees the glass as half full, while a pessimist sees it as half empty. Is it wiser to be an optimist or a pessimist?
- Do you consider yourself an organized person?
- What is your biggest regret?
- How important are wealth and material things to you?

Traps to Avoid

Sermonizing

One trap that some otherwise good writers fall into is lecturing a reader who should be assumed to be on their side of the issue. After a thoughtful, well-reasoned essay on why people turn to drugs, for instance, a writer might be tempted to end the essay with a statement like "Stay away from drugs—you'll be glad you did." Such a statement insults the reader, who should always be counted among the "good guys."

The only type of essay that should end with direct advice to the reader is one in which direct advice is given throughout, such as an essay entitled "How to Shop for a Used Car."

Starched Prose

Writers who speak in a natural voice throughout an essay sometimes stiffen up at the conclusion. They write starched prose like "As I have proven in this essay by discussing the above-mentioned points. . . ." These writers may simply be feeling the awkwardness of saying goodbye, or they may feel that an announcement of the conclusion is needed. It isn't. Even "in conclusion" is probably too much. Readers know when a writer is concluding because the writer stops developing specific points and begins to look once again at the big picture.

Armed with a set of specific concluding techniques, you can avoid the traps that snare some writers as they go about the difficult task of ending an essay.

Progressive Writing Assignment

Progressive Writing Assignment: Concluding the Essay

If your instructor has assigned the Progressive Writing Assignment, you have already completed your prewriting, a thesis and outline, an introduction, and three body paragraphs. In this chapter, you will write your conclusion. Recall that each assignment takes you a step further toward an essay and that you are now only a chapter away from a complete essay.

Topics and Tips

The Topics

Topic 1: Discuss three obstacles to your education.

Topic 2: Discuss your short-term goals, long-term goals, or both.

Topic 3: Discuss the values you have learned by observing members of your family.

Topic 4: Discuss your methods of coping with stress.

Tips for Concluding Your Essay

- For any of the topics in this assignment, a summary of the main points would be an appropriate concluding strategy, but consider other alternatives, too.
- If you used an anecdote or a particularly striking image in your introduction, consider using a full circle conclusion.
- Topics 1 and 2 might lend themselves to a prediction conclusion—a vote of confidence that you will overcome the obstacles to your education or will reach your goals.
- Check to make sure that you have not introduced any new material in your conclusion.

14

Definition and Classification

Professor Fogg's Lecture:

"Class, today's psychology lecture will be on defense mechanisms. Defense mechanisms are—**well,** the term is self-explanatory. They are part of everyone's personality, and there are—**well,** many types that work in various ways. The process through which they work is—**well,** different for each one, but our time for today is up. There will be a quiz over this material tomorrow. Class dismissed.

With each *well* uttered by the hypothetical professor above, students sink deeper into a well of confusion. The professor needs the techniques of definition, classification, and process to clarify the lecture. You can use these techniques in your writing to limit and order information and to answer the questions *What is it? How many different types exist?* and *How does it work?* Though this chapter presents each technique in isolation, you may eventually find yourself using the three techniques together to define an idea, show its different variations, and describe how it works.

Definition

When you think of definitions, you probably think of the dictionary. If you want to know the definition of *curmudgeon* or the difference between an *ectomorph* and an *endomorph,* you turn to the dictionary for definitions.

Similarly, when you want to define an idea or concept in detail, you may write a definition essay.

A dictionary entry provides a good example of a definition. Examine the sample dictionary definition of the word *burden,* then answer the questions that follow.

Sample Dictionary Definition

bur′ den (bēr′dən) *n.* **1,** something carried; a load. **2,** something borne with difficulty, as care, grief, etc. **3,** an encumbrance. **4,** a main theme; a refrain.

(from *The New American Webster Handy College Dictionary, New Third Edition.*)

■ Questions

1. Would you characterize the definition as brief or extended?
2. Does the entry provide any clue about how the person writing the entry felt about the subject, or is it strictly factual?
3. Does the dictionary definition include any examples?

As you noticed, a dictionary definition is extremely brief and entirely factual. However, there are two very brief examples in definition number two—*care* and *grief.*

A definition essay is like a dictionary definition in some ways. For example, a definition essay, like a dictionary definition, attempts to capture the essence of something—an object, a feeling, or a task—in words.

However, unlike the writer of a dictionary definition, you have the luxury of using many words in your definition essay. Instead of a four-word definition, you may have a four-hundred-word definition.

A definition essay might answer questions like the following:

- What is a status symbol?
- What are the characteristics of a leader?
- What does the word *duty* mean to you?

Using Examples in Definition Essays

Does it surprise you that the writer of a dictionary entry included an example? Dictionary entries often contain examples. Examples work well in definitions because they take an abstract idea, such as *devotion,* and make it into a concrete illustration, such as *My family tells me that my dog Lucky waits for hours at the window and barks with joy when he sees me on the front walk.*

Definitions tend to be general, and examples help to add the specificity that readers of both dictionaries and essays appreciate. Like the writer of the dictionary entry, you may decide to use an example to illustrate your definition. Instead of an example in a single word, however, you may provide an example in one or two sentences or even a whole paragraph.

■ Building Connections ■

In writing, using one method of development to support another is a common technique. Examples are often used to support and illustrate definitions. The more methods of development you know how to use, the more useful tools you will have in your writer's toolbox.

Subjective and Objective Definitions

As you examined the sample dictionary entry, you may have noticed that it was strictly factual, that it did not reflect its writer's opinion. Such factual definitions are called **objective definitions.** When you define something objectively, your task is relatively simple. An objective definition is a factual definition. You define a person, place, thing, or idea by providing facts such as physical characteristics, function or use, how it works, and its history. To define a mosquito objectively, for instance, you might say it is a winged insect that draws blood from humans and animals and sometimes spreads disease. An objective definition is the type that you would write when answering an essay question or writing a research paper.

A **subjective definition,** on the other hand, is a personal definition—one that reflects your attitude toward your subject. It may still follow the

* *Real-World Writing: Is Subjectivity Bad?*

How often have you heard people say, "Oh, that's *just* an opinion," as if opinions don't count? Such statements give subjectivity a bad reputation.

True, there are some forms of writing in which subjectivity is not appropriate—factual reports, encyclopedia entries, and scientific experiments, for example.

However, subjectivity is perfectly appropriate in many types of writing—letters to the editor, personal essays, and journal entries, to name a few. The best subjective writing is backed up by facts, so it's not *just* an opinion—it's a well supported, well thought out opinion.

same general pattern as the objective definition, but it goes beyond the merely factual. If you were defining a mosquito subjectively, you might say that it is a pesky insect that spoils summer evenings by hovering around its innocent victims, waiting for an opportunity to suck their blood.

A subjective definition, the kind found in personal essays and paragraphs, always reflects the writer's feelings about the subject. In a personal definition, a new parent might define love as a feeling that is overwhelmingly tender, yet fierce and protective. In contrast, someone who has recently been disappointed in romance might define love as a risky game that always ends in disappointment.

Exercise 1 Objective and Subjective Definitions

Read the two paragraphs below and answer the questions that follow.

Paragraph A

Denial is a type of psychological defense mechanism that allows a person to cope with a disturbing event by refusing to believe that it exists. For instance, a parent confronted with evidence that his child is using drugs might refuse to believe it. A person diagnosed with a serious illness, such as cancer, might believe that she is really healthy and that she has been misdiagnosed. When a loved one dies, the first reaction is often disbelief. Denial does not solve a problem, but it temporarily reduces the psychological discomfort that it causes.

Paragraph B

To some, pottery may be simply a craft, but to me, it is a kind of therapy. When I sit at my potter's wheel, I am in control. A lump of wet clay turns on the wheel and, under my hands, takes shape as a bowl or vase. As I shape the clay, life seems once again within my control. If I can shape clay into a pot, I can handle a difficult boss or a deadline at work. When I look at the lopsided pots and homely pitchers I made when I first started, then see the symmetrical urns and large, graceful bowls I now make, I have hope that whatever situation I am facing, whether it is a problem with my health or with a relationship, will improve. If practice can make me so much better at pottery, then practice will also help me to handle difficult times with grace and humor. Pottery always helps to restore my optimism and my sense of control.

- Which paragraph contains an objective definition? ______________________
- List an example used in each paragraph.

____

____

____

____

Wordsmith's Corner: Examples of Writing Developed by Definition

Below are two student essays developed by definition. Read each and answer the questions that follow.

Definition Essay 1

The writer of this essay takes an old subject—manners—and gives the reader an updated definition.

Manners for the Twenty-First Century

When the older man let the door swing shut behind him, I thought he did not see the woman entering the health club behind him. She caught the door before it shut and went through, holding it so I could enter behind her. As I walked into the men's locker room behind him, he said, "I don't hold doors for women anymore. These days, women will tell you off if you try to hold a door for them." I just looked at him, amazed. For most people, a changing world does not alter the need to be polite. The man's narrow-mindedness prompted me to construct my own definition of good manners for the twenty-first century.

First of all, politeness in the twenty-first century does not reinforce stereotypes. The "helpless woman" stereotype that may have once prompted men to hold doors for women is gone, but courtesy lives on. As a man, I should not hesitate to open the door for a woman, but it's also appropriate if she opens it for me. Stereotypes about people with disabilities need to be revised, too. They are not helpless, nor are they invisible. My friend Miko, who uses a wheelchair, says she appreciates it when people hold an elevator door for her. But she wishes they would look at her, not at the floor or at her companion. And while stereotypes about rank, race, or age might at one time have determined who was considered worthy of politeness, that is no longer the case. In the twenty-first century everyone from the bank president to the homeless person on the street is worth the effort of being polite.

Politeness in the twenty-first century also means considerately sharing space in a crowded world. Having good manners means not smoking in crowded public places where smoke might offend others. Increasingly, politeness has also come to include not wearing loud aftershave or cologne to the office or theater. Similarly, loud, boneshaking car stereos are usually enjoyed only by those who play them. Consideration for others means keeping the noise at a moderate level. While politeness might have once meant enjoying a conversation with a seatmate on a plane, now it often means leaving her alone to work on her laptop computer. The more crowded the world becomes, the more it is necessary to share space considerately.

Communications technology in the twenty-first century has brought a whole set of new rules. Taking a noisy beeper or cell phone into a theater or classroom is considered bad manners, as is hanging up on someone's answering machine after the beep has sounded. E-mail requires new rules, too. Sending e-mail without a subject line or trying to sell an exercise bike through company e-mail can waste people's time and is therefore considered a breach of etiquette. In e-mail messages or in computer chat rooms, typing in all capital letters is considered "shouting." The technology may be fairly new, but the basic principle of consideration for others has not changed.

Manners are not dusty relics of a former age. They change with the world and must be tailored to meet each new century. Manners for the twenty-first century, as in previous centuries, are simply rules that help the world run more smoothly.

Questions

1. Which introductory techniques does the writer use? Circle the correct answer.
   a. broad to narrow
   b. narrow to broad
   c. anecdote
2. Write the thesis statement on the line below. Does the writer's thesis indicate that his definition will be subjective or objective?

   ____

   ____

   ____

3. Write each topic sentence below.

   ____

   ____

   ____

   ____

   ____

   ____

4. Write in the space below each example that supports the topic sentence in the second body paragraph.

   ____

   ____

   ____

Definition Essay 2

The writer of this essay defines foot binding, a custom practiced for hundreds of years in China among the upper classes. The practice was officially banned by the Chinese government in 1911.

Bound by Tradition

As I lay nursing painful heel spurs that made the kitchen and the oatmeal raisin cookies my husband had baked seem impossibly far away, I began to reflect on the ancient Chinese custom of foot binding. When I first heard about it back in grade school, I was fascinated. It was, we were told, an ancient custom for Chinese girls to have their feet bound so that they would remain small. I pictured women in kimonos tottering merrily on tiny, delicate feet and wished that I had feet so small. Over the years, however, I have found an adult understanding and a darker definition of this ancient custom.

Binding the feet was a painful way to acquire what was then considered beauty. When, as a teenager, I read of a young girl who wept each time her feet were bound, it dawned on me for the first time that preventing the growth of a body part involved pain. Though some modern practices may seem strangely similar—torturing our feet into four-inch high heels or starving ourselves to pencil thinness, for example—at least we have a choice. An upper-class Chinese girl of that era had no alternative. Custom decreed that her feet be bound, and so her toes were folded under and her feet tightly wrapped in soaked bandages that shrank as they dried. The girl's parents believed they were ensuring her future, for no young man of good family could be expected to marry a woman with large peasant's feet.

Bound feet were also testament to a woman's aristocracy and marriageability. They served as public evidence that she was from a good and wealthy family. But there was a darker, more private reason that men liked bound feet: they were considered erotic. The bound foot was kept under wraps for the husband alone, to be admired behind closed doors. Well those doors might be closed, for the bindings concealed what to modern eyes would seem a shameful secret. Foot binding did not simply make feet small; it deformed them. The toes were folded permanently underneath the foot, making it misshapen and difficult to walk on. But at that time and in that place, the bound foot was considered more beautiful than the foot as nature created it.

The most horrible aspect of this ancient custom is that it deprived these supposedly privileged women of freedom. They never knew the childish pleasure of stomping through piles of crackling leaves just to hear the noise they made. As young women, they did not dance to the music of a lute under the full moon or romp through a sunlit garden with their dogs and children. It is doubtful that these women so much as walked to the kitchen for almond cookies and tea. As women of privilege, they were brought whatever they needed and were carried by servants wherever they wanted to go. If they were independent-minded women, if they would have preferred to range over the hills alone or to wander so far along a dry creek bed that they could no longer hear the bickering of servants or the shouting of children, no matter. They were carried, or they did not go.

As I reflected on that bitter bygone custom, I suddenly needed to feel my feet under me. My walk to the kitchen for the oatmeal raisin cookies was slow and painful, but I was thankful to walk on feet that would again dance, again hurry me forward on matters of no particular urgency, again run for joy. The cookies were plump and packed with raisins. I savored every bite.

Questions

1. Which two introductory techniques does the essay's introduction combine?
   a. broad to narrow and quotation
   b. narrow to broad and historical
   c. anecdote and historical
   d. anecdote and broad to narrow
2. In the space below, write the thesis statement of the essay.

   ____

   ____
3. In the space below, write the topic sentence of each supporting paragraph.

   ____

   ____

   ____

   ____

   ____

   ____
4. In the topic sentence of the third body paragraph, the word *most* indicates that the author is using
   a. chronological order.
   b. emphatic order.
   c. sandwich order.
5. Though the definition is partly subjective, revealing the writer's opinion, it also includes much objective detail. Circle the letter of the detail that is subjective.
   a. Foot binding involved wrapping the feet in soaked bandages that shrank as they dried.
   b. The toes were folded permanently underneath the foot, making it misshapen and difficult to walk on.
   c. The deliberate deforming of the foot is shameful.
   d. At that time, having bound feet made a woman more marriageable.
6. What type of conclusion does the essay have?
   a. prediction
   b. recommendation
   c. full circle

Topics for Writing Using Definition

Definition Assignment 1: Dueling Definitions

Journal Entry

Journal Entry 1: You are the owner of Rowf, a mixed breed dog. You become convinced that neutering Rowf is the best thing to do. It's best for Rowf, best for you, and best in terms of the pet population. Write a definition of neutering based on these beliefs.

Journal Entry 2: You are Rowf. Define neutering from the canine point of view. (Cat lovers—feel free to substitute a cat for Rowf.)

Definition Assignment 2: Definition of a Role

Essay

Write a definition essay about a role that you play in your life. It may be the role of student, friend, son or daughter, mother or father, husband, wife, or other significant other. It may be a work role, such as restaurant server, bank teller, or paramedic. Your definition will be a subjective one because you will infuse into it your enjoyment or dislike of the role and your attitudes toward it.

Definition Assignment 3: Defining an Activity

Essay

Write a definition essay on an activity that you enjoy, such as fishing, dance, aerobics, reading, or shopping.

Definition Assignment 4: What Is a Hero?

Essay

Write an essay giving your definition of a hero.

Begin by prewriting to generate a list of the characteristics of a hero. You will use these characteristics as a basis for your three body paragraphs. Then, make a list of people who possess these characteristics. These may be actual people (your sister; Dr. Martin Luther King, Jr.) or general categories (caregivers; firefighters). The people will serve as examples in your paragraphs.

Your thesis, then, will list the characteristics of a hero, and your paragraphs will illustrate those characteristics with specific examples.

Classification

Whether you know it or not, **classification** comes naturally to you. From the time you are born, you explore. You discover that some things are pleasurable and others are painful, that some things are edible and others are not. Those are your first lessons in classification.

By the time you reach adulthood, you divide people, articles of clothing, words, teachers, and ways of behaving into different types or categories so automatically that you are barely aware of it. When you answer a classmate's question, "What kind of teacher is Dr. Burton?" or reply to a friend who asks what kind of day you have had, you are classifying.

Writing a classification essay allows you to use your categorizing skills to answer questions like the ones that follow.

- What kinds of extracurricular activities benefit students most?
- What types of students do you least enjoy having as classmates?
- How would you classify the fans that you see at a football game?

Establishing a Basis for Classification

In the following list, which item does not belong?

Kinds of Teachers

a. the drill sergeant
b. the comedian
c. the sociology teacher

If you chose c, you are right. You have recognized, consciously or subconsciously, that the first two have the same basis for classification—teaching style. The third item has a different basis for classification—subject matter.

Building Connections

Classifications, especially those that are your own invention, may often begin with a definition. For example, if you classified *teacher* into three groups—the drill sergeant, the comedian, and the prima donna, you might begin each body paragraph with a definition: "The drill sergeant is a professor who runs the classroom as if it were boot camp."

When you write a classification essay, it is important that your classification have a single basis or underlying principle. If it does not, then your categories of classification may be so close that they overlap or so far-flung that they seem to have no connection with one another.

In the example above, "sociology teacher" overlaps all three categories since sociology teachers have a variety of teaching styles. A single basis for classification ensures that your categories of classification are separate and distinct.

Categories of classification that are too diverse can be illustrated with a different example. A writer who has listed "airplane" and "bus" under the heading "types of transportation" would not be likely to add "camel" to the list, even though a camel can be transportation in some parts of the world. The other two types are modern forms of mass transportation, so "camel" does not fit in.

EXERCISE 2 CLASSIFYING ITEMS IN A LIST

Fill in the blanks with the appropriate words to classify each list of items.

1. Kinds of ________________ Basis for classification: ________________

- **a.** dalmatian
- **b.** Labrador retriever
- **c.** cocker spaniel
- **d.** poodle

2. Kinds of ________________ Basis for classification: ________________

- **a.** French
- **b.** Italian
- **c.** ranch
- **d.** blue cheese

3. Kinds of ________________ Basis for classification: ________________

- **a.** heavy metal
- **b.** rap
- **c.** country
- **d.** pop

4. Kinds of ________________ Basis for classification: ________________

- **a.** carving
- **b.** fillet
- **c.** steak
- **d.** pocket

5. Kinds of ________________ Basis for classification: ________________

- **a.** rocky road
- **b.** Neapolitan
- **c.** fudge ripple
- **d.** coffee

6. Kinds of ________________ Basis for classification: ________________
   a. pepperoni
   b. sausage
   c. cheese
   d. mushrooms

7. Kinds of ________________ Basis for classification: ________________
   a. dining
   b. coffee
   c. end
   d. card

8. Kinds of ________________ Basis for classification: ________________
   a. skim (fat free)
   b. 1%
   c. 2%
   d. 4%

9. Kinds of ________________ Basis for classification: ________________
   a. rollerball
   b. ball point
   c. felt tip
   d. fountain

10. Kinds of ________________ Basis for classification: ________________
   a. bow ties
   b. elbows
   c. angel hair
   d. twists

Exercise 3 Finding a Basis for Classification

Part 1: Circle the letter of the item that does not belong in the following lists. Then write the basis for classification of the other items in the blank.

1. Cars Basis for classification: ________________
   a. Ford
   b. Mazda
   c. sports car
   d. Nissan

2. Cats — Basis for classification: ________________

   a. tiger
   b. tabby
   c. snow leopard
   d. cheetah

3. Restaurants — Basis for classification: ________________

   a. Mexican
   b. Italian
   c. Thai
   d. fast food

4. Schools — Basis for classification: ________________

   a. fewer than 200 students
   b. 201–500 students
   c. high school
   d. 501–1000 students

5. Dances — Basis for classification: ________________

   a. tango
   b. macarena
   c. senior prom
   d. electric slide

Part 2: As entry *d* in each list, add one item that fits the basis for classification.

6. Drugs
   a. caplet
   b. liquid
   c. patch
   d. ________________________________

7. Games
   a. solitaire
   b. hearts
   c. go fish
   d. ________________________________

8. Books
   a. geography
   b. biology
   c. history
   d. ________________________________

9. Tools
   a. trowel
   b. shovel
   c. hedge clippers
   d. ______________________________

10. Hair
   a. brown
   b. black
   c. red
   d. ______________________________

Exercise 4 Finding the Point that Does not Fit

The following paragraph contains one point that is on a different basis for classification than the other two. Read the paragraph, then answer the questions that follow.

Kinds of Exercisers

At the gym where I work out, three types of exercisers stand out from the crowd. The first type, the struggler, breaks into a sweat just at the sight of an exercise bike. Strugglers walk five laps around the track, then stop, huffing and puffing, to rest on a bench before attempting another few laps. In contrast to strugglers are the fashion plates, who always have the latest in exercise wear. Exercising in front of the mirror, fashion plates can admire their colorful leotards, smartly cut shorts, or new athletic shoes. Even when they exercise, fashion plates never have limp, straggly hair or sweat-stained clothing. They always look their best. Finally, there are the athletes, who do not mind working up a sweat and are dedicated to fitness. In aerobics class, they bounce higher than anyone else even after an hour on the treadmill. Before they leave, they may swim a few laps in the pool just to cool off. Whether they are suffering strugglers, self-absorbed fashion plates, or dedicated athletes, these exercisers are fun to watch as I struggle through my own workout.

1. Which type of exerciser is not classified on the same basis as the others?

____

2. What is the basis for classification of the other two points?

____

Wordsmith's Corner: Examples of Writing Developed through Classification

Below are two student essays developed through classification. Read each and answer the questions that follow.

Classification Essay 1

Drawing on observation and her own experience as a shopper, this writer divides shoppers into different categories.

Kinds of Shoppers

"Why do women love to shop?" my husband asks. I point out that it's a strange question from a man who, when it comes to pulling out a credit card, is quicker on the draw than a gunslinger in the Old West. I am convinced that men, despite their protests to the contrary, enjoy shopping as much as women do. But as a woman, I know female shoppers and I believe I know what motivates them. Some are bargain hunters, some are pleasure seekers, and others are social shoppers.

For bargain hunters, shopping is a game of strategy and skill, and saving money is the motivation. My friend Renee is a perfect example of a bargain hunter. She never shops without a plan. Her motto is "Never pay full price for anything." This past October, when the breeze picked up and the temperature dropped, we went shopping. I watched her bypass the tables of long-sleeved shirts and racks of dresses in deep colors with names like "pumpkin" and "eggplant." On a clearance table, she found marked-down shorts and tank tops in tropical colors. Then we went to the men's department, where she expertly searched through a picked-over display of short-sleeved shirts and khaki pants to find her husband's sizes. Buying clothes at the end of the season, she says, lets her buy twice the clothes at half the price.

Unlike the bargain hunter, a pleasure seeker shops because it feels good. Shopping is therapy, celebration, and comfort. I admit to being a pleasure seeker. If I am feeling down, the cure is a trip to the mall for aromatherapy at Lotions and Potions. Placing strawberry-guava shower gel, cucumber-mint facial masque, or mango-honey lip pomade into a wicker shopping basket, I feel my mood lift, and by the time I present my Visa card at the register, I am feeling downright cheerful. Celebrations call for a soft velour dress or just the right pair of earrings. Even an ordinary Saturday becomes special if I can pick up a novel or a few magazines and stop by Candyland for a treat to enjoy as I read. Shopping is always a mood enhancer for me.

For the last type of shopper, shopping is a social act. Social shoppers travel in pairs or threes or even groups of five or six. Laughing and chatting, they flit through the stores, fingering cashmere, modeling hats, and spritzing colognes on one another. Since the purpose of the trip is mainly social, making purchases is optional. One subgroup of the social shopping group, however, shops seriously, usually in pairs. These shoppers don't need a mirror; they have one another. Their voices ring through the dressing room: "Lydia, what do you think of this peach color on me?" "Mom, does this bathing suit make me look fat?" "Ooo-wee, girl, that skirt looks good on you!" If the shopping trip is fruitful, so much the better. If not, the social shopper is undaunted. There is, after all, a food court and a sit-down restaurant that serves yummy pumpernickel croutons with its salad. The social shopper almost never has a shopping trip she doesn't enjoy, unless she has to shop alone.

Why do so many women love to shop? The reasons are as varied as the individuals themselves. As long as money, pleasure, and companionship motivate humans, the bargain hunter, the pleasure seeker, and the social shopper will keep the cash registers humming at malls everywhere.

Questions

1. What type of introduction does this essay have?
   a. narrow to broad
   b. historical
   c. anecdote
   d. contrast
2. In the space below, write the thesis statement of the essay and the topic sentence of each body paragraph.

   ____
   ____
   ____
   ____
   ____
   ____
   ____
3. What is the basis for classification in this essay on types of shoppers?
   a. amount of money spent
   b. motivation for shopping
   c. type of merchandise bought
   d. type of store visited
4. Which body paragraph begins with a transitional topic sentence?

   ____
5. What type of conclusion does the essay have?
   a. prediction
   b. recommendation

c. summary
d. quotation

Classification Essay 2

The writer of this essay explores people's attitudes toward life.

Attitudes Toward Life

I have always heard it said that people are the same under the skin, and in many ways it's true. People have similar impulses, hopes, and dreams. However, people vary widely in their attitudes toward life.

A person with a negative attitude puts a pessimistic twist on life, even when good things happen. If she has front-row center seats at the concert, she complains that her neck hurts from sitting so close or that the music is too loud. If he has a new job, he complains that the hours are too long and the benefits inadequate. When I congratulated my friend Tim on his new job, his response was typically negative. "It's okay, I guess," he said, "but the money and the chances for advancement aren't that great. I'm just biding my time until something else comes along." Negative people can turn even good fortune into bad luck.

A positive person, on the other hand, can find the good in almost anything. My coworker Mario always says, "Something good is going to happen today." At first, I thought Mario's good cheer was just a false front. But I have worked with him for a while now and I have begun to see that there is nothing fake about his optimism. He really does look for good things to happen, and he sees failure as an incentive to work harder. Any doubt I had about Mario's attitude evaporated when he confided that his wife has cancer. "It's made me realize what's important in my life," he said, "and it's made me closer to her than ever before." Even tragedy has its positive side to a positive person like Mario.

The person with a wait-and-see attitude withholds judgment on everything. If you ask him how he is today, he may cautiously reply, "So far, so good." He sees no point in committing himself when unexpected disaster or great good fortune may befall him at any time. My elderly neighbor is a classic example of the wait-and-see person. The last time I saw her, I asked about her children and grandchildren. She told me that her daughter and son-in-law had just celebrated their twenty-fifth wedding anniversary. When I commented on how long their marriage had lasted, my neighbor shrugged. "Yes, I guess it's a good marriage," she said. "Time will tell."

Attitudes toward life shape the way we see the world. A negative person finds the bad in everything, while a positive person looks for the good. And the person with a wait-and-see attitude, like someone watching a play, sits back and waits for the next act to unfold.

■ Questions

1. What two techniques are used in the introduction?
   a. narrow to broad and contrast
   b. quotation and contrast
   c. anecdote and quotation
   d. anecdote and contrast
2. In the space below, write the thesis statement of the essay and the topic sentence of each body paragraph.

____

____

____

____

____

____

____

3. What basis does the author use to classify people's attitudes?
   a. gender of the person
   b. how the attitude was acquired
   c. type of attitude.
   d. age of the person
4. Which body paragraph contains three short examples?
   a. body paragraph 1
   b. body paragraph 2
   c. body paragraph 3

TOPICS FOR WRITING USING CLASSIFICATION

Classification Assignment 1: Kinds of People

Journal Entry

Write a journal entry classifying and describing one of the categories of people below.

gum chewers	doughnut eaters
complainers	speakers

Classification Assignment 2: Relationship in Ruins

Essay

Discuss the kinds of problems that can ruin a relationship. It is up to you to decide what the relationship is—it may be a romance, a friendship, a marriage, a student-teacher relationship, a relationship with a coworker, or a relationship with a neighbor. Choose the type of relationship that you wish to discuss, then write an essay about the types of problems that might ruin it.

Classification Assignment 3: Classy Classification

Essay

Write an essay classifying one of the following items having to do with classes.

assignments	tests
desks	schedules
professors	textbooks
classmates	note takers

Classification Assignment 4: It Takes All Kinds

Essay

Write a classification essay categorizing one of the types of people below.

15

Examining Logical Connections: Comparison-Contrast, Cause-Effect, and Argument

A salesperson is trying to convince a business owner to buy computer software.

"Okay," says the owner. "Tell me how your software is different from the program I already use."

"Ours is a very good product," says the salesperson.

"What effect will it have on my operations?" the owner asks.

"Our product is state of the art," says the salesperson.

"You have one minute," says the busy owner. "Tell me exactly why your product is the one I should buy."

"It's a great product," the salesperson replies.

Do you think that the salesperson in the example above was able to make a sale? Without techniques of comparison-contrast, cause-effect, and argument, no salesperson would ever close a deal and no lawyer would ever win a case in court. These techniques of logical thought are also indispensable in the academic world.

When you compare one alternative with another, when you look for causes and effects, or when you argue for a particular course of action, you are using logic to explore connections between ideas. If your logic is thin or your connections weak, your reader will notice. The methods in this chapter call for rational thought and careful planning. The skills that go along with these methods of development—pinpointing differences and similarities, discovering reasons, predicting results, and arguing an issue logically—are essential. These higher-order tools of thought can help you in the college classroom and beyond.

Comparison-Contrast

One of the most effective ways of describing an unfamiliar situation or object is by comparing or contrasting it with something familiar. When you make a **comparison,** you show how two things are similar. If a friend asks you about a class you are taking, you may describe it by comparing it to a class that the two of you have taken together. When you **contrast** two things, you show how they are different. If you are asked on a political science exam to discuss the legislative and judicial branches of the government, you may find yourself contrasting the ways each branch shapes the country's laws. In an English class, you may find yourself using both comparison and contrast to show how two writers develop similar themes in different ways. Used alone or used together, comparison and contrast are useful tools for any writer.

Comparison-contrast techniques are useful in answering questions such as those that follow.

- What are some of the differences between high school and college classes?
- Discuss the similarities and/or differences between your values and those of your parents.
- A line from the movie *Forrest Gump* says, "My mama always said life was like a box of chocolates. You never know what you're going to get." A line from an old song says, "Life is just a bowl of cherries." Now it's your turn to fill in the blank: Life is like a ______________. Discuss three ways in which life is like the word or phrase you chose.

Setting Up a Comparison-Contrast Paper

The first step in setting up a comparison-contrast composition is to choose your points of comparison or contrast and decide whether to compare or contrast. One way to decide is to prewrite. That way, you can see whether your primary focus is on comparison or on contrast. Below is a sample brainstorming for a paragraph or essay.

Brainstorming—Two Teachers

Kimball	Bettman
extremely good teacher	excellent teacher
liked by students	liked by students
✔ funny but disorganized lectures	✔ organized lectures—hints about test questions
✔ multiple-choice tests	✔ essay tests
✔ group project assignment	✔ research paper
easy to talk to	approachable and friendly

Though there are several points of comparison, the contrasting points "lectures," "tests," and "assignments" may make a more interesting paragraph than the points of comparison. These points will also be more valuable to a reader who is trying to decide which instructor to take.

The next step in planning the comparison-contrast paper is to decide whether to use a point-by-point pattern or a block pattern to discuss the points. In a point-by-point pattern, each point of comparison or contrast is considered separately. Below is a point-by-point outline that could be developed into a paragraph or essay.

* *Lectures*

Kimball: Humorous but disorganized

Bettman: Organized, gives hints

* *Tests*

Kimball: Multiple choice, tricky questions

Bettman: Essay questions require creative thought

* *Outside Projects*

Kimball: Group presentation

Bettman: Research paper

In a block pattern, information about one subject is presented in one big block, followed by information about the other subject in a second big block. A block outline is shown below.

Kimball:	Delivers humorous but disorganized lectures
	Gives tricky multiple-choice tests
	Assigns a group project
Bettman:	Delivers organized, hint-packed lectures
	Gives essay exams that require creative thought
	Assigns a term paper

Exercise 1 Recognizing Comparison-Contrast Patterns

Below are two paragraphs written from the outlines above. Read each paragraph and decide which is the point-by-point paragraph and which is the block paragraph.

Paragraph A

Mr. Kimball and Dr. Bettman are both excellent sociology teachers, but they are different in the way they lecture, test, and make assignments. Mr. Kimball makes jokes during class and throws out silly puns that make the class groan. He speaks quickly, so taking accurate notes can be difficult. Sometimes he gets sidetracked and forgets what he was talking about. Dr. Bettman does not tell jokes, but she is extremely organized. Her lectures are practically in outline form, and as she lectures, she gives hints about what might be on the test. The testing styles of the two teachers are also different. Mr. Kimball's tests are multiple choice, and he words questions so that students must read carefully. Dr. Bettman's tests are in essay format, and she expects students to use their knowledge in new and creative ways. The two instructors also differ in their assignment of outside projects. Mr. Kimball requires a group project and presentation. He asks for a typed list of references but no formal paper. Dr. Bettman, on the other hand, requires a research paper complete with a bibliography. Both are able instructors, but each approaches lecturing, testing, and outside projects in a different way.

Paragraph B

Mr. Kimball and Dr. Bettman are both excellent sociology teachers, but they are different in the way they lecture, test, and make assignments. During his lectures, Mr. Kimball makes jokes and throws out silly puns that make the class groan. He speaks quickly, so taking accurate notes can be difficult. Sometimes he gets sidetracked and forgets what he was talking about. His tests are multiple choice, and he words questions so that students must read carefully. Mr. Kimball requires a group project and presentation at the end of the term rather than a traditional term paper. In contrast, Dr. Bettman's style and classroom requirements are quite different. She does not joke during class, and she is extremely organized. Her lectures are almost in outline form, and she gives little hints about what might be on the test. Dr. Bettman's tests are in essay format, and she expects students to use their knowledge in new and creative ways. At the end of the term, she requires a research paper, complete with a bibliography. Both Mr. Kimball and Dr. Bettman are able instructors, but each approaches lecturing, testing, and outside projects in a different way.

1. The paragraph organized in point-by-point format is paragraph _____.
2. The paragraph organized in block format is paragraph _____.
3. Look at the two paragraphs. In which paragraph do you find more transitions?

   ____

   Why?

   ____

   ____

Building Connections

When you make comparisons or draw contrasts, *examples* are often useful in making the similarities or differences clear to your reader.

Wordsmith's Corner: Examples of Writing Using Comparison-Contrast

Below, see how two student writers use comparison-contrast. Read each essay and answer the questions that follow.

Comparison-Contrast Essay 1

This essay contrasts home ownership and apartment living. At what point in the essay are you certain which one the writer prefers?

The Advantages of Apartment Living

The other day, a friend asked, "When are you going to buy a house?" When I told him that my wife and I were happy in our apartment, he shook his head. "You don't know what you're missing," he said. I think I do. Natalie and I have talked about buying a house, but we always come to the same conclusion. Apartment living offers many advantages over home ownership.

First of all, apartment living gives us luxuries we could never afford if we owned a home. If we bought a home, it would be a small home in a modest neighborhood. We would be lucky to have a postage-stamp yard for recreation. Our security system would probably consist of a deadbolt lock on the door. Any home in our price range would certainly not have lighted tennis courts, a pool, and 24-hour security. In our apartment complex, we have all of those things. Anytime I like, I can go over to the courts for a set or two of tennis. Afterward, I can cool off in the clear blue water of our apartment complex's swimming pool. At night, I can sleep well, knowing that if thieves or vandals venture into the complex, there is on-site security to take care of them. Only apartment living can give me so many luxuries for such a small price.

As apartment dwellers, we are also more mobile than homeowners. If Natalie and I owned a home and one of us were offered a dream job in a distant city, we would have to put our home on the market and worry about whether it would sell. If it had not sold by the date of our move, we could entrust it to a real estate agent, or one of us could stay behind and try to sell it. In any case, it would be a burden to us until someone else bought it. Living in an apartment, we have none of those worries. The worst that could happen is that we would have to forfeit our deposit if we did not give adequate notice. If we had to move, we could leave right away and focus on settling into a new job and a new community.

Perhaps most important, apartment living frees us from the chores of home ownership. If the water heater, the air conditioner, or the refrigerator in our apartment breaks down, I don't pull out the owner's manual and call the parts store. I call the resident manager, who sends over a repair person. If the roof develops a leak or the outside of the building needs a coat of paint, I don't risk my neck climbing a shaky ladder, as a homeowner might. I know that the apartment complex will hire a roofer or painter to take care of the problem. And on Saturdays, when my homeowning friends are mowing lawns, cleaning gutters, or trimming shrubbery, I am relaxing in front of the television or enjoying a game of tennis. For an apartment dweller, routine chores are handled by the apartment complex's maintenance staff.

Some people enjoy home ownership in spite of the hassles that go along with it. But I prefer the luxury, mobility, and freedom from chores that apartment living offers.

Questions

1. In the space below, write the thesis statement of the essay.

___

2. In the space below, write the topic sentence of each paragraph.

___

___

3. Does the essay compare or contrast? What is being compared or contrasted?

4. In this essay, two of the three body paragraphs are in block format. Which paragraph is presented point by point? ______

Comparison-Contrast Essay 2

The writer of this essay uses comparison-contrast to show the world of work, past and present.

Working—Then and Now

When a reader wrote to the advice columnist Ann Landers saying he could not find a job in spite of a college degree and work experience, Ann suggested that perhaps the man's attitude was to blame. An avalanche of mail told Ann that she was behind the times. In the decades since Ann Landers began writing her column, the job market has undergone a mixed bag of changes. Today's workplace is more diverse, more demanding, and less secure than the workplace of the 1960s.

The most positive change in the workforce is that it has become more diverse. In the 1960s, executive jobs went mostly to white males, while women and minorities were steered toward secretarial or janitorial jobs. Today, an ever-widening crack in the door to the executive suite is admitting all ethnic groups and both genders. Minorities have moved from the mail room to the board room, and females from the typing pool to the executive suite.

There is likewise a diversity in mindset. Once, the "corporation man" was esteemed because his values and his ideas were likely to be in line with those of upper management. Now, however, employees are no longer expected to be yes-men or yes-women. Corporations now have become more creative and competitive, so the employee with a different slant on things is useful. Greater diversity has made today's workplace stronger and more vital.

Today's workplace also makes more demands on its workers' time than the workplace of the sixties. In those days, "nine to five" was the rule rather than the exception, and if a worker took an hour for lunch, the true workday was only seven hours long. The work week spanned Monday through Friday, and weekends were for rest. Today, split shifts, extended shifts, and brown-bag lunches at the desk are common. The downsized workforce of today means that the average worker simply has more to do, even if that work has to be done on weekends or after hours.

The most profound change in today's workplace is a change in the level of job security. When a college graduate from the class of 1965 went to work for a company like IBM, he expected to retire thirty-five years later with a gold watch and a fat pension. He could be assured that if he did his job reasonably well, he would not be fired. Today, however, the first job after college is seldom a permanent one. It is an item for the resume, a stepping stone to other jobs. Pensions have changed as well. Once totally financed by employers, pensions have evolved into 401k's and IRAs that are at least partially financed by employees themselves. The worst aspect of today's workplace is that good employees with many years of service have no guarantee of keeping their jobs. If the company downsizes to cut costs, the worker's job may be eliminated regardless of years of service.

Since the 1960s, the job market has changed drastically. Today's workers face a workplace that is more diverse, more demanding, and much less secure.

Questions

1. In the space below, write the thesis statement of the essay.

____

____

2. In the space below, write the topic sentence of each paragraph.

____

____

____

____

____

____

3. Does the essay compare or contrast? What is being compared or contrasted?

____

____

4. In this essay, two of the three body paragraphs are in block format. Which paragraph is presented point by point?

____

____

Topics for Comparison-Contrast Writing

Comparison-Contrast Assignment 1: Two by Two

Journal Entry

Write a comparison-contrast journal entry on one of the following topics.

two brands of pizza	two times of day or days of the week
two classrooms	two sports teams

Comparison-Contrast Assignment 2: Optimism and Pessimism

Essay

In an essay, discuss the differences in the way an optimist and a pessimist might approach life. It might help to select three areas, such as work, school, relationships, finances, or religion, and write a paragraph comparing and contrasting each point.

Comparison-Contrast Assignment 3: School Days

Essay

Write an essay explaining some of the differences between high school and college.

Comparison-Contrast Assignment 4: Today and Tomorrow

Essay

In five years, how will your life be different from the way it is today? In this essay, be sure to contrast the present and the future rather than simply discussing your plans for the future.

Cause and Effect

When you look for the **causes** of an event, you are looking for the reasons it happened. In other words, you are looking for answers to "why?" questions. Why did your last romantic relationship end badly? Why is your Uncle Leroy's car still humming along at 150,000 miles? Why are so many schools plagued by violence?

When you look for the **effects** of an action, you are looking for its results. You are answering the question "What would happen if . . . ?" What would happen if every community had a neighborhood watch? What would happen if you decided to devote just one hour a day to an important long-term goal? What is the effect of regular maintenance on an automobile?

When you explore both **cause and effect,** you look at both the reason and the result. You may explore actual cause and effect, as in "Uncle Leroy performs all scheduled maintenance on his car and changes the oil every 3,000 miles; as a result, his car is still going strong at 150,000 miles." You may also explore hypothetical cause and effect, as in "Many members of my generation are bored and cynical because everything—material possessions, good grades, and even the respect of others—has come to them too easily."

A cause-effect essay might be written in response to any of the following questions.

What are the causes of violence in schools?

What are the major effects of stress?

What are some of the reasons that people fear growing old?

Identifying Causes and Effects

A cause is a *reason.* If you are asking a "why" question, the answer is probably a cause. Why do toilets flush in a counterclockwise spiral above the equator and in a clockwise spiral below it? Why did I do so poorly on my history test? Why did the chicken cross the road? From the scientific to the silly, these "why" questions can be answered by finding reasons or causes.

An effect is a *result.* If you ask "What will happen if . . ." or "What were the results of . . . ," then your answer is an effect. What would the results be if the speed limit were lowered by ten miles per hour? What would happen if I set aside an hour a day to exercise? What would happen if I threw these new red socks into the washer with my white underwear? When you answer these and other "what if" questions, your answer is an effect.

Exercise 2 Causes or Effects?

For each topic listed, indicate whether an essay or paragraph on the topic would involve a discussion of causes (reasons) or effects (results).

_______ **1.** Why do so many people enjoy watching action-adventure films?

_______ **2.** What would the results be if private ownership of automobiles were phased out over a ten-year period?

_______ **3.** Why are so many American children overweight?

_______ **4.** Describe your reasons for attending college.

_______ **5.** What would happen if so-called recreational drugs were made legal for adult use and regulated in the same way as alcohol?

_______ **6.** What would happen if private ownership of handguns were banned?

_______ **7.** What bad habit have you broken lately? Why did you decide to break it?

_______ **8.** Do you recycle? Why or why not?

_______ **9.** What would be the effects of a mandatory parenting course for every first-time parent?

_______ **10.** What would be the effect if all nonviolent, first-time criminals had the option of performing community service and undergoing counseling as an alternative to prison?

Wordsmith's Corner: Examples of Writing Using Cause and Effect

Below are two examples of student writing dealing with causes and effects. Read each essay and answer the questions that follow.

Cause-Effect Essay 1

Our movement toward a twenty-four-hour society provided inspiration for the writer of this essay.

Open All Night

There was a time when the world woke with the sun and slept when darkness fell. In some places it is still that way, but in modern America, the line between night and day is becoming blurred. In the trend toward a twenty-four-hour society, the average American is being caught up in a cycle of unceasing activity.

For most Americans, the movement toward a twenty-four-hour society means that "nine to five" is no longer the rule at work. As factories install expensive technology that must run twenty-four hours a day to be cost effective, many workers find themselves pulling the night shift, twelve-hour shifts, or even split shifts. They become exhausted trying to maintain family relationships, attend school functions with their children, and catch a few hours' sleep during the day. The problem does not occur only among shift workers. Executives who used to leave their work behind them at the office now are given the mixed blessing of laptop computers, cell phones, and home fax machines that keep them in constant touch and make it harder to leave work behind. Americans increasingly complain that they are giving more and more of their lives up for work.

As America moves toward a twenty-four-hour society, people of all ages are playing harder and longer than ever before. A greater awareness of fitness means that many people get up before dawn to struggle to six A.M. aerobics or head for the gym for an evening tai chi class. For those seeking entertainment, the search can continue around the clock. All-night restaurants, skating rinks, movie houses, and miniature golf courses light up the night. Even child's play no longer stops at dusk. Little league fields are lighted for night games that sometimes start as late as 8:00 or 8:30 and last long past the time when children used to be in bed. Midnight basketball, which arose in cities as a way to keep teens off the streets and out of trouble, has become increasingly popular.

With the movement toward a twenty-four-hour society, there is also more to do at home than ever before. Decades ago, television and radio stations went off the air at midnight, but even at 3:00 A.M., today's couch potatoes can choose from a performance of Handel's *Messiah,* a Three Stooges film, or a rerun of *Green Acres.* No matter what time it is, there is no reason to put off Christmas shopping or filing income taxes. Catalog companies often have twenty-four-hour order lines, and the Internet is open twenty-four hours a day for shopping or downloading tax forms. And why shouldn't a homeowner go grocery shopping or start a painting project at 2:00 A.M.? The grocery store and the discount store are open twenty-four hours a day.

Now that the world never shuts down for rest, many people feel they must constantly seek some pleasurable or productive activity. These days, more Americans are living faster and enjoying it less.

Questions

1. In the space below, write the thesis statement of the essay.

____

____

2. In the space below, write the topic sentence of each paragraph.

____

____

____

____

____

____

3. Does the essay emphasize causes or effects? ______________
4. Identify the cause(s) and effect(s) discussed in the essay.

____

____

____

____

Cause-Effect Essay 2

In this essay, the writer discusses the burden of perfectionism.

The Effects of Perfectionism

Some people urge themselves to better performance with slogans like "Practice makes perfect." However, I am a perfectionist, and I have to remember another slogan: "Sometimes good is good enough." I stay away from proverbs that urge perfection. Over the years, I have noticed that the effects of perfectionism are mostly negative.

First of all, my perfectionism makes me anxious about high-pressure situations. In school, I worry about taking tests. The pressure is on because there is no way to go back or change my performance. As I enter the classroom on test day, I feel my hands becoming clammy and I worry that I will forget everything I have studied. Socially, I worry when I have to go to parties or meet new people. I am afraid that I will be dressed too casually or too formally, that I will forget someone's name, or that I won't be able to make small talk. Before I met my girlfriend's parents, I spent a week worrying about what I would say and how I would act. First impressions count, and with my perfectionistic nature, it was important to me to make a good impression.

Trying to do things perfectly often means that I do not do them quickly enough. Once, my perfectionism cost me my summer job at a car wash. On my first day, I was issued a t-shirt with a slogan on the back: "If you can read this, I'm moving too slowly." My job was to detail the cars after they came out of the automated washer. I would wipe the water from the car and polish the tires and rims, while my partner, Grady, cleaned the inside of the windows, polished the dash, and vacuumed the seats. Grady always finished before I did and had to help me with the rims and tires. When the manager thought we weren't working quickly enough, he would yell, "Hustle it up, guys!" But hurrying meant that dirt was left on the rims, watermarks on the car, and gray streaks on whitewalls, and my perfectionistic nature shrank from doing less than my best. I was forced to turn in my t-shirt before the month was over.

Perfectionism also makes me my own worst critic. I know that others do not see me as negatively as I see myself. To my teachers, I seem like a serious student who usually does well. To my friends and acquaintances, I am a funny, likeable guy, and to their parents, I am a well-mannered young man. Even my boss at the car wash could not deny that I worked hard. But I see only my failures. I see the question I missed on a test, not the ones I answered correctly. I notice my social blunders, not the times when I handle myself well. Perfectionism magnifies my faults and shrinks my good qualities. It means that no matter how hard I try or how well I do, there is one person that I can never please—myself.

Perfectionism affects my performance in high-pressure situations, the speed of my work, and the

```
way I see myself. It may be true that nobody is
perfect, but unfortunately, that has not stopped me
from trying.
```

Questions

1. In the space below, write the thesis statement of the essay.

   ____

   ____

2. In the space below, write the topic sentence of each paragraph.

   ____

   ____

   ____

   ____

   ____

3. Does the essay emphasize causes or effects? ________________
4. Identify the cause(s) and effect(s) discussed in the essay.

   ____

   ____

   ____

   ____

5. What two introductory techniques are used in this essay?
   a. anecdote and quotation
   b. quotation and contrast.
   c. broad to narrow and quotation

Topics for Practicing Cause-Effect Writing

Cause-Effect Assignment 1: Just Cause

Journal Entry

In a journal entry, discuss the causes of one of the following problems.

suicide among the elderly	homelessness
shoplifting	rudeness
stress or burnout	distrust between generations

Cause-Effect Assignment 2: A Milestone

Essay

Write an essay discussing the effects of an important event in your life. Some possibilities include the addition of a family member, the death of someone close to you, or a surprising discovery about yourself or someone you love.

Cause-Effect Assignment 3: A Painful Decision

Essay

Write an essay discussing the reasons for a painful decision in your life. A decision to divorce, to have an abortion or to give up a child for adoption, to break off a friendship, or to quit a job are some possibilities.

Cause-Effect Assignment 4: Healthful Effects

Essay

Write an essay describing the effects of exercise on a person's health, energy level, and self-esteem.

Argument

Though the word **argument** is sometimes used to mean a heated discussion or shouting match, the argument you make in an essay is of a cooler sort. Using pen and paper to explain your stand on an issue has its advantages—no one will interrupt you or try to outshout you. However, a good argument is more than just your opinion on an issue. It is your convincing, well-supported opinion. What matters is not which side you take, but how well and how strongly you support your views. Logic, a strong regard for truth, and solid examples are your allies in an argument essay.

Argument essays answer questions like the ones that follow.

- Is television a harmful influence on children?
- Should courses in consumer finance be required in high school?
- Is capital punishment an appropriate sentence for serious crimes?

Taking Sides

It has been said that there are two sides to every argument. Your essay, however, should favor just one side. In an argument essay, it is important to make your position clear and not waffle. Starting on the "pro" side of an argument and switching to the "con" side will not work. If you feel it is necessary to acknowledge the other side of the argument, try doing so in the introduction.

Introducing an Argument Essay

An introduction to an argument essay can be a **historical introduction** that provides background for your argument. It might also be a **contrast introduction** in which you briefly summarize the opposing view and then present your own. (See Chapter 11 for examples.) A third type of introduction that works well for an argument essay is the **concession introduction,** or "yes-but" introduction. In a yes-but introduction, you acknowledge the opposition's strong points before bringing in your own argument. This type of introduction makes your essay seem fair and balanced. In the example below, the writer concedes the strong points of the opposition's argument, then states his own thesis.

Example: Concession or Yes-But Introduction

Many a reluctant student is pulled from a warm bed for an eight o'clock class by a college attendance policy that limits the number of absences a student may accumulate. Such policies have the advantage of ensuring that the professor is not talking to an empty room at 8:00 A.M. on a frosty Monday morning. They also help many marginal students make it through a class. But these policies do more harm than good by treating college students like kindergartners, forcing students who know the material to sit in class anyway, and unfairly penalizing students who may be absent for legitimate reasons.

Will You Change Anyone's Mind?

A good argument is aimed at changing people's views. On some topics, a convincing argument may change someone's mind. On other topics, though, you will find it next to impossible to sway an opinion that may have been molded by a lifetime of experience. Particularly on such hot-button issues as abortion, assisted suicide, and the death penalty, the best you can realistically hope for is to open a window to your viewpoint. In this case, success means coaxing your reader to look through that window long enough to say, "I see what you mean, and I understand your point of view."

> **■ Building Connections ■**
>
> Arguing a point often involves *contrast* and *cause-effect.* Making an argument sometimes involves contrasting one side with another. An argument favoring a particular course of action (for example, making handgun ownership illegal) often involves examining the positive effects of that action.

Wordsmith's Corner: Examples of Writing Using Argument

Below are two student essays that argue a point. Read each essay and answer the questions that follow.

Argument Essay 1

Is it time to bench college athletes and let the scholars take the field? In this essay, one student speaks out.

Giving Academics the Edge

College athletic programs offer obvious benefits. Games bring money and recognition to the school. Athletic teams promote school pride and unity, and going to games can be fun. In spite of these benefits, the attention given to athletics shortchanges the majority of the students and forces scholarship to take a back seat. It is time for colleges to take the spotlight away from athletics and give academics the edge.

Special treatment for athletes sends the wrong message to other students. At some colleges, athletes are given their own dorms and a separate dining hall that provides special meals to help them reach the peak of physical condition. Coaches and staff watch over them carefully. If their grades lag, they are given tutoring and encouragement. These special privileges send the wrong message. College should be about academics, not athletics. If there are special dorms, they should be for students who are on academic scholarships. If there are special dining halls, they should serve "brain food" to students on the dean's list. And colleges should have a way of watching over every student. If an ordinary "C" student begins to lag behind, help and encouragement should be as immediate for her as it would be for a star athlete. The special privileges athletes enjoy should be spread among all students.

Expensive athletic facilities and equipment should not be used only by the teams. At the college level, sports should stress fitness and the joy of competition and should include everyone. It's time to open the basketball courts, unlock the weight rooms and saunas, and bring out the track and field equipment for everyone to enjoy. If students are to focus on academics, they need a healthy outlet for their energy. Encouraging every student—even the clumsy or the overweight, even the couch potatoes and the party people—to use these facilities for exercise would contribute to healthier bodies and minds for the whole student body.

Perhaps the worst consequence of shining the spotlight on athletics is that it takes the focus away from scholarship. Many talented students write computer programs, conduct experiments in physics or psychology, or write poems, stories and plays. The attention, however, is not on these students, but on the few who manage to move a pigskin-covered ball a few yards down a green field or who use their height and coordination to dunk a ball through a hoop. A focus on academics would give bright, successful students the attention they deserve. Then other students, seeing the recognition that scholarship brought, would be inspired to make the most of their own intellectual talents.

Sports programs have their place. However, when a school is more recognized for its athletic program than its academics or when athletes are seen as heroes by fellow students while scholars are dismissed as geeks and nerds, something is wrong. It's time for colleges to draft a new game plan, one that places the focus on academics.

Questions

1. In the space below, write the thesis statement of the essay.

____

____

2. In the space below, write the topic sentence of each paragraph.

____

____

____

____

____

____

3. The type of introduction used is
   a. contrast.
   b. concession (yes-but).
   c. broad to narrow.
4. List the three arguments that the writer makes against college athletic programs.

____

____

5. Do you agree or disagree with the writer's argument? If you agree, what further points could you make in support of it? If you disagree, what arguments would you make against it?

____

____

____

Argument Essay 2

The writer of this essay is willing to share the road, but thinks that truckers—and their rigs—should be held to a higher standard.

Curbing the Trucking Industry

Truckers have been called "the knights of the road," and for the most part, it's true. Drivers of the big rigs will usually change lanes to let a car onto the interstate, radio for help for a stalled car, or flash lights in a friendly warning that a speed trap lies ahead. Yet trucks cause problems, too. The trucking industry and the government should join forces to curb unsafe drivers, control pollution, and keep truckers away from residential areas.

The keys to controlling unsafe drivers are education and enforcement. Education for truckers should go beyond load limits and gear ratios. It should stress professional conduct. Most automobile drivers know the terror of having twenty tons of steel and cargo inches from their bumper, and quite a few have seen sleep-deprived truckers driving erratically. Education is one way to eliminate such dangerous behavior. For those who will not be educated, enforcement is the answer. Heavier penalties for speeding and reckless driving should be enacted and enforced. Drivers who drive under the influence of drugs or alcohol should face a mandatory minimum license suspension of one year and mandatory counseling. Those who repeat the offense should never be allowed behind the wheel of an eighteen-wheeler again. Education and enforcement will put dangerous truckers out of business and help the image of those who are already safe and courteous drivers.

Measures also need to be taken against two types of truck pollution: air pollution and ear pollution. Automobile emissions are strictly regulated, but "truck yuck" continues to pollute the air over interstates and cities. Like automakers, truck manufacturers should be required to develop and install better pollution control devices. Trucks that do not belch clouds of black, foul-smelling diesel smoke will be much more welcome on the road. Noise pollution is another problem that should be controlled. Many cities are filled with the deafening roar of large trucks, and the low rumble of an interstate highway is audible for miles in some places. Noise barriers around interstates and the development of quieter engines are two possible ways to mute the deafening roar of large trucks.

Finally, truck traffic through residential areas needs to be strictly limited. As cities and towns become more spread out and roads become better, trucks are encroaching on residential areas. They move cargo over roads that are not built for heavy vehicles. Their noise and pollution disturb the peace of the neighborhood, and their speed endangers children who play or ride their bikes in the streets. Laws are needed to preserve the peace of residential neighborhoods by keeping heavy trucks on the interstates and major roadways that are built to withstand truck traffic.

The trucking industry is essential, but like any other industry, it must be regulated to preserve safety, prevent pollution, and preserve the peace of residential neighborhoods.

Questions

1. In the space below, write the thesis statement of the essay.

____

____

____

2. In the space below, write the topic sentence of each paragraph.

____

____

____

____

____

____

3. What three changes would the writer like to see in the trucking industry?

____

____

4. What type of introduction does the writer use?
   a. anecdote
   b. historical
   c. concession (yes-but)

Topics for Writing Using Argument

Argument Assignment 1: Seeing Both Sides

Journal Entry

Choose any controversial issue that you feel strongly about and write a journal entry supporting your belief. Then, as an exercise in objectivity, write a journal entry supporting the opposing viewpoint.

Argument Assignment 2: Dangerous Drugs

Essay

In an essay, support your position on one of the following issues.

1. Should physicians be allowed to prescribe lethal doses or combinations of drugs to assist terminally ill patients in suicide?
2. Should the growing of marijuana for medical or personal use be legal?

Argument Assignment 3: School Days, Rule Days

Essay

Does your school have a policy or rule that makes you angry? If so, write an essay giving your reasons why the policy is unwise. Some students object to policies limiting the number of absences, while others fret at library policies that say a book may be checked out for only two weeks. Still others object to exams that all students must pass before graduating: sometimes these are tests of reading and writing ability, and at other times they are senior comprehensive exams in a student's major field. Brainstorming with other students will help to get your thoughts focused on your school's policies.

Argument Assignment 4: At Liberty

Essay

What is the most important freedom you have? Why is it important to you? Some of the freedoms that people in the United States take for granted are freedom to practice the religion of their choice; freedom to speak their mind, even against their government; freedom to move from place to place; and freedom to pursue any career they wish. Discuss in your essay one of these freedoms or any other that you value.

Topics for Combining Methods of Development

Comparison-contrast, cause-effect, and argument are methods of looking at the logical connections between ideas. How are they alike? How do they differ? How does one affect another, and what logical arguments can be made for or against an idea? The following assignments ask you to combine one or more methods of development.

Mixed Methods Assignment 1: Transportation

Essay: Contrast and Argument

Imagine that you are faced with one of the following decisions regarding transportation:

- Should I buy or lease a car?
- Should I buy a used car or a new car?
- Should I buy a car, or should I use public transportation?

First, choose one of the three questions as the basis for your essay. Contrast the two alternatives and make a recommendation (an argument) for the best alternative.

As you write each body paragraph, you may find advantages and disadvantages to each alternative. For example, that in terms of monthly payment, leasing a car is better than buying. However, buying a car may cost less in the long run since you own it when the payments are finished. If you have mixed results such as these, your conclusion will be a "decision paragraph" in which you weigh the arguments for and against each alternative and make a recommendation.

Mixed Methods Assignment 2: Argument For or Against Legalizing Marijuana

Argument Before the State Senate: Argument, Comparison-Contrast, and Cause-Effect

You are a state senator. One of your fellow legislators has placed a bill before the state senate advocating the legalization of marijuana for personal use. You are preparing a speech to argue for or against this proposal. In your argument, you may also want to compare or contrast marijuana with alcohol, a legal substance with similar effects. You may also wish to discuss the effects that legalizing marijuana may have on the people of your state.

Organize your paper as a speech, with an introduction mentioning the proposal to legalize marijuana and stating your position for or against the legalization of marijuana. The body of your speech will contain your arguments for or against the proposal. You should provide at least three strong arguments. Conclude by strongly urging your fellow senators to vote for or against the proposed law.

Mixed Methods Assignment 3: Poor Child, Poor Adult

Report: Comparison-Contrast, Cause-Effect, and Argument

Is it harder to be poor as a child or to be poor as an adult? In this essay, you will answer the question with an argument—that is, your thesis will state that it is harder to be poor as a child or that it is harder to be poor as an adult. Although the larger structure of the essay will be one of argument, you will also explore the effects of poverty on children and adults and contrast them to see which group would probably find poverty more difficult, thus bringing cause-effect and comparison-contrast techniques into your essay.

This is a surprisingly complex topic with strong arguments to be made for both sides. Before you write, prewrite thoroughly to explore the differing ways in which adults and children might experience poverty.

16 Writing Summary Reports

> It usually takes a long time to find a shorter way.
>
> —Author Unknown

While the saying above is probably intended as a warning against short-cuts, it could just as easily apply to writing a summary. Summarizing is a painstaking process, involving fully understanding the material to be summarized, determining the most important ideas, and condensing them in your own words. A summary may be a shorter way of saying something, but writing one is a time-consuming process.

Writing a Summary Report

A **summary report** condenses and presents information, often from a single source. When you write a summary, your goal is to concisely present information from an essay, article, or book so that your reader understands the main points. In a summary, present the author's ideas objectively, without including your opinion of them. At the end of your report, if the assignment calls for it, write a brief evaluation of the essay, article or book.

Five Steps in Writing an Article Summary

The following section shows you the steps in summarizing an article.

Step 1: Choose a Topic and Find Sources of Information

Your instructor may assign a topic or area of investigation or you may be asked to choose your own topic. Choose a topic that interests you and on which information is readily available.

Articles on your topic may be found in periodicals, databases, or on Internet sites. An overview of each type of information source is provided below.

Periodicals are publications such as newspapers, magazines, and scholarly journals that are published on a regular basis—daily, monthly, or quarterly, for example. Newspapers and magazines are written for the general public, while journals are written for scholars in a particular field.

Subscription and CD-Rom Databases

Periodical articles are also available through subscription databases or CD Rom databases. Most college libraries subscribe to databases such as ABI/INFORM, Academic Search Premier, ERIC, and Research Library. These databases may contain full-text articles from journals, newspapers, or magazines, or they may contain article abstracts. **Full-text articles** are complete articles, exactly as originally published. **Article abstracts** are summaries intended to help you decide if a particular article is appropriate for

What Does the Suffix of an Internet Site Mean?

An Internet site's suffix can tell you a bit about the person or group behind the site. Here's a key to decoding Internet suffixes.

.org: A nonprofit organization

.edu: A college or university

.gov: A U.S. government site

.com: A business or private individual

your purposes. If it is, you will need to find the original article in the periodical in which it originally appeared.

Internet Sources

Some websites may contain articles previously published in print sources; others may contain articles written for and published on the Internet. Internet sources vary widely in quality; it is up to you to evaluate the credibility of each site you visit.

■ Advice for Online Researchers ■

Go Online

Research used to mean poring through stacks of books and periodicals. Today, it usually means sitting in front of a computer screen. Even print sources must be located through online catalogs, indexes to periodicals, and databases. Even if you are comfortable using a computer, these resources may seem alien to you at first. If you need help, do not hesitate to ask for it.

Find a Friend

Find someone in class who will agree to be your research partner. You don't need an expert, nor do you need someone who is working on the same topic. All you need is someone who is willing to go through the process with you. The two of you can work side by side and handle the rough spots together.

Ask a Librarian

Librarians are experts in finding information, and they are there to help. Explain your project and the kind of information you are looking for, and a librarian will point you in the right direction.

Print the Information

When you find useful articles online, print them so that you will not have to find them again. Documentation of online sources requires that you note the database you are using and the date you accessed the information.

Be Patient

Be patient with yourself and with the process of finding information—it always takes longer than you think it will.

Step 2: Evaluate Sources of Information

Once you have found articles on your chosen topic, evaluate them to make sure they are suitable for your summary. Use the following criteria for evaluation to find suitable articles.

- **Length.** If an article summary covers all the major points in the article, it will probably be 25 to 50 percent of the length of the article. Therefore, if you are assigned a five-hundred-word summary, choose an article of between one thousand and two thousand words. These figures are only an approximation. The idea is not to choose an article so short that a few sentences can summarize it or one so long that you cannot summarize the entire article.
- **Readability.** In any article that you choose, expect to find unfamiliar terminology and concepts that are new to you. After all, the purpose of research is to learn something new. However, some articles are written for experts in the field and may be hard for a layperson to understand. If you read the article three times and still feel as though you are trying to comprehend ancient Egyptian hieroglyphics, choose another article.
- **Publication Date.** A publication date helps you to evaluate the timeliness of the source. In fields where change is rapid, such as medicine or computer technology, finding up-to-date-sources is essential.
- **Author.** Is the author an authority in the field? If not—if the author is a journalist, for example—does the author consult and quote credible, authoritative sources? These questions help you evaluate the authority and credibility of your source.

Step 3: Read Your Article Thoroughly

Before taking any notes, read your article through once or twice. Then, highlighter in hand, look for the following information.

- **Main and major ideas.** Read through the article, highlighting main and major ideas. Remember, main ideas are often found at the beginning of an article and repeated at the end. Major ideas are often stated at the beginning of a paragraph or after a headline, and they are often supported by examples. Don't worry if this step takes more than one reading.
- **Examples and supporting details.** Once you have found the main and major ideas, go back and highlight the supporting details and

examples that most directly support those ideas. A summary contains a minimum of the detail that fleshes out the main ideas, so be selective and choose only necessary and important details.

- **Information for the works cited list.** The final step in taking notes from your source is to write down the information you will need for your works cited list. In a summary of a single article, you have only one work to cite, but it is important to cite it correctly. A list of information needed for your works cited list follows.

  For all sources
  - Author
  - Title of article
  - Title of the magazine, journal, or newspaper in which the article was published.
  - Date of publication
  - Volume and issue number of periodical, if available
  - Page numbers

  For online sources, note the following additional information
  - Date of access
  - The URL (Universal Resource Locator, or complete web address) of an article from a website
  - The name of the database for articles accessed from subscription databases through a college (or other) library, and the name of that library

Step 4: Draft Your Paper

Drafting a summary report is similar to drafting an essay. Your draft should contain the following elements:

- **Introduction.** The introduction includes the author's name, the title of the article, and the central idea of the article.

Example

Interviews are crucial for both employer and prospective employee. The employer needs to find the best person for the job; the prospective employee wants a fulfilling job and perhaps even a career. In his article, "The Interview: Rights and Wrongs," David Butcher describes techniques that can be employed by both interviewer and job-seeker to make the interview process easier and more productive.

- **Body paragraphs.** The body paragraphs outline the most important points in the article. The topic sentence of each body paragraph should state the idea that the paragraph will develop and incorporate a reference to the author.

  Example

  Smith believes that the Internet can be especially beneficial for senior citizens.

  The inclusion of the author's name in each topic sentence makes it perfectly clear to the reader that you are still discussing the ideas of another person rather than your own ideas.

  The body paragraph itself will paraphrase the author's ideas; that is, you will state the ideas in your own words. Quoting the author is also permissible, but use quotations sparingly. Most of the summary should be in your own words.

- **Conclusion.** The conclusion sums up the author's ideas and presents your evaluation of or reaction to the article. Placing your evaluation in the conclusion is a way of clearly separating your reaction to the article from the summary, but if your evaluation is lengthy, you may place it in a final body paragraph before beginning the conclusion

Step 5: Format, Proofread, and Cite Your Source

The final draft of your paper will include proper formatting and a works cited page. Use the documentation style recommended by your instructor or follow the brief guide to MLA style that appears later in this chapter. Your instructor may also ask you to provide a copy of the article you are summarizing.

Paraphrasing: An Essential Skill

One of the most difficult tasks of writing a summary is to put an author's ideas in your own words. When you **paraphrase,** you capture an idea using your own sentence structure and your own words. Here are some pointers to help you when you paraphrase:

- It's always permissible to repeat key terms. If the author uses the term "geriatric medicine," there's no need to rephrase it as "medical care of the elderly."

- Unusual phrasings should be reworded. If the author refers to a spider web as "a spider's gossamer trap," a paraphrase should simply call it a spider web.
- The sentence structure of a paraphrase should vary from that of the original material.

Making the Switch to Academic Writing

As you move from personal writing to academic writing, you need a new set of strategies. Here are five helpful strategies for academic writing.

A Learning Approach

While personal writing allows you to write about the things you know best, academic writing requires a willingness to read, understand, and evaluate the ideas of others.

Objectivity

Personal writing is *subjective*—that is, it allows you to express your own feelings and opinions. Academic writing, on the other hand, is *objective*. It requires you to put aside your own opinions and to look without bias at the ideas of another person—even if you disagree with those ideas.

Knowledge of Key Terms

When you read and write about academic subjects, understanding key terms is essential. Make an effort to learn the meanings of unfamiliar terms. This essential step will help your comprehension of the article you are reading and will help you to use the terms knowledgeably in your writing.

Use of Third Person

When you write from personal experience, you often use the *first-person* pronouns *I, me*, or *my*. In academic writing, *third person* is preferred, even when you are expressing your own opinion. Thus you would write, "Several of Emily Dickinson's poems reflect an obsession with death," not "I think that Emily Dickinson's poetry reflects and obsession with death."

Careful Acknowledgment of Others' Work

If you are quoting or using the ideas of other writers, it is important to acknowledge your sources both informally within the text of your paper and formally through parenthetical references and a works cited page. Failure to acknowledge sources is called **plagiarism** and is considered cheating.

EXERCISE 1 RECOGNIZING EFFECTIVE PARAPHRASES

For the numbered items below, circle the letter of the better paraphrase.

1. Original material:

   From retail buying to bargain hunting, the Internet has revolutionized shopping. Shoppers used to be limited to the retail stores in their area; now, online stores across the country or even across the world are open to them if they have an Internet connection and a credit card. Shoppers can find items that are not available locally and can compare prices to get the best deal. Bargain hunters no longer have to get up early and spend a Saturday morning scouring area yard sales. Now they can sign on to E-Bay or similar auction sites to find secondhand items in a variety of places, from Alaska to Nebraska and beyond. Both buyers and sellers have benefited from the availability of online shopping.

   a. Because of the Internet, shoppers are no longer limited to stores within driving distance. Online shopping has made a wider range of goods available to both retail shoppers and bargain hunters. Online stores and auction sites have benefited both buyers and sellers.

   b. The Internet has revolutionized shopping from retail buying to bargain hunting. Shoppers are not limited to items that can be bought locally. From Alaska to Nebraska, online shoppers can get better deals from E-Bay other auction sites as well as from online retail stores the world over.

2. Original material:

   A cat's eye is different from a human eye in several respects. The first and most obvious difference is the shape of the pupil as it contracts. The pupil in a human eye is round, and when exposed to light, it contracts, retaining its circular shape. The round pupil of a cat's eye, on the other hand, contracts from each side to form an ellipse. Unlike a human eye, a cat's eye shines in the dark. A cat's eye contains a reflective layer of cells that picks up and reflects available light, enhancing the vision of these nocturnal animals. A final feature that distinguishes the cat's eye from a human eye is the nictitating membrane, an inner eyelid that serves to clean and protect the cat's eye.

   a. A cat's eye is different from a human eye in the shape of the pupil as it contracts. The pupil in a human retains its circular shape when it contracts, but the round pupil of a cat's eye contacts from each side to form an ellipse. Unlike a human eye, a cat's eye shines in the dark. Finally, a cat's eye has a nictitating membrane, an inner eyelid that cleans and protects the cat's eye.

   b. Though they perform the same function, a cat's eye and a human eye are different in some ways. While the pupil of a human eye remains rounds as it contracts, a cats pupil becomes elliptical. Cats' eyes also reflect in the dark, something a human eye cannot do. In addition, cats' eyes possess a protective inner eyelid called the nictitating membrane.

EXERCISE 2 PARAPHRASING SHORT PASSAGES

Paraphrase the following short passages.

Passage 1

Aggressive driving is characterized by the tendency to view driving as a competition rather than as a means of getting from one place to another. While most drivers are content to move along with the flow of traffic, aggressive drivers weave from lane to lane, seeking any advantage that will place them ahead of others. Aggressive drivers are also more likely to tailgate and honk the horn in an effort to intimidate other drivers or simply to move them along faster. When confronted with heavy traffic, aggressive drivers often engage in dangerous behavior such as passing on the right, using utility or turn lanes as driving lanes, and ignoring traffic signals. Paradoxically, aggressive drivers often pride themselves on their skill. They see other, more cautious drivers as the problem, not themselves.

Passage 2

The National Academies' Institute of Medicine now recommends an hour per day of total physical activity such as walking, stair-climbing, or swimming. Many Americans fall far short of reaching this goal. Some are still trying to catch up to the previous guidelines of thirty minutes of activity five days per week. A century ago, Americans would have found it easier to exercise for an hour per day. Without cars, people walked more, and without modern labor-saving devices, life required more physical exertion. Today, however, many Americans sit at a desk all day and come home to sit in front of a TV or computer. Even those who make an effort to exercise often find that they lack the time.

____

____

____

____

____

____

____

EXERCISE 3 SUMMARIZING A PASSAGE

In a paragraph, summarize the following longer passage. Use your paraphrasing skills to condense the ideas in the original material.

Developing Focus

One of the most valuable skills a student can develop is focus. **Focus** is the ability to concentrate on one thing for an extended period of time, shutting out everything else. The person who is focused has no trouble with homework; her mind is on the task until it is finished. The focused person has no trouble concentrating during a test. She does not even notice the voice of the lecturer in an adjacent classroom, the tapping pencil of the student two rows over, or her instructor's squeaking chair.

People differ widely in their ability to concentrate. Some seem capable of laserlike focus on any job until it is completed. Other are easily distracted, jumping up from homework to do a hundred small but suddenly urgent tasks as the homework gets pushed further into the background. Like any other skill, the ability to focus can be learned and reinforced through practice. To improve your ability to concentrate, start by establishing a set time and place to study. If possible, study at the same time and in the same place every day. Establishing a routine gives study the importance it deserves and helps make studying a habit. Then, to keep yourself on task, set a small timer as you begin studying. Start by setting the timer to go off after fifteen minutes. Until the timer goes off, give studying your full attention. If your mind wanders—and it will—pull it back to the task. Then reward yourself with something small: five minutes of solitaire on your computer or a trip to the refrigerator for a glass of iced tea. Time your reward, too—about five minutes should be sufficient. Then set the timer for another fifteen minutes.

As concentration becomes a habit, that habit will spill over into the classroom, too. You will be better able to focus on your instructor's words or on the test you are taking. If extraneous noises during test still distract you, invest in a pair of earplugs to shut out noise as you take your test.

The ability to concentrate is a necessary skill. Fortunately, it is a skill that can be improved with effort.

Brief Guide to MLA (Modern Language Association) Style

The following section outlines a few basic principles of MLA style. For complete information on MLA style, consult the *MLA Handbook for Writers of Research Papers*, available in most college libraries and bookstores.

Formatting Your Paper

- Double-space the paper, including the works cited page.
- Use one-inch margins.
- Indent paragraphs one-half inch.
- Do not use a title page. Instead, put your name, your instructor's name, your course name, and the date at the top of the first page, each on a separate line, each line flush with the left margin. Center the title above the first paragraph. This material, like the rest of your paper, should be double-spaced.

Price 1

Ferris Price

Dr. Ruby S. Acres

Business Administration 101

22 April 2003

Summary of "The Interview: Rights and Wrongs"

Referencing Sources Within Your Paper

Within your paper, MLA style requires **parenthetical references,** not footnotes. For a paragraph in which you mention the author's name, the only parenthetical reference necessary is a page number placed at the end of the paragraph. If you use a direct quotation, place a page number after the quotation.

Example

✔ According to Steven Pinker, the idea that parents are at fault if children turn out badly is an outgrowth of the "tabula rasa" or "blank slate" theory. This theory holds that cultural influence, not genetics, determines personality and character(16).

The Works Cited List

Use the following model entries as a guide to preparing your works cited list.

Journal Article

Shipman, Harry L. "Hands-on Science, 680 Hands at a Time." Journal of College Science Teaching 30.5 (2001): 318-21.

Magazine Article

Pinker, Steven. "The Blank Slate." Discover Oct. 2002: 34-40.

Newspaper Article

Hummer, Steven. "Surviving the Sweet Science." Atlanta Journal-Constitution 13 Oct. 2002: E-9.

Article on a Website

Dunleavy, M. P. "Twenty Ways to Save on a Shoestring." MSN/Money 29 Dec. 2001. 16 Oct. 2002. <http://moneycentral.msn.com/articles/smartbuy/basics/8677.asp.>

Note that the date of publication is followed by the date of access. The complete Internet address of the article is enclosed within carets.

Article Accessed from an Online Database

Zimbardo, Phillip G. "Time to Take Our Time." Psychology Today 35: 2 Mar/Apr 2002 Psychology and Behavioral Sciences Collection. EbscoHost. 10 Oct. 2002. Metro College Library.

Include the name of the database through which you accessed the article, the date of access and the library where you accessed it (if applicable).

Jackson, Carol D., and R. Jon Leffingwell. "The Role of Instructors in Creating Math Anxiety in Students from Kindergarten through College." Mathematics Teacher 92.7 (1999). ERIC. EbscoHost. 2 May 2003. GALILEO.

If your college is part of a larger university system that has a systemwide set of databases, reference that systemwide set of databases rather than the individual library.

A Model Summary Report

For her summary report, Sandra chose an article dealing with the evolutionary reasons behind negative emotions such as fear and anxiety. The article, along with Sandra's highlighting and annotations, appears on the following page, followed by the final draft of her summary report.

The Fears that Save Us
Diane Ackerman

main idea

Anxiety, dread, panic, aversion, depression—a small demonology of our age. It makes one anxious just to name them, and most people will eagerly perform any ritual, intone any magic that might keep such demons at bay. But, despite the disruptions that they cause us today, these demons once had a life-saving purpose. Just as physical pain warns us of potential damage to the body, emotional pains helped us avoid more complicated threats to life and limb.

Indeed, the full bouquet of our cherished traits and tastes, as well as the bestiary of our negative behaviors, evolved at a time when humans lived in small bands of hunter-gatherer scavengers. To us, their lives seem arduous and uncertain, but heaven knows what they would make of ours. The only thing is, we still navigate by their maps, still respond according to their instincts, still act like hunter-gatherers, though we grapple with problems they would not have encountered, understood, or valued.

anxiety — major point

example — usefulness of anxiety

Anxiety, that masochistic terrier of one's own devising, played a life-saving role in our ancestors' lives by alerting them to potential threats so they could plan a response. "A tiger may be in that grass," one instinctive train of thought might go. "It looks like the same sort of tall grass tigers hide out in. If a tiger is hiding there and attacks me, what would I do? Did I just see the grass move? Maybe not. On the other hand, maybe I'd better check again." Obsessive worry about nonexistent tigers might burn up needed calories, interfere with work and damage the body by flooding the tissues with cortisol, a stress hormone. Costly strategy, that, but one hungry tiger could result in instant death.

Evolution wagers risk against advantage. Better to agonize at every opportunity about a tiger than be wrong that one lethal time. The grinding down of one's spirit, hope, health, and sense of well-being doesn't matter; only one's ability to survive long enough to launch heirs. We face profound and trivial uncertainties: the possible effects of fluoride, a nuclear test in the South Pacific, deciding what to wear on a first date. Our penchant for anxiety doesn't sift what's important from that civilized heap. Worry kicks in even when we don't need it, want it or know how to stop it.

another type of anxiety

example — usefulness of r'ship anxiety

Anxiety about a relationship feels the worst of all, but ultimately it's a lifesaver. When you're faced with hunger, the elements, and wild animals, belonging to a loyal family group is your only hope.

Not belonging is one of those things to dread and worry endlessly about. You keep checking to be sure you won't be abandoned, won't be sacrificed if wild animals attack, won't be left to starve. Most of the time, these may be unfounded neurotic fears, but misread the situation once, overlook a warning sign, and you're dead.

Small wonder that loneliness frightens us. Even though being excluded isn't deadly today, the nerve it touches stretches down the arms of time to a world of distant relations who left us a bag of tricks we barely understand but which we enjoy, puzzle over and often misuse.

depression—major point

Faced with horrible adversity or nameless anxiety, the more vulnerable among us become depressed. In a sense, it's a form of temporary hibernation. Overloaded, a person winds down to a low-energy state, speaks and moves very little. Famine produces the same inert, energy-saving response. Depression also elicits concern and nurturing, and people tend to make allowances for the depressed person who may ignore the normal give-and-take of society, not meet the same schedules or obligations. "I'm helpless as a child," the posture says "Protect me, embrace me, tell the world I'm not available for a while."

usefulness of depression

low self-esteem—major point

We think of low self-esteem as an affliction, but it had important benefits too. Self-esteem helps one seize opportunities. But if our ancestors had been confident in every circumstance, they would have taken too many risks—like venturing alone into the wilderness—or they might have been tempted to pick fights, challenge leaders, not bother negotiating or create some other social havoc.

usefulness of low self-esteem

point—fewer positive emotions

Besides serenity, joy, excitement, thrill and desire, it may seem that we've evolved few positive emotions, or at least a wider and subtler range of negative ones. That may be because, when things are going well, only a few responses are needed. Everything is dandy, and we get on with tracking happiness like the elusive quarry it is.

possible reason

How odd to live in a country whose Constitution guarantees us the right to pursue happiness. In a recent study of thirty-nine cultures reported in Psychology Today, the U.S. ranked twelfth in perceived happiness. Citizens of Denmark, Finland, Norway, and Sweden were the happiest despite their gloomy weather. Surprisingly, people in France and Japan said they were among the least happy. Many cultures don't expect to be happy, though they're thankful for its state of grace. In collectivist countries such as China, an individual's wishing to be happy is thought selfish and therefore usefulness of happiness

prediction—more evolutionary changes

not a high priority. But we expect happiness, pursue it, feel wretched in its absence and experience sadness as a failure.

We sometimes feel serene, quiet, at rest—what we label "happy." When you're happy, the world is breaking someone else's heart. Of course, it may be nothing more than a sort of biological idle, the body being thrifty with its limited energy. Negative feelings burn up precious calories, so not to be in pain or at red alert feels good.

What continues to amaze me is how such mind-binding forces, ancient and powerful as glaciers, can be modified by circumstance to produce quirky individuals living unique and unpredictable lives. However tempting it may be to think evolution stopped with us—its crowning glory—in the grand scheme of things, we're newcomers. Our evolution isn't happening fast enough to be visible in our lifetime, but it's still under way as we eat, sleep, play, lust, worry, learn, work, dream. Heaven only knows what we will become.

1 inch

1/2 inch

Lopez 1

Sandra Lopez

Double-spaced throughout

Psychology 1101

Dr. Wilder

7 February 2004

Title Centered

Article Summary: "The Fears that Save Us"

Most people have heard of the "fight or flight" response, the rush of adrenalin that is blamed for everything from road rage to panic attacks. Most people have also heard that this response is left over from prehistoric days when a tiger might attack at any moment and a quick response could save a life. In her article, "The Fears That Save Us," Diane Ackerman takes the idea even further. She believes that a whole range of negative emotions can be traced to the prehistoric past, and that those emotions were once necessary to the survival of our earliest ancestors.

The first emotion that Ackerman discusses in terms of evolutionary value is anxiety. While constant worry may not seem useful today, our ancestors needed it. Ackerman points out that anxiety wastes time that might be used on more valuable pursuits, floods the body with stress hormones, and wears down an individual's sense of well-being. How could such a negative emotion have been useful to our ancestors? Ackerman suggests that constant anxiety about a tiger hiding in tall grass might have a big payoff if, just once, there really was a tiger and the watchfulness caused by anxiety saved a life. Ackerman also points out that anxiety over relationships can be traced to a very real threat. In prehistoric times, a person left alone might not survive.

Ackerman also has evolutionary explanations for depression and low self-esteem. Depression is an emotional retreat from the world, but it also saves the body's energy and brings a nurturing response from

Lopez 2

others, both of which could make survival more likely. Low self-esteem, seen as negative today, could have helped groups stay together by making it less likely that someone would challenge authority or fight.

Ackerman points out that, compared to the wide range of negative emotions, we seem to have developed few positive emotions. She suggests that positive emotions are not necessary for survival—when things are going fine, there's no need for a response. Happiness may be nothing more than a form of "biological idle"—a way of saving energy when there is no imminent danger. These responses are not the end of the evolutionary road, according to Ackerman. Evolution is a slow process, and while we will not see changes in our lifetime, they are certain to come.

Ackerman's article was valuable to me because it helped me to see negative emotions in a new light. This article also makes me wonder if I should evaluate my own negative emotions in terms of their usefulness. If I am worrying over a test or over a relationship, maybe that anxiety is a sign that I should take some action—or maybe not. Diane Ackerman's article, "The Fears That Save Us," was a fascinating look at how negative emotions may actually have had survival value for our earliest ancestors.

Lopez 3

Centered

Works Cited

First line is flush with left margin; any subsequent lines are indented one-half inch.

Ackerman, Diane. "The Fears That Save Us." Parade 26 Jan. 1997: 18.

Summary Report Assignments

Summary Report Assignment 1: Summarizing an Article about Your Career or Major

Write a summary of an article that deals with some aspect of your chosen career or major. The article may be one about job opportunities in your field, or it may focus on a particular issue central to your field. Follow the step-by-step process outlined in this chapter to find your article, evaluate it, read it to find the main ideas, and write your summary.

Summary Report Assignment 2: Summarizing an Article That Solves a Problem

Write a summary of an article that helps you solve a problem in your life. Whether you are trying to find ways to save more money, impress an interviewer, organize your time, choose an automobile, or eat more nutritiously, dozens of articles await you in the library or on the Internet. Because articles of this type vary widely in length, be sure to choose an article substantial enough to lend itself to summarizing. Follow the step-by-step process outlined in this chapter to find your article, evaluate it, read it to find the main ideas, and write your summary.

Summary Report Assignment 3: Summarizing an Article That Explores a Social Issue

Write a summary of an article that explores a current social problem. You will find articles on homelessness, drug abuse, domestic violence, school violence, and many more issues of current concern in the library or on the Internet. Articles may vary in length, so be sure to choose and article substantial enough to lend itself to summarizing. Follow the step-by-step process outlined in this chapter to find your article, evaluate it, read it to find the main ideas, and write your summary.

17 Writing a Research Paper

> Copy from one source, and it's called plagiarism; copy from several, and it's called research.
>
> —An old joke, source unknown

If you have ever written a research paper, you know that it involves much more than "copying from several sources." If you have written only personal essays, you will find that incorporating outside sources into a paper is a challenge. First, you must find the right sources, then you must carefully incorporate those sources and acknowledge their authors. However, a research paper is structurally similar to a personal essay, with an introduction that provides background and presents a thesis, body paragraphs that support the thesis, and a conclusion. It embodies all of the qualities of good writing—direction, unity, coherence, and support. As you write a research paper, you follow the familiar steps in the writing process. Prewriting and planning take longer with a research paper, because research is now a part of those preliminary steps. Drafting takes longer since each source must be acknowledged and a works cited page prepared. Revision and proofreading are, as always, the final steps in the process. The research paper provides new challenges, but the methods remain the same.

This chapter discusses the five steps in writing a research paper: creating a research question, finding and evaluating information, outlining and note taking, drafting, and formatting the paper and citing sources. It

Six Strategies for Academic Writing

Academic essays differ in several ways from personal essays and therefore require different strategies. Six strategies are listed below.

A Learning Approach

While personal writing allows you to write from your own experience, academic writing requires you to understand and evaluate the ideas of others. Therefore, academic writing requires a willingness to learn and to research.

Objectivity

Personal writing is *subjective*—that is, it allows you to express your own feelings and opinions on a topic. Academic writing, on the other hand, is *objective.* It requires you to put aside your own opinions and to look without bias at the ideas of another person—even if you disagree with those ideas.

Knowledge of Key Terms

Understanding key terms is essential in any field. When writing about a short story, for example, you might be asked to comment on *setting, character,* or *point of view* while your paper in psychology might discuss *internal and external locus of control.* When you write about a particular field, be willing to learn and use its key terms.

Use of Third Person

In personal writing, you often use *first person*—the pronoun *I.* In academic writing, *third person* is preferred even when you are expressing your own opinion. Thus you would write, "Several of Emily Dickinson's poems reflect an obsession with death," not "I think that Emily Dickinson's poetry reflects an obsession with death."

Analysis, Not Summary

In a research paper, it is usually not enough to simply summarize the ideas in an essay, article, or book. A research paper usually involves manipulating information: comparing, contrasting, categorizing, analyzing, or showing a progression through time. When you write a research paper, impose your own order on the material. Analyze, don't simply summarize.

Careful Acknowledgment of Others' Work

When you quote sources or paraphrase the ideas of other writers, it is important to carefully acknowledge your sources. Failure to do so is called **plagiarism** and is considered cheating.

provides discussion and practice of two essential research skills, summarizing and paraphrasing. The chapter ends with a brief guide to the MLA (Modern Language Association) style of writing research papers and a sample paper written and documented in MLA style.

Five Steps in Writing a Research Paper

Step 1: Find a Topic and Create a Research Question

Your instructor may assign a topic or area of investigation, or you may be asked to choose your own topic. Within the range of choices you are given, choose something that interests you. Once you have selected a topic, your next job is to narrow it by formulating a research question. In a personal essay, you would formulate a thesis at this point. However, research deals with a question to be answered, not a thesis to be proven, so writing a thesis at this point would be premature.

Just as a thesis statement provides direction for your essay, a research question provides direction for your research. For example, let's say that you decide your topic will be the Internet. When you look for articles on such a broad topic, you may find too much information. You will find information on the Internet as a business tool, a research tool, and a communication tool. You will find information on the history of the Internet and the future of the Internet. You will find articles on Internet addiction, the Internet and pornography, and the Internet and education. A research question will help you narrow your search to articles in one specific area.

Suppose you decide on the research question, *How can the Internet be made safer for children?* Now you have direction. You can focus your search on articles dealing with children and the Internet and Internet safety. However, remember that your research question is tentative. If you find a more interesting angle on your topic, don't be afraid to alter your question. If you cannot find enough information to answer your question, write a whole new question. It is easier to change the question or alter your angle of investigation before you have researched than it is later in the process.

Step 2: Find and Evaluate Information from Various Sources

Sources for information may include encyclopedias, books, periodicals, databases, and Internet sites. Once you have found source material, you will evaluate the material and determine its relevance to your research question.

Sources for Research

Different sources have different strengths and weaknesses. Some provide the latest information, some go into depth, and some provide a broad overview. Knowing the characteristics of various types of sources will help you select the right ones for your project.

General encyclopedias provide broad, general, factual information. They provide a broad overview and thus may be a helpful source of background information. However, they do not go into much depth and may not provide the latest information. Examples of general encyclopedias include *Encyclopedia Britannica, Compton's Encyclopedia, Funk and Wagnalls New World Encyclopedia,* and *World Book Encyclopedia.*

Subject encyclopedias focus on one specific area and go into greater depth than general encyclopedias. Examples of subject encyclopedias include the *Encyclopedia of Social Work,* the *Encyclopedia of Educational Research,* the *AMA Encyclopedia of Medicine,* and the *Encyclopedia of the Vietnam War.*

Books go into great depth and may be written by authorities in a particular field. Unless the books are recently published, however, they may not contain the most recent information.

Periodicals are publications such as newspapers, magazines, and scholarly journals that are published on a regular basis—daily, monthly, or quarterly, for example. Newspapers and magazines are written for the general public, while journals are written for scholars in a particular field. Recent periodicals of all types will contain current, up-to-date information.

Subscription and CD-ROM Databases

Most college libraries offer students access to subscription databases and CD-ROM databases from vendors such as EBSCOhost, GaleNet, First-Search, and ProQuest. Some of the more widely used databases, which may be available from one or more of the vendors, include *ABI/INFORM, Academic Search Premier, ERIC, Medline,* and *Research Library.* These databases may contain full-text articles from journals, newspapers, magazines, and encyclopedias, or they may contain article abstracts. **Full-text articles** in a database are exactly the same articles you would find in a periodical, so there is no need to locate the original periodical. **Article abstracts** are summaries of articles that appear in periodicals. To access the complete text of an abstracted article, locate a copy of the periodical in which it originally appeared.

Advice for Online Researchers

Get Ready to Go Online

Research used to mean poring through stacks of books and periodicals. Today, it usually means sitting in front of a computer screen. Even print sources must be located through online catalogs, indexes to periodicals, and databases. Even if you are comfortable using a computer, these resources may seem alien to you at first. But don't feel intimidated. Everyone has to start somewhere—even the librarians who are experts at finding information on the computer were beginners once. If you need help, do not hesitate to ask questions. As a researcher, part of your job is to ask questions and to seek help when you need it.

Find a Friend

It's a good idea to find someone in class who will agree to be your research partner. You don't need an expert, nor do you need someone who is working on the same topic. All you need is someone who is willing to go through the process with you. The two of you can work side by side and handle the rough spots together.

Ask a Librarian

Librarians are experts in finding information, and they are there to help. If you and your research partner need help, ask. Explain your project and the kind of information you are looking for, and a librarian will help you find it.

Print the Information

When you find useful articles online, print them so that you will not have to find them again. Just taking notes may not be sufficient. Documentation of online sources requires that you note the database you are using and the date you accessed the information. That information will be on your printout. The library may charge a minimal amount for printing, to cover costs of paper and ink.

Be Patient

Be patient with yourself and with the process of finding information. Finding information always takes longer than you think it will, and you may need to make several trips to the library before you have everything you need.

Internet Sources

Internet sources vary widely in quality, so it is necessary to be aware of the type of site you are visiting. If the site has the suffix *.gov,* it is an official government site. The suffix *.org* indicates a nonprofit organization. The *.edu* suffix is reserved for colleges and universities. Sites with this suffix may contain faculty and student home pages, official college information, and community outreach sites. The *.com* suffix denotes a commercial site, and anyone may set up a site with the suffix *.com.* It is up to you to evaluate the credibility of each site you visit.

Evaluating Sources: Four Questions to Ask

The four questions that follow will help you evaluate an article or book that you are thinking of using in your research.

- **When was it published?** A publication date helps you to evaluate the timeliness of the source. In fields where change is rapid, such as medicine or computer technology, finding up-to-date sources is essential.
- **Who wrote it?** Is the author an authority in the field? If not—if the author is a journalist, for example—does the author consult and quote credible, authoritative sources? These questions help you evaluate the authority and credibility of your source.
- **Is the coverage in-depth or is it an overview?** While an overview may provide good background information, you also need articles and books that cover your topic in depth.
- **Does it provide an answer to my research question?** Just because an article is on the topic you have decided to research does not mean that it answers the question you are trying to ask. Hint: If, after reasonable effort, you can't find articles that answer your question, ask a different question. Use the articles you have already scanned to help uncover other interesting research questions.

After evaluating your sources, you will have narrowed the choices to the articles, books, or websites that are most helpful to you. Check out books and photocopy or print items that cannot be checked out. Although you can take notes while you are in the library, it is a better idea to read through your sources, live with them for a while, and absorb the material before taking notes.

Step 3: Outline Your Paper and Take Notes from Your Sources

Once you have evaluated your sources and thoroughly read your source material, you are ready to organize your paper. Make a brief outline of the points you will make and the source or sources you will use to support each point. Then, take notes from your sources, choosing the material that most effectively supports the point you are making in your paragraph.

The first step in taking notes from your sources is to write down the information you will need for your works cited list. There is no more painful experience for a researcher than to discover, after the paper is written, that this basic information on the source has somehow disappeared. A list of information needed for your works cited list follows.

For all sources

- Author
- Title (If the source is contained within a larger work, make a note of both titles. For example, if your source is an article in a magazine, note the title of the article and the title of the magazine.)
- Date of publication
- Volume and issue numbers for periodicals
- Month, day (if available), and year for magazines or newspapers
- Page numbers

For online sources, note the following additional information:

- Date of access
- The URL (Uniform Resource Locator, or complete web address) of an article from a website
- The name of the database for articles accessed from subscription databases through a college library. In the case of subscription databases (for example, Academic Search Premier or Lexis-Nexis Academic Universe), also note the name of the library from which you accessed the database, even if you accessed your college library's website from your home computer. One exception: If your college participates in a systemwide database collection, such as the University System of Georgia's GALILEO, the University System of Maine's MARINER, or

California State University/California Community College's SEIR, reference the database collection rather than the specific library.

The next step is to take careful notes from your sources. As you note the information, also note whether you are directly quoting the material or paraphrasing it. Direct quotations should be used sparingly and only to highlight the most important points. Most of your paper should be in your own words. When you paraphrase, recheck your paraphrases to make sure your wording is not too close to that of the original material.

Step 4: Draft Your Paper

Drafting a research paper is quite similar to drafting a personal essay. Your draft should contain the following elements:

- An **introduction** that provides necessary background to the issue you have researched. The introduction should end in a thesis statement that directly answers the research question you have asked.
- Several **body paragraphs** beginning with **topic sentences** that state the point that the paragraph will support. Support in your body paragraphs will come from the sources that you found during your research. As you write the draft, make a note of sources and page numbers beside each paragraph.
- A **conclusion** that sums up your paper. A summary conclusion is always appropriate, but other possibilities include suggesting avenues for further research or proposing solutions to a problem.

Step 5: Format Your Paper and Cite Your Sources

The final draft of your paper will include proper formatting, parenthetical references, and a works cited page. Citing sources is considered so important that various academic disciplines have adopted their own methods of formatting papers and acknowledging sources. Fields such as psychology, sociology, nursing, and criminal justice generally use the **APA** style of documentation, as outlined in the *Publication Manual of the American Psychological Association.* Scholars in literature and the humanities often use the **MLA** style of the Modern Language Association, as outlined in the *MLA Handbook for Writers of Research Papers.* Researchers in history and the fine arts use the **Chicago** style developed by the University of Chicago

Press and outlined in the *Chicago Manual of Style* and *A Student's Guide for Writing College Papers.* When you are assigned a paper, use the documentation style recommended by your instructor. The brief guide to MLA style that appears later in this chapter may be used unless your instructor specifies another style.

Paraphrasing and Summarizing: Essential Research Skills

One of the most difficult tasks of writing a research paper is to put an author's ideas in your own words. When you *paraphrase,* you rephrase a sentence or paragraph using your own sentence structure and your own words. A *summary* involves exactly the same skills—capturing ideas in your own words—but with a longer piece of source material. You would normally paraphrase a sentence or a short paragraph but summarize a longer paragraph, a section of an article, or a chapter in a book. A paraphrase can usually capture an idea a bit more closely. When you have only a sentence or a short paragraph to paraphrase, you can express the author's idea fully in your own words. A summary of a chapter or of a long section of an article will be more general and will leave out the details. Both a paraphrase and a summary must be properly referenced as someone else's work.

Paraphrasing

A **paraphrase** captures an idea expressed in a short piece of writing, such as a sentence or paragraph. It is an author's idea expressed in your own words. Here are some pointers to help you when you paraphrase:

- It is always permissible to repeat key terms. If the author uses the term *geriatric medicine,* there is no need to rephrase it as "medical care of old people."
- Unusual phrasing should be rephrased. If the author refers to a spider web as "a spider's gossamer trap," a paraphrase should simply call it a spider web.
- A paraphrase is usually a bit shorter than the source material, but it captures the entire idea.
- The sentence structure of a paraphrase should vary from that of the original material.

Exercise 1 Recognizing Effective Paraphrases

For the two numbered items below, circle the letter of the better paraphrase.

1. Original material:

Unlike extraverts, introverts become worn out or at times overstimulated by the company of others. Therefore, introverts will seek solitude to regain their equilibrium and replenish their energy.

a. Because being with people is sometimes too exhausting or too exciting for introverts, they often need time alone to restore their energy and their balance.

b. Unlike outgoing people, introverts become fatigued or overexcited from the presence of other people. Therefore, introverts will search for seclusion to recover their balance and recapture their vigor.

2. Original material:

E-mail is less formal than a business letter or memo, but that does not mean that no rules apply. Sending e-mail without a subject line, sending crude jokes or lewd pictures, or sending mass e-mailings about free kittens or lost earrings are no-nos in the corporate world.

a. E-mail is more informal than some other forms of business communication, yet that does not mean that rules do not apply. Not having a subject line, sending dirty jokes or pornographic pictures, or e-mailing employees about lost glasses or free puppies is not proper in the world of business.

b. E-mail is an informal method of communication, but in a business situation, it is still inappropriate to send potentially offensive material or to mass mail messages that do not relate to business.

Exercise 2 Paraphrasing Short Passages

Paraphrase the following passages.

1. Many workers no longer receive a paycheck. Instead, their employers issue a plastic card that looks something like a credit card. Each payday, the employee's pay is made available electronically through any ATM.

____

____

____

2. Though the custom of "giving away" the bride now is strictly symbolic, among the ancient Romans it had a legal purpose. A Roman patriarch literally owned a daughter for a lifetime, even after she was married, unless he chose to formally transfer her and her possessions to her husband. To moderns, the ceremony may seem to exchange one kind of bondage for another, but ancient Romans probably saw it as liberating a daughter to live her own life as a married woman.

____

____

____

____

____

____

Summarizing

A **summary** is a statement of the main idea of a longer portion of a work. Like a paraphrase, a summary should restate the author's idea in your own words. Unlike a paraphrase, a summary does not need to capture the details of the paragraph or section of the work that you are summarizing. Therefore, a paragraph summary might be just a sentence or two, and a summary of a chapter might be just a paragraph or two.

Exercise 3 Recognizing Effective Summaries

For the two numbered items below, circle the letter of the better summary.

1. Original material:

   Convenience is the main advantage of shopping over the Internet. If you shop at a mall, you have to shop during the mall's hours of business. To do that, you have to get dressed, drive your car, use your gas, and find a parking space. With e-commerce, if you feel like shopping at midnight in pajamas and fuzzy bunny slippers, you can go right ahead. Get a cup of hot chocolate, sit at your computer, and shop at your convenience, not someone else's.

   a. Convenience is the main advantage of shopping over the Internet. While wearing fuzzy slippers, a person can sit at the computer with a cup of cocoa and shop at his or her convenience.

   b. Internet shopping at home is more convenient than mall shopping because one can shop at home without worrying about getting dressed, driving to a mall, or making it to a store before closing time.

2. Original material:

   Almost everyone has encountered a surly waiter or a rude clerk and wondered, "What is his problem?" The answer may lie in the amount of control the worker feels. Polite workers are most often those who feel they are in charge of their jobs and of their lives. They realize that life is what they make it, and they may as well make it pleasant. Impolite workers, on the other hand, may feel controlled. They feel manipulated and used by other people and by their employers. The only way they can retaliate is to be surly and rude.

a. Workers who feel in control of their jobs and lives are more likely to be polite than those who feel manipulated by employers.

b. Surly waiters and rude clerks are retaliating in the only way they know.

EXERCISE 4 SUMMARIZING SHORT PASSAGES

Summarize the following passages in a sentence or two.

1. Migraine researchers have recently confirmed what many *migraineurs,* or migraine sufferers, have known all along: weather can affect migraines. Specifically, falling barometric pressure can trigger a migraine in many people. People who possess what one sufferer terms a "weather head" often feel symptoms as a thunderstorm rolls in and the barometric pressure begins to fall. "I should have been a weather forecaster," jokes one longtime migraine sufferer. "I always know when a storm is coming."

____

____

____

2. What is the scientific method? The scientific method is a process of gathering and testing information. The four steps in the scientific method are observation, formulation of a hypothesis, prediction, and experimentation. The first step, observation, involves observing a particular phenomenon, usually over a period of time. In the second step, the scientist constructs a hypothesis that explains something about the phenomenon. In the third step, the hypothesis is then used to make a prediction about the phenomenon, an "educated guess" that the scientist must prove through the fourth step, experimentation. The experiment must be set up so that it can be repeated by the same scientist or by others to verify the results. If the experiment confirms the prediction consistently, the hypothesis becomes a theory, an assumption about the way the phenomenon works.

____

____

____

Guide to MLA (Modern Language Association) Style

The following section outlines some of the basic principles of MLA style. For complete information on MLA style, consult the *MLA Handbook for Writers of Research Papers,* available in most college libraries and bookstores.

Formatting Your Paper

- Double-space the paper, including the works cited page.
- Use one-inch margins.
- Indent paragraphs one-half inch.
- Do not use a title page. Instead, put your name, your instructor's name, your course name, and the date at the top of the first page, each on a separate line, each line flush with the left margin. Center the title above the first paragraph. This material, like the rest of your paper, should be double-spaced.

Roberts 1

Molly Roberts

Dr. L. A. Wade

Humanities 2112

22 April 2003

The Role of Women in Ancient Rome

Referencing Sources Within Your Paper

Within your paper, references to your sources are **parenthetical references,** not footnotes. MLA style calls for very brief references that interfere as little as possible with the flow of the text.

One thing to consider as you write your paper is whether to mention an author's name in the text of your paper or to put it in a parenthetical reference. A good rule of thumb is to use the author's name in the text of your paper if you are discussing that author's original research or ideas. If the author is reporting fact, as in a reference book, an interview, or a news story, put the author's name in a parenthetical reference.

The following examples show the MLA style of reference.

A Work by a Single Author

If you have already used the author's name in the sentence or paragraph where the parenthetical reference occurs, use the page number(s) alone as a reference.

✔ According to Merlin Stone, early societies were matrilineal because humanity had not yet figured out the role of men in producing children. To our earliest ancestors, females were the sole givers of life (10-11).

If you have not used the author's name in the sentence or paragraph, place the author's last name and the page number in parentheses after the quote or paraphrase of the author's words. Position the parenthetical reference as close to the end of the sentence as possible, but before the period that ends the sentence. No punctuation is needed between the author's name and the page number.

✔ A thirty-minute organizing session every Friday afternoon is recommended as a way to keep an office functioning smoothly (Morgenstern 109).

A Work by Multiple Authors

As with a single author, if the authors are already mentioned in the sentence or paragraph in which you discuss their work, the page number alone serves as the reference. If you have not mentioned the author's names, your parenthetical reference should include their last names separated by *and* along with the page number.

✔ Light waves from a an advancing light source become shorter and take on a blue tint, while light waves from a retreating body become longer and have a red tint. (Jones and Wilson 507)

✔ Because people tend to lose lean body mass as they age, older adults may become increasingly susceptible to the effects of alcohol. (Blow, Oslin and Barry 50-54).

Parenthetical references to a work by more than three authors should include the lead author's name and the abbreviation *et al.,* which means "and others."

✔ Unless parents are involved and patients are motivated, medical professionals may have little success in treating childhood obesity. (Story et al. 210).

A Work with No Author Listed

Some works, such as editorials, reports, web pages, and encyclopedia articles may have no author listed. Each parenthetical reference should include the first word of the title (unless it is *a, an,* or *the*) and the page number(s). Shortened book titles are underlined; article titles are put in quotation marks.

✔ In the wake of corporate accounting scandals, a ruling requiring company executives to certify the accuracy of their company's financial records may help to restore public confidence ("First" 6A).

✔ While early versions of the electronic pacemaker worked continuously, newer versions react to the patient's heartbeat and turn on only when they are needed ("Pacemaker").

Quote from an Interview or Reference to Another Author's Work

Use the abbreviation *qtd. in* (for *quoted in*) if you are quoting or paraphrasing someone who has been quoted in an interview. Also use *qtd. in* when you paraphrase or quote one author's paraphrase of another author's ideas, but only if you cannot obtain the original source. In other words, if Author A writes an article that paraphrases the ideas that Author B has written about, find Author B's article and use it as your source.

The example below is a paraphrase of an idea expressed by Holly Shimizu, executive director of the United States Botanic Garden, in an interview with Cassandra M. Vanhooser.

✔ Holly Shimizu, the executive director of the United States Botanic Garden, believes that Congress's willingness to fund a renovation of the

Washington, D.C., garden sends a message that plants are important (qtd. in Vanhooser).

The Works Cited List

The works cited list is double-spaced and alphabetized according to the last name of the author (or if no author is listed, by the first word of the title). The first line of each entry is flush with the left margin while subsequent lines are indented one-half inch. In MLA style, names of publications that would ordinarily be italicized are underlined for clarity, since some italic type styles can be difficult to read.

Print Sources and Personal Interviews

Documentation for print sources should include enough information so that other researchers would be able to locate and read the sources if they wished. The author's name, the title of the work, the date, and the page numbers (if it is a chapter or article) are all included in an entry on a works cited list. A citation for a personal interview includes the interviewee's name and the date of the interview. Use the following model entries as a guide to preparing your own works cited list.

Book by a Single Author

Schlosser, Eric. Fast Food Nation: The Dark Side of the All-American Meal. New York: HarperCollins, 2002.

Note: If more than one city is listed for the publisher, include only the first one mentioned.

Book by Two Authors

Halfacre, R. Gordon, and Anne Shawcroft. Landscape Plants of the Southeast. Raleigh: Sparks, 1997.

Journal Article

Cassady, Jerrell C., and Ronald E. Johnson. "Cognitive Test Anxiety and Academic Performance." <u>Contemporary Educational Psychology</u> 27.2 (2002): 270-295.

Magazine Article

Clark, Jane B. "As Seen on TV." <u>Kiplinger's</u> July 2002: 98-105.

Newspaper Article

Neuharth, Al. "Can We Curb Rude Cellphone Manners?" <u>USA Today</u> 19 Jul. 2002: A-13.

Encyclopedia Entry

"Post-traumatic Stress Disorder." <u>Gale Encyclopedia of Medicine</u>. 2nd ed. 2001.

Personal Interview

Borck, Pat. Personal Interview. August 22, 2002.

Online Sources

Documenting online sources is more complex than documenting print sources. The content of a print source will not change, but online sources often change and evolve. When a website is updated, its previous content may disappear forever. A site may move to a new server and change its web address entirely, or a library may drop its subscription to one database and pick up another. Because of these complexities, extra documentation is necessary for online sources of information.

Like a birdwatcher noting the sighting of a rare bird before it flies away, the online researcher needs to document when and where source material was viewed. The date that material was accessed, the name of the library that was used to access a subscription database, and the address of a website are necessary for the works cited list. For that reason, printing out material accessed online is strongly recommended. The date, the database used, and most other relevant information will be on the printed copy for easy reference.

Use the following models of online sources as a guide in preparing your list of works cited.

Article on a Website

Sahadi, Jeanne. "The Ideal Budget." CNN/Money 23 Jan. 2002. 12 Aug. 2002 <http://money.cnn.com/2002/01/23/pf/q_budgetideal/>.

This citation includes the author's name, article title, website name, date of article, date of access, and web address.

Article on a Website, No Author Listed

"Ten Tips for Successful Public Speaking." Toastmasters International. 1998-2001. Speaking Tips. 5 Feb. 2003 http://www.toastmasters.org/tips.asp

Since no author is listed, this citation includes the article title, organization that holds the website's copyright, copyright date, link followed from the home page, date of access, and web address.

Article Accessed from an Online Database

If you access a periodical or encyclopedia article from an online database, provide information about the original article and also information about the database from which you received it, the library where you accessed it (if applicable), and the date of access. If your college is part of a larger university system that has a systemwide set of databases, reference that systemwide set of databases rather than the individual library.

Lenzner, Robert, and Matthew Swibel. "Warning: Credit Crunch." Forbes 12 Aug. 2002 Research Library Periodicals. ProQuest. 1 Feb. 2003. Ferris College Library.

This citation includes the authors' names, article title, periodical, date of publication, name of online database, database vendor, date of access, and library where the article was accessed.

Umberson, Debra, Kristi William, and Kristin Anderson. "Violent Behavior: A Measure of Emotional Upset?" Journal of Health and Social Behavior 43.2 (2002). Research Library Periodicals. ProQuest. 2 May 2003. GALILEO.

This citation includes the authors' names, article title, periodical, volume and issue numbers, year of publication, name of online database, database vendor, date of access, and systemwide database name.

A Model Research Paper

1 inch

1/2 inch

Witt 1

Double-spaced throughout

Lilly Witt

Psychology 1101

Dr. Nemec

3 April 2004

Title Centered

The Purpose of Dreams

Factual reference; author's name in parenthetical reference.

Thesis statement. Reference to original ideas; author's name mentioned in paragraph.

Since ancient times, people have wondered about the scenes that play themselves out in the sleeping mind. What are dreams? Ancient cultures saw them as prophecies, as sources of inspiration, or as ways to heal the body or mind (Winson 54). Modern psychologists and biologists are also intrigued by the nature and purpose of dreams. Over the last century, dream research has evolved from Sigmund Freud's view of a dream as wish fulfillment to today's widely varying ideas about the practical role of dreams in human existence.

The most important early work on dreams was Sigmund Freud's The Interpretation of Dreams. First published in 1900, Freud's book debunked the idea that dreaming was merely a physical process (65). Instead, a dream was a mental process of wish fulfillment. The idea of a dream as the fulfillment of a wish was clear, Freud wrote, when a thirsty person dreamed of water or a hungry person of food. But how could anxious and unpleasant dreams fulfill a wish? In Freud's system, even nightmares concealed wishes carefully hidden from the dreamer by the unconscious mind. For Freud, the purpose of dreams was to allow the dreamer's wishes to come true, if only in sleep, while at the same time hiding and disguising wishes that might not be acceptable to the conscious mind (98–123).

Witt 2

Factual reference; author's name in parenthetical reference.

Since Freud's early work, much research has been done on dreams. A breakthrough came in 1953 with the discovery of REM (rapid eye movement) sleep, the stage of sleep in which the most vivid dreams occur (Fernald 166). Rather than rely on a sleeper's morning memories of dreams, today's sleep researchers work in sleep laboratories, where sensitive equipment alerts researchers when a sleeper falls into REM sleep. One point of agreement that most modern researchers share with Freud is that most dreams are prompted by events that occur during the day. In other words, dreamers process the day's events through dreams (Fernald 169). There, however, the agreement stops, and modern theories vary widely.

The abbreviation *qtd. in* is used with information from a published interview.

Many researchers believe that dreams play a role in learning. Stephen LaBarge of Stanford University's Sleep Disorder Clinic believes that one role of dreams is to move information from short-term memory to long-term memory. His studies show that people who are deprived of REM sleep find it difficult to "learn new skills, remember, or concentrate" (qtd. in Beaubien). Researcher J. Allan Hobson suggests that the information-processing function of REM sleep may include comparing old information with new and storing only what is new and different. Old information that is already in the memory is not stored again (295).

Paradoxically, it has also been proposed that the purpose of dreams is to help the dreamer forget. Biochemist Francis Crick, whose work on the structure of DNA won a Nobel Prize, has worked with Graeme Mitchison to discover why people dream. According to Crick and Mitchison, memory is stored in a "neural net" within the brain, a

Witt 3

system that allows a memory to be accessed from many different pathways instead of just one. The neural net has limited capacity, and the only way to keep it working properly is to flush out unneeded memories. It is through dreams and REM sleep that this process of "reverse learning" occurs (229–237). The reverse learning theory is supported by observations of two mammals that lack REM sleep, the dolphin and one species of anteater. These two mammals, Crick and Mitchison state, have unexpectedly large brains for their body size. It is possible, then, that the function of dreaming and REM sleep is "to make advanced brains more efficient and, in particular, to allow these brains to have a smaller size than they would otherwise have" (244).

Some of the most recent studies raise the possibility that dreams regulate moods. Rosalind Cartwright of the Sleep Disorder Service and Research Center believes that dreams help people to work through emotional problems. Dreams tend to be more negative than positive, providing "emotional homework" that allows a dreamer to work through problems. Dealing with negative emotions at night helps the sleeper to wake up in a better, more positive mood (qtd. in Beaubien).

Information from a published interview.

The idea that dreams regulate mood is confirmed by Milton Kramer and Mark Barasch. According to their studies, two possible scenarios may play out as a sleeper confronts emotional issues in dreams. The first scenario is similar to the one described by Cartwright. Dreams become progressively more positive as, dream by dream, the sleeper works through a problem. The sleeper awakes refreshed and in a positive mood. Sometimes, however, the dreams simply repeat the conflict again and again. In this case, the sleeper may wake up more irritable and depressed than he was when he went to sleep.

Omission of page number indicates that entire article is referenced or that a previously published article is published without page numbers on a website.

Witt 4

Why do dreams improve the moods of some people and worsen the moods of others? One of Rosalind Cartwright's studies points to an answer. The study compared clinically depressed people with people who were not depressed. Those who were not clinically depressed showed a normal pattern of mood improvement as dreams became more positive throughout the night. Most depressed patients, however, showed the opposite pattern: their dreams became less positive and their moods became progressively worse as morning drew near. However, one subset of depressed patients showed a normal pattern. Significantly, those were the ones whose depression was cured (qtd. in Neimark).

Information from a published interview.

If dreams have such a powerful effect on mood, can they be used deliberately to help people work through emotional issues and problems? The D.R.E.A.M.S. Foundation of Canada reports that it is possible to use dreams deliberately through a process called "dream incubation." The process involves focusing on the question before sleeping and forming the intention to have a dream that will shed light on the problem. Dreams may produce an obvious answer or they may require some interpretation. According to the Foundation's website, a trust in the process and a willingness to act on the insights that dreams provide will help to make the process work. The foundation reports that dreams may also be useful in solving creative and professional problems. For example, the Beatles' tune "Yesterday" and Samuel Taylor Coleridge's poem "Kubla Kahn" were inspired by dreams, and it is said that the golfer Jack Nicklaus worked out a problem with his golf swing in a dream ("Dreams").

First word of title is given for a page on a website with no author listed.

Most researchers agree that dreams have a purpose, but few can agree on what that purpose is. Dream research has moved away from

Conclusion sums up the paper's content.

Witt 5

Freud's idea that a dream is the mind's fulfillment of a wish. Modern researchers view the dream both as a way of learning and as a type of reverse learning that helps the brain purge unneeded memories. More recent research shows the dream as a regulator of moods, perhaps even as a tool that can be used deliberately to enhance mood and creativity. Whatever the purpose of dreams, they continue to be a source of fascination and speculation.

Works Cited page is separate, but numbering continues from previous pages.

First line is flush with left margin; subsequent lines are indented one-half inch.

Name of database.

Name of vendor.

Name of the library from which the database was accessed.

Volume and issue numbers of a journal.

Month and year of magazine.

Database collection shared by a university system or network of colleges is referenced rather than the name of the college library.

Volume and issue number of journal.

Witt 6

Works Cited

Beaubien, Greg. "In Your Dreams." Natural Way for Better Health Nov./Dec. 1995. 2 pp. Alt HealthWatch. EBSCOhost. 8 May 2003. Metro College Library.

Crick, Francis, and Graeme Mitchison. "REM Sleep and Neural Nets." Journal of Mind and Behavior 7.2-3 (1986): 229–49.

"Dreams—How to Apply and Benefit from Them." D.R.E.A.M.S. Foundation. 1996. 30 Apr 2003 <http://www.dreams.ca/apps1.htm>.

Fernald, Dodge. Psychology. Upper Saddle River, NJ: Prentice Hall, 1997.

Freud, Sigmund. The Interpretation of Dreams. Trans. Joyce Crick. New York: Oxford UP, 1999.

Hobson, J. Allan. The Dreaming Brain. New York: Basic Books. 1988.

Kramer, Milton and Mark Barasch. "Dreamspeak." Psychology Today. Sep./Oct. 2000, 56–61. Academic Search Premier. EBSCOhost. 7 May 2003. Metro College Library.

Neimark, Jill. "Night Life." Psychology Today. Jul./Aug. 1998. 3 May 2003. Platinum Periodicals. ProQuest. GALILEO.

Winson, Jonathan. "The Meaning of Dreams." Scientific American Special 12:1 (2002): 54–61.

Assignments for Writing a Research Paper

Choose one of the research assignments below. Follow the step-by-step process outlined in this chapter to complete the steps in writing a research paper: choosing a topic and creating a research question, finding and evaluating sources, outlining your paper and taking notes, drafting your paper, and finally, formatting your paper and citing your sources.

Research Assignment 1: Exploring an Issue in Education

Following the steps in research outlined in the chapter, explore and write about a current issue in education. Use one of the topics listed below or a topic of your own choosing. You may write about issues in higher education (on the college level), or you may choose to focus on an issue in secondary or elementary education. Focus your research on a single problem or issue within your chosen topic. For example, if you choose "disabilities," you might narrow your focus to a specific learning disability or to methods of making study materials more accessible to students with visual or hearing impairments.

Bilingual education	Gender equity
Disabilities	Nontraditional students in college
College access and admissions policies	Technology in education

Research Assignment 2: Exploring a Social Issue

Following the steps in research outlined in the chapter, explore and write about a current social issue. Use one of the topics listed below or a topic of your own choosing. Focus your research on a single problem or issue within your chosen topic. For example, if you choose drug abuse as your topic, your research question might focus on the problem of limited opportunities for rehabilitation and the possible solutions to that problem. If you choose domestic violence, your research question might focus on the effectiveness of services provided by domestic violence hotlines and "safe houses" for victims of abuse.

Alocoholism	Gangs	Drug abuse
Domestic violence	Poverty	Prisons

Research Assignment 3: Exploring an Issue in Health and Wellness

Following the steps in research outlined in the chapter, explore and write about an issue in health and wellness. Use one of the topics listed below or a topic of your own choosing. Be sure that your research question is issue-oriented. For example, rather than focusing on defining breast cancer, an issue-oriented paper would address a question such as which of several treatments works best.

Alternative medicine	Mental health
Diet	Pets and health
Breast cancer (or another disease)	Weight training (or another form of exercise)

Part 2
Grammar

Basic Grammar

Advanced Grammar

Punctuation, Word Choice, and Mechanics

18

Basic Grammar

Verbs and Subjects

A Journalist's Questions

~~Who?~~

~~What?~~

When?

Where?

Why?

If there were no verbs or subjects, the top two items in the list of traditional journalist's questions would be eliminated. Verbs tell *what* was done, while subjects tell *who* or *what* the sentence is about.

The **verb** of a sentence carries the action, if any, and directs that action to and from the other words in the sentence. Some verbs, called **linking verbs,** function as connectors for related words.

A **subject** is what the sentence is about. It is usually a noun or a pronoun. It is probably not the only noun or pronoun in the sentence, but it is the only one that enjoys such a direct grammatical connection to its verb. If you ask, "Who or what ____________?" putting the verb in the blank, the answer to your question is always the subject of the sentence.

Action and Linking Verbs

Verbs work in two ways within a sentence. Some verbs show the action, physical or mental, of the subject of the sentence. These verbs are called *action verbs*. Other verbs link the subject with other words in the sentence. These verbs are called *linking verbs*.

Action Verbs

Action verbs show physical or mental action performed by a subject. Look at the action verbs below, highlighted in italic print.

Examples

✔ Rachel *drove* to the doughnut shop. (physical action)

✔ She *bought* a dozen doughnuts and ate two on the way home. (physical action)

✔ She *wondered* why she found sweets irresistible. (mental action)

PRACTICE 1 RECOGNIZING ACTION VERBS

Underline the action verbs in the following sentences.

1. The judge's decision sparked controversy in the small community.
2. The twins' vivid red hair draws everyone's attention.
3. James worried about Monday's history test.
4. The cat leaped to the safety of the tree's lower branches.
5. The old car puttered along like a windup toy.

Linking Verbs

A **linking verb** links its subject with a word that describes it. The most common linking verb in English is the verb *to be*, in all its various forms: *is, are, was, were, has been, will be, could have been*, and so on. Look at the following examples to see how the verb *to be* functions as a linking verb.

Examples

✔ The dog *is* hungry.

The verb *is* links the subject, *dog*, with an adjective describing it.

✔ Ann *has been* a police officer for ten years.

The verb *has been* links the subject, *Ann*, with a phrase, *police officer*, that tells more about her.

✔ Tomorrow *will be* the last day to drop a class without penalty.

The verb *will be* links the subject, *tomorrow*, with a noun, *day*, that tells more about it.

Other common linking verbs include the verbs *to seem, to appear, to grow*, and *to become*. Verbs of the senses, such as *to smell, to taste, to look, to sound*, and *to feel*, can be action or linking verbs depending on how they are used.

Examples

L The dog *seems* friendly. (The verb links *dog* with the adjective *friendly*.)

L The gym socks *smelled* terrible. (*Smelled* is a linking verb—the socks are performing no action.)

A Monica *smelled* the perfume sample. (The verb *smelled* shows Monica's physical action.)

L The pumpkin pie *looks* tasty. (The verb links *pie* with the adjective *tasty*.)

A The dog *looks* forlornly at every passerby, hoping for a handout. (The verb shows the dog's physical action.)

The Linking Verb Test

To tell if a verb is a linking verb, see if you can substitute *is* or *was* in its place. If the substitution works, the verb is probably a linking verb.

Examples

? The crowd *grew* quiet as the conductor stepped onto the podium.

L The crowd ~~grew~~ *was* quiet as the conductor stepped onto the podium.

The substitution makes sense; therefore, *grew* is used here as a linking verb.

? The vines grew until they covered the cottage.

A The vines ~~grew~~ *were* until they covered the cottage.

The substitution does not makes sense; therefore, *grew* is used as an action verb.

? Michael stayed home from work because he *felt* sick.

L Michael stayed home from work because he ~~felt~~ *was* sick. (linking verb)

? Barbara *felt* the stress of the day dissolve as she stepped through the door of her apartment.

A Barbara ~~felt~~ *was* the stress of the day dissolve as she stepped through the door of her apartment. (action verb)

PRACTICE 2 RECOGNIZING ACTION AND LINKING VERBS

Underline the verbs in the following sentences. In the blank to the left of each sentence, write *A* if the verb is an action verb, *L* if it is a linking verb.

_____ **1.** Sharon is in a sour mood today.
_____ **2.** Emilio smelled the container to determine its contents.
_____ **3.** The bologna smells spoiled.
_____ **4.** The terrier leaped with joy as Nancy entered the house.
_____ **5.** Kim studied her sociology notes carefully before the test.
_____ **6.** The committee decided to postpone its meeting until Wednesday at noon.
_____ **7.** The small post office branch handles a large volume of mail.
_____ **8.** The ground is parched from lack of rain.
_____ **9.** The advertisement seems appealing.
_____ **10.** Too many drivers fail to use turn signals.
_____ **11.** Hisako grew tomatoes in a container on the patio.
_____ **12.** The audience grew restless when the singer was late.
_____ **13.** Yesterday Rozell tasted tiramisu, a layered Italian dessert, for the first time.
_____ **14.** The dessert tasted creamy and delicious.
_____ **15.** The burglar fled with over two thousand dollars in cash.

_____ **16.** Bernard felt sleepy all afternoon.

_____ **17.** Alanna pounded loudly on the door.

_____ **18.** The baker felt the silky texture of the flour between her fingers.

_____ **19.** On the upper right-hand corner of the envelope, Alex carefully pasted the stamp.

_____ **20.** Sandra looked through the tiny window at the front of the house.

Recognizing Verbs and Subjects

Finding the Verb

Finding the subject and verb of a sentence is easier if you look for the verb first. Below are some guidelines to help you spot the verb in a sentence.

1. **A verb may show action.**
   - ✔ The ancient elevator groaned to a stop on the second floor.
   - ✔ Larry wondered if he should take the stairs.
2. **A verb may link the subject to the rest of the sentence.**
   - ✔ The inspection sticker was three years out of date.
   - ✔ The old lion looked sleepy.
3. **A verb may consist of more than one word. Some verbs include a main verb and one or more *helping verbs.***
   - ✔ Jemal has been taking flute lessons for six years.
   - ✔ Katherine has not found the keys she lost yesterday.
   - ✔ Gwen might have been going to the library when we saw her this morning.
4. **Some verbs are compound verbs. Some subjects have more than one verb. When more than one verb goes with the same subject, the verb is called a *compound verb.***
   - ✔ The meteorologist pointed to a low-pressure system on the weather map and predicted rain.
   - ✔ The teller counted the bills twice and handed them to the customer.
   - ✔ I ate the asparagus and avocado casserole but did not like it.
5. **An infinitive (*to* + present tense verb) cannot act as a verb in a sentence.**
   - ✘ Paulo wanted to accept the award on his brother's behalf.

The phrase *to accept* is an infinitive and cannot be the main verb of the sentence. The verb in this sentence is *wanted*.

✔ Paulo wanted to accept the award on his brother's behalf.

✘ The actor's hair looked too smooth and full to be real.

The phrase *to be* is an infinitive, not the verb of the sentence. The verb in this sentence is *looked*.

✔ The actor's hair looked too smooth and full to be real.

6. **A verb form ending in *-ing* cannot act as a verb in a sentence unless a helping verb precedes it.**

✘ From the street came sounds of children playing.

Playing cannot be the verb because a helping verb does not precede it. The verb in this sentence is *came*.

✔ From the street came sounds of children playing.

✘ The setting sun sank below the horizon.

Setting cannot be the verb because a helping verb does not precede it. The verb in this sentence is *sank*.

✔ The setting sun sank below the horizon

✔ A crowd was gathering at the scene of the accident.

The verb in this sentence is *was gathering* (helping verb + main verb).

✔ James has been thinking about changing his major.

The verb in this sentence is *has been thinking* (helping verb + main verb).

PRACTICE 3 FINDING VERBS

Underline the verbs in each of the following sentences.

1. A strong breeze filled the sails of the small boat, pushing it toward the shore.
2. For her computer, Joy wants a wireless mouse and a flat-screen monitor.
3. Iced tea tastes refreshing on a hot day.
4. Mrs. Binks sat on her porch and waited for the mail to arrive.
5. I have been listening to the radio, hoping to hear my favorite song.
6. A person has a better chance of being struck by lightning than of winning the lottery.
7. Maud wondered why she had bought the black T-shirt with tarantulas on it.
8. Every morning, Anthony reads the comics page of the paper first.
9. Grandpa said the baby looked like him—bald and toothless.
10. Inch by inch, the tiny kitten climbed up the side of the bed.

Finding the Subject

Now that you can find the verb of a sentence, you can more easily find the subject of the verb. The easiest way to find the subject of a sentence is to find the verb first and work from there.

A subject answers the question "Who or what __________?" The verb fills in the blank. Be sure that the words *who* or *what* are stated before the verb, or you may find the object of the verb rather than its subject.

✔ The telephone rang, startling Raoul.

Who or what rang? The telephone rang. *Telephone* is the subject of the verb *rang*.

✔ The tour group will fly to Toronto on the six P.M. flight.

Who or what will fly? The tour group will fly. *Group* is the simple subject of the verb *will fly*. (The words *the* and *tour* are modifiers and are part of the complete subject.)

✔ Cedric and Joseph sat on the bench waiting for their mother.

Who or what sat? Cedric and Joseph sat. *Cedric and Joseph* is the compound subject of the verb *sat*.

✔ Carefully, Sandra measured the cinnamon and raisins and folded them into the bread dough.

Who or what measured? Sandra measured. *Sandra* is the subject of the verb *measured*. Who or what folded? Sandra folded. *Sandra* is the subject of the verb *folded*.

✔ Carefully, Sandra measured the cinnamon and raisins, and Brian folded them into the bread dough.

Who or what measured? Sandra measured. *Sandra* is the subject of the verb *measured*. Who or what folded? Brian folded. *Brian* is the subject of the verb *folded*.

PRACTICE 4 RECOGNIZING VERBS AND SUBJECTS

Find the verb in each sentence below and underline it twice. Then find the subject by asking "Who or what ____________?" Underline the subject once.

1. Casablanca is Adrienne's favorite movie.
2. Exhaustion showed in Hank's face.
3. Ophelia's college diploma hung on the wall of her office.
4. Dust clung stubbornly to the computer screen.
5. Tracy drove to the post office and mailed her package.

Recognizing Prepositional Phrases

A subject will not be part of a prepositional phrase. In many sentences, prepositional phrases intervene between subject and verb.

✔ The rim *of the glass* is chipped.

When we pick out the subject of the verb by asking "What is chipped?" it is tempting to say, "The glass is chipped." But *glass* cannot be the subject of the verb in this sentence. Grammatically, it already has a job:

■ Famous Prepositional Phrases ■

The prepositional phrases below have been used as titles for songs, television shows, movies, and books. How many do you recognize? Can you think of others?

Above Suspicion
Against the Wind
Around the World in Eighty Days
At Long Last Love
At the Hop
Behind Closed Doors
Behind Enemy Lines
Beneath the Planet of the Apes
Beyond the Sea
In Cold Blood
In Living Color
Of Mice and Men
On Golden Pond
On the Waterfront
Over the Rainbow
Under the Boardwalk
Under the Yum Yum Tree
Up a Lazy River
Up on the Roof
Up the Down Staircase

it is the object of the preposition. The subject of this sentence is *rim*. To avoid mistakes in picking out the subject of the sentence, cross out prepositional phrases before picking out subject and verb.

- **Prepositional phrases always begin with a preposition.** Prepositions are often short words like *of, to, by, for,* or *from*. They are often words of location, such as *behind, beside, beneath, beyond,* or *below*. Below is a list of common prepositions.

Frequently Used Prepositions

about	beneath	in	to
above	beside	into	toward
across	between	like	under
after	beyond	near	underneath
along	by	next to	until
along with	down	of	up
around	during	off	upon
at	except	on	with
before	for	outside	within
behind	from	over	without

- **Prepositional phrases always end with a noun or pronoun.** The object of a preposition, always a noun or pronoun, comes at the end of a prepositional phrase: of the *mongoose,* beside a sparkling *lake,* with *them,* to *James and Harlow,* within five *minutes.*
- **Prepositional phrases often have a three-word structure.** Often, prepositional phrases have a three-word structure: preposition, article (*a, an,* or *the*), noun. Thus phrases like *of an employee, under the car,* and *with a gift* become easy to recognize. But prepositional phrases can also be stretched with modifiers and compound objects: *beside Katie's bright blue dance shoes and pink-and-purple designer leotard*. More often, though, the three-word pattern prevails.

PRACTICE 5 ELIMINATING PREPOSITIONAL PHRASES

Cross out the prepositional phrases in the following sentences.

1. The vivid colors of the flowers in the blue bowl on the table brighten the room.
2. Outside the office, on the busy street, swarms of happy vacationers were leaving for weekend trips.

3. The point of Mr. Smith's remarks to the class was lost on Kendall, who dozed peacefully in the back row.
4. For dessert, I'll have a cup of coffee and a slice of that gooey, rich pecan pie.
5. The smell of freshly brewed coffee and frying bacon wafted through the open door of the small restaurant on the corner of Poplar and Main.

* *Real-World Writing: Is it okay to end a sentence with a preposition?*

How else would you say, "Will you pick me up?" or "I feel left out"?

Sometimes, what seems to be an objection to a preposition at the end of a sentence is really an objection to an awkward or redundant construction. "Where are you at?" will bring a scowl to any English teacher's face—not because it ends in a preposition, but because it is redundant: "where" and "at" are both doing the same job—indicating location.

But by all means, say "I have nothing to put this in" or "The dog wants to go out." Except in the most formal writing, ending sentences with prepositions is something almost everyone can live with.

Regular and Irregular Verbs

Regular verbs follow a predictable pattern in the formation of their **principal parts.** Every verb has four principal parts: the present-tense form, the past-tense form, the past participle (used with helping verbs), and the present participle (the *-ing* verb form used with helping verbs). Regular verbs add *ed* to form their past tense and past participles. Some examples of regular verbs appear below.

Examples of Regular Verbs

Present	Past	Past Participle	Present Participle
add	added	(have) added	(are) adding
change	changed	(have) changed	(are) changing
pull	pulled	(have) pulled	(are) pulling
walk	walked	(have) walked	(are) walking

Irregular verbs, on the other hand, follow no predictable pattern in their past and past participle forms. Sometimes a vowel changes: *sing* in the present tense becomes *sang* in the past tense and *sung* in the past participle. Sometimes an *n* or *en* will be added to form the past participle: *take* becomes *taken*, *fall* becomes *fallen*. Some verbs, such as the verb *set*, do not change at all. Others change completely: *buy* in the present tense becomes *bought* in the past and past participle.

Below are some common irregular verbs and their principal parts. If you are unsure about a verb form, check this list or consult a dictionary for the correct form.

Principal Parts of Common Irregular Verbs

Present	Past	Past Participle	Present Participle
be (am, are, is)	was (were)	(have) been	(are) being
become	became	(have) become	(are) becoming
begin	began	(have) begun	(are) beginning
blow	blew	(have) blown	(are) blowing
break	broke	(have) broken	(are) breaking
bring	brought	(have) brought	(are) bringing
burst	burst	(have) burst	(are) bursting
buy	bought	(have) bought	(are) buying
catch	caught	(have) caught	(are) catching
choose	chose	(have) chosen	(are) choosing
come	came	(have) come	(are) coming
cut	cut	(have) cut	(are) cutting
do	did	(have) done	(are) doing
draw	drew	(have) drawn	(are) drawing
drink	drank	(have) drunk	(are) drinking
drive	drove	(have) driven	(are) driving
eat	ate	(have) eaten	(are) eating
fall	fell	(have) fallen	(are) falling
feel	felt	(have) felt	(are) feeling
fight	fought	(have) fought	(are) fighting
find	found	(have) found	(are) finding
fly	flew	(have) flown	(are) flying
freeze	froze	(have) frozen	(are) freezing
get	got	(have) gotten (or got)	(are) getting
give	gave	(have) given	(are) giving
go	went	(have) gone	(are) going
grow	grew	(have) grown	(are) growing

Present	Past	Past Participle	Present Participle
have	had	(have) had	(are) having
hear	heard	(have) heard	(are) hearing
hide	hid	(have) hidden	(are) hiding
hold	held	(have) held	(are) holding
hurt	hurt	(have) hurt	(are) hurting
keep	kept	(have) kept	(are) keeping
know	knew	(have) known	(are) knowing
lay (put)	laid	(have) laid	(are) laying
lead	led	(have) led	(are) leading
leave	left	(have) left	(are) leaving
lend	lent	(have) lent	(are) lending
lie (recline)	lay	(have) lain	(are) lying
lose	lost	(have) lost	(are) losing
put	put	(have) put	(are) putting
ride	rode	(have) ridden	(are) riding
rise	rose	(have) risen	(are) rising
run	ran	(have) run	(are) running
see	saw	(have) seen	(are) seeing
set (place)	set	(have) set	(are) setting
sing	sang	(have) sung	(are) singing
sit (be seated)	sat	(have) sat	(are) sitting
speak	spoke	(have) spoken	(are) speaking
swim	swam	(have) swum	(are) swimming
take	took	(have) taken	(are) taking
tear	tore	(have) torn	(are) tearing
throw	threw	(have) thrown	(are) throwing
write	wrote	(have) written	(are) writing

Practice 6 Using the Correct Form of Irregular Verbs

Fill in the blank with the correct form of the verb shown to the left of each question. For help, consult the list of irregular verbs above.

(become) **1.** James has ________ an accomplished pianist.

(break) **2.** Ellen hopes she has not ________ her computer keyboard.

(drink)	**3.**	The dog ________ all the water in her bowl before we came home.
(eat)	**4.**	Have you ________ dinner?
(go)	**5.**	James has ________ to pick up his daughter.
(lead)	**6.**	The mother duck ________ her ducklings across the busy intersection.
(lend)	**7.**	The bank ________ Miguel the money to buy a car.
(run)	**8.**	Alisha ________ across the street, hoping to catch the bus.
(see)	**9.**	When Greg ________ his test grade, he felt relieved.
(swim)	**10.**	When Tamiko had ________ for half an hour, she got out of the pool.

Puzzling Pairs

Some irregular verbs are easily confused with other words. The following section will help you make the right choice between *lend* and *loan, lie* and *lay*, and *sit* and *set*.

Lend and *Loan*

Lend is a verb meaning "to allow someone to borrow," as in "*Lend* me ten dollars until payday," or "She *lent* her book to another student." *Loan* is a noun meaning "something borrowed," as in "He went to the bank for a mortgage *loan*."

Examples

✘ I was not sure the bank would *loan* me the money.

✔ I was not sure the bank would *lend* me the money.

✘ Mrs. Timmons *loaned* her son the money for tuition.

✔ Mrs. Timmons *lent* her son the money for tuition.

> ** Real-World Writing: Lend? Loan? Who Cares!*
>
> People who care about English also care about the distinction between *lend* and *loan*. Though the use of *loan* as a verb is widespread, it is not considered acceptable by careful writers and speakers of English.
>
> Therefore, it's best to avoid such constructions as "Loan me a quarter for the telephone," or "He loaned me his car."

PRACTICE 7 USING *LEND* AND *LOAN*

For each sentence, choose the correct word.

1. I promised my grandmother I would pay back the (lend, loan), but she said, "Consider it a gift."
2. Derek tries not to (lend, loan) books he wants to keep.
3. Shakespeare wrote, "Friends, Romans, countrymen, (lend, loan) me your ears."
4. Amy is irresponsible with money; she needs a (lend, loan) before each payday.
5. Would you mind (lending, loaning) me a hand?

Lay and *Lie*

Lay and *lie* are often confused, partly because their forms overlap. The present tense of the verb *lay* and the past tense of *lie* are both the same: *lay*. Look at the chart below to see the different forms of each verb.

Present	Past	Past Participle	Present Participle
lay (put)	laid	(have) laid	(are) laying
lie (recline)	lay	(have) lain	(are) lying

- The verb *lay* means to *put* or *place*. It always takes an object; that is, there will always be an answer to the question, "Lay what?"

Examples

verb object
✔ Horace lays his work problems aside before he walks into his house.

verb object
✔ Jessica laid her duffel bag on a bench in the locker room.

verb object
✔ Spiros has laid the brick for his patio, and he promised he would help me with mine.

verb object
✔ Preston and I are laying the groundwork for our project.

- The verb *lie* means to *recline*. It does not take an object.

Examples

verb
✔ Since Anna broke her ankle, she lies around watching soap operas all day.

✔ The turtle lay (verb) upside down in the middle of the highway, unable to right itself.

✔ I have lain (verb) on that soft couch for too long; now my back is aching.

✔ The flashlight was lying (verb) on the mantel where Kaya had left it.

PRACTICE 8 USING *LAY* AND *LIE*

Underline the correct verb forms in the paragraph below.

Before the sun rose, Martin went out to pick up the newspaper that was [1](laying, lying) in his driveway. Because it was dark, he did not even see the small shape that [2](laid, lay) in the street just past his mailbox. Inside the house, he [3](lay, laid) the paper on the kitchen counter, fixed a bowl of cereal for himself, and opened a can of food for his golden retriever, Bart. But when he went to the back door to call Bart, the dog did not come. "He must have jumped the fence again," Martin thought. "I'll have to [4](lay, lie) down the law to that crazy dog." But when Martin pulled out of his driveway to go to work, he saw Bart [5](laying, lying) beside the road. The dog [6](lay, laid) so still that Martin thought he was dead. As he bent down, Martin heard a soft whine, so he picked the dog up and gently [7](lay, laid) him in the back seat of the car. At the vet's office, Dr. Jordan said, "I'll have to [8](lay, lie) it on the line. Bart's injuries are serious, and it will be twenty-four hours before we can make any real predictions. That night, Martin [9](lay, laid) awake for a long time. When he called Dr. Jordan the next morning, the vet said, "Bart's a strong dog. I think he's going to make it." As he [10](lay, laid) the telephone receiver back in its cradle, Martin breathed a sigh of relief. It would not be a day for goodbyes.

Sit and *Set*

The verb *sit* means to take a seat or to be located. It does not take an object.

Examples

✔ The house sits (verb) on a hill overlooking the lake.

✔ Phooey sat (verb) beside her bowl wearing a look that said "feed me."

✔ The children have sat (verb) in front of the television for too long.

✔ The Arnolds' car is sitting (verb) in the driveway, so they must be at home.

Set means to put or place. The verb *set* always takes an object; that is, you will always find an answer to the question, "Set what?"

Examples

✔ Set (verb) the groceries (object) on the counter.

✔ On New Year's Eve, Janis set (verb) her goals (object) for the year.

✔ I believe I have set (verb) the tomato plants (object) too close together.

✔ The students believe the teacher is setting (verb) standards (object) that they cannot meet.

PRACTICE 9 USING *SIT* AND *SET*

Underline the correct verb forms in the sentences below.

1. The cat (sits, sets) in the window, entertained for hours by the sparrows outside.
2. The letter carrier (sat, set) the package beside the door.
3. While the grownups were (sitting, setting) on the porch, Billy scrawled abstract designs on the living room wall.
4. (Sitting, setting) at the table, Bonita (sat, set) her goals down in writing.
5. Craig's bread machine has (set, sat) on the shelf ever since he bought it.

Review Exercises

Complete the Review Exercises to see how well you learned the skills addressed in this chapter. As you work through the exercises, go back through the chapter to review any of the rules you do not understand completely.

Review Exercise 1 Finding Subjects and Verbs

Cross out prepositional phrases in the following sentences. Then underline the subject once and the verb twice.

1. In many homes, the kitchen is the hub of family activity.
2. The television has been blaring loudly in the living room almost all day.
3. The kite sailed majestically upward, then spiraled to earth.
4. The coffee in this pot tastes bitter and strong.
5. The meeting of the planning committee might be rescheduled.
6. The dog has been drinking from your glass of water.
7. The lack of space in my office may force me to dispose of some of my books.
8. Anita longed for a new car to replace her unreliable old clunker.
9. Computers were supposed to create a "paperless office."
10. Instead, they generate even more paper.

Review Exercise 2 Finding Subjects and Verbs

Cross out prepositional phrases in the following sentences. Then underline subjects once and verbs twice.

1. The sleeping cat woke when Mattie went into the kitchen.
2. Some of the leftovers in this refrigerator should be thrown out.
3. The dictionary's cover was tattered and worn.
4. The sound of the gong reverberated throughout the auditorium.
5. Selenium is believed to play a role in cancer prevention.
6. Tim glanced in the mirror at his shaggy hair and decided to get a haircut after work.
7. The company's apology came too late for Claire.
8. Jake and Mike are fraternal twins but do not look much alike.
9. The melon, grown in poor, sandy soil, barely reached the size of a baseball.
10. The witness could not recollect the color of the robber's shoes.

Review Exercise 3 Puzzling Pairs

Choose the correct form of the following verbs.

1. (Sit, Set) down and make yourself comfortable.
2. In the summer, Kristen enjoys (laying, lying) on the beach.

3. James was sorry he had (lent, loaned) his circular saw to Matt.
4. Pablo has promised to (lend, loan) his expertise when we paint the set.
5. A shining ribbon of discarded cans (lay, laid) alongside the road.
6. The rivals shook hands and (lay, laid) their differences aside.
7. Barbara has (laid, lain) in the sun too long.
8. Joan called and asked, "Are you busy or are you just (sitting, setting) around?"
9. Can you (loan, lend) me a pencil?
10. The compact disks, removed from their cases, were (laying, lying) on the table.

Review Exercise 4 Using Irregular Verbs

Fill in the blank with the correct form of the verb shown to the left of each question. For help, consult the list of irregular verbs in this chapter.

(lie) 1. Nicole walked along the stretch of sand, occasionally stopping to pick up one of the shells that __________ scattered along the shoreline.

(burst) 2. The child stood in the supermarket aisle, crying because his balloon had __________.

(fly) 3. The nest was deserted; the nestlings had long since __________.

(put) 4. Howard brought the groceries in and __________ them away immediately.

(fall) 5. When Alison __________ on the track, everyone rushed over to ask if she was hurt.

(begin) 6. It is distracting when people enter the theater after a performance has __________.

(tear) 7. An hour ago, the cat __________ out of the house, and I haven't seen him since.

(spend) 8. I __________ $35 and left the grocery store with just one small bag.

(fight) 9. When they were young, the sisters __________ continually.

(throw) 10. Quinton __________ the ball too hard and pulled a shoulder muscle.

Review Exercise 5 Using Irregular Verbs

Fill in the blank with the correct form of the verb shown to the left of each question. For help, consult the list of irregular verbs in this chapter.

(bring) **1.** After she was hired, the new manager __________ a measure of stability to the department.

(rise) **2.** After the dough had __________, Mary shaped it into loaves.

(ride) **3.** Mr. Smith said he had not __________ a bicycle since he was a child.

(see) **4.** Yesterday I __________ a wasp's nest in our garage.

(drink) **5.** Who __________ all the diet cola?

(lay) **6.** Harriet __________ a blanket across the sleeping child.

(break) **7.** The company __________ with tradition by adding athletic shoes to its line.

(go) **8.** Betty __________ to work before the sun rose.

(lose) **9.** Adam has __________ the combination to the safe.

(drive) **10.** Four police cars have __________ past within the last hour.

19 Subject-Verb Agreement

The Question

How can I get on with writing
When subjects and verbs are always fighting?

The Answer

Plural paired with singular
Can't seem to get along,
And singular with plural
Just doesn't quite belong.

But singular and singular
Will need no referee,
And plural paired with plural
Is in perfect harmony.

In grammatical relations
You'll achieve tranquility
By using combinations
That never disagree.

Fortunately, the rules for agreement between subjects and verbs are much simpler than the rules for human relationships. All of the rules for subject-verb agreement presented in this chapter have the same idea behind them: **A singular subject requires a singular verb, and a plural subject requires a plural verb.**

The Basic Pattern

Since most subject-verb agreement problems occur in the present tense, let's begin by looking at a present-tense verb as it moves through the first, second, and third person.

	Singular	Plural
First person	I walk	we walk
Second person	you walk	you walk
Third person	he, she, it walks	they walk

PRACTICE 1 CONJUGATING A VERB

All regular verbs follow the pattern above. Using the sample above as a model, fill in the forms of the verb *call* in the spaces below.

	Singular	Plural
First person	I ________	we ________
Second person	you ________	you ________
Third person	he, she, it ________	they ________

Did you remember to put the *s* on the third-person singular form? Notice that it is only in the third person that the singular form is different from the plural form. Notice, too, that the third-person verb pattern is exactly the opposite of the pattern you see in nouns. When you look at the noun *cat*, you know that it is singular and that the plural form is *cats*. But verbs in the third person, present tense, work in exactly the opposite way. The third-person singular form of the verb ends in *s*, not the plural form. When you see the verb *walks*, you know it is singular because it ends in *s*.

Examples

A third-person singular subject and verb usually follow the pattern shown below:

> The *cat walks*. (The singular noun does not end in *s*; the singular verb does end in *s*.)

A third-person plural subject and verb usually follow this pattern:

The *cats walk*. (The plural noun ends in *s*; the plural verb does not end in *s*.)

> *** *Memory Jogger***
>
> If you have trouble with third-person verbs, remember the following verse.
>
> The Singular S
> When verbs are in the present tense,
> You never need to guess.
> The singular third-person verb
> Always ends in s.

PRACTICE 2 CONJUGATING VERBS

On your own paper, fill in the first-, second-, and third-person forms of the following regular verbs: *inspire, locate, dance, resist, type*. Remember to add the *s* to the third-person singular form.

Verbs Ending in *-es*

Look at the regular verb *confess* in the present tense. Here, when the verb already ends in *s*, the third-person singular form also changes, adding an *es*.

	Singular	Plural
First person	I confess	we confess
Second person	you confess	you confess
Third person	he, she, it confess**es**	they confess

Using Third Person

Third person is sometimes confusing. One reason is that it is the only person where the verb form changes. The biggest reason, however, is that third person includes much more than just the pronouns *he, she, it*, and *they*. Third-person singular also includes any noun or pronoun that can be replaced by *he, she*, or *it*. *James, Ms. Smith, cat, table, child, one, bank teller*, and *Abraham Lincoln* are all third-person singular. Thus, each requires a present tense verb ending in *s* or *es*.

Any noun or pronoun that can be replaced by *they* is third-person plural. The *Joneses, both, washer and dryer, beds, automobiles,* and *several* are words that could be replaced by *they*. Thus, all are third-person plural and require a present-tense plural verb, the form that does not add *s* or *es*.

The Verb *to be*

Now look at the most common irregular verb, the verb *to be*.

	Singular	Plural
First person	I am	we are
Second person	you are	you are
Third person	he, she, it **is**	they are

Notice that the pattern still holds: the third-person singular form of the verb always ends in *s* or *es*.

A Fundamental Rule

Knowing the pattern that present-tense verbs follow should make it a bit easier to apply the fundamental rule of subject-verb agreement:

A singular subject requires a singular verb, and a plural subject requires a plural verb.

Examples

Susan (S) takes (V) a walk every morning before leaving for work. (singular subject, singular verb)

A hurricane (S) spins (V) in a huge circle around a central eye. (singular subject, singular verb)

Ice cream shops (S) do (V) most of their business during the summer months. (plural subject, plural verb)

In the kitchen of the new restaurant, crates (S) of dishes and glassware wait (V) to be unpacked. (plural subject, plural verb)

PRACTICE 3 MAKING SUBJECTS AND VERBS AGREE

Underline the correct verb form in each of the following sentences.

1. Roberto (insists, insist) on biking every day, rain or shine.
2. If Karen (impress, impresses) the interviewer, she will have a good chance to get the job.
3. The cuckoo clock (squawks, squawk) loudly on the hour and half hour.
4. The names of Trevor's goldfish (is, are) Moe, Larry, and Curly.
5. The speckled jellybeans (tastes, taste) like buttered popcorn.
6. The cat had found the jellybeans, and they (was, were) scattered across the floor.
7. An airline's reputation (suffers, suffer) when one of its planes crashes.
8. Because the sisters (is, are) so busy, they rarely see one another.
9. Ms. Roberts (quiz, quizzes) her students on grammar every week.
10. For breakfast, Lauren (insist, insists) on eating sugary cereal with multicolored marshmallows.

Problems in Subject-Verb Agreement

Prepositional Phrase between Subject and Verb

One problem in subject-verb agreement occurs when a prepositional phrase comes between a subject and a verb, making it easy to make mistakes. Crossing out prepositional phrases will help you remember this important rule:

The subject of a verb is not found in a prepositional phrase.

Example 1

Consider the following problem in subject-verb agreement:

The members of the softball team (practices, practice) every afternoon until five.

Which verb is correct? If you look for the subject by asking the question, "Who or what *practices* or *practice*?" it might seem logical to say, "The *team* practices, so *team* is the subject of the sentence and *practices* is the verb." However, *team* cannot be the subject of the sentence because it already has a job: It is the object of a preposition, and *the subject of a sentence is never found in a prepositional phrase.*

Incorrect Solution:

✗ The members of the softball team practices every afternoon until five.

Correct Solution: Cross out prepositional phrases to find the subject.

✔ The members ~~of the softball team~~ (practices, practice) ~~every afternoon until five~~.

Example 2

✔ The color ~~of the draperies~~ matches the stripe woven ~~into the fabric of the sofa~~.

The verb agrees with its subject, *color,* not with the object of the preposition.

Practice 4 Eliminating Prepositional Phrases

In the sentences below, cross out prepositional phrases to find the subject of the sentence. Then, underline the subject and double-underline the correct verb.

1. The hands on the clock (seems, seem) to have stopped.
2. The layers of grime on the old desk (obscures, obscure) its beautiful finish.
3. The loudness of the music in the aerobics room of the fitness center (makes, make) Yolanda's head ache.
4. As the stairs of the escalator (disappears, disappear) into the floor, a child stands watching in amazement.
5. The computers in the library of the college (attracts, attract) many students.

Indefinite Pronouns as Subjects

Problems in subject-verb agreement are also likely to occur when the subject is an **indefinite pronoun,** a pronoun that does not refer to a specific person or thing. The following indefinite pronouns are always singular and require singular verbs.

each	everybody	everyone	anything
either	nobody	one	everything
neither	somebody	someone	nothing
anybody	anyone	no one	something

> ** Memory Jogger*
>
> Remember the singular indefinite pronouns more easily by grouping them:
>
> Each, either, neither
>
> All the bodies (anybody, everybody, somebody, nobody)
>
> All the ones (anyone, everyone, someone, one, no one)
>
> All the things (anything, everything, something, nothing)

Examples

> If no one comes to their yard sale, Pat and Amy will donate the goods to charity.

The subject *no one* is singular, as is the verb *comes*.

> Each ~~of the party guests~~ has been asked to bring an inexpensive gag gift.

The singular verb *has been asked* agrees with the singular subject *each*. The plural object of the preposition, *guests*, does not affect the verb.

PRACTICE 5 MAKING VERBS AGREE WITH INDEFINITE PRONOUNS

In each of the following sentences, cross out prepositional phrases and underline the verb that agrees with the indefinite pronoun subject.

1. Neither of the contestants (was, were) prepared to lose.
2. Everybody on the street (pass, passes) the homeless man without a backward glance.
3. No one in any of my classes (has, have) taken a class from Dr. Mason.
4. Something on the bottom of Sidney's shoes (makes, make) them stick to the floor as he walks.
5. Everything on the table (looks, look) good to me.

Subject Following the Verb

Problems in subject-verb agreement are also likely to occur when a subject follows the verb. In most English sentences, the subject comes before the verb. However, the subject follows the verb in these situations:

1. when the sentence begins with *here* or *there*
2. when the sentence begins with a prepositional phrase that is immediately followed by a verb
3. when the sentence is a question

Examples

There are no more tissues left ~~in the box~~.

The plural subject *tissues* requires the plural verb *are*. The word *there* is not the subject of the sentence.

On top of the refrigerator sit my lost keys.

The prepositional phrases *on top* and *of the refrigerator* are immediately followed by a verb. Since the subject is never found in a prepositional phrase, it must be somewhere after the verb. The plural verb *sit* agrees with the plural subject *keys*.

What was the answer to the first question?

The singular subject *answer* follows the singular verb *was*.

What were the answers to the first two questions?

The plural subject *answers* follows the plural verb *were*.

PRACTICE 6 MAKING VERBS AGREE WITH SUBJECTS THAT COME AFTER VERBS

Cross out prepositional phrases in each of the following sentences. Then underline the subject and double-underline the correct verb.

1. Nestled in the little valley (was, were) a cluster of houses.
2. Why (is, are) Trevor's parents moving to Detroit?
3. Here (is, are) the study guides you asked for, Jonathan.
4. (Does, Do) Angelica know that her paper is due on Friday?
5. There (wasn't, weren't) any newspapers left at the bookstore.

Compound Subjects

Compound subjects may also cause confusion in subject-verb agreement. The rules for subject-verb agreement with compound subjects are outlined in the sections that follow.

Compound Subjects Joined by *and*

Because *and* always joins at least two elements, compound subjects joined by *and* require a plural verb. Remember this rule:

Compound subjects joined by *and* require a plural verb.

Look at the following sentence:

Keisha and her brother (is, are) scheduled to arrive today.

If you look at the sentence and ask *how many* will arrive, subject-verb agreement should be easy. *More than one* will arrive, so the logical choice is the plural verb *are*.

Keisha and her brother are scheduled to arrive today.

Examples

A good book *and* a warm fire are ideal companions on a winter night.

Patience *and* persistence pay.

A bent umbrella, an old chair, *and* a discarded mop sit forlornly beside the trash can.

Tall pines *and* scrub oaks dot the landscape.

PRACTICE 7 MAKING VERBS AGREE WITH SUBJECTS JOINED BY *AND*

Cross out prepositional phrases, then underline the verb that agrees with each compound subject.

1. A bright-eyed Raggedy Ann doll and a tattered bear (adorns, adorn) the bookshelf in Kim's room.
2. Cold pizza and a moldy scrap of cheese (was, were) the only food in Foster's refrigerator.
3. A bowl of cold ice cream and a hot bath (awaits, await) Kim at the end of the day.
4. Two plates of spaghetti with meatballs, two salads, a glass of iced tea, and one cup of coffee (costs, cost) less than ten dollars at the Coffee Cup Cafe.
5. A monster truck show and a trip to the drive-through window of a fast food restaurant (was, were) not Gayle's idea of a good time.

Compound Subjects Joined by *or, either/or,* or *neither/nor*

When subjects are joined by *or, either/or,* or *neither/nor,* it is not always possible to use logic to determine whether the verb will be singular or plural. Therefore, one rule applies to all compound subjects joined by *or, either/or,* or *neither/nor.*

When a compound subject is joined by *or, either/or,* or *neither/nor,* the verb agrees with the part of the subject closer to it.

Consider the following sentence:

Keisha or her brother (is, are) scheduled to arrive today.

How many will arrive today? *Just one* will arrive: either Keisha *or* her brother, so using the singular verb *is* makes logical sense. The singular verb *is* also agrees with *brother,* the part of the subject closer to the verb.

Keisha or her brother is scheduled to arrive today.

Now, let's change the sentence a bit.

Keisha's brothers or her parents (is, are) scheduled to arrive today.

How many will arrive? In this sentence, *more than one*—either *brothers* or *parents.* It makes sense, then, to use a plural verb. The plural verb *are* also agrees with *parents,* the part of the subject closer to the verb.

Keisha's brothers or her parents are scheduled to arrive today.

The next two sentences do not respond to logical examination.

Keisha or her parents (is, are) scheduled to arrive today.

Keisha's parents or her brother (is, are) scheduled to arrive today.

How many will arrive? There is no way to tell. Simply follow the rule and make the verb agree with the part of the subject closer to it.

Keisha or her parents are scheduled to arrive today.

Keisha's parents or her brother is scheduled to arrive today.

Examples

A term paper *or* an oral report is required ~~in Mr. Hanson's class~~.

A term paper *or* two oral reports are required ~~in Mr. Hanson's class~~.

Either two oral reports *or* a term paper is required ~~in Mr. Hanson's class~~.

Neither the cats *nor* the dog shows any interest ~~in the parakeet~~.

~~Among the requirements~~ was listed an associate's degree *or* five years ~~of experience~~.

PRACTICE 8 MAKING VERBS AGREE WITH SUBJECTS JOINED BY *OR*, *EITHER/OR*, OR *NEITHER/NOR*

Cross out prepositional phrases, then underline the verb that agrees with each compound subject.

1. Garlic bread or dinner rolls (is, are) served with the meal.
2. Either the neighbors or my mother (watches, watch) my house while I am on vacation.
3. Neither Ms. Pitts nor Mr. Shaw (possesses, possess) the qualities that the personnel director looks for in a manager.
4. A thunderstorm or a hailstorm (is, are) expected later this afternoon.
5. Neither going to a movie nor eating at a trendy restaurant (appeal, appeals) to Jenae.

Review Exercises

Complete the Review Exercises to see how well you learned the skills addressed in this chapter. As you work through the exercises, go back through the chapter to review any of the rules you do not understand completely.

REVIEW EXERCISE 1

Underline the correct verb in each sentence below.

1. The persistent ringing of the alarm clock (wakes, wake) Shawn every morning at six.

2. Books from the library (is, are) an inexpensive form of entertainment.
3. Each of the kittens (has, have) found a good home.
4. Neither of the witnesses to the crime (tells, tell) the same story.
5. The shampoo and the conditioner (smells, smell) good, but neither is worth five dollars.
6. The flowers and the grass (has, have) dried out in the dry weather.
7. Neither Benjamin nor his professors (was, were) told that he would receive the award.
8. In an emergency, salt or baking soda (substitutes, substitute) for toothpaste.
9. How (does, do) Angela and Dennis get away with being late every day?
10. There (is, are) few students remaining on campus after exams are over.

Review Exercise 2

Write *correct* in the blank if the italicized verb agrees with its subject. If the verb is incorrect, write the correct form in the blank.

_______ 1. The potholes in the parking lot *make* driving difficult.

_______ 2. The purpose of the two assignments *was* not clear to the students.

_______ 3. One of the librarians *are* holding a book for me.

_______ 4. Everybody in the front of the classroom *seem* to make good grades.

_______ 5. A bowl of cereal and a chocolate-chip cookie *is* all I have eaten today.

_______ 6. Apples and bananas *was* at the top of Avery's shopping list.

_______ 7. Beatrice's uncle or her aunt always *comes* to her rescue when she runs out of money.

_______ 8. The blue notebook or the two red ones *belongs* to Mickey.

_______ 9. Why *has* class *been canceled* today?

_______ 10. Here *is* the assignments for the next two weeks.

Review Exercise 3

In each set of sentences, cross out the two verbs that do not agree with their subjects. Then write the correct verb forms on the lines provided.

1. The two quizzes in math class was not difficult, but the test was very hard. However, the last two problems on the test was for extra credit.

   Sentence 1: __________ Sentence 2: __________

2. Not one of the animals in that pet shop look very healthy. An animal adopted through the Humane Society cost much less, and spaying or neutering is included in the fee.

   Sentence 1: __________ Sentence 2: __________

3. Neither Tanya nor her friends was able to find a job as a grocery store cashier. Neither of the grocery stores were hiring.

   Sentence 1: __________ Sentence 2: __________

4. A college diploma or a technical school certificate are required by most employers these days. As a result, people of all ages is attending these schools.

   Sentence 1: __________ Sentence 2: __________

5. "Why is the lines always so long in this bank?" Stephanie complained. "There is just not enough tellers to help all of the customers."

   Sentence 1: __________ Sentence 2: __________

Review Exercise 4

In each set of sentences, cross out the two verbs that do not agree with their subjects. Then write the corrected verbs on the lines provided.

1. One of the purposes of children's games are to teach. I sometimes wonder what the violence in so many video games teach children.

   Sentence 1: __________ Sentence 2: __________

2. Keith and Valerie always budgets carefully and cut out coupons from the Sunday paper to save a few extra dollars. But it seems as if bills or an unexpected emergency take whatever they manage to save.

   Sentence 1: __________ Sentence 2: __________

3. Our neighborhood used to be quiet and peaceful, but now that there is a gas station and a shopping center two miles down the road, traffic has increased. Why have the city's zoning board approved commercial development so close to quiet residential districts?

   Sentence 1: __________ Sentence 2: __________

4. When an outbreak of influenza occurs, attendance at the elementary schools always drop. Some parents keep their kids at home just to insure that the children doesn't come in contact with anyone who is infected.

   Sentence 1: __________ Sentence 2: __________

5. Neither the cat nor the dog have been fed this morning. What is the chances of running out of cat food and dog food at the same time?

   Sentence 1: __________ Sentence 2: __________

Review Exercise 5

Find and correct the ten subject-verb agreement errors in the following paragraph.

[1]My friend Helen believe that she is addicted to shopping. [2]She says that whenever she feels depressed or disappointed, the neon lights and large department stores of the local mall seems to draw her right in. [3]As she wanders around the department stores, displays of stylish clothing catches her eye, and she starts to forget her problems. [4]On the racks in front of her hang the answer to her problems. [5]By the time one of the salesclerks offer to show her to a dressing room, her mood has improved considerably. [6]As she tries on clothing, she begins to feel that a new dress or a pair of jeans are just what she needs. [7]Before she knows it, she is standing at the register with an armload of clothes, and there are a charge slip or a check in front of her waiting to be signed. [8]As she walks to her car, pleasure and satisfaction washes over her, and everything is right with the world. [9]But by the time she gets home, the logical part of her mind have begun to take over. [10]She realizes she has bought unnecessary items and know she will be back at the store tomorrow to return them.

1.	______________________	**6.**	______________________
2.	______________________	**7.**	______________________
3.	______________________	**8.**	______________________
4.	______________________	**9.**	______________________
5.	______________________	**10.**	______________________

20 Run-on Sentences

> "Hi. How are you?"
>
> "Oh, you wouldn't believe the things that have been happening lately I got a job did I tell you that the last time I saw you I don't remember and anyway I'm working with Angela you remember her from high school she sat in the second row near the window in our homeroom well she and I are dating now can you believe it my old car you know the one I was driving last year the transmission just tore up completely and I had to get rid of it my dad cosigned for a loan though and I got the one over there walk on over with me and I'll show it to you hey, are you listening to me?"

What Is a Run-on Sentence?

A **run-on sentence** is not one sentence, but two or more, run together without proper punctuation, like the sentences in the box above. Reading a run-on sentence is like listening to a person speaking so quickly that the words pour out in a breathless jumble. You get the general idea, but you may lose track of where one thought ends and the next begins. The sentence below is a run-on.

✗ Two pieces of paper slipped out of Desmond's notebook a student walking by picked them up and ran down the hall after Desmond.

By examining the sentence, you can probably decide where the first thought ends and the second begins—between *notebook* and *a student*.

Grammatically, too, you can figure out why the thoughts should be separate. Each has a subject and a verb and is an **independent clause,** a clause that can stand alone as a sentence or that can be combined with other clauses in specific patterns.

Another type of run-on is called a **comma splice** because two independent clauses are spliced, or joined, with a comma.

✘ Two pieces of paper slipped out of Desmond's notebook, a student walking by picked them up and ran down the hall after Desmond.

The first step toward writing paragraphs and essays that are free of run-on sentences is to learn to recognize run-ons and comma splices. When you see a sentence that you believe is a run-on, test it. Read the first part. Is it a sentence that could stand alone? If your answer is yes, read the second part, asking the same question. If your answer is again yes, the sentence is probably a run-on.

PRACTICE 1 RECOGNIZING RUN-ONS AND COMMA SPLICES

In each sentence, underline the spot where the run-on occurs. Mark *RO* in the blank to the left of the sentence if the sentence is a run-on, *CS* if it is a comma splice.

_____ **1.** An old, bent woman trudged alongside the busy highway she wore several layers of clothing and pushed a shopping cart laden with her belongings.

_____ **2.** The computer screen was hard to read, light from the window created a reflection on the screen's surface.

_____ **3.** Fitness is important to Sandra, she jogs every morning.

_____ **4.** "What does it take to be successful?" Anthony asked his boss Ms. Gray told him, "You have to be willing to make a lot of mistakes."

_____ **5.** Vanessa's brother goes to the university her sister attends a technical school.

_____ **6.** The store will open in the morning, it is closed for inventory today.

_____ **7.** Yesterday's meeting was supposed to last for an hour one hour and forty-five minutes later, it was still in progress.

_____ **8.** Maureen had a part-time job, an active social life, and a full load of courses after she received her first test grade, she decided she needed to spend more time on her coursework.

_____ **9.** No matter how many times Antwan went by his instructor's office, she wasn't there after a while, he decided he needed to make an appointment.

_____ **10.** The microwave's buzzer sounded dinner was ready.

Correcting Run-ons

Five methods of correcting run-ons are presented in the following sections. The first three methods are simple; the remaining two are more complex. Learning all five methods will give you more than just ways to correct run-ons; it will give you a variety of sentence patterns and transitional words to use in your writing.

Method 1: Period and Capital Letter

Correcting a run-on with a period and capital letter is the easiest method to use. The hard part is knowing when and how often to use it. Short, single-clause sentences can emphasize ideas by setting them apart. Too many short sentences can make your writing seem choppy and disconnected.

Pattern: Independent clause. Independent clause.

Put a period between the two sentences. Use a capital letter to begin the new sentence.

Example

✗ The technician flipped a switch red and green lights blinked on the control panel.

✓ The technician flipped a switch. Red and green lights blinked on the control panel.

PRACTICE 2 CORRECTING RUN-ONS WITH A PERIOD AND CAPITAL LETTER

In each sentence, underline the spot where the run-on or comma splice occurs. Write *RO* in the blank to the left of the sentence if it is a run-on, *CS* if it is a comma splice. Then correct each sentence using a period and a capital letter.

_____ **1.** Nonessential water usage has been banned, people are asked not to wash their cars or water their lawns until the drought ends.

____

_____ **2.** Rosie walked over to a display of books she picked up a novel by Stephen King.

____

_____ **3.** In the checkout line, Olivia dropped a quarter it rolled across the floor until an elderly man placed his foot on it to stop its progress.

____

_____ **4.** Wearing his bathrobe, Lou sleepily walked to the end of the driveway, he picked up the newspaper and headed back toward the house.

____

_____ **5.** Americans are becoming more aware of the need to exercise the sale of treadmills, stationary bikes, and weight training equipment has increased over the last decade.

____

Method 2: Comma and FANBOYS Conjunction

Coordinating conjunctions, or FANBOYS conjunctions, are among the most useful and powerful connecting words in the English language. If you can remember the nonsense word FANBOYS, you can remember the seven coordinating conjunctions: **f**or, **a**nd, **n**or, **b**ut, **o**r, **y**et, **s**o.

Pattern: Independent clause, and independent clause.

When a FANBOYS conjunction is used with a comma to separate two clauses, the comma goes before the FANBOYS conjunction.

Example

✗ Andrea had the day off, she went shopping.

✔ Andrea had the day off, so she went shopping.

** FANBOYS Conjunctions*

for	and	nor	but	or	yet	so

Practice 3 Correcting Run-ons with a *FANBOYS* Conjunction

In each sentence, underline the spot where the run-on or comma splice occurs. Write *RO* in the blank to the left of the sentence if it is a run-on, *CS* if it is a comma splice. Correct each run-on or comma splice by using a comma and a FANBOYS conjunction.

_____ **1.** The house was painted brown the shutters and trim were red.

____

_____ **2.** The letter carrier had never seen the two dogs before, she approached them cautiously.

____

_____ **3.** The park was overgrown with weeds the city workers were on strike.

____

_____ **4.** Eating raw eggs used to be considered healthy now people worry about the dangers of salmonella.

____

_____ **5.** Karen is a grouch when she first wakes up, after her first cup of coffee, she feels human again.

____

Method 3: Semicolon

Using a semicolon to join clauses works best with ideas that are closely connected and need no transitional word to explain the connection between them. The semicolon is the grammatical equivalent of a period, but the first letter of the clause after the semicolon is *not* capitalized.

Pattern: Independent clause; independent clause.

The semicolon goes between the two clauses.

Example

✘ The book section is to the right as patrons enter the library, journals and periodicals are to the left.

✔ The book section is to the right as patrons enter the library; journals and periodicals are to the left.

Practice 4 Correcting Run-ons with a Semicolon

In each sentence, underline the spot where the run-on occurs. Write *RO* in the blank to the left of the sentence if it is a run-on, *CS* if it is a comma splice. Then correct the sentences using a semicolon alone.

_____ **1.** Registration for classes will be held until Thursday the late registration period runs through Monday.

____

_____ **2.** Stephanie bought a five-year-old Toyota, newer cars were too expensive.

____

_____ **3.** Marcy fell from a swing and broke her arm at recess, the school could not immediately reach either of her parents.

____

_____ **4.** Jason buys a lottery ticket every week, he calls it his retirement plan.

____

_____ **5.** Books lined the shelves in the small classroom, maps were displayed on the walls.

____

Method 4: Semicolon and Transitional Expression

A run-on sentence may also be corrected with a connecting word or phrase that functions as a transitional expression, underscoring the relationship between the two clauses.

Pattern: <u>Independent clause</u>; therefore, <u>independent clause</u>.

A semicolon precedes the transitional expression and a comma follows it. With the words *thus* and *then*, the comma is often omitted.

Example

✘ Traffic was heavy the rain made it almost impossible to see the road.

✔ Traffic was heavy; furthermore, the rain made it almost impossible to see the road.

Connectors Used with a Semicolon

accordingly	as a result	finally
also	besides	for example

for instance	instead	on the other hand
furthermore	meanwhile	then
however	namely	therefore
in addition	nevertheless	thus
in fact	of course	

PRACTICE 5 CORRECTING RUN-ONS WITH A SEMICOLON AND TRANSITIONAL EXPRESSION

In each sentence, underline the spot where the run-on occurs. Write *RO* in the blank to the left of the sentence if it is a run-on, *CS* if it is a comma splice. Then correct the sentence using a semicolon and an appropriate transitional expression.

_____ **1.** Denice thought she could get by without studying, her grades suffered.

____

_____ **2.** The lake was beautiful and clear, cans, bottles, and fast-food wrappers littered the beach alongside it.

____

_____ **3.** Philip looked at expensive stereo equipment for hours, he decided that what he had was good enough.

____

_____ **4.** Dogs have lost their position as the most popular pet, more Americans now have cats than dogs.

____

_____ **5.** In relatively wealthy countries, people can afford to have pets in some countries, dogs and cats are used as food.

____

Method 5: Dependent Word

Placing a dependent word in front of an independent clause makes it a dependent clause, a clause that can no longer stand on its own as a sentence. It now *depends* on the sentence it is attached to and can no longer be separated from it.

Example

Each of the independent clauses shown below stands on its own as a sentence.

independent clause — independent clause

The orchestra began to play. Fireworks appeared in the night sky.

When the word *as* is added to the first clause, it becomes a *dependent clause.* Now, it cannot stand on its own but must depend on—or remain attached to—the independent clause.

dependent clause — independent clause

As the orchestra began to play, fireworks appeared in the night sky.

Two Patterns Using the Dependent Clause

Sentences containing dependent clauses take on various patterns. Two of those patterns are shown below. In the first pattern, the dependent clause introduces the sentence and is followed by a comma. In the second pattern, the dependent clause ends the sentence.

Pattern 1: Dependent clause as an introductory clause

As dependent clause, independent clause.

When the dependent clause acts as an introductory clause, a comma follows it.

Example

✘ Margaret walked into her office, the phone began to ring.

✔ As Margaret walked into her office, the phone began to ring.

Pattern 2: Dependent clause last

Independent clause as dependent clause.

When the dependent clause comes last in the sentence, no comma is used.

✔ Margaret walked into her office as the phone began to ring.

Commonly Used Dependent Words

after	as if	as though
although	as long	because
as	as soon as	before

even though	though	whenever
if	unless	where
once	until	wherever
since	what	which
so that	whatever	while
that	when	who

PRACTICE 6 CORRECTING RUN-ONS WITH A DEPENDENT WORD

In each sentence, underline the spot where the run-on occurs. Write *RO* in the blank to the left of the sentence if it is a run-on, *CS* if it is a comma splice. Correct the following run-ons, using a different dependent word with each sentence.

_____ **1.** The throbbing in Charles's jaw became worse he picked up the phone to call the dentist.

____

_____ **2.** The setting sun painted the lake red-gold, the breeze ruffled its mirrored surface.

____

_____ **3.** A water shortage developed the city imposed a ban on outdoor watering.

____

_____ **4.** The women's softball team has won every game this season, the men's team has turned in its worst performance ever.

____

_____ **5.** Helen won tickets to the concert she is looking for someone to go with her.

____

A Special Case: The Word *That*

Occasionally, the dependent word *that* is implied rather than stated in a sentence. The sentence may look like a run-on, but it is not.

Example

✔ The mechanic didn't think he could fix the car.

Five Ways to Correct Run-on Sentences

Method 1: Period and Capital Letter

Pattern: Independent clause. Independent clause.

Method 2: Comma and FANBOYS Conjunction

Pattern: Independent clause, and independent clause.

A comma goes before the FANBOYS conjunction in this pattern.

FANBOYS Conjunctions

for and nor but or yet so

Method 3: Semicolon

Pattern: Independent clause; independent clause.

Method 4: Semicolon and Joining Word

Pattern: Independent clause; therefore, independent clause.

A semicolon goes before the joining word and a comma follows it.

Exceptions: With the words *thus* and *then,* the comma is often omitted.

Joining Words Used with a Semicolon

also	however	of course
as a result	in addition	on the other hand
besides	in fact	then
finally	instead	therefore
for example	meanwhile	thus

Method 5: Dependent Word

Pattern 1: Although dependent clause, independent clause.

When a dependent word begins the sentence, a comma is used between the dependent and independent clause.

Pattern 2: Independent clause when dependent clause.

When the dependent clause ends the sentence, a dependent word separates the clauses.

Dependent Words

although	because	that	whenever
as	before	though	where
as if	if	unless	wherever
as long	once	until	which
as soon as	since	whatever	while
as though	so that	when	who

This sentence could be mistaken for a run-on. "The mechanic didn't think" has a subject, *mechanic*, and a verb, *did think*, and is not preceded by a dependent word. It could stand alone as a sentence. "He could fix the car" also has a subject, *he*, and a verb, *could fix*. It, too, could stand alone as a sentence. But is the sentence a run-on? No. The two thoughts are connected by the implied dependent word *that*. The meaning of the sentence is "The mechanic did not think *that* he could fix the car." Sentences in which the dependent word *that* is implied do not need correction—it is not even necessary to insert the word *that*.

PRACTICE 7 RECOGNIZING AN IMPLIED *THAT*

Write *OK* by the sentences that contain the implied word *that*. Write *RO* by the run-ons.

_____ **1.** The lawyer had a feeling her client was withholding information.

_____ **2.** On the desk sat a mystery novel Becky had not read.

_____ **3.** On the desk sat a mystery novel Becky had not read it.

_____ **4.** Last night Andrew dreamed he had forgotten to take his final exams.

_____ **5.** Jason was afraid his instructor would find out he had cheated on the exam.

_____ **6.** In the parking lot, Lauren ran over a nail it went through the bottom of her tire and out the sidewall.

_____ **7.** The technician at the tire store told her it would be too dangerous to patch the sidewall.

_____ **8.** Lauren had planned to buy a new pair of shoes she bought a tire instead.

_____ **9.** As the police officer wrote the ticket, she reminded Bryan his driver's license would need to be renewed in a month.

_____ **10.** The ceiling fan cooled the room an air conditioner would have done a better job.

Review Exercises

Complete the Review Exercises to see how well you have learned the skills addressed in this chapter. As you work through the exercises, go back through the chapter to review any of the rules you do not understand completely.

Review Exercise 1

Correct the ten run-on sentences below, using each of the five methods at least once. Rewrite the corrected portion of each sentence on the line provided.

1. The bus was late this morning the driver was delayed by a wreck on Miller's Hill Road.

   ____

2. Zandra likes her unusual name she wonders how some parents can saddle their children with names like "Bob" or "Ann."

   ____

3. We met our new neighbors today, their names are Gary and Vicki.

   ____

4. Vijay worked for two hours on his research paper then he went out for pizza with his friends.

   ____

5. The shallow lake near the college is a popular gathering place everyone calls it Lake Knee Deep.

   ____

6. In the clear night sky, the Belt of Orion shone brightly Tasha could not find the Big Dipper.

   ____

7. The Andersens didn't have time for a camping trip, they pitched their tent in the back yard for a weekend mini-vacation.

   ____

8. Sonya's job in the Gaslight Grill pays less than minimum wage her tips, however, more than compensate for her low wages.

   ____

9. The gym was crowded at 6:00 P.M., Bert had to wait fifteen minutes for a treadmill.

   ____

10. Seven fragile cups sat in a row on the cupboard shelf, the eighth lay in pieces on the tile floor.

    ____

Review Exercise 2

Correct the ten run-on sentences below, using each of the five methods at least once. Rewrite the corrected portion of each sentence on the line provided.

1. Chandra is a vegetarian her husband complains he has not seen a hamburger for months.

   ____

2. Alex answered the telephone only silence greeted him on the other end.

   ____

3. Jan likes blues and rock, her husband prefers Beethoven and Bach.

   ____

4. Highlighters are useful for marking textbooks experts say only 10 to 20 percent of the material should be highlighted.

   ____

5. Orientation and study skills courses are a good way to learn to adjust to the demands of college many students say they benefit from such courses.

   ____

6. A roll of pennies contains fifty pennies a roll of nickels contains only forty nickels.

   ____

7. Bank tellers count money rapidly they always count it twice to make sure the amount is correct.

   ____

8. Smoke billowed from the forest fire the sky turned a muddy brown.

   ____

9. Annette always forgot to water the plants on her porch they eventually died.

   ____

10. Tyler is an optimist he always looks at the positive side of any situation.

    ____

Review Exercise 3

Correct the two run-ons in each of the following sentence groups, writing your corrections on the lines provided.

1. My little brother wastes time playing video games, then he claims he was too busy to do his homework. Yesterday, his teacher sent a note home to my parents now Caleb has to show Mom his finished homework before he plays video games.

____

____

2. Alfreda gets her oil changed at Lube'n'Go, her husband goes to Slick City and pays twice as much. Alfreda does not understand why he continues to pay exorbitant prices, he claims, however, that Slick City does a better job.

____

____

3. Society's expectations about education have changed, many years ago, a high school diploma was considered adequate for most people. Now, employers are demanding a more educated workforce most high school graduates go on to college or technical school before beginning their chosen careers.

____

____

4. Adults returning to school often have been in a job for many years they return to school to advance their skills or increase their chances for promotion. Others are women who have been out of the workforce raising children they know that a college diploma can make them more employable and help to raise their standard of living.

____

____

5. News is readily available from a variety of media, including radio and TV it is even available through a computer. Many people prefer to read a newspaper it is portable, can be read anytime, and offers more depth than many other sources of information.

____

____

Review Exercise 4

Correct the two run-ons in each of the following sentence groups, writing your corrections on the lines provided.

1. Marian is trying to save money on her grocery bill she cuts coupons, watches the sales, and shops carefully. Her husband Pete is not as frugal with one trip to the grocery store, he can destroy Marian's entire budget.

____

____

2. Pirby, Nick's Persian cat, loves to sleep in the sun it warms his old bones. As the day progresses, the sunlight inches across the floor Pirby moves with it.

____

____

3. After work each day, Henry works in his garden he is proud of the results of his hard work. Henry's nephew Billy visited last weekend he trampled most of Henry's flowers into the ground.

____

____

4. The Naturally Organic Foods Company hired an artist to draw a new label for its line of soups the design was similar to that of another company. The company sued Naturally Organic Foods had to redesign its label.

____

____

5. Art, the assistant salad chef at Fisher House, likes to play practical jokes he once tossed a plastic cockroach in with the salad. The cockroach was served to a customer Art's boss was not amused.

____

____

Review Exercise 5

Correct the ten run-on sentences in the following paragraph, writing your corrections on the lines provided.

[1]Roberto has never forgotten his first night on the job at the Stake-Out Steak House it was a disaster. [2]Jan, who had been assigned to train him,

asked him to take beverages to a table of four then she left to take another order. [3]Carefully, Roberto drew coffee from the large urn on the counter in back and then looked around in confusion where was the tea? [4]He saw a large refrigerator in the tray assembly area, he thought he might find tea there. [5]From the refrigerator he withdrew a large, heavy jug of brown liquid he poured a tall glassful over ice. [6]He felt self-sufficient and proud, he garnished the glass with a lemon slice and took the beverages to the table. [7]He walked away from the table, the customer called him back, handed him the glass of tea, and said, "Are you trying to poison me?" [8]Roberto cautiously sniffed the brown liquid, then drew back in horror, it was vinegar. [9]Roberto apologized, explaining that it was his first night on the job, to his relief, the man at the table began to laugh. [10]Roberto thought, "I guess I'll laugh about this someday, it won't be today."

1. ______________________________
2. ______________________________
3. ______________________________
4. ______________________________
5. ______________________________
6. ______________________________
7. ______________________________
8. ______________________________
9. ______________________________
10. ______________________________

21

Sentence Fragments

To whoever finds this–

I know I am dying. But the secret of my family's treasure shall not die with me. I pass it on to you now.

Here are specific directions to reach it. It is buried in the Oza

on a piece of land deeded to me by my grandfather. Take Rout

en turn left, walk four paces, and dig beside the old well.

But beware the curse. If you do not

it means certain death.

Good luck–you will need it.

Whoever finds the letter above is likely to be frustrated because it is only a fragment. Important elements are missing. Readers are similarly frustrated by sentence fragments because they leave out important elements of a sentence.

What Is a Sentence Fragment?

A **sentence fragment** is an incomplete sentence. It may be a dependent clause that cannot stand on its own, or it may lack a subject, a verb, or both. If you read a fragment by itself, without the other sentences that surround it, you will usually recognize that it does not express a complete thought. It is only a part, or fragment, of a sentence.

Examples

✘ Many animals hibernate in winter. *Including woodchucks, ground squirrels, and frogs.*

✘ On Saturday morning, Alvin spent an hour raking leaves. *And sweeping them from his carport.*

The italicized word groups are sentence fragments—pieces of sentences that cannot stand alone.

Dependent Clause Fragments

✘ Jarrod said he did not finish his term paper. *Because his computer had crashed.*

✘ *When Alice arrived at 10:15.* The exam had already started.

Each of the italicized fragments above is a **dependent clause fragment.** A dependent clause fragment always begins with a dependent word. To fix a dependent clause fragment, attach it to a complete sentence. Removing the dependent word will also fix the fragment, but the dependent word may be necessary to strengthen the logical connection between two ideas.

✔ Jarrod did not finish his term paper because his computer had crashed.

✔ Jarrod did not finish his term paper. His computer had crashed.

✔ When Alice arrived at 10:15, the exam had already started.

✔ Alice arrived at 10:15. The exam had already started.

> *** *Punctuation Pointer***
>
> Use a comma to attach a dependent clause fragment at the beginning of a sentence.

Commonly Used Dependent Words

after	as	as long as
although	as if	as soon as

because	so that	whenever
before	that	where
even though	though	wherever
how	unless	which
if	until	while
once	what	who
since	when	whoever

PRACTICE 1 CORRECTING DEPENDENT CLAUSE FRAGMENTS

Correct the dependent clause fragments in the following exercise by attaching them to an independent clause. Write the corrected portion of each sentence on the line provided.

1. Tamika complained that her car did not run well. Unless she used premium gasoline.

   ____

2. Ray wondered what was wrong with the compact disc changer. That he had bought just two weeks ago.

   ____

3. Since Andrea is cold-natured and her roommate is not. They are always battling over the thermostat.

   ____

4. If Jeff did not set his clock fifteen minutes fast. He might never be on time.

   ____

5. The suspect admitted that she had shot her husband. Because the poison she was giving him had not worked quickly enough.

   ____

Verbal Phrase Fragments (*to, -ing,* and *-ed*)

✘ Anita's dog was a familiar sight in the neighborhood. *Running through yards and tearing up flowerbeds.*

✘ *To relax and to develop her creative abilities.* Ann decided to take an art class.

✘ *Bored by his job in a warehouse.* Evan bought a lawn mower and cut grass to earn money.

The examples above are **verbal phrase fragments.** A verbal phrase fragment begins with a verb form that is not used as a main verb. Verbal phrase fragments include *to* fragments, *-ing* fragments, and *-ed/-en* fragments.

Correct verbal phrase fragments by attaching them to a complete sentence.

✔ Anita's dog was a familiar sight in the neighborhood, running through yards and tearing up flowerbeds.

✔ To relax and to develop her creative abilities, Ann decided to take an art class.

✔ Bored by his job in a warehouse, Evan bought a lawn mower and cut grass to earn money.

to Fragments

Correct *to* fragments by connecting them to a sentence or by adding a subject and verb, as shown in the examples below.

Examples

✘ The auto repair shop has begun to open on weekends. To accommodate customers who work during the week.

✔ The auto repair shop has begun to open on weekends to accommodate customers who work during the week.

✘ To ensure that we would not forget to tip him. The server asked, "Do you want change back?"

✔ To ensure that we would not forget to tip him, the server asked, "Do you want change back?"

✘ James programmed his VCR before he left the house. To make sure he would not miss even one inning of the ball game.

✔ James programmed his VCR before he left the house. He wanted to make sure he would not miss even one inning of the ball game.

> ** Punctuation Pointer*
>
> A *to* fragment attached to the beginning of a sentence is followed by a comma because it is an introductory phrase. A *to* fragment connected to the end of the sentence needs no comma.

PRACTICE 2 CORRECTING *TO* FRAGMENTS

Underline and correct the *to* fragments in the following exercise. Write the corrected portion of each sentence on the line provided.

1. To give his students plenty of writing practice. The teacher assigned journals.

   ____

2. To give herself a break from the computer. Nora took her dog for a walk.

   ____

3. Samuel was surprised. To see the package outside his door.

   ____

4. To mark his place in his book. Henry used a dollar bill.

   ____

5. Radio stations often hold contests. To keep listeners tuned in.

   ____

-ing Fragments

To correct an *-ing* fragment, connect it to the rest of the sentence with a comma. You may also correct it by adding a subject and a helping verb.

✘ Peering out the window and checking her watch every five minutes. Charlene waited for her guests to arrive.

✔ Peering out the window and checking her watch every five minutes, Charlene waited for her guests to arrive.

✘ Rachel spent the afternoon at home. Listening to her new CD and reading magazines.

✔ Rachel spent the afternoon at home, listening to her new CD and reading magazines.

Sometimes, the *-ing* word may be the second or third word in the fragment.

✗ James hopped into his car and left the restaurant's parking lot. Not realizing that he had left his bucket of chicken on top of the car.

✓ James hopped into his car and left the restaurant's parking lot, not realizing that he had left his bucket of chicken on top of the car.

> ** Punctuation Pointer*
>
> Usually, *-ing* fragments can be connected to the rest of the sentence with a comma.

PRACTICE 3 CORRECTING *-ING* FRAGMENTS

Underline and correct the *-ing* fragments in the following exercise. Write the corrected portion of each sentence on the line provided.

1. Puffing as if she had run a marathon. Bonita completed her first lap on the circular track.

   ____

2. The vines grew thick on the abandoned house. Obscuring the windows and part of the front door.

   ____

3. Riding in the back of the pickup truck. The dog wobbled unsteadily as his owner rounded a curve.

   ____

4. Sneaking cigarettes, playing her music too loud, and visiting a male resident after curfew. Aunt Matilda has broken most of the nursing home's rules.

   ____

5. Leslie complains that her neighbor's children are allowed to run wild. Playing loudly in the street until past midnight.

   ____

-ed and *-en* Fragments

Another kind of fragment begins with an *-ed* or *-en* verb form, or past participle. If the verb is a regular verb, the verb form will end in *-ed,* like the verbs *walked, called,* and *plotted.* If the verb is irregular, then the verb form will end in *-en* or in another irregular ending. *Broken, grown, found, bought,* and *written* are some of these forms. (For other examples, see the list of irregular verbs in Chapter 18.) This type of fragment is usually corrected by connecting it to a complete sentence.

✗ Spaced evenly and set in rows. The desks seemed ready for the fall term.

✓ Spaced evenly and set in rows, the desks seemed ready for the fall term

✗ Everyone looked at the white rabbit. Held by the top-hatted magician.

✓ Everyone looked at the white rabbit held by the top-hatted magician.

✗ Caught with his car full of stolen property. The thief could only confess.

✓ Caught with his car full of stolen property, the thief could only confess.

PRACTICE 4 CORRECTING *-ED* AND *-EN* FRAGMENTS

Underline and correct the *-ed* and *-en* fragments in the following exercise. Write the corrected portion of each sentence on the line provided.

1. Next week, students are invited to a career fair and resume workshop. Presented by the college's career counseling office.

____

2. Cleaned and pressed at the local cleaners. Eldon's old sport coat looked like new.

____

3. Drawn by the smell of food. The dog decided to join our picnic.

____

4. Kevin has kept his old model trains. Stored on a shelf in a closet in his parents' house.

____

5. Encouraged by her parents. Dawn decided to apply for the scholarship.

____

Missing-Subject Fragments

Fragments beginning with a joining word such as *and, or, but,* or *then* followed by a verb are **missing-subject fragments.** The subject of the verb is usually in a previous sentence. Connect the fragment to the sentence or add a subject to begin a new sentence.

✗ Woodrow held up his prize fish and posed for the camera. Then fell off the end of the fishing pier.

✔ Woodrow held up his prize fish and posed for the camera, then fell off the end of the fishing pier.

✗ The hurricane changed course and seemed to falter. But gathered strength again before it hit the coast.

✔ The hurricane changed course and seemed to falter but gathered strength again before it hit the coast.

✔ The hurricane changed course and seemed to falter. But it gathered strength again before it hit the coast.

PRACTICE 5 CORRECTING MISSING-SUBJECT FRAGMENTS

Underline and correct the missing-subject fragments in the following exercise. Write the corrected portion of each sentence on the line provided.

1. The cat ate the hamburger. But refused the bun.

   ____

2. The baseball player emerged from the dugout. And waved his cap to acknowledge the cheering fans.

   ____

3. At the side of the road, the collie looked both ways. Then crossed the street.

   ____

4. On her days off, Ebony reads a book. Or surfs the Internet on her computer.

   ____

5. Every morning, a wily squirrel bounds into Maurice's backyard and heads for the bird feeder. Then eats the food Maurice has put out for the birds.

   ____

* Real-World Writing: Is it okay to start a sentence with but?

Yes and no. Grammatically, it is correct to start a sentence with *but* or any other FANBOYS conjunction. However, your instructors may discourage the practice, for two good reasons.

1. Beginning a sentence with *but* is an informal technique. It may work in personal essays but should not be used in formal compositions such as research papers. (This text, you may have noticed, takes an informal, conversational approach, addressing you directly and occasionally using a FANBOYS conjunction to begin a sentence.)
2. Using *but* to begin a sentence can be addictive. *But* is the strongest contrast signal in our language, and it's easy to overuse.

The bottom line: Use conjunctions to begin sentences only if your instructor gives the green light, and then use them sparingly.

Example and Exception Fragments

Fragments often occur when a writer decides to add an example or note an exception. Example fragments often begin with *such as, including, like, for example,* or *for instance.* Exception fragments often begin with *not, except, unless, without,* or *in spite of.* To fix the fragment, connect it to the sentence with which it logically belongs. If the fragment begins with *for example* or *for instance,* it is often best to make the fragment into a separate sentence.

✗ Hollis becomes nervous in high-pressure situations. Such as exams and interviews.

✔ Hollis becomes nervous in high-pressure situations, such as exams and interviews.

✗ Lindsay is trying to put herself through college. Without any help from her parents.

✔ Lindsay is trying to put herself through college without any help from her parents.

✗ Classes with labs require more time than other classes. For example, biology and French.

✔ Classes with labs require more time than other classes. For example, biology and French take more of my study time than history or math.

* Punctuation Pointer

Usually, you can connect fragments beginning with *such as, including, not, especially,* and *in spite of* with a comma, and fragments beginning with *except, unless, without,* and *like* with no punctuation.

A fragment beginning with *for example* or *for instance* may be attached with a comma if it immediately follows the idea it illustrates: **The chef enjoyed cooking with beans, for example, lima beans, garbanzo beans, and kidney beans.** If the idea that the example illustrates is expressed earlier in the sentence, place the example in a new sentence: **Beans are the specialty of the house at Rizzoli's Restaurant. For example, the chef makes delicious dishes from lima beans, garbanzo beans, and kidney beans.**

PRACTICE 6 CORRECTING EXAMPLE AND EXCEPTION FRAGMENTS

Underline and correct the example and exception fragments in the following exercise. Write the correction on the line provided.

1. Natalie sets aside specific times to study and lets nothing interfere with her plans. Unless something more interesting comes along.

   ____

2. Leonard complained that nothing grew in his garden. Except weeds.

   ____

3. Thirty years ago, office workers had to get along without modern equipment. Such as computers, copiers, and fax machines.

   ____

4. On New Year's Eve, Alexandra vowed to give up all sweets. Especially chocolate.

   ____

5. If everyone would cooperate, it would be easy to solve some of the community's problems. For example, litter on public streets.

   ____

Prepositional Phrase Fragments

A prepositional phrase, alone or within a series, cannot function as a sentence. Correct a prepositional phrase fragment by connecting it to a sentence with which it logically belongs.

✘ Hamilton finally found his lost history book. In a large mud puddle on the street beside the student union.

✔ Hamilton finally found his lost history book in a large mud puddle on the street beside the student union.

✘ On her way to a three o'clock job interview at Stanfield Corporation. Melanie became lost.

✔ On her way to a three o'clock job interview at Stanfield Corporation, Melanie became lost.

> *∗ Punctuation Pointer*
>
> Use a comma behind introductory prepositional phrases. No punctuation is required to connect a prepositional phrase to the end of a sentence.

Practice 7 Correcting Prepositional Phrase Fragments

Underline and correct each of the following prepositional phrase fragments. Write your correction on the line provided.

1. After searching frantically for half an hour, Amanda finally found her lost keys. Under a bunch of bananas on the kitchen counter.

   ____

2. In a hanging philodendron on the front porch. The bird had built her nest.

   ____

3. On a sandy beach with a frosty strawberry slush in her hand. Morgan found contentment.

   ____

4. Because she had stayed up all night to study, Deb fell asleep. During the exam.

   ____

5. In a pond beyond the city limits. James and his father fish on the weekends.

____

Review Exercises

Complete the Review Exercises to see how well you have learned the skills addressed in this chapter. As you work through the exercises, go back through the chapter to review any of the rules you do not understand completely.

Review Exercise 1

Underline and correct each fragment in the exercise below. Write your correction on the line provided.

1. In their cabin beside the lake. The Millers displayed photos of fish they had caught and released.

   ____

2. Because of numerous complaints. The city council passed a law prohibiting obscene bumper stickers.

   ____

3. Tom enjoys all aspects of cooking. Except chopping onions and garlic.

   ____

4. Uncle Walter raised his parrot lovingly. Giving it affection and teaching it to curse in seven languages.

   ____

5. It took three people to carry the prize-winning pumpkin. Which weighed almost 100 pounds.

   ____

6. The preschool teacher says jokingly that Sharma is a born rebel. Because she always colors outside the lines.

   ____

7. Found beside a dumpster. The coffee table looks good with a coat of paint.

   ____

8. Harriet went over to the candy dish. And picked out all the licorice drops.

   ____

9. The child tried to stay awake all night. To see if the tooth fairy was real.

____

10. We left the house forty-five minutes early. To take the car to the dealership.

____

Review Exercise 2

Underline and correct each fragment in the exercise below. Write your correction on the line provided.

1. Except for the shower, which produced just a small dribble of water. The hotel room was comfortable and inviting.

____

2. Although Mu Lan is happy to be attending college in the United States. She misses her family in Beijing.

____

3. When they went on vacation, the Colesons packed everything they thought they would need. But did not consider the possibility of snow.

____

4. The young man wore a green shirt. That said, "My parents were kidnapped by aliens and all I got was this lousy T-shirt."

____

5. Worn through at the toe and battered from use. Jennifer's sneakers need to be replaced.

____

6. With the top down and the music turned up loud. Anita sailed down the moonlit highway.

____

7. Cheering loudly and clapping rhythmically. The audience demanded an encore.

____

8. Interrupted by dozens of long commercials. The TV show ground slowly toward its conclusion.

____

9. Ayesha went to the library to return a book. That was three weeks overdue.

____

10. At the garage sale, Mark looked at the worn wooden desk. And wondered if it would fit into the back of his vehicle.

____

Review Exercise 3

Underline and correct the two fragments in each numbered item below. Write your corrections on the lines provided.

1. Because grass grows quickly in the South and weeds abound. Many residents plant thick, slow-growing grasses. Such as centipede.

____

____

2. After he had gone through registration. Edward stood in line at the bookstore. He glanced through his textbooks. And remarked to the student behind him that it was going to be a long semester.

____

____

3. Though it is common to hear of people hiring gardeners or housekeepers. It is possible to hire someone to do almost any kind of chore. Including shopping or standing in line.

____

____

4. The teacher said that she could always tell. Which students in her class were computer literate. They were the ones who knew how to turn on the computers. And find the Solitaire game.

____

____

5. Before the annual Easter egg hunt, volunteers hid Easter eggs. In bushes, behind benches, and in clumps of grass. They worked for hours hiding eggs. That the children would find in minutes.

____

____

Review Exercise 4

Underline and correct the two fragments in each of the following. Write your corrections on the lines provided.

1. High-fashion models wear extreme styles. That most women would not wear. For example, skimpy dresses and sheer tops.

____

____

2. One town in Spain holds a tomato festival. In its town square every year. Residents gather in the square. And throw tomatoes at one another until the pavement is inches deep in goo.

____

____

3. As the hunter traipsed through the snowy woods. His boots crunched loudly in the snow. The noise carried through the forest. Warning every animal within half a mile.

____

____

4. Though the old rotary phone is battered and cracked. It still works as well as it did twenty years ago. However, it does not have programmable speed dial. Or even touch tone capability.

____

____

5. Inside the top drawer of the desk, Nick found a stapler, two rolls of pennies, a lime-green note pad, a yellow highlighter, and five catnip mice. That belonged to his five cats. The drawer seemed to hold everything. Except the computer diskette he was looking for.

____

____

Review Exercise 5

Underline and correct the ten fragments in this exercise. Write your corrections on the lines provided.

[1]The kitchen workers at Arturo's Pizza have invented several games. [2]To relieve boredom when business is slow and Arturo, the owner, is not around. [3]One of their favorite games is "dough ball." [4]Which is a game of catch played with a baseball-sized ball of pizza dough. [5]When they tire of "dough ball." [6]They play "doughboy." [7]This game involves mixing a batch of extremely wet, sticky dough. [8]Then throwing it at each other. [9]At the end of the game, the person with the most dough stuck to him loses. [10]And has to clean up the mess. [11]The kitchen workers have recently invented another game. [12]That they call "beef darts." [13]The object of the game is to earn points. [14]By throwing small balls of raw hamburger at a pizza-sauce target painted on the wall. [15]As their games become more elaborate and messy. [16]The likelihood that they will be caught increases. [17]But they have been lucky. [18]So far. [19]Whenever Arturo returns to the restaurant. [20]The kitchen is spotless and the employees are hard at work.

22

Pronoun Case

The Pronoun

It substitutes for any noun you can name,
Improving coherence and flow.
So it is no wonder that people proclaim
This noun's a pro.

No matter what the verse above seems to suggest, pronouns are not simply nouns that have turned professional. **Pronouns** are words that stand in for nouns or for other pronouns. They are useful words that keep writers and speakers from tedious repetition of words.

However, the rules that govern pronoun use are complex, and confusion over pronoun use is common. If you have ever hesitated between "Stacy and me" or "Stacy and I," or wondered whether to say "between you and I" or "between you and me," this chapter will help you find the answers.

Subject and Object Pronouns

Personal pronouns (*I, we, you, he, she it, they*) refer to specific people or things. These pronouns take different forms, called **cases,** as they perform different jobs in a sentence. Look at the example that follows to see how the first person pronoun *I* changes form as its role in a sentence changes.

✔ *I* borrowed a book from the library and forgot about it. Early this week, the library sent *me* a notice saying the book was overdue.

Subject pronouns (*the subjective case*) are used as subjects or subject complements. Some commonly used subject pronouns are *I, we, you, he, she, it,* and *they.*

✔ *I* know James well; *we* have been friends for years.

✔ If *you* are looking for paper clips, *they* are in the desk drawer.

✔ Allison was told that the finalists were John and *she.*

Object pronouns (*the objective case*) are used as objects of verbs or prepositions. Some commonly used object pronouns are *me, us, you, him, her, it,* and *them.*

✔ Rachel spoke to her parents and promised to visit *them* in the weekend.

✔ The police officer was happy to give directions to Raul and *me.*

Subject Pronouns

In most instances, you probably use the subject form of the pronoun correctly without thinking about it. You probably haven't said, "Me went to the park" since you were three years old. However, using the subject form becomes trickier when a *compound subject* is used. Is it "Tiffany and her went to the concert" or "Tiffany and she went to the concert"? Usually, trying the sentence with the pronoun alone will help you hear the correct answer. Without *Tiffany and,* the sentence becomes clear. "*She* went to the concert" is correct, not "*Her* went to the concert."

Example

? *Him and his brother* went hunting this morning.

Step 1: To determine if the sentence is correct, try the pronoun alone.

✘ *Him* ~~and his brother~~ went hunting this morning.

✘ *Him* went hunting this morning.

Step 2: If the pronoun sounds incorrect, try changing the form.

✔ *He* went hunting this morning.

✔ *He and his brother* went hunting this morning. (corrected sentence)

PRACTICE 1 USING SUBJECT PRONOUNS

Underline the correct pronoun in each of the following sentences. To determine the correct pronoun form, try the pronoun alone without the compound element.

1. Cynthia and (I, me) played two games of tennis yesterday afternoon.
2. Cecil and (they, them) are meeting us over at the new ice-skating rink.
3. I heard that Wally and (she, her) had made the highest grades in class.
4. (He and I, Him and me) have been friends since grade school.
5. Do you think that you and (I, me) could study our grammar together tomorrow?

Subject Pronouns with Linking Verbs

"Hello?"

"May I speak to Tanisha Jones, please?"

"This is she."

"Hello, Tanisha, this is Randall Groover from your biology class. I was wondering . . ."

This polite exchange is typical of the way many telephone conversations begin, and it illustrates a rule that many people use in telephone conversations but ignore otherwise: When a pronoun renames the subject (that is, when it is a *subject complement*) and follows the verb *to be* or any *linking verb,* that pronoun takes the subject form.

Examples

✔ The keynote speaker [subject] will be [linking verb] she [subject complement]. (not *her*)

✔ It is *I*. (not *me*)

✔ If you are looking for Mr. Smith, that is *he* in the blue jacket. (not *him*)

✔ Ms. Smith, you say it was the defendant who robbed you. Look at him carefully. Can you be absolutely sure it was *he*? (not *him*)

PRACTICE 2 USING SUBJECT PRONOUNS AFTER LINKING VERBS

In each sentence, underline the correct pronoun.

1. I would have spoken to Randy, but I wasn't sure that it was (he, him).
2. If you need to speak with the manager, that is (she, her) at the desk by the window.
3. You said you were looking for your gloves. Are these (they, them)?
4. "Who is it?" said Sandra. "It is (I, me)," said Ken.
5. I have talked to Professor Smalls before, but I did not know at the time that it was (she, her).

Object Pronouns

Object pronouns are used as objects of verbs and prepositions. Again, problems with object pronouns commonly occur in compound constructions. These problems can usually be resolved by isolating the pronoun.

Example

? The supervisor asked *Lou and I* to work overtime.

✘ The supervisor asked Lou and *I* to work overtime.

✘ The supervisor asked *I* to work overtime.

✔ The supervisor asked *Lou and me* to work overtime.

Object Pronouns with *between*

Object pronouns always follow the preposition *between*. Thus, it is always *between you and me, between us and them, between him and her, between Larry and him.*

✘ Just between you and *I,* I heard that Alan has found a new job in Phoenix.

✔ Just between you and *me,* I heard that Alan has found a new job in Phoenix.

✘ The argument was between Leo and *she;* I tried to stay out of it.

✔ The argument was between Leo and *her;* I tried to stay out of it.

> *✻ Grammar Alert*
>
> Pronouns are often misused with *between.* Remember to use the object form: between you and *me, him, her,* or *them.*

PRACTICE 3 USING OBJECT PRONOUNS

Underline the correct pronoun in each of the following sentences.

1. Renata told Sandra and (I, me) where to recycle our glass bottles and aluminum cans.
2. When we went to see the performance at the Grand Opera House, Fran sat between Gerard and (I, me).
3. Anna gave Clay and (she, her) an extra pair of tickets to Tuesday's performance of *Big River.*
4. Someone told Catherine and (I, me) that the wildlife park was worth visiting.
5. It is a small apartment, but it is perfect for Connie and (he, him).

Intensive and Reflexive Pronouns

Personal pronouns also take on forms known as *intensive* and *reflexive forms.* These pronouns are the *-self* pronouns: *myself, ourselves, yourself, himself, herself, itself,* and *themselves.*

Intensive Pronouns

Intensive pronouns are used for emphasis. They let a reader know that an action was performed by or directed toward *only* the person or thing that the pronoun refers to. It is easy to identify intensive pronouns. Since they are used strictly for emphasis, a sentence would make perfect sense and have the same meaning if the intensive pronoun were left out.

✔ The dean *herself* approved Joseph's schedule.

✔ The fire damage was confined to the building *itself* and did not extend to the grounds.

✔ To save money on his home renovation, John did all the painting and tile work *himself.*

Reflexive Pronouns

Reflexive pronouns show that an action was performed by someone on himself or herself (or by something on itself).

✔ Mac accidentally cut *himself* with a knife.

✔ The oven cleans *itself* with no need for chemicals or elbow grease.

✔ The executive blamed *herself* for the company's problems.

PRACTICE 4 RECOGNIZING INTENSIVE AND REFLEXIVE PRONOUNS

Underline the *-self* pronoun in each sentence below. Then, in the blank provided, write *I* if the pronoun is an intensive pronoun and *R* if it is a reflexive pronoun.

_____ **1.** Eric talked himself into taking a job that he really did not want.

_____ **2.** Isabella decided to do the job herself.

_____ **3.** The mayor himself took the children on a tour of City Hall.

_____ **4.** Donald decided to buy himself a birthday present—a new computer.

_____ **5.** I know that the store is closing because the owner himself told me.

Problems with Intensive and Reflexive Pronouns

Intensive and reflexive pronouns are often used incorrectly in compound subjects or objects. Look at the examples below.

> ** Grammar Alert!*
>
> The *-self* pronouns are never used as subjects.

Example

✘ Ernie and myself fixed the leaky pipe with duct tape.

When you leave out the compound element, the problem is easier to spot:

✘ Myself fixed the leaky pipe with duct tape.

A subject pronoun is needed to correct the sentence:

✔ I fixed the leaky pipe with duct tape.

✔ Ernie and I fixed the leaky pipe with duct tape.

Example

✘ "Molly makes her mother and myself very proud," said Mr. Roberts.

When you leave out the compound element, the problem is easier to spot:

✘ "Molly makes myself very proud," said Mr. Roberts.

An object pronoun is needed to correct the sentence:

✔ "Molly makes her mother and me very proud," said Mr. Roberts.

> ** Grammar Alert!*
>
> Never use *hisself, theirself,* or *theirselves.* They are not words. *Himself* and *themselves* are the proper forms.

PRACTICE 5 AVOIDING ERRORS WITH *-SELF* PRONOUNS

Underline the correct pronoun in each sentence.

1. Andrea looked at (her, herself) in the mirror and decided that she needed a haircut.
2. Gavin saved his money so that his wife and (he, himself) could go to Hawaii for their vacation.
3. The argument eventually divided the entire office, but it started between Mike and (me, myself).
4. Marion was proud because she had tiled the entire bathroom wall (she, herself), and it looked like a professional job.
5. Vanessa could not wait until summer when (she, herself) and her friends could go to the lake every day.
6. My sister and (I, me, myself) are always competing against one another," Yolanda said. "In sports and academics, we always try to outdo one another."
7. The store manager (him, himself) interviewed Quinton for the job.

8. Gary wanted to make breakfast for (him, himself), but he had no bread, eggs, or milk.
9. "The boat belongs to my brother and (me, myself)," said Miguel.
10. The governor gave (he, himself) good marks for improving the state's economy.

Review Exercises

Complete the Review Exercises to see how well you have learned the skills addressed in this chapter. As you work through the exercises, go back through the chapter to review any of the rules you do not understand completely.

Review Exercise 1

Underline the correct pronoun in each sentence.

1. The prize money was divided between Sarah and (he, him, himself).
2. Ms. Carlson (her, herself) will meet with you before next month.
3. If you are going out for lunch, come along with Darren and (I, me, myself).
4. Frank says that Consuelo and (he, him) may be transferred.
5. That is the woman that Sammy introduced me to last week—at least I think it is (she, her).
6. Since none of the hotels took pets, Brianna wondered where Bongo and (she, her) would stay that night.
7. Martha reminded (she, herself) that she had promised to call her mother in the morning.
8. The senator complained that the media's attitude toward (he, him) and his fellow members of Congress had changed over the years.
9. Sabrina, a college sophomore, said that (she, her) and her friends were not as likely to be drug users as people of her parents' generation.
10. Aunt Harriet said that if I needed a place to stay, Uncle Edgar and (she, her) would be glad to put me up for a few days.

Review Exercise 2

Underline the correct pronoun in each sentence.

1. When she was offered a transfer, Alice said that (she, her) and her family would need to discuss it first.

2. Laney said that she would pick up Meiko and (I, me) on her way to the mall.
3. "Even though we live far apart now, my brother and (I, myself) always try to get together at least once a year," Jake said.
4. The basketball player tried to resolve the problems between (her, herself) and her coach.
5. When Ron went to the ATM to withdraw cash, the machine said that (he, him) and his wife had no money in their account.
6. "When I graduate," said Angela, "the first thing I will do is buy (me, myself) a new car."
7. The best candidates for the plant manager's job are John and (she, her).
8. Quinton told his mother that he did not know how he could ever repay (she, her) and his father for all they had done for him.
9. "If you don't want that old bicycle," Eric said, "my brother and (I, me) can repair it and use it."
10. Can you keep a secret, just between you and (I, me)?

Review Exercise 3

Underline the correct pronoun in each sentence.

1. The two-year-old insisted that she could tie her shoes (her, herself).
2. Jason said that Sam and (he, him) were meeting at the work site tomorrow morning.
3. The cat sat on the porch, giving (it, itself) a leisurely bath.
4. Harry asked me to give the report to Shamika and (he, him) when I was finished with it.
5. "Parker and (I, me) are going fishing on Saturday, rain or shine," said Andrew.
6. Carla wondered whether (she, her) and her sister would ever be on good terms again.
7. The two recipients of the Award for Overall Excellence were Wakendra and (she, her, herself).
8. The dean said that (she, herself) and other members of the administration wanted to meet with representatives of the student body.
9. If there are any problems with the new computer program, please call Pakhi or (I, me, myself).
10. If you need a ride, George and (I, me) can take you.

Review Exercise 4

Underline the two errors in each of the following sentences. Then write the corrected sentence on the lines below.

1. The last time that Jim and myself ate at Galileo's, the server was rude to he and I.

2. Sandra told Eric and I that her and her parents plan to visit in March.

3. Mr. Smith testified that the agreement between the defendant and himself had never included murder. "He may have made an agreement of that sort with someone," Smith said. "But it was not me."

4. "This merger will not only benefit my employees and myself today," said the company's chief executive officer, "but it will also carry we and our stockholders toward a more prosperous future."

5. Brenda and him are scheduled to take their graduate school entrance exams on Saturday. I told her that you and me would have our fingers crossed for them.

23

Pronoun Agreement, Reference, and Point of View

Abbott:	I'm telling you Who is on first.
Costello:	Well, I'm asking YOU who's on first!
Abbott:	That's the man's name.
Costello:	That's who's name?
Abbott:	Yes.
Costello:	Well, go ahead and tell me.
Abbott:	Who.
Costello:	The guy on first.
Abbott:	Who!

From Abbott and Costello's "Who's on First?"

Abbott and Costello's classic comedy routine deliberately causes confusion through use of pronouns. Sometimes, writers unintentionally cause confusion through errors in pronoun reference, agreement, and point of view. Each sentence below contains a pronoun error. Can you figure out why the pronouns in bold type are incorrect?

✘ The coffee shop usually closes at midnight, but on Sundays, **they** close at 6:00 P.M.

✘ Josh told Marquez that **he** needed to work on his social skills.

✘ Clara did not get the job she wanted, but what can **you** expect if you go to an interview in jeans and a ripped t-shirt?

Each of the sentences above contains a pronoun error that could cause confusion for the reader. The first sentence contains an error in pronoun agreement. The pronoun *they* is plural, but the word it refers to is singular. The corrected sentence is below.

✔ The coffee shop usually closes at midnight, but on Sundays, it closes at 6:00 P.M.

The second sentence contains an error in pronoun reference. The reader cannot be sure whether *he* refers to Josh or Marquez. The corrected sentence clears up the confusion:

✔ Josh told Marquez, "I need to work on my social skills."

The third sentence contains an error in pronoun point of view. The writer switches from the third person (the job *she* wanted) to the second person (what can *you* expect).

✔ Clara did not get the job she wanted, but what can she expect if she goes to an interview in jeans and a ripped t-shirt?

Keeping your writing free of errors in pronoun agreement, reference, and point of view ensures that your reader will move through your work smoothly and without confusion.

Pronoun Agreement

Pronoun agreement means that a pronoun must agree in number with the word it refers to. In other words, a singular pronoun can refer only to a singular noun or pronoun, and a plural pronoun can refer only to a plural noun or pronoun.

The word that a pronoun refers to is called its **antecedent.** An antecedent may be a noun or pronoun, or even a compound construction, such as *pens and pencils* or *Sam or Lilah.*

Examples

antecedent (hammer) — pronoun (it)

✔ Julian picked up the hammer and put it in the toolbox.

In the sentence above, the singular pronoun *it* refers to one word in the sentence, the singular word *hammer*.

antecedent (upholstery tacks) — pronoun (them)

✔ Julian picked up the upholstery tacks and put them in the toolbox.

In the above sentence, the plural pronoun *them* refers to the plural antecedent *tacks*.

(antecedent: measuring tape and the staple gun; pronoun: them)

✔ Julian picked up the measuring tape and the staple gun and put them in the toolbox.

Above, the plural pronoun *them* refers to the compound antecedent *measuring tape and staple gun.*

Problems in Pronoun Agreement

Errors in pronoun agreement occur when a singular pronoun is used to refer to a plural word or when a plural pronoun is used to refer to a singular word.

Examples

Error in Pronoun Agreement:

(singular: post office; plural: they)

✘ Sarita went to the post office, but they were already closed.

Corrected:

(singular: post office; singular: it)

✔ Sarita went to the post office, but it was already closed.

Error in Pronoun Agreement:

(plural: cookies; singular: it wasn't)

✘ Rick ate the cookies even though he knew it wasn't good for him.

Corrected:

(plural: cookies; plural: they weren't)

✔ Rick ate the cookies even though he knew they weren't good for him.

(plural: cookies; reworded to eliminate pronoun: eating sweets)

✔ Rick ate the cookies even though he knew eating sweets wasn't good for him.

Practice 1 Making Pronouns Agree

Underline the correct pronoun in each sentence below.

1. The tenor had a rich, strong voice. (It, They) filled the small auditorium without the aid of a microphone.
2. Sharon is prone to migraines, but she has found that avoiding caffeine and chocolate keeps (it, them) to a minimum.

3. My mother likes to shop at Barton's because (it is, they are) locally owned.
4. Sanjay lost his driver's license last week; today he is going to the Division of Motor Vehicles to have (it, them) replaced.
5. The leaves on the peace lily have lost (its, their) shine.

Pronoun Agreement with Indefinite Pronouns

The following indefinite pronouns are always plural.

both few many several

Examples

plural / plural
✔ Both of the children had chocolate on their faces.

plural / plural
✔ Many of the courses in the catalog should be removed because they are seldom offered.

The following indefinite pronouns are singular or plural, depending on their antecedents.

all any most none some

Examples

plural / plural / plural
✔ All of the pines were cut down because they were diseased.

singular / singular / singular
✔ We ate all of the noodle soup in one sitting. It was delicious.

plural / plural / plural
✔ None of the children seemed afraid as they came forward to pet the boa constrictor.

singular / singular / singular / singular
✔ None of the coffee had been drunk, but Karen threw it away because it was starting to look like sludge.

The following indefinite pronouns are always singular.

anybody	either	neither	one
anyone	everybody	nobody	somebody
anything	everyone	no one	someone
each	everything	nothing	something

> *** *Memory Jogger***
>
> Remember the singular indefinite pronouns more easily by grouping them:
>
> | | |
> |---|---|
> | *each* | all the *bodies* |
> | *either* | all the *ones* |
> | *neither* | all the *things* |

Examples

✗ Somebody (singular) called you, but they (plural) didn't leave a message.

✔ Somebody (singular) called you, but he (singular) didn't leave a message.

✗ Each (singular) of the team members has their (plural) own particular strength.

✔ Each (singular) of the team members has her (singular) own particular strength.

Pronouns and Gender Fairness

Gender fairness means using gender-neutral terms such as *server, police officer*, and *firefighter*. It means not stereotyping professions: Gary Kubach is a *nurse*, not a *male nurse*; Sarita Gray is a *doctor*, not a *woman doctor*. Naturally, gender fairness also includes avoiding descriptions of women solely in terms of their looks or of men solely in terms of their bank accounts. Those things are fairly simple. The area of gender fairness and pronouns, however, requires more thought. Using *he or she* or *his or her* is often awkward, and constructions such as *he/she* or *(s)he* are downright ungraceful. How, then, can a writer's language be unbiased, graceful, and grammatically correct, all at the same time? There are several possible solutions.

Example

✗ Nobody (singular) has received their (plural) grades from the last term yet.

This sentence contains an error in pronoun agreement. The singular indefinite pronoun *nobody* does not agree with the plural pronoun *their*. The following section shows several ways to correct pronoun agreement errors such as this one while remaining gender-fair.

Solution 1: Choose a gender and stay with it throughout a single example or paragraph. Then, in your next example or paragraph, switch to the other gender.

singular plural
✗ Nobody has received their grades from the last term yet.

singular singular
✓ Nobody has received his grades from the last term yet.

singular singular
✓ Nobody has received her grades from the last term yet.

Solution 2: Use a "his or her" construction. Because this solution is grammatically correct but stylistically awkward, use it in situations where you will not have to repeat the construction.

singular plural
✗ Nobody has received their grades from the last term yet.

singular singular
✓ Nobody has received his or her grades from the last term yet.

Solution 3: Use plural rather than singular constructions.

singular plural
✗ Nobody has received their grades from the last term yet.

plural plural
✓ The students have not received their grades from the last term yet.

Solution 4: Remove the pronoun agreement problem by removing the pronoun.

singular plural
✗ Nobody has received their grades from the last term yet.

✓ Nobody has received grades from the last term yet.

singular singular plural
✗ Each manager has the same job description, yet each has developed their own style.

✓ Each manager has the same job description, yet each has developed an individual style.

PRACTICE 2 MAKING PRONOUNS AGREE

Correct the pronoun agreement errors in each sentence below. Use all four of the solutions listed above.

1. Both of the restaurant patrons had finished his coffee.

____

2. I do not agree with you, but everybody is entitled to their own opinion.

____

3. Does everybody know what their schedule will be for next month?

____

4. Nobody on the *Titanic* realized that the trip might be their last.

____

5. Neither of the prisoners had seen their children for months.

____

6. Each member of the audience took away their own special memory of the singer's performance.

____

7. If one of the librarians is not busy, maybe they can help you.

____

8. Everyone ate as if they were starving.

____

9. If someone finds my wallet, maybe they will turn it in.

____

10. Few of the students finished his or her test.

____

Pronoun Reference

If a sentence has problems with **pronoun reference,** then either a pronoun has no antecedent or it has more than one possible antecedent.

Pronoun Reference Problem: No Antecedent

A pronoun that does not logically refer to any noun or pronoun has no antecedent.

Examples

✘ When I went to the bank to cash my check, *she* asked for two forms of identification.

✘ Mary applied for a scholarship, but *they* said she didn't meet the requirements.

To correct the problem, replace the pronoun with a more specific word.

✔ When I went to the bank to cash my check, *the teller* asked for two forms of identification.

✔ Mary applied for a scholarship, but *the committee* said she didn't meet the requirements.

Practice 3 Correcting Problems in Pronoun Reference

Correct the pronoun reference problems in each of the following sentences.

1. Carrie tried to avoid taking college algebra, but they said she had to have it.

____

2. We had looked forward to the concert, but they were so loud we could not enjoy the music.

____

3. When Tomas went to the FotoMart to pick up his vacation photographs, they gave him pictures of a baby's christening by mistake.

____

4. April stopped by the dry cleaners on her way home from work, but her husband had already picked it up.

____

5. James called the computer repair shop after he turned it on and could not get his mouse or his keyboard to work.

____

Pronoun Reference Problem: Two Possible Antecedents

When a pronoun could logically refer to either of two words, it has two possible antecedents.

Examples

? ? pronoun
The supervisor told Mary that she had been nominated for an award.

It is unclear whether Mary or her supervisor has been nominated. To clarify, show the supervisor's exact words.

antecedent pronoun
✔ The supervisor said, "Mary, you have been nominated for an award."

antecedent pronoun
✔ The supervisor said, "Mary, I have have been nominated for an award."

✘ The doctor told Clara she needed to exercise daily.

The pronoun *she* could refer to Clara or to the doctor. To clarify, use a direct quotation or reconstruct the sentence.

✔ The doctor told Clara, "You need to exercise daily."

✔ The doctor advised Clara to exercise daily.

Practice 4 Using Quotations to Correct Pronoun Reference Problems

Correct each of the pronoun reference problems by using a direct quotation.

1. The veterinarian told Mrs. Hughes that she had given Lucky the wrong medication.

   ____

2. Joel told his son that he would have to turn down the television.

   ____

3. Marinda told the driver of the BMW that the accident had been her fault.

   ____

4. J. J. told his brother that he had drunk too much to drive.

   ____

5. Annie reminded her neighbor that she had something that belonged to her.

   ____

Special Pronoun Reference Problem: *This* and *Which*

The pronouns *this* and *which* are so often used incorrectly that you should check them every time you see them in your writing.

When you see the pronoun *this* in a sentence, particularly if it begins the sentence, ask the question, "This what?" If you cannot put your finger on a noun that answers that question, then *this* probably has no antecedent.

Example

✗ Many people in the world go to sleep hungry every night. With better management of the world's resources, we could do something about *this*.

✗ It has come to our attention that many residents are keeping pets in violation of the no-pet rule. *This* will no longer be tolerated.

There are two quick ways to fix the problem. The first is to place a noun that answers the question "This what?" immediately after the word *this*.

✔ Many people in the world go to sleep hungry every night. With better management of the world's resources, we could do something about *this problem*.

✔ It has come to our attention that many residents are keeping pets in violation of the no-pet rule. *This situation* will no longer be tolerated.

The second solution is to take out the pronoun and replace it with an appropriate word or phrase.

✔ Many people in the world go to sleep hungry every night. With better management of the world's resources, we could do something about *hunger*.

✔ It has come to our attention that many residents are keeping pets in violation of the no-pet rule. *Pets* will no longer be tolerated.

Problems with *which* often require you to reconstruct the sentence.

Examples

✗ People throw litter on the highway, which is a problem.

In the sentence above, the pronoun *which* does not have an antecedent—that is, there is no single noun or pronoun that it refers to. *Which* could refer to litter or to the highway, but more likely it refers to the whole idea of "people throwing litter."

To fix problems with *which*, reconstruct the sentence to eliminate the pronoun.

✔ Littering is a problem on the highway.

✘ The summer term is shorter, which means that classes move at a faster pace.

✔ The summer term is shorter, so classes move at a faster pace.

PRACTICE 5 CORRECTING VAGUE USES OF *THIS* AND *WHICH*

Find and correct the vague uses of *this* and *which*.

1. When I drive in for my ten o'clock class, the parking lot is always full. School officials should do something about this.

____

2. The landlord of that building has evicted several elderly citizens, which has outraged many people.

____

____

3. Kendra will be the first in her family to earn a college degree. This makes her whole family very proud.

____

4. The card on Ann's door said, "Sorry we missed you! A representative of Double Jeopardy Insurance will be back to see you later this week. If this is not convenient, please call to let us know."

____

5. Rita tried to work thirty hours a week and attend school full time, but this turned out to be more difficult than she had imagined.

____

____

6. Sandra's class was canceled, which will cause her graduation to be delayed.

____

7. Demetria is having problems in school because her parents are going through a divorce. This is always hard on children.

____

8. Ernest decided to get revenge on his bank by leaving a dead fish in his safety deposit box, which might have worked if the box had not been rented in Ernest's name.

____

____

9. Some people believe that lightning never strikes the same place twice, but this is incorrect.

____

10. The police chief's daughter was arrested for stealing, which must have been embarrassing to the chief.

____

Pronoun Point of View

It is important to avoid unnecessary shifts in **point of view,** that is, shifts from one person to another. The chart below shows common first-, second-, and third-person pronouns in their singular and plural forms.

Point of View	Singular	Plural
First person (the person speaking)	I	we
Second person (the person spoken to)	you	you
Third person (the person spoken about)	he, she, it singular indefinite pronouns (each, either, neither . . .)	they

Examples

✗ Leon (3rd person) does not like to check books out of the city library because you (2nd person) have to return the books after just two weeks.

The sentence contains an unnecessary shift in point of view. *You* do not have to return books; *Leon* has to return them. Notice, below, that the verb must also be changed.

✓ Leon (3rd person) does not like to check books out of the city library because he (3rd person) has to return the books after just two weeks.

✘ The members (3rd person) of the class need to get together to study our (1st person) notes.

✔ The members (3rd person) of the class need to get together to study their (3rd person) notes.

✔ We (1st person) need to get together to study our (1st person) class notes.

Practice 6 Correcting Problems in Pronoun Point of View

Correct the point of view problems in the following sentences.

1. Max was disappointed in his poor test grade, but you can't expect good grades without studying.

____

2. I don't plan to take a physical education class during the summer term; July is too hot for them to exercise outside.

____

3. I will never eat in that restaurant again. You spend half an hour waiting for a server and another forty-five minutes waiting for food.

____

4. Raj is looking for a used guitar, and he thinks you can find one at a shop called Play It Again.

____

5. Maggie drinks orange juice every morning because it is good for you.

____

Review Exercises

Complete the Review Exercises to see how well you have learned the skills addressed in this chapter. As you work through the exercises, go back through the chapter to review any of the rules you do not understand completely.

Review Exercise 1

Choose the correct alternative in each of the sentences below. Then, in the blank to the left of the sentence, indicate whether the problem is one of agreement (singular with singular, plural with plural), reference (making sure the pronoun has a clear antecedent), or point of view (making sure there are no shifts in person).

_____________ 1. Someone left (her, their) shower gel in the locker room.

_____________ 2. When Kevin asked if he could have an extra day to write his paper, (she, the professor) told him that a letter grade would be deducted for every day the paper was late.

_____________ 3. Dennis likes to sit near the door because (you are, he is) the first one to leave.

_____________ 4. The woman tried to put a coin in the expired parking meter as a ticket was being written, but (he, the police officer) told her it was too late.

_____________ 5. Everyone on the team has (his, their) own opinion about the new coach.

_____________ 6. Westside High School will name (its, their) new football coach by the end of February.

_____________ 7. Sam told Mr. Perkins (that his dog had been digging up his flowerbed again, "Your dog has been digging up my flowerbed again.")

_____________ 8. Francine bought a security system for her home. She is a pilot and (she has, they have) to be away for days at a time.

_____________ 9. Some hockey fans have suggested that a section of the arena be set aside for nondrinkers, and (this, the idea) is under consideration.

_____________ 10. Kim sat at the computer and navigated the Internet as her daughter gave her instructions. (This, The situation) amused Kim's husband.

Review Exercise 2

Find and correct the pronoun reference, agreement, or point of view error in each of the following sentences.

1. Hannah threw away the shampoo and the conditioner because it made her scalp itch.

____

2. "I don't care if everybody else pierces their navel," said Katie's mother. "You can't get yours pierced until you're eighteen."

____

3. "Someone needs to turn the heat up," said Greg. "This room is so cold that even a sweater doesn't keep you warm."

____

4. Brian watched the giraffe in fascination. You could sense the animal's contentment as it browsed on leaves at the top of a small tree.

____

5. Without fear, the children grabbed the handholds and scaled the surface of the climbing wall, which terrified some of their parents.

____

6. Neither of the babysitters was sure that they could sit for Joshua on Friday night.

____

7. Janie's horoscope said, "Don't turn your back on money and love." Janie said she would never turn her back on it.

____

8. Most of the pups advertised for sale in the newspaper have not had its shots.

____

9. "Yesterday it was fifty-two degrees outside and today it's eighty," complained Grandpa. "If a person doesn't like the weather, you can just wait twenty-four hours, and it will change."

____

10. Each of the job candidates said they enjoyed working with people.

____

Review Exercise 3

Find and correct the two errors in pronoun agreement, reference, or point of view in each of the numbered items below.

1. I hate going to the library because they always ask for my student ID when I check a book out. The problem is that you don't always have the ID handy.

____

____

2. Anyone who needs to register for classes should see their advisor this week. This will enable him to sign up for classes without waiting in long lines.

____

____

3. Every morning, if the weather is nice, Frank sits on his deck and enjoys the newspaper and coffee. This helps him to relax before a busy day at work. Frank believes you should always take a few minutes for quiet relaxation each day.

____

____

4. Andrea told Joann that she was late to work again. Anyone who is late for work too often is in danger of losing their job.

____

____

5. As he left the theater, Joe wondered how they could charge $8.00 for such a bad movie. He grumbled that their popcorn had been stale, too.

____

____

Review Exercise 4

Find and correct the two errors in pronoun agreement, reference, or point of view in each of the numbered items below.

1. The local car wash gives anyone a free car wash on their birthday. This generates good will and brings people back to the car wash on other days during the year.

____

____

2. Someone left their sunglasses and car keys sitting on the lunch counter. Chances are that the person will return to pick it up.

____

____

3. Irvin told Tom he needed to lose some weight. Irvin added, "I think you can lose more weight by exercising than by restricting food."

____

____

4. Bill did not buy a cellular phone because he thought someone might eavesdrop on your conversations. He had also heard they caused cancer.

____

____

5. Sean saw that someone had left their headlights on. He was afraid to try to open the door to turn it off because people might think he was trying to steal the car.

____

____

Review Exercise 5

Find and correct the error in pronoun agreement, reference, or point of view in the paragraph below.

[1]Nell, my roommate, has a King Tut glitter pyramid on her desk, and when anyone sees it, they can't resist picking it up and shaking it. [2]It is modeled along the lines of those plastic snow globes that you see in stores around Christmas. [3]The difference is that they put a golden replica of Tutankhamen, the boy king, inside a plastic pyramid. [4]It is filled with glittery flakes, and like golden sand, it spreads out to the four corners of the pyramid. [5]Nell turns the pyramid upside down and lets all of the glitter collect at the top of the pyramid; then you flip it quickly. [6]This sends a golden stream of glitter onto the boy king's head. [7]When the pyramid is shaken, flakes of gold rise and swirl, and it hides Tut's face. [8]Nell says her little pyramid is practical as well as entertaining because they make good paperweights.

1. ____
2. ____
3. ____
4. ____
5. ____
6. ____
7. ____
8. ____

Editing Exercises: Basic Grammar

The following exercises allow you to test the grammar skills you have learned in Chapters 18 through 23. The exercises focus on verbs, pronouns, run-on sentences, and sentence fragments.

Basic Grammar: Five Editing Exercises

Editing Exercise 1 Subject-Verb Agreement and Run-ons

In the following paragraph, correct the subject-verb agreement errors and run-ons.

6 subject-verb agreement errors
2 run-on sentences
2 comma splices

[1]Why does men find the entire question of clothing so much simpler than women do? [2]The answer lie in the differing approach of each sex toward clothing. [3]Most women uses the "outfit" concept of dressing. [4]In this system, each of a woman's dresses, sweaters, and skirts have to be accessorized with the proper shoes, belt, undergarments, jewelry, and hosiery. [5]A woman may own a mid-calf black skirt, a knee-length blue dress, and tan slacks, however, only her long slip, silver-buckled belt and black shoes go with the mid-calf black skirt. [6]If she chooses to wear the blue dress or tan slacks, she must choose a different slip, belt, and shoes the system is complicated, so women spend a lot of time choosing their clothing. [7]Men, on the other hand, follows the "uniform" concept of dressing. [8]If the dress code in his office require a man to wear a shirt and tie, he will wear a shirt, a tie, and a pair of pants every day. [9]His underwear will go with any shirt or pair of pants he has in his wardrobe except for coordinating the color of his tie with the color of his shirt, he has little to worry about. [10]Men spend less time thinking about

what they wear, their system of choosing clothes is a simpler one.

1. ____________________
2. ____________________
3. ____________________
4. ____________________
5. ____________________
6. ____________________
7. ____________________
8. ____________________
9. ____________________
10. ____________________

Editing Exercise 2 Run-ons and Fragments

In the following paragraph, correct the fragments, run-ons, and comma splices.

5 fragments
2 run ons
3 comma splices

[1]Last spring, when I decided to plant a vegetable garden. [2]I discovered that gardening has its unpleasant aspects. [3]Two hours in the garden convinced me of one fact gardening is a dirty job. [4]Even though I wore gardening gloves, dirt found its way under my fingernails, my shoes and jeans were caked with mud. [5]After half an hour of gardening. [6]I discovered a second unpleasant aspect of gardening—heat. [7]The sun beat down on me as I worked. [8]Causing beads of sweat to pop out on my forehead and run into my eyes. [9]Sweat stung my eyes and soaked my t-shirt I was extremely uncomfortable. [10]The dirt and the heat were bad enough, pesky bugs and slimy worms were even worse. [11]The sweat attracted flies, they hovered and buzzed around my head. [12]When I turned over the soil with my trowel, I unearthed slimy worms and grubs that squirmed palely in the sunlight. [13]Then burrowed back into the dark earth. [14]A ripe tomato from the garden may taste better than one from the grocery store. [15]But is not worth the trouble it takes to grow it.

1. ______________________________
2. ______________________________
3. ______________________________
4. ______________________________
5. ______________________________
6. ______________________________
7. ______________________________
8. ______________________________
9. ______________________________
10. ______________________________
11. ______________________________
12. ______________________________
13. ______________________________
14. ______________________________
15. ______________________________

Editing Exercise 3 **Verbs, Run-ons, and Fragments**

In the following paragraph, correct the verb errors, run-ons, and fragments.

3 subject-verb agreement error
2 comma splices
2 fragments
2 irregular verb errors
1 run-on

[1]I can't recall the exact moment when my cat Molly become the true head of the household. [2]Molly came to me as a tiny, defenseless kitten, the neighbor who convinced me to take Molly said that she was the runt of the litter, the kitten that no one wanted. [3]She stood trembling in a cardboard box. [4]Looking up through moist, blue-green eyes and mouthing the first of many silent meows that soon reduced me to a lowly member of her entourage.

[5]Over the past few months, the trembling kitten has growed strong and sure, quickly gaining control of the family. [6]She meow loudly if left alone for long without attention. [7]Molly will not be ignored; she hops into my lap and looks offended. [8]If I don't drop everything and pay attention to her. [9]In the morning, she slides a paw under the bedroom door and rattle it loudly to awaken her human servants if breakfast is late. [10]She refuses to eat inexpensive store-brand cat food; instead, she insist on small, expensive cans of name-brand food. [11]If she wants to come in or go out, her meow takes on a demanding tone it almost sounds as if she is saying, "Now!" [12]Molly commands naturally and without a second thought, the timid, trembling kitten is gone forever.

1.	______________	**7.**	______________
2.	______________	**8.**	______________
3.	______________	**9.**	______________
4.	______________	**10.**	______________
5.	______________	**11.**	______________
6.	______________	**12.**	______________

Editing Exercise 4 **Fragments and Pronouns**

In the following paragraph, correct the sentence fragments and pronoun errors.

6 fragments
4 pronoun errors

[1]Smoking may be a vile and harmful habit, but workplaces can go too far. [2]In penalizing employees who smoke. [3]While few would want to work in an office thick with smoke. [4]Employers could provide smoking lounges for employees who smoke. [5]Instead, sending workers outside in twenty-degree weather to shiver and smoke. [6]Some workplaces won't allow you

to smoke anywhere on company property. [7]Smokers must wait a jittery eight hours before lighting up. [8]Or use their lunch hour to drive off company property to smoke. [9]To keep insurance costs down. [10]Other companies forbid smoking entirely. [11]An employee who is caught smoking, even at home, faces dismissal from their job. [12]Employees who smoke may be more likely to become ill and to use his or her insurance benefits, but the same can be said of people who eat cholesterol-rich diets and even those who are depressed. [13]What's next, a company representative knocking on your door for a refrigerator inspection or a mood check? [14]Companies should back off and show a little more tolerance. [15]Toward employees who smoke.

1. ____________________
2. ____________________
3. ____________________
4. ____________________
5. ____________________
6. ____________________
7. ____________________
8. ____________________
9. ____________________
10. ____________________
11. ____________________
12. ____________________
13. ____________________
14. ____________________
15. ____________________

Editing Exercise 5 Subject-Verb Agreement, Fragments, Run-ons, and Pronouns

In the following paragraph, correct the fragments, run-ons, and errors in pronoun use and subject-verb agreement.

3 subject-verb agreement errors
2 fragments
2 comma splices
3 pronoun errors

[1]The gym where I work out have both advantages and disadvantages. [2]One of the biggest advantages are that Rocky's is just a five-minute drive from

my home and my work. [3]It is easy to stop by on your way home from work or to drive over for a quick workout on weekends. [4]In addition, the gym is open 24 hours a day for people like myself who have busy schedules. [5]Though no staff members are on duty at night. [6]Security is adequately provided by cameras, a key card entry system, and a huge plate glass window that make the interior of the gym visible from the street. [7]In addition, unlike many gyms, Rocky's does not require a lengthy contract, a member can choose a month-to-month contract instead of a long-term commitment. [8]The disadvantages of Rocky's includes a lack of locker room space. [9]If a member comes straight from work, they have to change into workout gear in the tiny restroom and stow work clothing on one of the open shelves. [10]Since a staff member is on duty only a few hours a day, from ten A.M. until five P.M. [11]Members who work out in the mornings or evenings have no one to answer questions or help them with unfamiliar equipment. [12]However, the advantages of the gym far outweigh the disadvantages, I enjoy my membership at Rocky's.

1. ______________________
2. ______________________
3. ______________________
4. ______________________
5. ______________________
6. ______________________
7. ______________________
8. ______________________
9. ______________________
10. ______________________
11. ______________________
12. ______________________

24 Misplaced and Dangling Modifiers

The Brush-off

The English major caught his eye,
He smelled her sweet perfume.
He said, "While dancing cheek to cheek,
Romance is sure to bloom."

She said, "To say romance can dance
Is silly from all angles,
And I could never love a man
Whose modifier dangles."

While dangling and misplaced modifiers probably won't ruin your next romance, they may confuse your readers. That's reason enough to learn what they are and how to avoid them.

Look at the two versions of the sentence below:

✘ *Perched at the top of the flagpole,* Orville saw a red-tailed hawk.

✔ Orville saw a red-tailed hawk *perched at the top of the flagpole.*

The words in italic type are modifiers. A **modifier** is a word, phrase, or clause that gives information about another word. In the sentences above, the placement of the words *perched at the top of the flagpole* makes a great deal of difference. It is easy to imagine a bird sitting on top of the flagpole, but the idea of Orville perched there does not seem logical.

Although they are not always as obvious as the problem in the example above, problems with modifiers are always problems in logic. If you approach this chapter—and your writing in general—with the idea that good writing should above all make sense, you will have an easier time spotting and correcting misplaced and dangling modifiers.

Misplaced Modifiers

✘ Hot off the griddle, the family enjoyed pancakes.

Do you see what is not logical about the sentence above? Of course. The family is not hot off the griddle, the pancakes are. This type of modifier problem is called a **misplaced modifier.** The modifier *hot off the griddle* is misplaced to modify *family* instead of *pancakes.* To fix a misplaced modifier, remember this principle: **A modifier should be placed as close as possible to the word it modifies.**

✔ The family enjoyed pancakes hot off the griddle.

Examples

✘ The dog was examined by a veterinarian that had just had a litter of puppies.

The sentence seems to suggest that the veterinarian had given birth to puppies. Putting the modifier *that had just had a litter of puppies* closer to the word it modifies makes the meaning clear.

✔ The dog that had just had a litter of puppies was examined by the veterinarian.

Reconstructing the sentence is also a possibility.

✔ The veterinarian examined the dog that had just had a litter of puppies.

✘ Hisako watched the movie eating popcorn.

The sentence is worded as though *the movie* ate the popcorn.

✔ Eating popcorn, Hisako watched the movie.

✗ Pregnant and tired-looking, the old man gave his seat to the young woman.

It sounds as though the old man has defied the laws of nature.

✓ The old man gave his seat to the pregnant and tired-looking young woman.

PRACTICE 1 CORRECTING MISPLACED MODIFIERS

Correct the misplaced modifiers in the following sentences.

1. Antoinette walked the dog wearing high heels.

 ____

2. Sam placed the suitcase on the bed that he was going to carry on the trip.

 ____

3. The man kept a close eye on the toddler sitting on a bench and smoking a cigar.

 ____

 ____

4. Snapping and growling, the letter carrier was afraid to approach the dog.

 ____

5. The student visited the office of the English professor who needed tutoring in grammar.

 ____

 ____

Single-Word Modifiers

A misplaced modifier that is a single word may be more difficult to spot, but the idea is still the same: an error in logic needs to be corrected.

The words *almost, just, nearly,* and *only* are often carelessly misplaced in sentences. Look at the following example to see the difference that word placement can make:

✓ *Only* James tasted the melon. *(no one but James)*

✓ James *only* tasted the melon. *(only sampled the melon,* or possibly, *no one but James)*

✔ James tasted *only* the melon. *(nothing but the melon)*

✔ James tasted the *only* melon. *(the only melon available)*

✔ James tasted the melon *only*. *(nothing but the melon)*

Next, look at the following examples of illogical modifier placements and corrections:

✘ While watching the football game, Kyle *almost* ate a whole pizza.

If he *almost* ate it, he thought about eating but never actually took a bite. The writer more likely means something like "he ate eight of the ten pieces."

✔ While watching the football game, Kyle ate *almost* a whole pizza.

✘ Cara *nearly* spent a hundred dollars at the mall.

If she *nearly* spent a hundred dollars, she thought about it but decided to keep her money. A more probable meaning is shown below.

✔ Cara spent *nearly* a hundred dollars at the mall.

✘ Because she felt ill, Miriam *just* ate a few bites of chili.

Because *just* can mean "just now" or "only," placement is important. *Just ate* suggests the meaning *just now ate,* but the writer more likely means *ate only a few bites.*

✔ Because she felt ill, Miriam ate *just* a few bites of chili.

✘ Though she received many toys for Christmas, Amber *only* played with her teddy bear.

If she played with the bear and nothing else, then she played with *only* her teddy bear.

✔ Though she received many toys for Christmas, Amber played with *only* her teddy bear.

Practice 2 Using Single-Word Modifiers

Place the listed modifier in the sentence to make each sentence match its intended meaning. The first one is done for you.

1. The distraught mother believed the child was gravely ill.
Modifier to insert: only
Intended meaning: No one but the mother believed it.
New sentence: Only the distraught mother believed the child was gravely ill.

2. The distraught mother believed her child was gravely ill.
Modifier to insert: only
Intended meaning: The mother had no other children.
New sentence: ______________________________

3. Kim ate a whole bucket of popcorn at the movies.
Modifier to insert: nearly
Intended meaning: She ate all but a handful or two.
New sentence: ______________________________

4. After buying lunch, Mollie had enough for bus fare home.
Modifier to insert: just
Intended meaning: She would have no money left after paying her fare.
New sentence: ______________________________

5. Leo said, "Mandy, I agreed to watch your poodle for one hour."
Modifier to insert: just
Intended meaning: He agreed to one hour only; Mandy has been gone two hours.
New sentence: ______________________________

6. Simon's reading speed test shows he reads 400 words per minute.
Modifier to insert: almost
Intended meaning: He reads 394 words per minute.
New sentence: ______________________________

7. Dion bypassed the appetizers because he was watching his weight.
Modifier to insert: only
Intended meaning: His diet was the sole reason.
New sentence: ______________________________

8. Deborah took a job in Seattle for $30,000 per year.
Modifier to insert: almost
Intended meaning: She thought about it but did not take the job.
New sentence: ______________________________

____

9. Jarvis took a job in Louisville for $25,000 per year.
Modifier to insert: almost
Intended meaning: The job pays a bit less than the figure mentioned.
New sentence: ______________________________

____

10. Marisa says her math professor is grumpy on days that end in *y*.
Modifier to insert: only
Intended meaning: The professor is grumpy just on the days mentioned.
New sentence: ______________________________

____

PRACTICE 3 CORRECTING MISPLACED MODIFIERS

Correct the misplaced one-word modifiers in the following sentences.

1. We almost saw ten of our friends at the concert.

____

2. Chad nearly got two weeks' vacation last month.

____

3. Alice only waited on four tables of customers all evening.

____

4. Though Benjamin was speeding, the police officer just let him off with a warning.

____

5. Sandra almost sent out resumés to twenty different companies.

____

6. Giorgio nearly wrote a paper of five hundred words.

____

7. After his surgery, Karl said, "It only hurts when I laugh."

____

8. The candidate said he only wanted one thing—our vote.

____

9. The list of people Ben wanted to invite almost included all his friends.

____

10. Grover only gave his love to one woman.

____

Dangling Modifiers

Unlike a misplaced modifier, which needs to be moved closer to the word it modifies, a dangling modifier has no word to modify.

✘ With a wave of his wand, the rabbit was pulled from the magician's hat.

The phrase *with a wave of his wand* has no word in the sentence to modify. The only two possibilities are *rabbit* and *magician's hat,* neither of which is likely to wave a wand. To fix the misplaced modifier, you have to put a magician in the sentence. The easiest way to fix a dangling modifier is to give it a word to modify. Place the word immediately after the dangling modifier.

✔ With a wave of his wand, **the magician** pulled a rabbit from his hat.

The sentence may also be reconstructed.

✔ As the magician waved his wand, he pulled a rabbit from his hat.

✘ Waking from a nightmare, Makeisha's alarm buzzed loudly.

Obviously, it is Makeisha who has had a nightmare, not her alarm. The easiest way to fix the sentence is to put the word *Makeisha* (not the possessive form *Makeisha's*) immediately after the modifier.

✔ Waking from a nightmare, **Makeisha** heard her alarm buzz loudly.

But it is also permissible to reconstruct the sentence entirely.

✔ The alarm buzzed loudly as Makeisha awoke from a nightmare.

✔ Makeisha's alarm buzzed loudly as she awoke from a nightmare.

✘ By carefully constructing a resumé, the potential employer is impressed.

It is not the employer who constructs the resumé, but the applicant. The sentence can be fixed by indicating, immediately after the modifier, who constructed the resume.

✔ By carefully constructing a resumé, an applicant can impress a potential employer.

The sentence can also be reworked entirely.

✔ A carefully constructed resumé can impress a potential employer.

✘ Bored and restless, the minutes seemed to crawl.

Who was bored and restless? (If the sentence does not say, the decision is yours.)

✔ Bored and restless, **I** felt the minutes crawl.

✔ Because **Sherman** was bored and restless, the minutes seemed to crawl.

✘ Listless and feverish, the pediatrician suspected the flu.

Sometimes, the only solution is to reconstruct the sentence. If you try putting the child after *listless and feverish,* you will probably change the meaning of the sentence.

✔ The pediatrician suspected that the listless and feverish child had the flu.

✔ Because the child was listless and feverish, the pediatrician suspected the flu.

PRACTICE 4 CORRECTING DANGLING MODIFIERS

Correct the dangling modifiers in the sentences below.

1. Walking across the tile floor, the coffee cup slipped from my hand.

____

2. Unhappy with his current job, Malcolm's resumé was updated and employment ads scanned.

____

____

3. Blinded by the setting sun, Janna's car nearly ran off the road.

____

4. By spending hours in the library, careful research for a term paper can be done.

____

5. Whistling cheerfully, the luggage was loaded into Quinton's trunk.

____

Review Exercises

Complete the Review Exercises to see how well you have learned the skills addressed in this chapter. As you work through the exercises, go back through the chapter to review any of the rules you do not understand completely.

Review Exercise 1

Rewrite the sentences to correct the italicized misplaced or dangling modifiers.

1. *After sitting in a jar of brandy for a month,* Mrs. Smith decided that her "drunken peaches" were ready to serve.

____

____

2. *Speaking in a stern voice,* the children soon became quiet.

____

3. The bride walked down the aisle with her father *dressed in a white satin gown.*

____

4. *Working with full concentration,* the hours passed quickly.

____

5. *Hanging on a chain,* Melinda wears her child's picture around her neck.

____

6. *Sitting on the deck,* the light became too dim for reading.

____

7. *By shopping early for Christmas,* a last-minute rush will be avoided.

____

8. Jared *almost* saved 15 percent of his income last year.

____

9. *With a huge yawn,* Al's TV was turned off and the door was locked.

____

10. *Paying for my groceries,* the clerk said that the store was going out of business.

____

____

Review Exercise 2

Correct the dangling and misplaced modifiers in the following sentences.

1. Hanging in the sky like a giant Christmas ornament, Beth looked up at the moon.

____

____

2. Stark and filled with angles, the abstract painting almost won all the awards.

____

3. Liberally fertilized and given just the right amount of light, Samantha was sure that her African violets would thrive.

____

____

4. By changing the oil every three thousand miles, a car will last longer.

____

5. Albert replaced the light over the stove that had burned out.

____

6. Bianca bought presents and hid them for her children in the closet.

____

7. By advertising in the newspaper, Helen's yard sale was successful.

____

8. Paco almost took six bags of aluminum cans to the recycling center.

____

9. Well aged and giving off a foul odor, Frank decided he did not like the Limburger cheese.

____

____

10. Freshly poured and smooth as glass, the worker looked with pride at the new driveway.

____

____

Review Exercise 3

Place the listed modifier in the sentence to make each sentence match its intended meaning. The first one is done for you.

1. The applicant for the job was offered half the salary she expected.
   Modifier to insert: only
   Intended meaning: Just one person applied.
   New sentence: The only applicant for the job was offered half the salary she expected.
2. The applicant for the job was offered half the salary she expected.
   Modifier to insert: only
   Intended meaning: She was offered $15,000 per year; she expected $30,000.
   New sentence: ______________________________
   ____
3. Carol has been interested in science since she was twelve years old.
   Modifier to insert: nearly
   Intended meaning: She was eleven years, ten months, and two days old when she first discovered an interest in science.
   New sentence: ______________________________
   ____
4. The carrels in the library are reserved for graduate students.
   Modifier to insert: just
   Intended meaning: The carrels are for graduate students only.

New sentence: ____

____

5. Olen said, "Sandy, I finished mopping the floor an hour ago, and you tracked in mud."

Modifier to insert: just

Intended meaning: She tracked mud within the last minute or so.

New sentence: ____

____

6. Perry told the officer, "I was going under fifty miles per hour."

Modifier to insert: just

Intended meaning: He was going 49.5 miles per hour.

New sentence: ____

____

7. The officer replied, "Sir, you were going sixty-five."

Modifier to insert: almost

Intended meaning: He was going 64.5 miles per hour.

New sentence: ____

____

8. I gave Mary twenty dollars.

Modifier to insert: almost

Intended meaning: I thought about it but did not give it to her.

New sentence: ____

____

9. I gave Mary twenty dollars.

Modifier to insert: almost

Intended meaning: I gave her $19.72.

New sentence: ____

____

10. The gas station accepts cash or credit cards after dark.

Modifier to insert: only

Intended meaning: It accepts those forms of payment and no other after dark.

New sentence: ____

____

Review Exercise 4

Underline and correct the two misplaced or dangling modifiers in each sentence group.

1. My mother did the best she could for my brothers and me. As a single mother with three children, few luxuries were available. By working long hours for little pay, the basic needs of life were met.

____

____

2. Sharon saw a polar bear visiting the zoo on Sunday. Sitting on a block of ice, she noticed that although his fur was white, his nose and paw pads were coal black.

____

____

____

3. Shakira almost had to wait three hours to see the doctor. Waiting for hours with no magazines to read, the doctor must not have cared how the patients felt.

____

____

____

4. Last week, my six-year-old and I visited the Humane Society to pick out a puppy. Furry and cute, my daughter was captivated by a white terrier that she named Roscoe. Though not yet paper trained, my daughter loves Roscoe so much that I don't mind cleaning up his messes.

____

____

____

____

5. Leah nearly took piano lessons for two years, but she can't play a note. Her brother, on the other hand, plays beautifully. Interested in music even as a child, a career in music seems right for Daniel.

____

____

____

____

Review Exercise 5

Find and correct the misplaced and dangling modifiers in the following paragraph.

> [1]Creamy, sweet, and irresistible, Betty does crazy things to feed her addiction to chocolate. [2]Last Monday, desperate for chocolate, a thunderstorm did not deter her from going out for candy. [3]Squinting past the windshield wipers, sheeting rain poured as she splashed into the parking lot of Food Town. [4]Minutes later, wet but triumphant, her purchase was made. [5]The store nearly charged five dollars for the candy, but she did not mind. [6]She munched on it straight from the bag as she drove on the seat beside her. [7]Eating and driving at the same time, an accident was barely avoided when she swerved to keep from hitting a pedestrian. [8]She only saw him at the last minute. [9]Then, struck by a bolt of lightning, she saw a huge tree that had split down the middle. [10]She realized that she had taken unnecessary risk in going out for candy in a thunderstorm that she did not really need at all.

1. ______________________________
2. ______________________________
____
3. ______________________________
____
4. ______________________________
5. ______________________________
6. ______________________________
7. ______________________________
____
8. ______________________________
9. ______________________________
____
10. ______________________________
____

25

Parallel Structure

Choose the best answer to complete each sequence.

1. **a**, **b**, **c**, ______	a. **t** b. **z** c. **d**
2. ↘, ↗↗, ↘, ↗↗, ______	a. ↗ b. ↗↗ c. ↘
3. 20, 40, 60, ______	a. 10 b. 120 c. 80
4. ⧉, ▣, ______	a. • b. □ c. ⊡

If you chose *c* each time, you are correct. Your mind was responding to the patterns you saw developing in each sequence. Patterns are pleasing to the human mind, and that is why parallel structure works.

In any famous speech, such as Abraham Lincoln's Gettysburg Address or Martin Luther King, Jr.'s "I Have a Dream," you hear the regular, memorable rhythm of **parallel structure**—parallel words, parallel phrases, and parallel clauses. You see it in good writing, too, lending elegance to ordinary sentences. Once you are used to seeing parallel structure, anything else seems awkward. Look at the following lists to see examples of nonparallel and parallel structure.

Examples

✗ Nonparallel:

eating at fast-food places

to snack on sweets and chips

avoiding exercise

The phrase *to snack on sweets and chips* is not parallel with the *-ing* constructions of the other two phrases.

✔ **Parallel:**

eating at fast-food places

snacking on sweets and chips

avoiding exercise

All phrases in the revised list have the same structure; that is, they are parallel.

✘ **Nonparallel:**

medium blue

light gray

with a bright orange hue

✔ **Parallel:**

medium blue

light gray

bright orange

✘ **Nonparallel:**

studied for her midterm exam

worked on her term paper

researching at the library was also done

✔ **Parallel:**

studied for her midterm exam

worked on her term paper

researched at the library

PRACTICE 1 USING PARALLEL STRUCTURE

Each of the following lists contains one item that is not parallel. Cross out the nonparallel item and reword it to make it parallel with the other items. Then write the reworded version on the line provided.

1. sitting on the deck
reading a book
to swat at mosquitoes

____

2. calm
had an easygoing personality
friendly

____

3. frustrated by deadlines
under pressure from her boss
hassled by customers

____

4. a beautiful campus
excellent food service
dorm rooms that are large

____

5. the fact that it was unheated
it had no television
it had no lights

____

In sentences, items given equal emphasis should be parallel in structure whenever possible. These items include words, phrases, and clauses in pairs or lists. Look at the following examples of nonparallel and parallel structure within sentences.

Examples

✘ The chef *chopped* the garlic and then *was sprinkling* it on the pizza.

✔ The chef *chopped* the garlic and then *sprinkled* it on the pizza.

✘ Alberto is sometimes late for class because he has to *wait* for elevators, *looking* for access ramps, and *navigate* his wheelchair through crowded hallways.

✔ Alberto is sometimes late for class because he has to *wait* for elevators, *look* for access ramps, and *navigate* his wheelchair through crowded hallways.

✘ Kristi hoped for a roommate who was *quiet, studious, and who was also friendly.*

✔ Kristi hoped for a roommate who was *quiet, studious, and friendly.*

✘ James feared *he would fail* but knew *quitting was not an option.*

✔ James feared *he would fail* but knew *he could not quit.*

Practice 2 Using Parallel Structure

Each of the following sentences contains one item that is not parallel. Cross out the nonparallel item and reword it to make it parallel with the other items. Then write the reworded version on the line provided.

1. Swimming, jogging, and to waterski are my athletic sister's favorite pastimes.

 ____

2. The squirrel leaped from the roof, had scampered up a tree, and watched us from the safety of a high branch.

 ____

3. For dinner, Lisa had iced tea, a tomato sandwich, and she also ate a salad.

 ____

4. Mandy could not concentrate because the dogs were barking, the children were whining, and because the television also blared.

 ____

5. Ed's yard sale table looked good once he stripped the old paint, the rough spots had been sanded, and painted the table white.

 ____

Review Exercises

Complete the Review Exercises to see how well you have learned the skills addressed in this chapter. As you work through the exercises, go back through the chapter to review any of the rules you do not understand completely.

Review Exercise 1

Each of the following lists contains one item that is not parallel. Cross out the nonparallel item and reword it to make it parallel with the other items. Then write the reworded version on the line provided.

1. to have a rewarding career
 buying a comfortable home
 to have healthy children

 ____

2. dirty
 old
 having many dents

 ____

3. supported by his family
with encouragement from his teachers
admired by his friends

____

4. covers that were warm
soft pillows
freshly laundered sheets

____

5. that the test was fair
if it covered assigned chapters
that students had time to finish

____

____

6. barking loudly
a fieree growl
jumping at the fence

____

7. pressed trousers
starched shirt
shoes that had been shined

____

8. on street corners
in bowling alleys
grocery stores

____

9. without a cent to his name
lonely
homeless

____

10. go down two blocks
turn left
at the light you will turn right

____

Review Exercise 2

In each of the following sentences, one italicized item is not parallel. Cross out the nonparallel item and reword it to make it parallel with the other items. Then write the reworded version on the line provided.

1. When it's time to study, Carl always remembers that he has to *do his laundry, shop for groceries,* or *his car needs washing.*

____

2. Today the children want *to go to the movies* and *visiting the museum.*

____

3. Kevin's project failed because he ran *out of time, out of money,* and *he also had bad luck.*

____

4. The tail of a comet always *points* toward the sun, while the nose *is pointed* away from the sun.

____

5. Grandma says she remembers when gas stations *filled the tank,* ~~*they would*~~ *check the oil,* and *washed the windshield.*

____

6. Before going to bed, Kay checked to make sure *her children were in bed* and *that she had locked the door.*

____

7. Real estate agents say that there are three important considerations when buying property: *location, where it is located,* and *location.*

____

8. The lion's *scratched nose* and *ear that was torn* bore testimony to the many battles he had fought.

____

9. Sam said he was having *problems at work, problems with his math class,* and *health problems.*

____

10. "My neighbors are a pain," said Michelle. "*Their music is loud, their yard is messy,* and *they have children who are rude.*"

____

Review Exercise 3

Each of the following sentences contains one item that is not parallel. Cross out the nonparallel item and reword it to make it parallel with the other items. Then write the reworded version on the line provided.

1. Magazines devoted to news, science magazines, and science fiction novels are Sierra's favorite reading material.

____

2. Next fall, Gus plans to take English, biology, and a course in sociology.

____

3. The eerie old house was filled with musty corridors, stairs that creaked, and dark, curtained rooms.

____

4. "If I have my family, my home, and I suppose a job could be added to the list, then I have everything I need," said Clarice.

____

5. Ants zigzagged along the flagstone path; some traveled toward the anthill, and others were traveling away.

____

6. When baby animals play, they are really learning how to behave socially and how hunting is done.

____

7. After the flood, Don's basement was filled with water, mud covered his floor, and his lawn was carpeted with debris.

____

8. Because of good weather and the traffic was light, Alex made the trip in less than two hours.

____

9. Sarita says she barely has time for work between attending night school and because she has to chauffeur her kids to their softball games.

____

10. On weekends, Daniel likes to spend time with his kids, working in his garden, and restoring his old Chevrolet.

____

Review Exercise 4

Each of the following sentences contains one item that is not parallel. Cross out the nonparallel item and reword it to make it parallel with the other items. Then write the reworded version on the line provided.

1. Careful planning and to make wise use of time are skills that make anyone's life easier. However, it is easier to talk about them than doing them.

____

____

2. One room of the art museum contained modern oil paintings, statues, and also it contained furnishings. The chairs were low, pretzel-shaped, and they were uncomfortable.

____

____

3. Along the riverwalk, a young couple strolled with a baby carriage, two teens executed elaborate moves on skateboards, and on a bench watching the

sunset sat two old men. Nearby, a pretzel vendor furled the umbrella over his cart and was closing down for the day.

____

____

4. For her English class, Marcy has to keep a journal, a term paper, and read a novel. She says she may have to cut back her work hours and giving up some of her extracurricular activities.

____

____

5. The personal ads contained requests for a sensual woman, a woman with a slim build, and even a "red-hot mama." "Isn't there someone who just wants a woman who is fun and has intelligence?" Sara complained.

____

____

Review Exercise 5

Each of the sentences in the following paragraph contains one item that is not parallel. Cross out the nonparallel item and reword it to make it parallel with the other items. Then write the reworded version on the line provided.

[1]Being a professional astronomer requires many years of study, but to be an amateur astronomer is probably within your reach. [2]Astronomy is a hobby that is rewarding, relatively inexpensive, and it will fascinate you. [3]To reap the rewards of astronomy, you must have the patience and be willing to learn the positions of planets and stars in the night sky. [4]Patience pays off with the ability to pick out the constellations, the planets, and to point out the stars. [5]Amateur astronomy does not have to empty your wallet or leaving you broke. [6]Some amateurs invest in expensive telescopes; inexpensive binoculars are purchased by some; others simply use their eyes. [7]Astronomy is at its most fascinating when a meteor shower is in progress or there is a comet passing by. [8]Your friends will be impressed when you can

spot the heavenly visitors and pointing them out to others. [9]You will find your knowledge is in demand as "comet craze" or "mania about meteors" grips your friends and acquaintances. [10]Astronomy can capture your imagination and helps you understand the universe from your own back yard.

1. ______________________________

2. ______________________________

3. ______________________________

4. ______________________________

5. ______________________________

6. ______________________________

7. ______________________________

8. ______________________________

9. ______________________________

10. ______________________________

26

Verb Shifts

> A Shifty Excuse
>
> "I brought my term paper with me, Professor Lipton, but when I opened my notebook, it's gone. I can't print out another copy because the file was eaten by the computer."

The excuse above is shifty—but not just because it is unconvincing. It contains two common types of **verb shifts.** The first sentence contains an unnecessary shift from past tense to present tense, and the second contains an unnecessary shift from active voice to passive voice. In this chapter, you will learn to correct unnecessary shifts from past to present tense and to make necessary shifts into the past perfect tense. You will also learn to recognize active voice and passive voice and to correct unnecessary shifts between the two.

Shifts in Tense

Verb tenses give the English language its sense of time, its sense of *when* events occur. The timeline below shows six verb tenses, and the chart below the timeline briefly explains how each tense is used.

Verb Tense Timeline

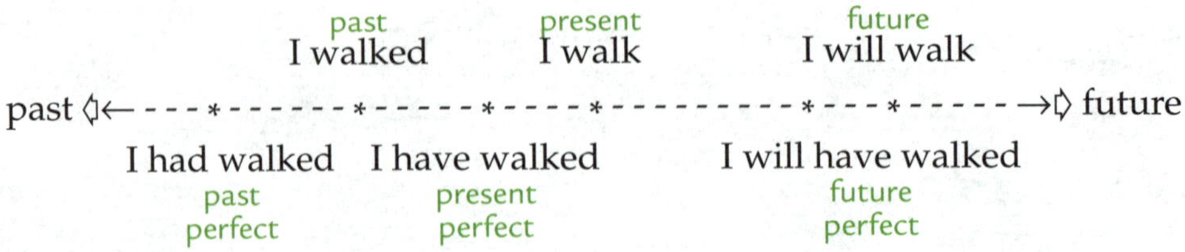

Verb Tense Chart

⇦⇦⇦	Furthest in the past; happened before another past action	past perfect *had* + *-ed* verb form	I *had walked* up the stairs, and I was out of breath.
⇦⇦	In the past; happened before now.	past *-ed* verb form	I *walked* all the way around the nature trail.
⇦•	In the past but extending to the present	present perfect *have* or *has* + *-ed* verb form	I *have walked* every day for the last month. He *has walked* a mile already.
•	Happens regularly or often, or is happening now.	present base verb form or base verb + *-s*	I *walk* at least five miles a week. She *walks* quickly.
⇨	Happens in the future but before another future event	future perfect *will have* + *-ed* verb form	By the time you join me on the track, I *will have walked* at least two miles.
⇨⇨	Happens at some time in the future	future *will* + base verb	I *will walk* with you tomorrow if we both have time.

Avoiding Unnecessary Tense Shifts

With so many ways of designating time, it is easy to make mistakes. The most common error in verb tense is an unnecessary shift from past tense to present tense. A writer may become so caught up in describing a past event that it becomes, at least temporarily, a part of "the now." Look at the following examples to see the difference between a necessary shift and an unnecessary shift in verb tense.

Examples

Necessary Shift:

✔ Coral was (past) a poor student in high school, but she is doing (present) well in college.

Since the sentence above refers to both the *past* (high school) and the *present* (college), the verb tense shift is necessary.

Unnecessary Shift:

✘ When Joe came (past) into the room, he breaks (present) into a big smile and says (present), "Guess what?"

Since the action in this sentence is a single, continuous event, there is no need for a shift to present tense. To correct an unnecessary tense shift, decide which tense is appropriate and use that tense for all verbs in the sentence.

Corrected:

✔ When Joe came (past) into the room, he broke (past) into a big smile and said (past), "Guess what?"

Unnecessary Shift:

✘ Annie boarded (past) the bus, and she sees (present) her friend Chloe sitting in a window seat.

Corrected:

✔ Annie boarded (past) the bus, and she saw (past) her friend Chloe sitting in a window seat.

PRACTICE 1 MAINTAINING CONSISTENT TENSE

Underline the correct verb in each sentence.

1. When Amanda finally arrived at the restaurant, her friends (have, had) already ordered.
2. The plumber knocked on the door, checking his watch impatiently, but no one (is, was) home.

3. The car rounded the corner too quickly, skidded on the wet pavement, and (slams, slammed) into a telephone pole.
4. Every day, Horace works in his garden until the sun (falls, fell) below the horizon.
5. The trees in the front yard look beautiful all year long; however, they (bloom, bloomed) only in spring.

PRACTICE 2 Correcting Unnecessary Tense Shifts

In each of the following sentences, correct the unnecessary shift from past to present.

1. Yoshi had just settled down to watch the ball game when suddenly his cable goes out.

____

____

2. The plane gained speed as it moved down the runway, and then it is airborne.

____

____

3. Edward accidentally left his headlights on, so his car battery dies before he gets out of class.

____

____

4. After I had put my heart and soul into studying the first six chapters, the professor moves the test to next Friday.

____

____

5. The troops moved quietly, knowing enemy soldiers are nearby.

____

____

Providing Necessary Tense Shifts

Another common type of verb tense error is likely to occur when a writer needs to shift from the past tense into the more distant past, using the past perfect tense. Often, writers omit this needed shift and stay in the simple past tense, thus taking the risk of confusing the reader.

Examples

✘ By the time Jill woke (past) up, her husband made (past) coffee.

Made coffee is further in the past than *woke up. Had* needs to be used to push *made* to a time before that indicated by the simple past tense verb *woke.*

✘ The minister said a prayer at the grave of Florence Jones, who attended his church.

Without *had,* the two verbs in the sentence are, as far as the reader can tell, occupying the same space in the past. Look at the corrected versions of the sentences:

✔ By the time Jill woke (past) up, her husband had made (past perfect) the coffee.

✔ The minister said (past) a prayer at the grave of Florence Jones, who had attended (past perfect) his church.

Notice in the example below that if the sequence of events is clearly shown in other ways, the past perfect tense is not needed:

✔ Carl made coffee *before* Jill woke up.

Practice 3 Making Necessary Tense Shifts

In the following sentences, provide the necessary shift to the past perfect tense by using *had* + the past participle (the *-ed* or *-en* form of the verb). Some of the verbs in the sentences below are irregular and do not form their past participle by adding *-ed.* (If you are uncertain of the past participle of irregular verbs, consult the list in Chapter 18.)

1. I was stranded on a lonely road, and I left my cell phone at home.

____

____

2. When the landlady called about the rent, I told her I mailed it.

____

____

3. When Vijay asked his daughter if she had homework, she told him she finished it.

____

____

4. When someone asked Michael for a cigarette, he said he quit smoking.

___

___

5. The dog ate as if no one fed him for days.

___

___

Active and Passive Voice

Active voice means that the subject of a verb performs the action described by the verb, as in the following sentence:

Tom ate the hamburger.

In this sentence, *Tom,* the subject, performs the action described by the verb *ate.* Rewritten in **passive voice,** the sentence looks like this:

The hamburger was eaten by Tom.

What has changed? Simply put, the subject of the verb is not *acting,* but is *acted upon.* The subject *hamburger* performs no action, but instead is acted upon by the person who eats it. Notice, too, another hallmark of the passive voice: the verb contains a helping verb that is a form of the verb *to be.* Though an active voice verb also may have a helping verb such as *is, was, were, have been, will be,* or another form of *to be,* a passive voice verb *always* has a helping verb. Another hallmark of the passive voice is the *by* construction that sometimes tells who or what acted upon the subject.

** Memory Jogger*

In *active voice,* an action is done *by* the grammatical subject.

In *passive voice,* an action is done *to* the grammatical subject.

Practice 4 Examining Active and Passive Voice Verbs

Look at the following sets of sentences and answer the questions about them. The first one is done for you.

Set 1

Active: The National Weather Service predicts rain for tomorrow.

The subject of the verb is National Weather Service.

The verb that shows the action done *by* the subject is predicts.

Passive: Rain is being predicted for tomorrow by the National Weather Service.

The subject of the verb is rain.

The verb that shows the action done *to* the subject is is being predicted.

Set 2

Active: Andrea read the book over the weekend.

The subject of the verb is ________________.

The verb that shows the action done *by* the subject is ________________.

Passive: The book was read by Andrea over the weekend.

The subject of the verb is ________________.

The verb that shows the action done *to* the subject is ________________.

Set 3

Active: Terrell completely reorganized the company's delivery system.

The subject of the verb is ________________.

The verb that shows the action done *by* the subject is ________________.

Passive: The company's delivery system was completely reorganized by Terrell.

The subject of the verb is ________________.

The verb that shows the action done *to* the subject is ________________.

Set 4

Active: In the bottom of the ninth inning, the Expos won the game.

The subject of the verb is ________________.

The verb that shows the action done *by* the subject is ________________.

Passive: In the bottom of the ninth inning, the game was won by the Expos.

The subject of the verb is ________________.

The verb that shows the action done *to* the subject is ________________.

Set 5

Active: After the park closes, work crews rake leaves, sweep sidewalks, and clean restrooms in preparation for the next day.

The subject of the verb is ________________.

The verbs that show the action done *by* the subject are ________________ ____________.

Passive: After the park closes, leaves are raked, sidewalks are swept, and restrooms are cleaned in preparation for the next day.

The subjects of the verbs are ________________________.

The actions done *to* the subjects are ______________________________.

Uses of Active and Passive Voice

Active voice, with its directness and vitality, is stronger than passive and is preferred in most situations. There are times, however, when you may want to emphasize the recipient of the action rather than the actor. At those times, use passive voice. If you were composing a paragraph about an old mansion, you would probably say "The Wetherby mansion was built in 1897 by Augustus L. Wetherby," not "Augustus L. Wetherby built the Wetherby mansion in 1897." If your paragraph were about Augustus Wetherby, however, the second sentence would be a better choice. While active voice is ordinarily preferred, decisions about active and passive voice depend on the focus and purpose of each sentence.

Shifts between active and passive voice are avoided unless they are necessary, as in the following sentence:

The entire nation mourned (active) when President John F. Kennedy was assassinated (passive).

The shift is necessary because to stay in active voice the writer of the sentence would have to take the focus away from Kennedy by writing a sentence like this one: "The entire nation mourned when Lee Harvey Oswald assassinated President John F. Kennedy."

Writing Sentences in Active and Passive Voice

To avoid unnecessary shifts between active and passive voice, you need to be able to recognize and write sentences in both voices. The next section of the chapter will give you practice in switching from passive to active voice and from active to passive voice.

Switching from Passive to Active Voice

To switch from passive voice to active voice, first determine who or what acts upon the subject of the sentence. Then rewrite the sentence to make that actor the subject.

Examples

Passive: The contract was drawn up by the company's lawyers.

Since the sentence is in passive voice, you know that the subject, *contract,* is acted upon. To switch this sentence to active voice, first look for the word or phrase that tells who or what acted upon the subject. In a passive voice sentence, the information will come after the verb. In this sentence, *the company's lawyers* drew up the contract. Next, make that word or phrase the subject of the sentence. Finally, change the verb to active voice—in this case, by removing the helping verb and converting it to simple past tense.

Active: The company's lawyers drew up the contract.

Sometimes, the *by* construction will be omitted, and you will need to mentally fill in the blank to put an actor into the sentence:

Passive: The prisoner was sentenced to life without parole.

The sentence does not say who sentenced the prisoner, but logic tells you that it must have been a judge. To rewrite the sentence in active voice, supply the missing judge as the subject of the sentence:

Active: The judge sentenced the prisoner to life without parole.

Practice 5 Changing Passive to Active Voice

Each of the following sentences is in passive voice. Rewrite each sentence in active voice.

1. The chairs were ordered by Herman on May 12.

____

2. The wedding was attended by one hundred people.

____

3. At the scene of the crime, an address book containing names of suspected drug dealers was found by police.

____

____

4. In English class today, our graded essays were returned.

____

5. The clock was sent to us by Aunt Matilda and Uncle Norris.

____

Switching from Active to Passive Voice

To switch from active voice to passive voice, reverse the position of the actor (the subject of the verb) and the recipient of the action (the object of the verb).

Examples

Active: The cheering fans watched the game.

The actor (the subject of the verb) is *cheering fans.* The recipient of the action (the object of the verb) is *the game.* To convert the sentence to passive voice, switch the positions of the two. Then change the verb to passive voice by adding a helping verb:

Passive: The game was watched by hundreds of cheering fans.

Here is a second example:

Active: The Committee for Park Beautification and the Citizens' Council planted fifty new trees in Gregory Frasier Park.

Passive: Fifty new trees were planted in Gregory Frasier Park by the Committee for Park Beautification and the Citizens' Council.

PRACTICE 6 CHANGING ACTIVE TO PASSIVE VOICE

Each of the following sentences is in active voice. Rewrite each sentence in passive voice.

1. Children's drawings and magnets of various types covered the refrigerator door.

____

____

2. The technician expertly cleaned and repaired the old lawnmower.

____

____

3. The head chef supervised the cooking and menu planning in the restaurant.

____

____

4. Women of ancient times washed clothes in streams and rivers.

____

____

5. The ringing of the telephone broke Bonnie's concentration.

____

____

Correcting Shifts in Voice

When an unnecessary shift in voice occurs within a sentence, rewrite the sentence so that it is in one voice. (Active voice is usually preferred.)

Examples

Unnecessary Shift:

✗ Before I left (active) for the airport, a phone call was made (passive) to confirm my reservations.

Corrected:

✔ Before I left (active) for the airport, I called (active) to confirm my reservations.

Unnecessary Shift:

✗ George's car needed (active) work, so it was left (passive) at the shop.

Corrected:

✔ George's car needed (active) work, so he left (active) it at the shop.

PRACTICE 7 CORRECTING SHIFTS IN VOICE

Each of the following sentences contains a shift in voice. Cross out the passive voice portion of each sentence and rewrite it in active voice. The first one is done for you.

1. The dog's former owner had abused it, but ~~it was treated well by Sarah~~.

   The dog's former owner had abused it, but Sarah treated it well.

2. We had plenty of cake left over, but all of the fruit had been eaten by the guests.

3. By the time we came home, all the food in the dog's bowl had been eaten.

4. Fran wrote the letter, but it was signed by all ten of us.

5. Because the plants were carefully watered and fertilized by Martin, they were tall and healthy.

6. Icicles hung from the trees like Christmas decorations, and the street was covered by a glassy sheet of ice.

7. Chelsie was serious about sticking to her budget, so every expenditure was recorded.

8. At the salon, Andrea's hair was expertly cut and styled by the beautician while the manicurist buffed and painted her nails.

9. Firefighters arrived on the scene, and the blaze was soon extinguished.

10. As we sat on the porch, a siren was heard.

Review Exercises

Complete the Review Exercises to see how well you have learned the skills addressed in this chapter. As you work through the exercises, go back through the chapter to review any of the rules you do not understand completely.

Review Exercise 1

The italicized portions of the following sentences contain unnecessary shifts in voice or tense, or a verb that needs to be shifted from the past to the past perfect tense. Correct the problem in each sentence.

1. Kendall is graduating in June, and *a celebration party is being given by him.*

2. I saw Mark at the grocery store, and *he says,* "Have you seen Vernon lately?"

3. We offered Jim dinner, but he said *he ate.*

4. Sandra and Tom were pronounced husband and wife, and then *they light* a single candle to symbolize their union.

5. When the jury walked into the courtroom, everyone tried to read the jurors' expressions to see what verdict *had been reached.*

6. As they walked through the produce department, Lynn and her mother picked up bananas, pears, and apples, and then *they decide* to get some cherries, too.

____

____

7. We discussed the price and the terms of payment, and *the deal was sealed* with a handshake.

____

____

8. Karen *already worked* an eight-hour shift and did not appreciate being asked to work overtime at the last minute.

____

____

9. Last night, as we sat down to the first family dinner we had had all week, *the phone rings.*

____

____

10. Evelyn felt she should have been promoted before Bill because *she worked* at KC Corporation for five years longer than he.

____

____

Review Exercise 2

The italicized portions of the following sentences contain unnecessary shifts in voice or tense, or verbs that need to be shifted from the past to the past perfect tense. Circle *a, b,* or *c* to indicate the type of problem in each sentence; then correct the problem.

1. In the morning, we left our beds unmade, and when we came back to the hotel room, the housekeeping staff *cleaned the room and made up the beds.*

   The problem in this sentence is

   a. a shift in voice

   b. a shift between past and present tense

   c. past tense verbs that need to be further in the past (past perfect)

____

____

2. We walked into the house, and May and Chad were sitting there with smug smiles, as *if they know a secret* that we didn't.
The problem in this sentence is
   a. a shift in voice
   b. a shift between past and present tense
   c. a past tense verb that needs to be further in the past (past perfect)

___

___

3. In the stands, hockey fans danced the Hokey-Pokey and the Macarena *while hot dogs, soft drinks, and beer were sold by vendors.*
The problem in this sentence is
   a. a shift in voice
   b. a shift between past and present tense
   c. a past tense verb that needs to be further in the past (past perfect)

___

___

4. Out in the yard, the two dogs worried a small rodent *that had been caught by them.*
The problem in this sentence is
   a. a shift in voice
   b. a shift between past and present tense
   c. a past tense verb that needs to be further in the past (past perfect)

___

___

5. When Jack got to the veterinarian's office with Prince, he realized he *left* the dog's urine sample in the refrigerator at home.
The problem in this sentence is
   a. a shift in voice
   b. a shift between past and present tense
   c. a past tense verb that needs to be further in the past (past perfect)

___

___

Review Exercise 3

The italicized portions of the following sentences contain unnecessary shifts in voice or tense, or verbs that need to be shifted from the past to the past perfect tense. Circle *a, b,* or *c* to indicate the type of problem in each sentence; then correct the problem.

1. On Harold's first day of work, his supervisor called him into the office and *says*, "If you are honest, prompt, and hardworking, you will succeed here."
   The problem in this sentence is
   a. a shift in voice
   b. a shift between past and present tense
   c. a past tense verb that needs to be further in the past (past perfect)

   ____

   ____

2. When Jane arrived home, *her husband left a note*, "Gone to grocery store. Home soon."
   The problem in this sentence is
   a. a shift in voice
   b. a shift between past and present tense
   c. a past tense verb that needs to be further in the past (past perfect)

   ____

   ____

3. I was driving along Straight Street when *a truck runs a red light and hits my car.*
   The problem in this sentence is
   a. a shift in voice
   b. a shift between past and present tense
   c. a past tense verb that needs to be further in the past (past perfect)

   ____

   ____

4. Carlotta tried to pick up the heavy packages with one hand and hold onto her toddler with the other. Though several people were standing in line with her, *not one offer of assistance was made.*
   The problem in this sentence is
   a. a shift in voice
   b. a shift between past and present tense
   c. a past tense verb that needs to be further in the past (past perfect)

   ____

   ____

   ____

5. Ingrid came home and said she was certain *she made a good impression* at her interview.
   The problem in this sentence is

a. a shift in voice

b. a shift between past and present tense

c. a past tense verb that needs to be further in the past (past perfect)

____

____

Review Exercise 4

Correct the voice or tense problem in each sentence.

1. The clerk asked me if I ordered from the company before.

____

____

2. The crew was almost finished polishing the floor in the hallway when the power goes out and the machinery whines to a halt.

____

____

3. The rain was pelting down in sheets, so Anthony pulls off the road under an interstate bridge.

____

____

4. Helen is a perfectionist; if a job is done by her, it is done right.

____

____

5. The telephone rang, and Meg answers it right away.

____

____

6. On his trip home, Larry tried to visit his friend Carl, but Carl moved.

____

____

7. It was not Emma's day. She waited in the rain for the bus, but when it came, the driver didn't see her and just passes by.

____

____

8. When I asked Mary about the quilt hanging on her wall, she said she had it for years.

9. The room was a disorderly array of books, papers, and potted plants, and a cat is curled up in the only chair.

10. David loves to garden. This year, peas, tomatoes, and beans were planted by him.

Review Exercise 5

Each sentence in the following paragraph contains a voice or tense problem. Correct the problem by rewriting a verb in past tense or past perfect tense or by changing a passive voice construction to active voice.

[1]Yesterday, as I ran my Saturday errands, some of the people who were seen by me made me think of Robert Burns' poem about seeing ourselves as others see us. [2]At the drugstore, I see a woman in tight jeans, a stained shirt, and huge pink curlers. [3]If she thought of how others might view her before she left the house, she might have taken the time to change clothes and comb out her hair. [4]One young man drove through a downtown street with his stereo at full blast, not caring that others might not like the same music that was liked by him. [5]He may have seen himself as sophisticated; to others on the street that day, he is an annoyance. [6]An attractive middle-aged woman in a business suit did not behave attractively toward the poodle that walks beside her. [7]She jerked its leash and speaks harshly to it, revealing a bad temper under a polished exterior. [8]Finally, disgusting behavior was exhibited by one man as he sat at a traffic light. [9]He casually picks

his nose as if his car had rendered him invisible. [10]On that Saturday, some people were seen by me who could not see themselves as others saw them.

1. ____________________
2. ____________________
3. ____________________
4. ____________________
5. ____________________
6. ____________________
7. ____________________
8. ____________________
9. ____________________
10. ____________________

Editing Exercises: Advanced Grammar

Advanced Grammar: Three Editing Exercises

Editing Exercise 1 Misplaced Modifiers, Dangling Modifiers, and Parallel Structure

Correct the following misplaced and dangling modifiers and parallel structure errors.

6 parallel structure errors
4 dangling and misplaced modifiers

[1]Stress is a normal response to change, good and bad, in people's lives, and everyone nearly experiences stress. [2]*Eustress* (from the Greek root *eu*, meaning *good* or *well*) is stress in response to a positive event such as going on vacation, to win the lottery, or receiving a job promotion. [3]Deciding whether to buy a Mercedes or a BMW with lottery winnings, the pressure may seem overwhelming. [4]Eustress, however, is temporary; families remember the beauty of a wedding and forget that they almost spent all the time prior to the wedding squabbling over trivial things. [5]*Distress,* stress in response to negative events, presents more serious problems and causing more harm. [6]This type of stress is often a response to traumatic events such as loss of a job or a family member dies. [7]Having lost the status and income that a job provides, anger and despair can overwhelm a person who has been fired or downsized. [8]Anger, nightmares, or to lose weight are often the results of distress. [9]Chronic stress is also said to contribute to illnesses such as heart disease, depression, and having some form of cancer. [10]The good news is that for most people, stress and its symptoms fading and disappear after a period of adjustment.

1. ______________________________

2. ______________________________

3. ______________________________

4. ______________________________

5. ______________________________

6. ______________________________

7. ______________________________

____

8. ______________________________

9. ______________________________

10. ______________________________

Editing Exercise 2 Misplaced and Dangling Modifiers, Parallel Structure, and Verb Shifts

Correct the following misplaced and dangling modifiers, parallel structure errors, and shifts in verb tense and voice in the following paragraph.

3 parallel structure errors
2 misplaced and dangling modifiers
3 shifts in verb tense
2 shifts in voice

[1]I enjoy observing my fellow coffee drinkers when I visited the coffee shop each morning. [2]One older gentleman, an absentminded coffee drinker, pays no attention to the coffee that is drunk by him. [3]He may be reading a newspaper, jot notes on a pad, or talking to the server. [4]As he picks up his coffee, he never looks at it; he just raised the cup to his lips and drinks. [5]Paying no attention, a fly in the coffee would probably never be noticed. [6]Another coffee shop customer, a middle-aged woman, plays with her coffee, with her cup, and spoon. [7]As she sits, she picks up the cup and sets it in the saucer, is playing with the handle of the cup, or

stirs the coffee, but I never see her drink. [8]Another regular is a young man who obviously loves coffee with a mustache. [9]Cradling the cup in his hands, he sniffs the rich aroma of his coffee, then closes his eyes blissfully as the coffee is drunk. [10]For me, one of the pleasures of drinking coffee is watching my fellow coffee drinkers as I drank my morning coffee at the Mug and Spoon.

1. ______________________________
2. ______________________________
3. ______________________________
4. ______________________________
5. ______________________________
6. ______________________________
7. ______________________________
8. ______________________________
9. ______________________________
10. ______________________________

Editing Exercise 3 Verb Shifts, Parallel Structure, and Dangling or Misplaced Modifiers

In the following editing exercise, correct the following verb shifts, parallel structure errors, and dangling or misplaced modifiers.

3 shifts in tense
1 shift in voice
2 dangling modifiers
1 misplaced modifier
3 parallel structure errors

[1]The city sprawls out for miles, but no matter where I drive, I see the fragile-looking woman I called "the walking lady." [2]Crowded with speeding cars, I see her in the summer, walking along a dangerous four-lane highway. [3]Her fair skin is

sheltered from the sun by a flowered umbrella, but her wavy blonde hair was straggly and damp in the humid summer air. [4]Her shoes are not the sturdy athletic shoes that people wear for exercise, but flats that are worn, flimsy, and looking much too loose for her feet. [5]In winter, I see her walking the narrow downtown streets in the pouring rain, the biting wind, and the snow that falls. [6]Wearing a thin coat, the same fragile shoes enclose her wide, flat feet. [7]One spring day, sitting on a bench in the park, she walked right past me. [8]Up close, her blonde hair looked thin, her bare legs were mapped with blue veins, and swollen ankles also were a problem. [9]She looked straight ahead as she walks, and a quiet dignity surrounded her like an eggshell enclosing a yolk. [10]She is still seen by me as she walks the city's streets and highways, and I always wonder how she lives, where she eats, and most of all, why she endlessly walks.

1. ______________________________
2. ______________________________
   ____
3. ______________________________
4. ______________________________
5. ______________________________
6. ______________________________
7. ______________________________
8. ______________________________
9. ______________________________
10. ______________________________

27 Commas

Unreliable Rules

"When in doubt, leave it out."

"Put a comma where there is a natural pause."

"Sprinkle them sparingly, like salt."

There are so many comma rules that, in desperation, people often resort to makeshift rules like the ones above. Unfortunately, these blanket statements don't always work. When it comes to commas, rules—and exceptions—abound. The rules presented in this chapter will give you a head start in coping with the complexities of comma usage.

Commas to Set Off Introductory Words, Phrases, and Clauses

Use commas after an introductory word, phrase, or clause.

Examples

Instead, Van decided to take the summer off.

The next morning, the newspaper reported the election results.

Since the class did not meet yesterday, Mitzi spent the day in the library.

PRACTICE 1 USING COMMAS WITH INTRODUCTORY ELEMENTS

Insert commas after introductory words, phrases, and clauses.

1. Reluctantly the instructor agreed to postpone the test.

   ____

2. When Kim plays video games she shuts out the world.

   ____

3. During the seventh-inning stretch Harry Caray led the fans in "Take Me Out to the Ball Game."

   ____

4. In fact the car has had very few problems.

   ____

5. Yawning loudly Eric said, "Is it morning already?"

   ____

Commas to Join Items in a Series

When a series of three or more words, phrases, or clauses is connected with *and* or *or*, place a comma after each item except the last one. The final comma goes before *and* or *or*.

> ** Real-World Writing*
>
> In journalism, it is becoming customary to omit the comma before *and*, *or*, or *nor* when items are joined in a series. Academic usage is more traditional and favors keeping the final comma.

Examples

Iguanas, chameleons, and salamanders were Ted's passion when he was seven.

Motorcycles, off-road vehicles, and cars are his passion at seventeen.

The dog had tracked mud across the porch, into the kitchen, and up the stairs.

The doctor asked Neville if the pain occurred before he ate, after he ate, or while he ate.

If only two items appear in the series, no comma is used.

> Stacy said her two worst vices were soap operas and talk shows.
>
> Arnold was slowed by a traffic tie-up in the tunnel and a wreck near the downtown connector.
>
> Jason takes care of his parents because they are old and because they once took care of him.

Practice 2 Using Commas to Join Items in a Series

Insert commas to join words, phrases, and clauses in a series of three or more. Write *correct* below the sentence that does not need a comma.

1. Mycology is the study of yeasts molds mushrooms and other fungi.

   ____

2. The ancient Maya restricted the consumption of cocoa to the aristocracy because of the cost of growing the beans and the labor involved in processing them.

   ____

3. The dog looked as if he had been dipped in water coated with dirt and set out to dry.

   ____

4. The children watched in fascination as the magician reached into his hat pulled out a dove and released it into the air.

   ____

5. Students screamed as the lights flickered the alarm sounded and the elevator jerked to a halt.

   ____

Commas to Join Independent Clauses

Use a comma with a FANBOYS conjunction *(for, and, nor, but, or, yet, so)* to join independent clauses.

Examples

> Harrison thought that researching would be the easy part of his project, but it turned out to be the hardest.

I feel exhausted already, and tomorrow is just Tuesday.

Karen's sinus medication makes her sleepy, so she avoids taking it during the day.

Do not use a comma if the FANBOYS connects verb to verb rather than clause to clause. In other words, do not use a comma unless there is a complete sentence on both sides of the FANBOYS.

Ernestine lay in a hammock and read a book.

Nick looked for his glasses but couldn't find them.

Alberto couldn't decide whether to sign up for biology in the fall or wait until spring.

PRACTICE 3 USING COMMAS TO JOIN INDEPENDENT CLAUSES

Place commas before FANBOYS conjunctions that join two independent clauses. One of the sentences does not need a comma.

1. The weeds were tall and the mower died whenever Helen tried to cut through them.

   ____

2. The upholstery was worn and faded but the couch was still comfortable.

   ____

3. Leo received a credit card in the mail but did not remember requesting it.

   ____

4. Lorenzo was studying so he let the answering machine pick up his calls.

   ____

5. "You can pay now or you can take up to ninety days to pay on our easy credit plan," said the salesclerk.

   ____

Commas Around Interrupters

An **interrupter** is a word, phrase, or clause inserted into a sentence to give more information about some element within the sentence. An interrupter is never essential to the structure of the sentence. If you took it out, the sentence would still make perfect sense.

Examples

The dog, tail wagging, bounded toward its owner.

The student, disappointed by her grades, withdrew from the course at midterm.

PRACTICE 4 USING COMMAS AROUND INTERRUPTERS

Insert commas around interrupters in the following sentences.

1. The interruption brief as it was distracted Heather and made it hard for her to focus on her work again.

   ____

2. Mr. Angelo a friend of my family runs the delicatessen on Third Street.

   ____

3. Breanna sighing heavily opened her book to study.

   ____

4. The banana apparently left by one of the children lay forgotten in the back seat until it was brown and shriveled.

   ____

5. Lava lamps which first appeared in the 1970s became popular again in the 1990s.

   ____

Commas with Direct Quotations

A **direct quotation** is an exact repetition of the words that someone speaks or thinks. When a comma is used with a direct quotation, it is always placed in front of the quotation mark.

1. When a direct quotation is followed by a tag (such as *he said*), a comma goes after the quoted words and *in front of the quotation mark:*

   "I think I can find the information I need on the Internet," Javier said.

2. When a tag leads into a direct quotation, a comma goes after the tag and *in front of the quotation mark:*

   Sophie said, "If I had the time, I would audit a world history class."

3. When a sentence is written as a split quotation, commas are placed *in front of the quotation marks:*

   "If it had not been for Hal," said the supervisor, "I don't know what we would have done."

PRACTICE 5 USING COMMAS WITH DIRECT QUOTATIONS

Insert commas to set off direct quotations in the following sentences.

1. Karin asked "Would you mind helping me move this ladder?"

   ____

2. "If you are not going to watch television" said Patrick "let me have the remote control."

   ____

3. "I can never remember where I put my keys" said Mike.

   ____

4. "You may like that herbal tea" said Gerry "but it tastes like dishwater to me."

   ____

5. Ben Franklin said "Lost time is never found again."

   ____

Commas in Names and Dates

When a professional title or family designation follows a name, it is set off with commas.

The woman's name tag read, "Judy Smith, L.P.N."

Raymond J. Johnson, C.P.A., rented an office on Second Street.

When you write the month, day, and year, a comma goes between the day and year.

The Declaration of Independence was signed on July 4, 1776.

When you write just the month and year, no comma is used.

The Declaration of Independence was signed in July 1776.

PRACTICE 6 USING COMMAS IN NAMES AND DATES

Insert commas as needed in the following sentences. One sentence needs no comma.

1. Dave says he quit smoking on January 1 1999.

 ____

2. The letter was addressed to Jeana S. Reynolds D.D.S., but there was no return address.

 ____

3. Avery says he will graduate in June 2007.

 ____

4. Carl Grollier C.P.A. will hold a seminar on the new tax laws.

 ____

5. Jonathan Burns M.D. has been our family doctor for five years.

 ____

Review Exercises

Complete the Review Exercises to see how well you have learned the skills addressed in this chapter. As you work through the exercises, go back through the chapter to review any of the rules you do not understand completely.

REVIEW EXERCISE 1

Insert commas where they are needed in the sentences below.

1. Infotainment is a store that sells books compact discs and videos.

 ____

2. In fact only 12 percent of the students surveyed said they had seriously considered dropping out during their first year of college.

 ____

3. Kudzu a vine native to Japan now flourishes throughout the South.

 ____

4. At the end of June 1998 Felicia graduated from the university.

 ____

5. As the plane disappeared into the clouds Andrea turned away from the window and walked slowly toward the parking lot.

____

6. Broken shells dead jellyfish and tangled seaweed were left behind by the receding tide.

____

7. Darlene knew she was too ill to work but she still felt guilty about calling in sick.

____

8. The computer disk had a gummy substance on it and Raoul was afraid to put it into the disk drive.

____

9. A graduation tassel a pair of fuzzy dice and a pine air freshener hung from the car's rearview mirror.

____

10. Renaldo the dispatcher on duty said that it had been a quiet night.

____

Review Exercise 2

Insert commas where they are needed in the sentences below.

1. Yolanda found a cat toy a dusty sock and a fuzzy piece of Halloween candy under the couch.

____

2. Janis Monroe R.N. was staffing the phone lines at Ask-a-Nurse.

____

3. When Rakesh picked up the telephone he heard no dial tone.

____

4. The driver of the red sports car unaware of the state trooper's presence whipped past at 85 miles per hour.

____

5. In the garage piles of *National Geographics* were stacked against one wall as high as Nell's shoulders.

____

6. With only one day left before finals students flocked to the library's study rooms.

____

7. The courtyard was filled with students chatting studying or just enjoying the spring weather.

____

8. The phone book listed the accountant as Harold Smith C.P.A.

____

9. Driving down the lonely stretch of highway, Paul saw asphalt pastureland and cattle bunched under the occasional shade tree.

____

10. When Kendrick saw the puddle on the kitchen floor he realized his attempts to fix the dishwasher had been unsuccessful.

____

Review Exercise 3

Insert commas where they are needed in the sentences below. Each of the questions contains two types of problems that require the addition of a comma or commas.

1. "I can be a full-time student" said Kasey "or I can be a full-time worker. However I can't do both."

____

____

2. Because Ashley won the coin toss she was the one who chose the toppings for the pizza. She ordered mushrooms black olives onions and pepperoni.

____

____

3. Putting toe tags on the preserved frogs planting clues to point to the "murderer" and letting the students serve as coroners were ways to get students interested in dissection. "Science can be fun as well as educational" said the teacher.

____

____

____

4. The apartment was small cramped and dark. "I can't believe the landlord wants $500 a month for this place" said Felice.

____

____

5. "The label on this freezer bag says June 6 1998," Harold told his wife. "Should I throw the bag away or should we keep it as a souvenir?

____

____

Review Exercise 4

Insert commas where they are needed in the sentences below.

1. Even as an adult Jamie remembers a particular Christmas from his childhood. On the evening of December 24 1979, Santa Claus did not visit the Thaxton household.

____

____

2. Sounding cranky Melissa sleepily answered the phone. "This had better be important" she told the caller.

____

____

3. As he came in from his morning run Andre kissed his daughter. "You smell like an old, sweaty shoe" she told him.

____

____

4. Clouds slid in from the west and the wind began to pick up. "At least the rain will cool things off" said Calvin.

____

____

5. A golf ball had smashed through the window striking the television. Glass lay on the windowsill on the floor and on the arm of the sofa.

____

____

Review Exercise 5

Insert commas where they are needed in the paragraph below. Each sentence contains one type of comma problem, which may require more than one comma to correct.

[1]For many people waiting is a fact of life. [2]People wait in train stations doctor's offices and employment offices. [3]However people's attitudes about waiting are even more interesting and varied than the places where they wait. [4]My dentist Jack Davis values his time and his patients' time. [5]"I hate to wait" he says "so I don't keep my patients waiting, either." [6]Some people become angry and they make sure that those who keep them waiting get the message. [7]One of my neighbors once told me "If I'm kept waiting more than an hour, I send a bill for my time." [8]Other people endowed with more philosophical natures try to make waiting productive. [9]These are the people who are seen in airport terminals and doctors' offices reading books knitting or catching up on their correspondence. [10]Though some endure it more patiently than others waiting is a fact of life for everyone.

1. ____
2. ____
3. ____
4. ____
5. ____
6. ____
7. ____
8. ____
9. ____
10. ____

28

Other Punctuation

. ? ! ; : — ( )

Punctuation marks other than the comma are the focus of this chapter. Some of these punctuation marks, such as the period and the question mark, are quite familiar to you. Others, such as the dash and the colon, are more exotic and less often used. This chapter reinforces the familiar and introduces the less familiar marks of punctuation.

End Punctuation: Period, Question Mark, and Exclamation Point

The period, the question mark, and the exclamation point are all forms of **end punctuation;** that is, they signal the end of a sentence.

The Period

The **period** is used to mark the end of a sentence that makes a statement.

Examples

✔ The stereos advertised at Electronix Unlimited were gone by the time Frank got there.

✔ The elephant's trunk was ringed with deep wrinkles.

Periods are also used to signal an appropriate abbreviation. Except for abbreviations in courtesy titles, such as *Mr., Ms., Dr.,* and *Rev.,* used before proper names, do not abbreviate words in your paragraphs and essays.

Examples

✘ Jas. has an appt. with the dr. on Wed. afternoon.

✔ James has an appointment with the doctor on Wednesday afternoon.

✔ James has an appointment with Dr. Davis on Wednesday afternoon.

The Question Mark

A **question mark** is used at the end of a direct question.

✔ What time are we leaving?

✔ Did you know that the bar code system used in retailing was invented in 1970?

No question mark is used with an indirect question.

✔ I wonder why Ursula always wears black.

✔ Mr. Smith asked why the meeting was being held on Friday.

The Exclamation Point

Exclamation points are used to show extreme excitement or surprise. They are seldom needed in a college essay. Unless you are quoting someone who has just discovered that the building is on fire (or has another reason for extreme excitement), there will be few opportunities to use an exclamation point. Interjections such as "Ouch!" and "Yikes!" are followed by exclamation points but are seldom needed for college writing. So use exclamation points when you quote someone who is shouting or speaking excitedly. Otherwise, let your words, not your punctuation, convey the excitement of your essay.

Examples

✘ I noticed an orange glow under the door, and I realized that my house was on fire!

✔ I noticed an orange glow under the door, and I realized that my house was on fire.

✘ I reached for the doorknob! It was hot!

✔ I panicked and reached for the doorknob. It was as hot as a live coal.

✔ "Fire!" I yelled.

PRACTICE 1 USING END PUNCTUATION AND APPROPRIATE ABBREVIATIONS

In each sentence, correct an inappropriate abbreviation or place a period after an appropriate abbreviation. Then place end punctuation (period, question mark, or exclamation point) where needed.

1. Did Rev Madison really order fourteen boxes of your daughter's Girl Scout cookies

____

____

2. I asked the prof if I could make up the test, but she said it was too late

____

____

3. "Look out" Ms Muller yelled as the child stepped into the path of the oncoming truck.

____

____

4. Aunt Daisy wants to know if we can take our vacation in Oct to come to the family reunion

____

____

5. After I graduate, I hope to work for a big automobile corp like Ford

____

____

The Semicolon

Semicolon to Join Independent Clauses

A **semicolon** may be used with a transitional expression between independent clauses or may be used alone between independent clauses that are closely related. (For a more detailed discussion of this use of the semicolon, see Chapter 20, "Run-on Sentences.")

Examples

✔ The office's trash can was much too small; it had to be emptied twice a day.

✔ Elise was half an hour late; furthermore, she took an extra fifteen minutes for lunch.

Semicolon to Join Items in a List

Ordinarily, items in a list are joined by commas. However, if the items themselves contain commas, avoid confusion by using semicolons to join the items.

Examples

✔ The plane made stops in Richmond, Virginia; Atlanta, Georgia; and Houston, Texas.

✔ The journal article was written by Samuel Ellis; Jametta Holly, Ph.D.; and Laramie Spicer, M.D.

PRACTICE 2 USING SEMICOLONS

Use semicolons in the following sentences to join independent clauses or items in a series.

1. The crowd fell silent not even a cough could be heard.

____

____

2. Mike's performance on the tennis court was better than usual however, he still lost the match.

3. Almost everyone knows what happened on July 4, 1776 December 7, 1941 and November 22, 1963.

4. In spite of her poor prognosis, the woman did not die in fact, she outlived her doctor.

5. The cathedral gave the impression of immense height its spires seemed to reach the clouds.

Colons and Dashes: Formal and Informal Punctuation

The Colon

The **colon** is used to introduce a list, a restatement, or a clarification. The single most important thing to remember when you use a colon is that a complete sentence *always* comes before the colon.

1. A colon is sometimes used to introduce a list. A complete sentence must come before the colon.

Examples

✗ In her purse Dot carried: a pen, a checkbook, her credit card, and a lipstick.

This sentence is incorrect because a complete sentence does not come before the colon. Below, the sentence is corrected.

✔ In her purse Dot carried the necessities: a pen, a checkbook, her credit card, and a lipstick.

It is also correct—and sometimes simpler—to integrate a list into a sentence without using a colon.

✔ In her purse Dot carried a pen, a checkbook, her credit card, and a lipstick.

2. A colon is used to introduce a restatement or clarification of an idea. A complete sentence must come before the colon.

Examples

✔ Brian says his kids have just one method of locomotion: running.

The word *running* restates and clarifies *method of locomotion.* It is introduced with a colon.

✔ The workers were enthusiastic in their praise of Ed's managerial style: he believed in fixing the problem, not in fixing the blame.

The colon introduces a clarification of *Ed's managerial style.*

The Dash

While the colon is a formal mark of punctuation, the **dash** is informal. Like a colon, a dash is used to introduce a list, restatement, or clarification. A dash is also used to set off material that a writer wants to emphasize.

1. A dash introduces a list or restatement. When used in this way, a dash must be preceded by a complete sentence. A dash is typed as two hyphens, with no spaces before or after.

Examples

✔ In her purse Dot carried the necessities—a pen, a checkbook, her credit card, and a lipstick.

The dash is used here to introduce a list.

✔ Brian says his kids have just one method of locomotion—running.

The dash is used here to introduce a restatement and clarification of *method of locomotion.*

2. A dash is used to set off material that the writer wants to emphasize.

Examples

✔ It was her kindness—not her money or her fame—that made people love her.

A more formal way of punctuating this sentence would be to use commas to set off the interrupter: *It was her kindness, not her money or her fame, that made people love her.*

✔ The office was such a mess—books scattered on the floor, papers and unopened mail stacked on the desk—that Natalie was not sure where to start.

One way of expressing the idea in the sentence more formally would be to use two sentences: *The office was such a mess that Natalie was not sure where to start. Books were scattered on the floor; papers and unopened mail were stacked on the desk.*

Parentheses: Tools of Understatement

While dashes emphasize, **parentheses** downplay or de-emphasize. Parentheses are used to enclose material that a reader could skip over without missing the more important ideas.

Examples

✔ The Drama Club will meet in the Humanities Conference Room (Room 222, Stetson Hall) at 1:00 P.M. on Tuesday, May 26.

✔ Ann knew the apartment was not for her. She hated the color of the walls (mint green), didn't like the location (Bass Road), and was horrified at the price ($800 per month).

PRACTICE 3 USING COLONS, DASHES, AND PARENTHESES

Rewrite each of the following sentences as indicated, punctuating the italicized portion of the sentence with a colon, a dash (or dashes), or parentheses.

1. Jeremy brought several items with him to the beach. He brought *a radio, a Frisbee, a beach towel, sun block, and a cooler filled with sandwiches and soft drinks.*

   Directions: Rewrite as one sentence, with a colon introducing the list. Remove words as needed.

   ____

   ____

2. Tiana bought her textbook, *Understanding Psychology,* secondhand for only eighteen dollars.

   Directions: De-emphasize the title of the textbook.

   ____

   ____

3. Professor Jones says that if he were stranded on a desert island, he would need just one thing: *a copy of the complete works of Shakespeare.*

   Directions: Set off the restatement in an informal way rather than a formal way.

   ____

   ____

4. The tie *(the same one he wore every Friday)* was black with bright yellow happy faces.

   Directions: Emphasize the parenthetical material. Assume that the context is informal.

   ____

   ____

5. The speaker emphasized the difficulties of entrepreneurship—*the long hours, the crushing responsibility, and the uncertainty that the hard work will pay off.*

   Directions: Introduce the list in a formal way.

   ____

   ____

Review Exercises

Complete the Review Exercises to see how well you have learned the skills addressed in this chapter. As you work through the exercises, go back through the chapter to review any of the rules you do not understand completely.

Review Exercise 1

Look at the punctuation printed in color in each sentence; then briefly explain the rule that justifies its use. The first one is done for you.

1. When Grandma's palm itched, she always said it meant she was going to receive money.

   A period is used to end a sentence that makes a statement.

2. Carl asked, "Is the crossword puzzle in the sports section of the newspaper today?"

3. Maryann said she needed only three simple things: food, shelter, and unlimited money.

4. The circus (which has been held over until October 30) features clowns, animal acts, and a death-defying high wire act.

5. The hamburger—the first thing I had eaten all day—was juicy and delicious.

6. It was a typical Fourth of July; the beach was crammed with picnicking families.

7. "Wait! You forgot your change!" the cashier called after the customer.

8. Hazel's exams are on Friday, May 18; Monday, May 22; and Wednesday, May 23.

9. The car's ashtray was filled with change—mostly quarters for paying tolls.

____

____

10. The review exercise was long and tedious; Carol thought she would never finish.

____

____

Review Exercise 2

Fill the blank(s) in each sentence with a period, question mark, exclamation point, semicolon, colon, dash (or dashes), or parentheses. On some questions, more than one answer may be possible. Be sure you can justify the answer you choose.

1. Sam slowed to 75 when he saw the car __ the one with the siren and flashing lights __ pull up behind him.

____

2. Though the 1960s were a time of political passion, concern for the environment, and dedication to peace and equality, they are linked to less elevated pursuits by a slogan of sixties youth __ "Sex, drugs, and rock and roll."

____

3. "Run for your lives __" the firefighter shouted.

____

4. The requirement can be fulfilled by taking an American history course __ History 2510 or 2520 __ or by taking an exam.

____

5. "Curses __" spat the villain, twirling his black mustache.

____

6. Holidays will be observed on Thursday, November 27 __ Friday, November 28 __ Thursday, December 26 __ and Friday, December 27.

____

7. The pushpin had fallen from the bulletin board and lodged in the rug behind the desk __ Marcie hoped Gato would not eat it.

____

8. "Why was I born __ Why do I exist __" Arturo moaned, banging his head on the desk.

____

9. Crumpling his test paper into a ball, Martin felt himself seized by quiet determination __ he would not fail again.

____

____

10. The change in Brad's pocket __ two quarters and a nickel __ was not enough to get a snack from the vending machine.

____

Review Exercise 3

In each sentence, add a period, question mark, exclamation point, semicolon, colon, dash (or dashes), or parentheses.

1. From the armchair came the sound of the dog's gentle snoring

____

____

2. "Have you had a homeowner's insurance audit lately" asked the voice on the phone.

____

____

3. The editorial questioned whether a weapon particularly a handgun did more to harm than to protect the individual citizen.

____

____

4. "Drop the gun now" the officer shouted.

____

____

5. Before calling a plumber, try using Drano available in grocery stores to clear the drain.

____

____

6. The article was entitled "Is Your Diet Making You Fat"

____

____

7. The psychic claimed to have Dahlia's lucky numbers 4, 17, 18, 36, and 48.

____

____

8. The awards were presented to the following students: James Hay, Biology Award Brenda Haller, Mathematics Award Stephanie Sawyer, Outstanding Social Sciences Student Award and Abercrombie Fincher, Mentor Program Award.

____

____

____

____

9. The Pilchers were obviously not at home a week's worth of newspapers was piled in their driveway.

____

____

10. The new uniforms orange with yellow trim were universally hated by the company's employees.

____

____

Review Exercise 4

Fill in the blanks below with the correct punctuation.

[1]My Aunt Susie has been trying to lose weight __ she calls it "the battle of the bulge" __ for at least forty years. [2]She says that weight control has changed in three ways over the years __ the foods allowed, the role of calorie counting, and the emphasis on exercise. [3]When she first began trying to lose weight, her family physician __ who has since retired __ told her to cut out all breads. [4]Dr __ Smith told her to eat plenty of protein, including bacon and beef. Now, bread is allowed on diets __ however, meats are limited. [5]Aunt Susie also remembers making lists and writing down every

calorie she ate: one carrot, 25 calories __ one chocolate chip cookie, 100 calories __ one slice of bread, 60 calories. [6]When she went on her latest diet, she asked, "Should I count calories __" [7]Her nutritionist told her that today, the emphasis is on watching fat intake and eating nutritiously __ very low calorie diets are strictly discouraged. [8]In the past, doctors prescribed one exercise __ pushing away from the table. [9]Now, the leader of Susie's diet group ends each meeting by yelling, "Get out there and move __" [10]Methods of weight loss have changed __ unfortunately, losing weight remains as difficult as ever.

29 Word Choice

Cleaning the Language Closet

"Let's see. I'll put my everyday, informal language at the front of the closet so it will be handy. Hmmm . . . some of this slang is getting pretty outdated—'a happenin' dude?' I need to get rid of that! Oh, look! My formal language! It's so elegant. I'll put it in boxes for special occasions, and—what's this? Look at all this pretentious phrasing! I can get rid of it. There! My language closet looks better already!"

Words, like articles of clothing, are chosen for comfort and appropriateness. You would not wear grass-stained tennis shoes to the opera or rent a tuxedo or a diamond tiara for a trip to the laundromat. Your word choice is probably similarly appropriate. For instance, you would not greet a prospective employer with "Yo!" or a casual acquaintance with "Good afternoon, ma'am." Already, then, you have practice in exercising good judgment in word choice. This chapter helps you to fine-tune that judgment and to recognize categories of word choice that are generally not appropriate for college writing: slang, clichés, wordiness, and pretentious writing.

Slang

People enjoy using **slang** because it is informal, up-to-the-minute, and fun. Just as a common language is a bond among those who speak it, so is slang a bond among the members of the groups who use it. Yet the very things that make slang appealing in conversation make it unsuitable for writing to a broad audience. Writing requires a common language and is usually more formal than conversation. In addition, no writer wants to use words that may be out of date if an audience reads them years later. Slang expressions such as *the bee's knees, hunky-dory,* and *daddy-o* may have sounded up-to-the-minute decades ago, but now they are relics of another time.

Group Exercise 1 Discussing Slang Terms

Form small groups. Try to include both sexes and as many different ages and ethnic groups as possible. Each group member should write down five slang terms and then share the list with other group members. Are some of the terms different? (The more diverse the group, the more likely that it will generate a variety of slang.) Are there any slang expressions that not all group members are familiar with? What conclusions can the group draw about the use of slang? Choose one spokesperson to report the group's findings, along with a few of the most interesting slang terms, to the class.

PRACTICE 1 AVOIDING SLANG EXPRESSIONS

Underline the two slang expressions in each sentence; then substitute more traditional word choices.

1. I decided that Vincent van Gogh was a few sandwiches short of a picnic, especially after I read that the dude had cut off his own ear.

____

____

2. Raymond was supposed to take an exam yesterday, but he blew it off so he could catch a few z's.

____

____

3. Allison bombed her last test because she never hit the books.

____

____

4. We were hyper about the exam, but the professor told us to chill.

____

____

5. Sam needed to study, but instead he was zoned out in front of the tube all evening.

____

____

Clichés

While slang is fresh and new, **clichés** are expressions used so often for so long that they have become worn out. The cliché *burn the midnight oil,* for instance, is a relic of a time when working until midnight meant lighting an oil lamp. Because they are easy to remember and widely used, clichés are often the first expressions that come to mind. It takes a deliberate effort to recognize them and eliminate them from your writing. Look at the following list of clichés. Can you think of others?

a heart of gold	cream of the crop	handwriting on the wall
apple of my eye	dead as a doornail	happy as a clam
at the drop of a hat	eat like a bird	on thin ice
burn the midnight oil	fit as a fiddle	sick as a dog

PRACTICE 2 AVOIDING CLICHÉS

Underline the two clichés in each sentence; then rewrite the sentence to eliminate the clichés.

1. Some older people become sick or depressed, but my grandmother is fit as a fiddle and happy as a clam.

____

____

2. Sara eats like a horse, but she is still as thin as a rail.

____

____

3. I heard that Mrs. Jones was as sick as a dog and probably not long for this world.

____

____

4. When office gossip landed Kerry in hot water with her boss, she decided to take the bull by the horns.

5. Preston has been on thin ice at work for some time now, and if you ask me, the handwriting is on the wall.

Wordiness

Wordiness sometimes happens when writers do not take the time to be concise. The shortest and simplest way of expressing an idea is usually the best way.

The words and phrases below contribute to wordiness and can usually be omitted:

basically	~~basically~~ performs no function in most sentences
definitely	is ~~definitely~~ a space-waster
in my opinion	usually weakens a sentence ~~in my opinion~~
the fact is that	~~The fact is that~~ facts, like opinions, can usually be stated without preamble
totally	usually ~~totally~~ unnecessary
very	can ~~very~~ often be omitted

The phrases below are wordy and can usually be shortened and strengthened.

Wordy	Concise
at the present time	now, today
due to the fact that	because, since
for the reason that	because, since
in point of fact	in fact
in today's society	today
long in length	long

Examples

✗ The course was *definitely* a good introduction to the *basic fundamentals* of algebra.

✓ The course was a good introduction to the fundamentals of algebra.

✗ *Due to the fact that* we are understaffed *at the present time,* Linda has a good chance of being hired.

✓ Since we are understaffed, Linda has a good chance of being hired.

PRACTICE 3 ELIMINATING WORDINESS

Rewrite the sentences to eliminate wordiness.

1. During the solar eclipse of the sun, the light outside seemed blue in color.

   ____

2. James counted the amount of money he had on his person, and it totaled to a sum of eight dollars.

   ____

3. The form basically asked us to list the annual salary that we receive each year.

   ____

4. In point of fact, the key to success in today's society is a good education.

   ____

5. I found it hard to get up at six A.M. in the morning due to the fact that I had studied until midnight.

   ____

Pretentious Writing

Wordy and pretentious writing are two separate problems, but they often go hand in hand. **Pretentious writing** occurs when writers try to impress by using many words where one would do or by using a long word where a short one would serve better. Few words are pretentious in every context, but if the language seems too elevated or too technical for the situation, the writer is probably showing off. Good writers choose words not for their length but for their precision and appropriateness. In other words, good writers use words to clarify rather than to confuse.

Examples

✘ Due to the fact that Kim has minimized her physical energy output of late, she has observed a considerable increase in poundage.

✔ Because Kim has not been exercising lately, she has gained weight.

✘ There is no location that is quite comparable to one's own domicile.

✔ There's no place like home.

Practice 4 Eliminating Pretentious Writing

Rewrite the sentences to eliminate pretentious writing.

1. Due to the fact that precipitation was anticipated, I took the precaution of bringing my umbrella.

____

____

2. I endeavored to contact Andrea yesterday, but to no avail.

____

____

3. Joe scrutinized his timepiece and concluded that he would not be punctual in his arrival to class.

____

____

4. When we were youths, Paco and I resided in the same neighborhood. We have enjoyed an amicable interpersonal relationship ever since.

____

____

5. The automobile sales representative asked Leon if he was prepared to affix his signature to a contractual agreement.

____

____

Group Exercise 2 **Confident? Go solo!**

In small groups, "translate" the following sentences, written here for you in both slang and pretentious language. Then rewrite the same thought in clear, concise language.

Sentence Group 1

Slang: The driver of the car was busted by the fuzz because he was wasted.

Pretentious writing: The driver's obvious inebriation caused him to be detained and incarcerated by officers of the law.

Your revision: ____

____

Sentence Group 2

Slang: I know I can blow this test away if I hit the books and burn the midnight oil.

Pretentious writing: Doubtless, application of fundamental study techniques for a protracted interval of time will produce the desired result of successful completion of the examination.

Your revision: ____

____

Sentence Group 3

Slang: I could really dig some new threads, but I have maxed out my plastic.

Pretentious writing: I long to attire myself in the latest styles, but I find myself in the unfortunate circumstance of having strained my current line of credit to the utmost.

Your revision: ____

____

Sentence Group 4

Slang: The dude will be fired if he doesn't quit copping an attitude around the higher-ups.

Pretentious writing: The individual in question will find himself among the unemployed unless he can cease behaving in an insolent manner while in the presence of persons in positions of authority.

Your revision: ____

____

Sentence Group 5

Slang: It's beyond me how my kid's preschool teacher keeps it together with all those rug rats raising a ruckus.

Pretentious writing: It is difficult to fathom how my offspring's preschool teacher maintains her mental equilibrium in the face of the pandemonium created daily by her young charges.

Your revision: ______________________________

____

Review Exercises

Complete the Review Exercises to see how well you have learned the skills addressed in this chapter. As you work through the exercises, go back through the chapter to review any of the rules you do not understand completely.

Review Exercise 1

In the blank, indicate whether the italicized expressions are slang, clichés, wordiness, or pretentious writing. Then rewrite the sentence to correct the problem in word choice.

__________ **1.** Jessica *dined upon a sumptuous repast* of microwaved ramen noodles.

____

____

__________ **2.** Janice said her boss would *go ballistic* if she came in late for work.

____

____

__________ **3.** Ahmed *kept his nose to the grindstone* and finally finished his term paper.

____

____

_____ **4.** Paulo was sorry he could not come with us, but he had *prearranged plans that he had made at an earlier time.*

_____

_____

_____ **5.** *In conclusion, I would like to sum up by saying that* having a semi-pro baseball team will benefit the city in several ways.

_____

_____

_____ **6.** Professor Smith was *as pleased as punch* with the grades on the last exam.

_____

_____

_____ **7.** By the time I left class, I was *as hungry as a bear.*

_____

_____

_____ **8.** After the guests *scarfed up* all the food, they went home.

_____

_____

_____ **9.** A scrawny cat *reposed upon* the lid of a garbage can.

_____

_____

_____ **10.** Grover Cleveland was born in 1837, served two terms as president, and *kicked the bucket* in 1908.

_____

_____

Review Exercise 2

Underline and correct the two word choice problems in each sentence below.

1. We all thought Harold was as guilty as sin, but he swore he was innocent as a lamb.

____

____

2. I hit the sack early last night, and almost before my head hit the pillow, I was sawing logs.

____

____

3. When the sound of a heartbeat persists in continuing, the narrator of "The Tell-Tale Heart" is definitely unnerved.

____

____

4. John wishes to obtain gainful employment to optimize his cash-flow situation.

____

____

5. Lorenzo bought a pair of really cool shades at the mall, and he paid big bucks for them, too.

____

____

Review Exercise 3

Some slang expressions have alternate meanings that are not slang. For each of the sentence pairs in the exercise, choose the expression from the list below that fits both sentences in the pair. Then write the slang meaning of the expression and the standard meaning of the expression in the blanks provided.

bag	cool	gross	ticked off
bug	crash	shaft	toast
bust	freak		

1. Sentence pair 1

   a. Sarah was really ______________ when she found out she hadn't made the basketball team.

   b. As the students filed into the exam room, the proctor checked his roster and ______________ each name.

   Slang meaning: ____

   Standard meaning: ____

2. Sentence pair 2

   a. "I am calling to report an error," said Mr. Sneed. "Not a ______________ error, but an error nevertheless. I ordered a ______________ of pencils, but I counted them twice, and one is missing. There are only 143 in the box."

   b. "I don't know what that was that the dining hall served for lunch," said Steve, "but it was so ______________ I couldn't eat it."

   Slang meaning: ______________________________

   Standard meaning 1: ______________________________

   Standard meaning 2: ______________________________

3. Sentence pair 3

   a. Kim's parents were horrified by her tattoo, but Kim thought it was ______________.

   b. At this time of year, days are warm but nights are ______________.

   Slang meaning: ______________________________

   Standard meaning: ______________________________

4. Sentence pair 4

   a. One of these days the campus police are going to ______________ me for parking in the faculty lot.

   b. On the piano a folder of sheet music lay next to a ______________ of Mozart.

   Slang meaning: ______________________________

   Standard meaning: ______________________________

5. Sentence pair 5

   a. When Elaine woke up, she realized she had slept through her alarm. "I'm late for work," she moaned. "I'm ______________."

   b. When Elaine looked in the cabinet, she saw that she was out of cereal. "I'll have ______________," she decided.

   Slang meaning: ______________________________

   Standard meaning: ______________________________

6. Sentence pair 6

   a. Marina yawned as she got up from the couch. "It's late," she said. "I'm going to ______________."

   b. Edgar screamed as the car hurtled toward a stand of trees, "Look out!" he yelled. "We're going to ______________!"

   Slang meaning: ____

   Standard meaning: ____

7. Sentence pair 7

   a. The young woman carried a large canvas tote that said "Art is my ______________."

   b. The cashier asked Paul if he wanted his groceries in a paper or plastic ______________.

   Slang meaning: ____

   Standard meaning: ____

8. Sentence pair 8

   a. The children were warned repeatedly not to go near the old mine ______________ .

   b. After his divorce, Earl went down to the honky-tonk, ordered a root beer, and stood by the jukebox playing his favorite country song, "She Got the Gold Mine, I Got the ______________."

   Slang meaning: ____

   Standard meaning: ____

9. Sentence pair 9

   a. Unexpectedly in early April, a ______________ snow-storm blanketed the area.

   b. "All of a sudden Amy started yelling and throwing things," said Jonathan. "I knew she was angry, but I never expected her to ______________."

   Slang meaning: ____

   Standard meaning: ____

10. Sentence pair 10

a. "I'm trying to watch this program," Elena told her little brother. "Don't _____________ me."

b. Under a picture of a giant cockroach, the caption on the billboard read, "See a _____________? Call Rid-a-Pest."

Slang meaning: ______________________________

Standard meaning: ______________________________

Review Exercise 4

Rewrite the sentences below to correct word choice problems.

1. It was the unanimous consensus of all the members that the club should not meet the Wednesday before Thanksgiving, so the meeting was postponed until a later time.

____

____

2. Later this evening, I shall avail myself of the dormitory's convenient laundry facilities.

____

____

3. Brian says he got ripped off by the car dealership when he bought his first car. Now he wishes he hadn't been so clueless.

____

____

4. Due to the fact that he has not learned his way around campus, Louis is basically late for every class.

____

____

5. When my little brother rubs me the wrong way, I just tell him to take a hike.

____

____

Review Exercise 5

Correct the ten errors in word choice in the letter below.

Dear Mom and Dad,

[1]I was really bummed out to hear that Dad sprained his ankle. [2]Dad, I hope by now you are fit as a fiddle. [3]I am battling a cold—I took some cold capsules, but the nostrum failed to effect a cure.

[4]The earthquake we had the other day was just a mild tremor, but everyone was running around like chickens with their heads cut off. [5]However, we all came through the ordeal unscathed. [6]Some people actually slept through the quake, but they were few in number.

[7]I was reading the local rag the other day and saw an article about the company where you work, Mom. [8]The article said the company is raking in the dough since it changed its marketing strategy. [9]Let me say prior to concluding this letter that I was proud to know you were behind that strategy.

[10]Right now it's dullsville around here, but I'll write more when I have news.

Love,

Sam

30 Words Commonly Confused

```
Bob—
Just a quick e-mail too say thanks for
you're advise to use a spelling checker
on my last essay. Its a relief to know
I have less errors and that I won't
loose points for poor spelling.
                         Kim
P.S. I ran this through the spelling
checker, to. Can you tell?
```

Although Kim's e-mail has no misspelled words, it contains several errors involving words that are commonly confused. This chapter helps you to avoid the kinds of errors that Kim has made—errors that a spelling checker cannot catch.

Words Commonly Confused

a, an The article *a* is used before consonant sounds. The article *an* is used before vowel sounds.

> **a** cat, **a** sandy beach, **a** widely held opinion; **an** advanced class, **an** egg, **an** ostrich.

But you must base your choice on the consonant or vowel *sound.* Some words, such as those beginning with a silent *h* or with a *u* that is pronounced like *y,* require careful treatment. If the *h* is silent, *an* is used—**an** honor, but **a** house. If a *u* is pronounced like the consonant *y,* the word is preceded by *a*—**a** used car but **an** uncle.

✔ In the music store, Bob looked at **a** guitar, **a** used snare drum, **a** ukulele, and **a** harmonica. As he waited for **a** salesclerk, he saw **a** customer—obviously not **an** honest person—steal **a** guitar pick. Bob wondered if he should alert **an** employee, but the thief quickly moved to **an** exit and left the store.

accept, except To *accept* is to take or believe; the word *except* means *but* or *with the exception of.*

✔ I cannot **accept** your excuse; everyone **except** you has finished the project.

advice, advise *Advice* is a noun; one gives advice or asks for it. *Advise* is the verb form; one person *advises* another.

✔ I needed some **advice** about fertilizer, so I asked Tim to **advise** me.

affect, effect *Affect* is the verb form. It means *alter* or *influence. Effect* is the noun form. It means *result.*

✔ Will the weather **affect** the turnout for the concert?

✔ The **effect** of the tornado was devastating.

all right, ~~alright~~ *All right* is the only correct spelling. It is never all right to write *alright.*

✔ Tina said that the change in the schedule was **all right** with her.

alone, along To be *alone* is to be by yourself. If someone else is *along,* you aren't alone.

✔ I didn't want to be **alone,** so I took my dog Beebo **along.**

a lot, ~~alot,~~ allot *A lot* is always written as two words, never *alot.* When you mean *much* or *many,* it's considered better form to use a word such as *much, many, several,* or a specific amount instead of *a lot.* The word *allot* means to *allow* or *set aside* for a special purpose: *The Student Affairs Committee allotted two thousand dollars to the college's debate team.*

✔ **acceptable:** Vicki's grandmother has several old Barbie dolls that are worth **a lot** of money.

✔ **better:** Vicki's grandmother has several old Barbie dolls that are worth **over a hundred dollars each.**

among, between *Among* is used with three or more persons or things; *between* is used with two.

✔ Chadrick found it easy to choose **among** the cars on the lot, but he found it difficult to choose **between** a lease option and a purchase agreement.

breath, breathe *Breath* is the noun form: A person can take a breath or be out of breath. *Breathe* is the verb form: Someone may *breathe* heavily after exercising.

✔ "Please don't **breathe** on me," said Amelia, "you have morning **breath.**"

by, buy *By* means *beside* or *through. Buy* means *to purchase.*

✔ Nick said he was going **by** the store because he needed to **buy** some cat food.

feel, fill *Feel* means to touch or to experience emotions. Some writers confuse it with *fill, to make full.*

✔ I **feel** there are better ways to **fill** my time than to watch television.

fewer, less Use *fewer* when writing about something you can count; *less* if you would measure it in some other way. Specifically, if you could put a number in front of a word (five acres), use *fewer.* If you cannot put a number in front of a word (~~five~~ land), use *less.* You would write *fewer* rocks but *less* sand, *fewer* cookies but *less* flour.

✔ Because Raj is working **fewer** hours, he is making **less** money.

good, well *Good* is an adjective that answers the question "What kind?" *Well* is an adverb that answers the question "How?" or "In what manner?" Therefore, a person writes a *good* essay. (*Good* answers the question, "What kind of essay?") But he writes it *well.* (*Well* answers the question, "How did he write it?")

✔ Jennifer is a **good** student, but she did not do **well** on the last test.

himself, ~~hisself~~ The word is always *himself,* never *hisself.*

✔ Phillipe congratulated **himself** for getting a good deal on the used washer.

its, it's *Its* is the possessive pronoun. *It's* always means *it is* or *it has.*

✔ The old sofa has served **its** purpose, but **it's** time to get a new one.

knew, new *Knew* is the past tense of *know; new* means *not old.*

✔ Frances **knew** it would be costly to fix her old television, so she decided to do without until she could afford a **new** one.

know, no *Know* means *to understand; no* means *not any* or the opposite of *yes.*

✔ "Rex does not **know** what '**no**' means," said Rita as her dog chewed the sofa.

loose, lose *Loose* is the opposite of *tight; lose* is the opposite of *find.*

✔ Anthony's watch was so **loose** that he was afraid he would **lose** it.

obtain, attain To *obtain* is *to get* or *to acquire.* To *attain* is *to reach.* A person *obtains* an education but *attains* a goal.

✔ **Obtaining** a job in the field of genetic engineering is a goal Mai has always hoped to **attain.**

past, passed *Past* means *beyond* or *before now. Passed* means *went by.*

✔ "In the **past,** I might have **passed** that car," said Elise, "but now I'm a more cautious driver."

peace, piece *Peace* means *calm* or *tranquility; piece* means a *part.*

✔ Kendra knew she would get no **peace** until she gave Trinket a **piece** of her hamburger.

plain, plane *Plain* refers to flat land or means *clear* or *unadorned. Plane* is a form of air transportation, a carpenter's tool, or a geometric surface.

✔ It's **plain** that Kendall is afraid to travel by **plane.**

principal, principle *Principal* means *chief* (*principal* reason) or *a person in charge of a school* (*principal* of Westmore High). A *principle* is a policy or a rule.

✔ Al's **principal** purpose in life is to make money, and he does not mind sacrificing his **principles** to do it.

✔ The school's **principal** tries to set a good example for her students.

quit, quite, quiet To *quit* is to stop. *Quite* means *very,* and *quiet* means *hushed.*

✔ "Please be **quiet,**" Cliff whispered to his son. "I will be **quite** angry if you don't **quit** making noise in church."

regardless, ~~irregardless~~ Regardless of the number of times you may have seen it, *irregardless* is not a word. The word is *regardless.*

✔ **Regardless** of her doctor's warnings, Hazel plans to fly to Tucson for her granddaughter's graduation.

themselves, ~~themself~~, ~~theirself~~, ~~theirselves~~ The word is always *themselves.*

✔ After they painted the living room, Bettina and Tom decided to give **themselves** a day off.

then, than *Then* is used to show time or cause and effect; *than* is used to compare.

✔ Call me tomorrow; by **then** I will have an answer.

✔ If rainfall is not sufficient, **then** crops will be poor.

✔ Fat takes up more space **than** muscle because it is less dense.

there, their, they're *There* is used to mean *in that place* or to start a sentence or clause. *Their* means *belonging to them,* and *they're* means *they are.*

✔ "**They're** here already!" Kim yelled as her aunt and uncle pulled into the driveway.

✔ "**There** are fewer insects in Wisconsin," said Sal, who had lived **there.**

✔ "I need to take Freon and Chill to the vet; **their** vaccinations are due," said Stacy.

through, threw *Through* means *within, between,* or *finished. Threw* is the past tense of the verb *throw.*

✔ After they were **through** with their picnic, they **threw** their paper plates and napkins in a nearby trash can and went on a stroll **through** the park.

two, too, to *Two* refers to the number two; *too* means *also* or indicates an excessive amount. Any other use requires *to.*

✔ Alfredo said he wanted **to** go **to** the beach **too,** but I told him we had **too** many people unless someone else agreed **to** drive so that we could take **two** cars.

weather, whether, rather *Weather* includes natural phenomena such as temperature, rainfall, and wind velocity. *Whether* indicates the existence of two possibilities and is often paired with *or not. Rather* indicates a preference.

✔ The **weather** was too cold for our picnic on the beach.

✔ Tahia is not sure **whether** to take a computer course or a biology course.

✔ Would you **rather** eat barbecue at Lee and Eddie's or Satterfield's?

where, were *Where* rhymes with *air* and refers to *place. Were* rhymes with *fur* and is a past tense form of the verb *to be.*

✔ When you did not answer the phone, I wondered **where** you **were.**

Review Exercises

Complete the Review Exercises to see how well you have learned the skills addressed in this chapter. As you work through the exercises, go back through the chapter to review any of the rules you do not understand completely.

Review Exercise 1

Refer to the explanations in this chapter to choose the correct word from each of the pairs in the following sentences. Underline the correct choice.

1. There was (a, an) editorial in this morning's paper that I found (quite, quiet) interesting.

2. Giselle asked Marc (rather, whether) he would prefer to stay home or go (alone, along) with her.
3. Although she went (threw, through) all her desk drawers, Kim could not find the report or remember (were, where) she had put it.
4. "My ex-husband should be ashamed of (himself, hisself) for getting so far behind on child support," said Laurie. "I can't even afford to (buy, by) the children new school clothes."
5. The new homes (were, where) attractively priced but had only (too, to, two) bedrooms.

Review Exercise 2

Refer to the explanations in this chapter to choose the correct word from each of the pairs in the following sentences. Underline the correct choice.

1. Alfred said that all he wanted was a little (piece, peace) and (quite, quiet).
2. "I'll be (alright, all right) when I catch my (breath, breathe)," said Jay.
3. When his painting did not win (a, an) award at the art show, Henri remarked, "I was just born to (loose, lose)."
4. Everyone (except, accept) Sanders made it (through, threw) the obstacle course.
5. "I would not (advice, advise) traveling by (plain, plane) during the month of August," the fortuneteller told Paige.

Review Exercise 3

Find and correct the two word choice errors in each of the numbered items below.

1. Marie found it hard to choose between the seventeen books on the life of Emily Dickinson. "If there were less books it would be an easier choice," she said.

   ____

   ____

2. "I don't think computers will ever be smarter then humans," said Jeff. "A computer is just a adding machine with a few extra features."

   ____

   ____

3. "Ms. Jordan said I did good on the test," said Vernell. "She also said that hard work would help me obtain my goals."

4. After saving all year, Milton and Deloris treated theirselves too a trip to Disney World.

5. "I am trying to get more exercise and consume less calories," said Willie. "I fill a lot more energetic, too."

Review Exercise 4

Find and correct the two word choice errors in each of the numbered items below.

1. Michelle new that a lie would get her out of working late. However, she decided to stick to her principals.

2. Eric's hamster got out of it's cage last night. He wondered weather his mother would be angry that it had gotten loose.

3. Stan said he couldn't except Rachel's resignation while tempers were running high. "Think about it tonight, and then tell me how you fill," he said.

4. Andrew said that their were less people at the concert than he had expected to see.

5. As she turned to look at the clock, Althea saw that ten minutes had past while she had been standing in line. "I new I should not have come to the post office on my lunch hour," she thought.

Review Exercise 5

Correct the word choice error in each sentence of the paragraph below.

[1]When I was a child, my parents took my sister and me too the circus. [2]I can remember walking threw the flaps of a large circus tent and sitting on tiered bleachers around a center ring. [3]The circus began with clowns on bicycles circling the ring, waving at the crowd, and tooting their bicycle horns as they past. [4]They were followed by tumblers who flipped and rolled across the ring and a contortionist who twisted herself into pretzel shapes and did everything accept turn herself inside out. [5]Next came a beautiful woman in a spangled bodysuit standing on the back of a elephant. [6]Finally, the ringmaster called for complete quite for the dangerous trapeze act, performed without a net. [7]No one in the audience seemed to breath as the trapeze artists, a man and a woman, began to swing in wider and wider arcs above the heads of the audience. [8]The woman launched herself into the air, were she seemed to hang suspended, arms outstretched for her partner. [9]Then, with a smack that I could hear in the hushed air, they firmly caught one another buy the wrists. [10]As I left the circus that day, I remember telling my parents that I wanted to go their again soon.

31 Capital Letters

i LOv yOu
mOM!!!!
MaX
AgE 4

When you learned to print your first awkward letters as a child, you slowly began to learn the rules of capitalization. You learned to capitalize your own name, the first letter of a sentence, and the pronoun *I*. This chapter reviews these fundamentals as well as many of the fine points of capitalization.

Capital Letters to Begin Sentences

Capitalize the first word of a sentence or a direct quotation.

Examples

The woman told a reporter that she was walking down the street when a cat fell on her head.

In some places, snow tires are a necessity.

Martino said, "I hope you remembered to mail the birthday card to Dad."

Capitalization of Words Referring to Individuals

Names and the Pronoun *I*

Capitalize people's names and the pronoun *I*.

Examples

I heard that James Maldonado made the hockey team.

Mr. Benton, the music professor, told Khadijah that she had a musical-sounding name.

Family Relationships

Family Designations Used in Place of a Name

Capitalize a word that designates a family relationship if it is used in place of a name. To make sure that the word is used as a name, try substituting a name for the word. If it is used as a name, the substitution will sound natural.

Examples

✔ I drove Mother to her doctor's appointment.

I drove ~~Mother~~ Ella Satterfield to her doctor's appointment.

"I drove Ella Satterfield to her doctor's appointment" sounds natural, so the capitalization of *Mother* is correct.

Try your own substitution in the next sentence. If substituting a name for *Grandpa* sounds natural, the capitalization is correct.

"I will not retire," Grandpa said, "because I'd rather wear out than rust out."

Family Designations Used with Possessives and Articles

No capital letter is used when family designations such as father, mother, or great-uncle Elmo are preceded by a possessive pronoun (*my, her, his, their*), a possessive noun (*Ted's, Penny's*), or an article (*a, an,* or *the*). For additional proof, try directly substituting a name for the family designation. It will sound awkward.

Examples

✔ My grandmother manages an income tax preparation business.

My ~~grandmother~~ Sally Lewis manages an income tax preparation business.

"My Sally Lewis" does not sound natural, confirming that the word *grandmother* need not be capitalized.

✔ I took my mother to her doctor's appointment.

In this sentence, substituting a name does not work. "I took my Ella Satterfield to her doctor's appointment" sounds awkward.

Professional Titles

Do not capitalize professional titles unless they are used immediately before a name.

Examples

Harold Smith is my family *doctor*.

I took the children to *Dr*. Harold Smith for their vaccinations.

Antoinette Wheatley is my American history *professor*.

I am taking American history with *Professor* Antoinette Wheatley.

PRACTICE 1 CAPITALIZING WORDS REFERRING TO INDIVIDUALS

Correct the two capitalization mistakes in each sentence.

1. aunt Florence said Timothy was brave when the Doctor gave him his shots.

   ____________________ ____________________

2. My Grandmother said, "be careful what you wish for; you might get it."

   ____________________ ____________________

3. Sam and elaine are going to take professor Edith Cartwright's drama class next fall.

   ____________________ ____________________

4. Aunt Phoebe told uncle Bill that my Grandmother was losing her memory.

   ____________________ ____________________

5. Mrs. harris called her City Council Representative and said, "Please, Councilwoman Jones, can't you do something about the potholes in Broad Street?"

__________________ __________________

Capitalization of Words Referring to Groups

Religions, Geographic Locations, Races, and Nationalities

Capitalize words that refer to specific religions, geographic locations, races, and nationalities.

Examples

People who consider themselves multiracial may have trouble filling out a form that asks if they are Asian, Caucasian, African American, Hispanic, or Native American.

Though Ilsa is originally from Denmark, she considers herself a New Yorker. She collects African art, drinks Irish whiskey, and drives a German car.

Ann was brought up as a Catholic, but she now considers herself a Buddhist.

Organizations, Businesses, and Agencies

Capitalize specific names of organizations, businesses, and government agencies.

Examples

Haley belongs to the Spanish Club, Phi Beta Kappa, and the Association of Engineering Students.

Sam works at the Criterion Corporation, and his wife works at IBM.

After Ami graduates, she wants to work for the Internal Revenue Service.

Do not capitalize nonspecific or generic organization names.

Examples

Cliff is active in the church and is also a member of the choir.

As a top executive in a large corporation, Ms. Simmons often travels on the company plane.

After Ami graduates, she wants to work for the government.

PRACTICE 2 CAPITALIZING WORDS REFERRING TO GROUPS

Correct the two capitalization mistakes in each sentence below.

1. Talisha hopes her Government job at the bureau of alcohol, tobacco, and firearms will not be affected by budget cuts.

   ____

2. The funds raised by shriners go to the scottish rite children's hospital.

   ____

3. When he began working for general motors, Allan joined the Union.

   ____

4. Some of the faculty at the College belong to the american association of university professors.

   ____

5. Our Company buys its paper and office supplies from office depot.

   ____

Capitalization of Words Referring to Time and Place

Dates, Days, Holidays, and Seasons

Capitalize months of the year, days of the week, and names of holidays.

Examples

Memorial Day is officially celebrated on the last Monday in May.

Christmas, Hanukkah, and Kwanzaa all fall in December.

Do not capitalize the names of the four seasons.

Marcy wants to do some spring cleaning before her children get out of school for the summer.

Place Names

Capitalize *specific* place names.

Examples

On our trip to Atlanta, we visited Six Flags Over Georgia, the High Museum of Art, and Ebenezer Baptist Church, where Dr. Martin Luther King, Jr., preached.

We also saw a show at the Fox Theater and took in a Braves game at Turner Field.

Starla said that when her little sister graduates from Westside High School, she plans to attend Spelman College.

The robber ran out of the First National Bank and tore down State Street.

Do not capitalize *general, nonspecific* place names.

On our trip to Atlanta, we visited an amusement park, an art museum, and the historic church where Dr. Martin Luther King, Jr., preached.

We also saw a show at a theater and took in a Braves game at the stadium.

Starla said that when her little sister graduates from high school, she plans to attend college.

The robber ran out of the bank and tore down the street.

Compass Points

Do not capitalize compass points unless they refer to a specific geographical area.

Examples

Head east on Eisenhower Parkway; then take Interstate 75 north until you reach Exit 255.

Having lived on the West Coast all his life, Doug found it hard to adjust to the heat of the South.

PRACTICE 3 CAPITALIZING WORDS REFERRING TO TIME AND PLACE

Correct the two capitalization mistakes in each sentence below.

1. When we visited Washington, D.C., we visited the Lincoln Memorial, the white house, and other Historic Places.

   ______________ ______________

2. If a person is at the exact center of the north pole, can he move without going South?

   ______________ ______________

3. People living in new mexico sometimes have trouble convincing people that they live in the united states.

   ______________ ______________

4. When he visited his old High School, Ed was shocked to realize that the Principal was younger than he was.

   ______________ ______________

5. The state of west Virginia is known for its beautiful blue ridge mountains.

   ______________ ______________

Capitalization of Words Referring to Things and Activities

School Subjects

Do not capitalize subjects studied in school unless they are part of a specific course title.

Examples

Diego is taking history, English, and biology this term.

Diego is taking History 2212, English 1151, and Biology 2202 this term.

Diego is taking World Civilization, Introduction to Poetry, and Principles of Biology this term.

Titles

Capitalize titles of novels, short stories, poems, newspapers, magazines, articles, works of art, television shows, movies, and songs and other musical works. There are exceptions to many rules in English, and this rule has more exceptions than most. Some newspapers and journals capitalize only the first word in the title of an article. Some writers, like e. e. cummings, do not follow the conventional rules of capitalization. In general, when you write about an article, a poem, or any other piece of writing, preserve the title as it was published.

Otherwise, follow these rules: Capitalize the first word of a title. Do not capitalize articles (*a, an, the*) or short prepositions (*to, of, from,* and similar short prepositions) unless they are the first word in a title. Capitalize all other words.

Examples

Hoshiko read an article in *Archaeology* called "Faces from the Past."

The class read *Hamlet* and *Death of a Salesman.*

Andre wrote his paper on "The Weary Blues" by Langston Hughes and "kitchenette building" by Gwendolyn Brooks. (In this example, Gwendolyn Brooks's title has been written just as it was published.)

With at least three more hours to drive, Fay and Lamar regretted having taught their children the words to "It's a Small World."

Consumer Products

For consumer products, capitalize the brand name but not the general product name. Often, the general product name is omitted.

Examples

My mother always washes her clothes with Tide detergent and Downy fabric softener.

My mother always washes her clothes with Tide and Downy.

A Nissan broke down in front of the drive-through at Wendy's.

Abbreviations

Capitalize some common abbreviations. Abbreviations of organizations, corporations, and professional designations are capitalized. Some examples include NBC, AFL-CIO, FBI, NAACP, CIA, UPS, C.P.A., M.D., Ph.D., D.D.S. The disease AIDS is always written in all capitals.

PRACTICE 4 CAPITALIZING WORDS REFERRING TO THINGS AND ACTIVITIES

Correct the two capitalization mistakes in each sentence below.

1. At Seaside Snacks, we ordered two diet cokes and two bags of fritos.

   ______________ ______________

2. Monica opened a can of friskies cat food and a can of bumble bee tuna, but her finicky cat refused them both.

   ______________ ______________

3. Andy reads the new york times or watches nbc to get the latest news.

   ______________ ______________

4. Since she was out of Folger's Coffee, Edna decided to have some Lipton Tea.

   ______________ ______________

5. The article in time was called "cartoons are no laughing matter."

   ______________ ______________

Review Exercises

Complete the Review Exercises to see how well you have learned the skills addressed in this chapter. As you work through the exercises, go back through the chapter to review any of the rules you do not understand completely.

REVIEW EXERCISE 1

Correct the two capitalization mistakes in each sentence below.

1. Valerie used to buy her children's clothes at wal-mart, but now the kids think they need expensive tommy hilfiger clothing.

   ______________ ______________

2. Samantha told her Mother that she liked only green giant vegetables.

_______________ _______________

3. Santa claus sat in the middle of the shopping mall, calling out, "ho, ho, ho!" to passing children.

_______________ _______________

4. I went to High School with Andrew, but I did not know he had gone to work for the fbi.

_______________ _______________

5. Ms. Chatfield warned the girl scout troop, "never get in a car with anyone you don't know."

_______________ _______________

Review Exercise 2

Correct the two capitalization mistakes in each sentence below.

1. Trey enjoys watching elmer fudd and bugs bunny on television.

_______________ _______________

2. After leaving the town of east point, the bus headed West on Route 27.

_______________ _______________

3. The crowd at three rivers stadium stood to sing "the star-spangled banner."

_______________ _______________

4. As Edward watched reruns of the twilight zone, he munched lay's potato chips.

_______________ _______________

5. Some birds, such as the scarlet tanager, live in north america during the summer and migrate to south america in the winter.

_______________ _______________

Review Exercise 3

Correct the two capitalization mistakes in each sentence below.

1. The bainbridge bass club is sponsoring a fishing tournament at lake seminole.

_______________ _______________

2. The aids support group met at the unitarian universalist church.

__________________ __________________

3. When jimmy tried to buy a pack of camel cigarettes at the convenience store, the clerk asked him for proof of age.

__________________ __________________

4. Anthony Small is President of the local chapter of the afl-cio.

__________________ __________________

5. On the first sunday in march, the Packards will have their family reunion.

__________________ __________________

Review Exercise 4

Correct the twenty capitalization errors (two per sentence) in the paragraph below.

[1]Every morning, my retired neighbor, mrs. grimes, takes a brisk walk down harrison street. [2]In her nikes and her chicago cubs hat, she is a familiar sight to people along her route, which never varies. [3]She walks south toward bob's handi-mart, where she pops in for her morning cup of maxwell house coffee. [4]She chats with hassan, who works the cash register, and buys a copy of the snellville times. [5]Then she walks west down pauldo avenue toward st. luke's church. [6]At the church, her route veers north past the ymca and the little row of shops on milk street. [7]At wet pets, the tropical fish store, she stops to look in the window at the colorful fish and the stacked displays of hartz mountain fish food. [8]Then she walks on past emil's cut and style and baskin-robbins. [9]If she continued north, she would pass woodrow wilson high school and the washington memorial library. [10]instead, she turns back onto harrison street and heads home.

1. ____________________________________

2. ____________________________________

3. ____________________________________

4. ______________________________

5. ______________________________

6. ______________________________

7. ______________________________

8. ______________________________

9. ______________________________

10. ______________________________

32 Apostrophes

The best
apple's
50¢ each

The handmade sign above announces a roadside vendor's stand. The vendor's apples may be the best, but his use of the apostrophe leaves a great deal to be desired. Can you pinpoint the problem? If you can't now, you will be able to by the time you finish this chapter, which outlines the two main uses of apostrophes: to form contractions and to show possession.

Apostrophes in Contractions

Contractions are informal or conversational shortenings of words: *can't* for *cannot, doesn't* for *does not,* and *it's* for *it is* or *it has.* Contractions are used in informal writing but are generally inappropriate for formal or scholarly writing. You will find contractions in some journalistic writing, in some textbooks, in works of fiction, and in informal essays. Contractions are considered inappropriate in reports of academic research and in legal documents. Your instructor will specify the level of formality you should use in your essays and other writings.

To form a contraction, replace omitted letters with a single apostrophe. Close any spaces between words.

Examples

isn't = is not

hasn't = has not

couldn't = could not

don't = do not

won't = will not (an irregular contraction: the i in will changes to an o)

wouldn't = would not

Practice 1 Using Apostrophes in Contractions

Make a contraction of each of the following expressions. Be sure to place an apostrophe where letters are omitted, not in the space between the words.

1. he is ______________
2. I am ______________
3. could not ______________
4. does not ______________
5. she is ______________
6. it is ______________
7. they are ______________
8. I will ______________
9. that is ______________
10. cannot ______________

Practice 2 Using Apostrophes in Contractions

In each sentence below, supply the missing apostrophe in the contraction and write the contraction in the blank provided.

________ **1.** Kwan says shes playing in the soccer tournament next Saturday.

________ **2.** Rodney hasnt heard from either of the firms where he applied.

________ **3.** This isnt the first time Jingles has deposited a dead mouse on the doormat.

________ **4.** Its a cool, cloudy day, perfect for travel.

________ **5.** "After Ive finished my degree," said Philip, "I hope to go on to veterinary school."

________ **6.** "Sorry," said the clerk, "but were out of the nine-grain bread."

________ **7.** "Isnt that the same outfit Professor Smith wore last Tuesday?" whispered the student.

________ **8.** When Karen couldnt find a parking place near her favorite store in the mall, she left.

________ **9.** I have been trying to figure out this math problem for half an hour, so please dont tell me the answer is obvious.

________ **10.** "Wait right here," said James. "Ill be back."

Apostrophes to Show Possession

If you could not use apostrophes to show **possession,** you would have to rely on long, tedious constructions such as "I drove the car of my father to the house of Ray to study for the test of tomorrow," instead of "I drove my father's car to Ray's house to study for tomorrow's test."

Making Nouns Possessive

There are two rules for making nouns possessive.

Rule 1: Add an apostrophe and *s ('s)* to form the possessive of singular nouns and of plurals that do not end in *s.*

Examples

the bowl that belongs to the cat = the *cat's* bowl

the ring of the telephone = the *telephone's* ring

the cover of the book = the *book's* cover

the work of a day = a *day's* work

the vegetable garden belonging to Daphne = *Daphne's* vegetable garden the books that belong to the children = the *children's* books

the office of my boss = my *boss's* office

the boots of Jess = *Jess's* boots

PRACTICE 3 USING APOSTROPHES TO SHOW POSSESSION

Practice rule 1 by converting the ten expressions in the exercise to possessives using *'s*.

1. The flame of the candle = ______________________________
2. The red dress belonging to Cherie = ______________________________
3. the lecture of Professor Ross = ______________________________
4. the tools of the artist = ______________________________
5. the meeting of next month = ______________________________

> * *Grammar Alert!*
>
> When a singular word ends in *s*, it is also acceptable to use an apostrophe alone to make it possessive: *Mr. Jones'* job, *Dickens'* novel, the *boss'* office, the *crabgrass'* rapid growth.

Rule 2: Add an apostrophe (') to form the possessive of plural nouns that end in *s*.

Examples

the cheers of the soccer fans = the *soccer fans'* cheers

the lawn belonging to the Smiths = the *Smiths'* lawn

the aroma of the flowers = the *flowers'* aroma

PRACTICE 4 USING APOSTROPHES TO SHOW POSSESSION

Practice rule 2 by converting the ten expressions in the exercise to possessives using an apostrophe.

1. the names of my uncles = ______________________________
2. the litter box of the cats = ______________________________

3. the exhaustion of the workers = ______________________
4. the salaries of the athletes = ______________________
5. the taste of the cookies = ______________________
6. the demographic makeup of the classes = ______________________
7. the water levels of the lakes = ______________________
8. the disastrous vacation of the Robinsons = ______________________
9. the barking of the neighborhood dogs = ______________________
10. the voices of the speakers = ______________________

PRACTICE 5 USING APOSTROPHES TO SHOW POSSESSION

Convert the ten expressions in the exercise to possessives by adding *'s* or by adding an apostrophe after the *s*.

1. the hum of the air conditioner = ______________________
2. the hands of the clock = ______________________
3. the faces of the students = ______________________
4. the prices of Tire Mart = ______________________
5. the exasperation of Mr. Pless = ______________________
6. the importance of the idea = ______________________
7. the haircuts of the men = ______________________
8. the brilliant idea of Sam Perato = ______________________
9. the itch of the mosquito bites = ______________________
10. the Internet address of IBM = ______________________

Distinguishing Possessives from Simple Plurals

To use apostrophes correctly, it is important to distinguish between possessives and simple plurals. A plural may be followed by a verb, a prepositional phrase, or by nothing at all. Words that show possession will end in *s,* like plurals, but will be immediately followed by something that is being possessed, as in *"Mom's homemade chicken and dumplings"* or the *"horse's mane."*

Possessive (Apostrophe Used)	Plural (No Apostrophe Used)
Amy's computer	computers used in class
a day's work	days in a month
Mother's Day	Mothers Against Drunk Driving
a king's ransom	kings in the seventeenth century
the tornadoes' fury	several tornadoes
the washer's spin cycle	the broken washers

PRACTICE 6 DISTINGUISHING POSSESSIVES FROM PLURALS

In each sentence, underline the noun that ends in *s*. If the noun is possessive, write *possessive* in the blank provided. If the noun is simply a plural, remove the apostrophe and write the corrected plural form in the blank. The first one is done for you.

parents 1. Sometimes I think my parents' are hopelessly old fashioned.

______ 2. The dog's collar looked too tight.

______ 3. The speaker's viewpoint is controversial; therefore, a large turnout is expected.

______ 4. Our debate team and those of several other schools' will be participating.

______ 5. Since no one used them anymore, the typewriters' were placed in storage.

______ 6. Near the window, the sun had faded the carpet's color.

______ 7. The Smith's have lived next door to me for nearly a year.

______ 8. The oldest resident of the neighborhood has lived here for thirty year's.

______ 9. The manatee's body looks heavy and awkward, but it swims easily.

______ 10. For older adults, the benefit's of weight training include improved coordination and stronger muscles and bones.

Possessive Forms of Pronouns

Personal pronouns (*I, we, you, he, she, it,* and *they*) have their own possessive forms that never require an apostrophe. These forms include *my, mine, our, ours, your, yours, his, hers, its, their,* and *theirs.*

Its and *It's*

The pronoun that is the focus of the most confusion is *its.* Since the possessive form of a pronoun never takes an apostrophe, *its* is the possessive form, meaning *belonging to it. It's,* the form with the apostrophe, always means *it is* or *it has.*

Examples

The lawnmower seems to have lost *its* pep.

It's too hot to mow, anyway.

Practice 7 Using *Its* and *It's* Correctly

Underline the correct form of *its* or *it's* in the following sentences.

1. "(Its, It's) evident that you did not study," Professor Tate told the student.
2. The car was new, and (its, it's) owner had parked it in the far end of the parking lot to prevent it from being scratched.
3. That novel has been on the bestseller list for ten weeks, and (its, it's) still number five.
4. The mail truck slowly made (its, it's) way through the neighborhood.
5. Caroline has put off filing her health insurance paperwork, so (its, it's) piling up on her desk.

Proofreading for Apostrophe Errors

Apostrophes Incorrectly Omitted from Possessives

To find apostrophes incorrectly omitted from possessives, check each noun ending in *s* to see if it is followed by something it possesses.

✗ The corner delis roast chicken is the best in town.

Does *roast chicken* belong to *delis?* Yes. But does the apostrophe go before or after the *s?* Look for clues to whether the original word (before it was made possessive) was intended to be singular or plural. The main clue lies in the word best. Only one deli would have the *best* chicken. In addition, the deli is described as *the corner deli,* and there is unlikely to be more than one deli on the corner.

✔ The corner deli's roast chicken is the best in town.

✘ The girls bikes had been left lying in the carport.

Bikes belong to *girls,* but does the apostrophe go before or after the *s?* Since there is more than one bike, there is probably also more than one girl. The word *bikes* also ends in *s.* Does anything belong to *bikes?* No, the word is simply a plural and is correct without an apostrophe.

✔ The girls' bikes had been left lying in the carport.

PRACTICE 8 CORRECTING APOSTROPHE ERRORS

Supply the omitted apostrophes in the following sentences.

1. The cars windshield had been cracked by a grapefruit-sized hailstone.

____

____

2. The judge imposed the maximum sentence because of the thiefs lack of remorse.

____

____

3. The car lots no-haggle prices make it attractive to many potential buyers.

____

____

4. The restaurants atmosphere was pleasing; candles glowed on the tables and the musicians played softly in the background.

____

____

5. The painters said it would take about three days work to finish the exterior of the house.

____

____

Review Exercises

Complete the Review Exercises to see how well you have learned the skills addressed in this chapter. As you work through the exercises, go back through the chapter to review any of the rules you do not understand completely.

Review Exercise 1

Convert the ten expressions in the exercise to possessives using an apostrophe or *'s*.

1. the glare of the lamp = ______________________________
2. the snarl of a wild animal = ______________________________
3. the closing of the stores = ______________________________
4. the pages of the calendar = ______________________________
5. the harpoon belonging to Ed = ______________________________
6. the corona of the sun = ______________________________
7. a vacation of two weeks = ______________________________
8. the opinion of Amelia = ______________________________
9. the daily rounds of the mail carrier = ______________________________
10. the pattern of the curtains = ______________________________

Review Exercise 2

Each of the following sentences has an omitted apostrophe in a contraction or a possessive form. Cross through the error; then, in the blank, write the word with the apostrophe placed correctly.

__________ **1.** Ron couldnt tell which of the twins was Daria.

__________ **2.** The restaurants breakfast menu featured pancakes and waffles.

__________ **3.** An ice pack helps to reduce the swelling in Carolyns sprained ankle.

__________ **4.** The sales of tabloids often depend on their headlines sensationalism.

__________ **5.** Anita sat on a beach towel and stared out at the oceans broad expanse.

__________ **6.** "Salary is important," said Amin. "But its job satisfaction that really matters."

__________ **7.** Memos, notes, and photographs entirely covered the bulletin boards surface.

__________ **8.** The buildings tumbledown appearance made it a neighborhood eyesore.

__________ 9. The vet said that the dogs operation should not be postponed.

__________ 10. Some scientists questioned the two researchers techniques.

Review Exercise 3

Each of the following sentences contains two omitted apostrophes. Cross through the error; then, in the blanks, write the words with the apostrophes placed correctly.

1. Though researchers are uncertain of the role of dreams, having dreams and getting a good nights sleep are important to a persons overall health.

   ____________________ ____________________

2. The nursing homes smoke alarms were checked twice a month for the residents safety.

   ____________________ ____________________

3. The clocks hands seemed to move at a turtles pace.

   ____________________ ____________________

4. The childrens whispers made their parents wonder what mischief was brewing in the youngsters minds.

   ____________________ ____________________

5. "Ive noticed youre not very talkative today," said Kim's mother.

   ____________________ ____________________

Review Exercise 4

Each numbered item contains two omitted apostrophes in a contraction or a possessive form. Cross through the errors; then write the correct form of each word in the blank provided.

1. The coachs enthusiasm fanned the teams desire to win.

   ____________________ ____________________

2. "Its been cool for July," said Mavis. "Usually, the months temperatures are in the nineties by now."

   ____________________ ____________________

3. Sundays newspapers, stacked and bundled for citywide distribution, awaited the carriers arrival.

   ____________________ ____________________

4. The two would-be robbers thought the convenience store was an easy target, but an off-duty police officers vigilance prevented them from carrying out their plans. "Im glad Officer Bell was around," said the owner of the store.

____________________ ____________________

5. Because she didnt want to spill the contents, Daisy held tightly to the watering cans handle.

____________________ ____________________

Review Exercise 5

Correct the ten apostrophe errors in the restaurant review below. Apostrophes may be misplaced, missing, or unnecessary.

[1]Restaurant Review: Leos Seafood House

[2]On Friday nights, theres always a line at Leo's Seafood House, and this past Friday was no exception. [3]The wait was short, however, and once we were seated, I ordered the Catch of the Day—grilled tuna—and my companion ordered the Fishermans Platter. [4]Service was slow, and our salads, a blend of greens topped with tomatoes and croutons, were just a memory by the time the entree's arrived at our table. [5]My companions' Fisherman's Platter was a sizzling delight with its crisply fried shrimp, tender flounder, and butter-drenched scallops. [6]The Catch of the Day, on the other hand, smelled as though it had been left to decay in the hold of a fishing boat while the fishers took two week's vacation. [7]The tuna was crisply grilled, but even a dousing of lemon could not disguise it's fishy flavor. [8]The server was apologetic and didnt mind substituting the more expensive Captain's Feast at no extra charge. [9]Dessert was a deliciously cold raspberry sorbet for me and Banana's Foster for my companion. [10]In spite of slow service and a Catch of the Day that should have been thrown back, its evident that there's a good reason for the lines outside Leo's on Friday nights.

1. ______________________________
2. ______________________________
3. ______________________________
4. ______________________________
5. ______________________________
6. ______________________________
7. ______________________________
8. ______________________________
9. ______________________________
10. ______________________________

33

Quotation Marks, Underlining, and Italics

Academic Shorthand Symbols

1. " "
2. ______________
3. *italics*

Quotation marks, underlining, and italics are visual signals that give a reader information that would otherwise have to be conveyed in words. They say, "Someone is speaking or thinking"; "These words are a title of a long work"; or "These words are the title of a short work." Quotation marks, underlining, and italics are a kind of academic shorthand that enhances your ability to communicate within the academic world.

Quotation Marks to Signal Quotations

Direct Quotations

Quotation marks are used to signal a **direct quotation;** that is, they are placed around the exact words that someone speaks, writes, or thinks. As you look at the following examples, notice that when a comma or period comes at the end of a quotation, it is always placed inside the quotation mark. When a direct question is quoted, the question mark also goes inside the quotation marks.

Examples

"I'll wait for you in front of the fountain," said Paul.

Ann said, "I have so much research to do that I might as well pitch a tent in the library."

The clerk told the customer, "I can't help you now. It's time for my break."

The child asked, "Why don't people have fur?"

"Did you have a good time?" asked Harry.

PRACTICE 1 USING QUOTATION MARKS WITH DIRECT QUOTATIONS

Following the models above, place quotation marks around each of the direct quotations below and add a comma or question mark where needed.

1. I wish it were Friday thought Sandra.

   ____

2. Did we do anything in class yesterday Tim asked the professor.

   ____

3. A sign on the hairstylist's mirror read I'm a beautician, not a magician.

   ____

4. I always read the comics first said Harold.

   ____

5. This milk is expired. I should throw it away said Tom.

   ____

Split Quotations

Some direct quotations are *split quotations*. Below are two rules for splitting quotations.

1. When you split a sentence, use commas to set off the tag (such as *she said*) that tells who said or thought the words you are quoting.

   "If I've missed the bus," thought Alexandra, "I'll have to walk."

2. When there is a complete sentence before and a complete sentence after the tag, put a comma after the first sentence and a period after the tag.

   "There's nothing good on TV," said Rick. "Let's go for a walk around the neighborhood."

PRACTICE 2 Using Quotation Marks with Split Quotations

Following the models above, place quotation marks around each of the direct quotations below and add commas where they are needed.

1. Tonight will be clear with temperatures in the fifties said the meteorologist. Tomorrow, though, we can expect rain.

   ____

   ____

2. The elevator business is just like any other said the technician. It has its ups and downs.

   ____

   ____

3. Because Grandfather hated labels said Emil he always said 'human' when someone asked his race.

   ____

   ____

4. Go directly to jail the Monopoly card read. Do not pass go; do not collect $200.

   ____

   ____

5. For my birthday this year Carlton told his wife I'd like a gift certificate to the car wash.

   ____

   ____

Indirect Quotations

An **indirect quotation** is a paraphrase. It repeats the essence of what a person said, and it may repeat some or all of the words, but it is not a word-for-word quotation. The word *that* is stated or implied before an indirect quotation. Finally, an indirect quotation is not set off by quotation marks.

Examples

Truman said that he had lost his best pen.

Truman said he had lost his best pen.

The two examples above are indirect quotations. They do not repeat Truman's exact words (Truman did not use the words *he* and *his*). The word *that* is stated in the first example and implied in the second. Therefore, no quotation marks are used.

PRACTICE 3 RECOGNIZING DIRECT AND INDIRECT QUOTATIONS

On the line provided, label each quotation direct *(D)* or indirect *(I)*.

_____ 1. Earl said, "I might have gotten a better grade on the test if I had read the book."

_____ 2. Earl said that he might have gotten a better grade on the test if he had read the book.

_____ 3. The customer at table five said she needed extra salad dressing.

_____ 4. The bumper sticker said, "My other car is a piece of junk, too."

_____ 5. "If you are going to the post office," said Ann, "would you mind mailing my package?"

_____ 6. Brittany said, "Here, Mom. I drew this alligator for you at school."

_____ 7. James asked, "How much fertilizer should I feed the fern?"

_____ 8. James asked how much fertilizer he should feed the fern.

_____ 9. The mechanic told me I should have my car's oil changed every 3,000 miles.

_____ 10. Joy said that she could live without television but would be lost without her computer.

PRACTICE 4 RECOGNIZING DIRECT AND INDIRECT QUOTATIONS

On the line provided, label each quotation direct *(D)* or indirect *(I)*.

_____ **1.** The applicant said, "I have experience in both pediatric and geriatric nursing."

_____ **2.** The applicant said she had experience in both pediatric and geriatric nursing.

_____ **3.** The post card read, "Wish you were here in Jamaica."

_____ **4.** Two out of three people surveyed said that the governor was doing a good job.

_____ **5.** Pat said, "I don't care if it is on sale; I save even more by not buying it."

_____ **6.** The article said that people who ate soup before meals consumed fewer calories than those who did not eat soup.

_____ **7.** The child said he knew nothing about the overturned flowerpot.

_____ **8.** "I'm sorry," said Althea, "I let my temper get the best of me."

_____ **9.** "Would you like fries with that?" asked the fast-food clerk.

_____ **10.** The salesperson said that the store had a no-hassle return policy.

Quotation Marks, Underlining, or Italics to Set Off Titles

Quotation marks, underlining, and italics act as academic shorthand to signal a title.

Quotation Marks

Quotation marks set off titles of short works, including chapter titles, essays, episodes of a television series, newspaper and periodical articles, poems, and short stories.

1. Chapter titles: "Revising and Proofreading," "Introducing the Essay"
2. Essays: "Migraine Blues," "Should College Athletes Be Paid?"

3. Individual episodes of a TV series: "The Soup Nazi" *(Seinfeld)*, "Hawaii: Crucible of Life" *(Nova)*
4. Newspaper articles: "Climbers feared dead on Everest," "Braves Beat up Pirates Again"
5. Poems: "To His Coy Mistress," "Harlem"
6. Short stories: "The Smallest Show on Earth," "A Good Man Is Hard to Find"

> ** Grammar Alert!*
>
> When you write *about* an essay, place the title of the essay within quotation marks. When you type the title of *your* essay on a cover sheet or at the head of the essay, do not use quotation marks.

Underlining and Italics

Use of italics is the accepted way of setting off titles of longer works in published material; however, underlining has long been an acceptable substitute in handwritten, typed, and word-processed materials. Although word-processing software has the ability to reproduce italic type, the Modern Language Association still recommends the use of underlining for clarity. If you are writing on a computer, use underlining in place of italics if you are following MLA style. Otherwise, ask your instructor's preference. If you are hand writing or typing, use underlining.

Instructions for the exercises in this text tell you to underline, since you will probably use pen and paper for the exercise. Keep in mind, though, that underlining and italics do the same job.

The titles of the following types of works are underlined or italicized.

1. Books: <u>A Tale of Two Cities</u>, <u>The Latin Deli</u>
2. Comic strips: <u>Jumpstart</u>, <u>Blondie</u>
3. Newspapers: <u>Miami Herald</u>, <u>Wall Street Journal</u>
4. Anthologies (collections) of poetry or short stories: <u>The Poem: An Anthology</u>, <u>The Best American Short Stories: 1998</u>
5. Music albums: <u>Life After Death</u>, <u>Turnstiles</u>
6. Television programs: <u>The CBS Evening News</u>, <u>Oprah</u>

7. Movies: Jurassic Park: The Lost World, On the Waterfront
8. Works of art: Mona Lisa, Nude with a Hat

PRACTICE 5 USING QUOTATION MARKS AND UNDERLINING WITH TITLES

In each of the following sentences, use quotation marks or underlining to set off titles.

1. Tonight's episode of Nature is entitled Extraordinary Dogs.

2. For next week, the professor assigned a chapter called Memory in the book Psychology: An Introduction.

3. Jason's favorite cut on Best of the Blues is Stormy Monday.

4. The class read a poem by Gwendolyn Brooks called kitchenette building.

5. The newspaper headline read Dow up 130 points, but Ann did not feel any richer.

6. Many people know that Aretha Franklin recorded Respect, but few know that Otis Redding wrote it.

7. Carlos read Great Expectations for the third time.

8. Steve wondered why his wife was reading a magazine article called No More Chubby Hubby.

9. Before final exams, Pat tacked a poster of Edward Munch's painting The Scream above her desk.

10. Carol's favorite comic strip is For Better or For Worse.

Review Exercises

Complete the Review Exercises to see how well you have learned the skills addressed in this chapter. As you work through the exercises, go back through the chapter to review any of the rules you do not understand completely.

Review Exercise 1

Place quotation marks around direct quotations in the following sentences and place commas and question marks where they are needed.

1. Something is going on. It's too quiet in here said Francine.

2. I don't care if the pet store is giving away free goldfish said Clark's mother. We already have enough pets.

3. Vernon said This looks like a catalog for people with more money than sense.

4. Do you know how far it is to the stadium the customer asked the clerk.

5. When we tried to see the movie said Curtis there was a line halfway around the theater.

____

____

Review Exercise 2

Place quotation marks around direct quotations in the following sentences. Two of the sentences are indirect quotations that do not require quotation marks.

1. The angry woman said My appointment was for two-thirty, and I have been waiting for an hour.

____

____

2. The veterinarian said Puddles was improving but should remain hospitalized for at least two more days.

____

____

3. Every work week should be a four-day week said Carla.

____

____

4. When her children cleaned the entire house and mowed the lawn, Paula said it was the best Mother's Day gift she had ever received.

____

____

5. Did you say this was thyme? said Paul. It looks like a weed to me.

____

____

Review Exercise 3

Use underlining or quotation marks to set off titles in each of the following sentences.

1. In his book, Born to Rebel, Frank J. Sulloway says that birth order affects a person's tendency to defy authority.

____

____

2. Chapter 14, Psychological Disorders, is the most interesting chapter in our psychology textbook.

____

____

3. On Friday night, Kiku stayed up late watching Chiller Theater.

____

____

4. Andrew's Scottish grandfather believes there's no sweeter sound than Amazing Grace played on the bagpipes.

____

____

5. John Williams has composed music for movies such as Jaws, E.T., Star Wars, and Jurassic Park.

____

____

6. Derek swears there is a country song called If My Nose Were Full of Nickels, I'd Blow It All on You.

____

____

7. The Complete Works of Shakespeare, Annie's text for English 252, must weigh at least ten pounds.

____

____

8. My grandmother enjoys watching Bogie and Bacall films such as To Have and Have Not, The Big Sleep, and Key Largo.

____

____

9. David Hockney's painting, A Bigger Splash, contains no human figure, just a splash made by a diver entering a pool.

____

____

10. A small headline at the top of the page said Suspect arrested in Tuesday's robbery.

____

____

REVIEW EXERCISE 4

In the following paragraph, place quotation marks around direct quotations. Use underlining or quotation marks to set off titles. Do not place indirect quotations in quotation marks.

[1]When Samantha unlocked her door last night and walked into her apartment, she was startled to hear the familiar voices of her mother, father, and sister yelling, Surprise! [2]On the kitchen table sat a beautifully decorated cake that read Happy Birthday Samantha. [3]After Samantha blew out the candles and cut the cake, her sister said That's not all. We have presents for you. [4]Samantha said that they shouldn't have gone to so much trouble, but she reached eagerly for her presents just the same. [5]A small package from her sister contained the CD The Ultimate Otis Redding. [6]Samantha put the CD on her player, and as Try a Little Tenderness played in the background, she opened the present from her parents. [7]It was software and a book called Understanding Your Computer. [8]Samantha said, Thanks, Mom and Dad, but I don't have a computer. [9]Look on your desk, said her dad. [10]As she admired her computer, Samantha said that it had been the perfect birthday.

Editing Exercises: Punctuation, Word Choice, and Mechanics

Punctuation, Word Choice, and Mechanics: Three Editing Exercises

Editing Exercise 1 Punctuation, Word Choice, and Mechanics

Correct the following errors in punctuation, word choice, and mechanics.

1 quotation marks/underlining error
1 word choice error
2 apostrophe errors
1 capitalization error
2 punctuation errors
3 words commonly confused

[1]Susan Vreeland's novel, "Girl in Hyacinth Blue," traces a painting from its current owner's hands back to the moment of its origin. [2]The painting depicts a young chick sitting by the window, lost in thought, her sewing forgotten in her lap. [3]In a series of vignettes, Vreelands story traces the painting through its various owners. [4]A professor's love of the painting, which he believes to be a Vermeer, is overshadowed only buy his guilt. [5]He is consumed by the knowledge that his father, a Nazi, took it from a jewish family as he sent them off to die in a prison camp. [6]In another vignette a married man keeps the painting because it reminds him of a lost love. [7]Another story tells of a father who sells the painting to feed his child after the child's mother is hanged! [8]As the story winds back threw the centuries through owner after owner, only the painting remains the same, luminous and beautiful, a scrap of ordinary life captured on canvas. [9]As the owner's admire the luminous beauty of the painting, so may readers appreciate the luminous quality of Vreeland's writing and the poignancy of the characters as scraps of their extraordinary lives are captured on paper. [10]<u>Girl in Hyacinth Blue</u> is a novel too be savored and enjoyed.

1. ______________ 6. ______________
2. ______________ 7. ______________
3. ______________ 8. ______________
4. ______________ 9. ______________
5. ______________ 10. ______________

Editing Exercise 2 Commas, Quotation Marks, Capital Letters, and Apostrophes

Correct the following errors in punctuation, word choice, and mechanics.

2 comma errors
2 quotation marks errors
3 capitalization errors
3 apostrophe errors

[1]When I see Aunt Rita today I see a person whose life has been altered by pain. [2]When I was a child, Rita taught me to throw a softball and trudged through the woods helping me to earn my nature badge for girl scouts. [3]When I was a teenager, Rita would come by on Saturday's and propel me out the door for a day of shopping at the mall. [4]She was full of energy then but she has changed. [5]Now, when I stop by her house, I might see my Aunt walking slowly and painfully out to her mailbox at midday, still in her bathrobe. [6]Its not age that wears her down; instead, it is the chronic pain of severe and crippling arthritis. [7]If I ask her to go out to lunch with me, she often says, Sorry, "it's not a good day." [8]Ritas pain is like a miserly hand that doles out freedom in small pinches. [9]A line by T. S. Eliot says, "I have measured out my life in coffee spoons". [10]I was never sure what the line meant until I saw how Rita's Arthritis forces her to weigh every action she takes against the pain it may cause.

1. ______________ 4. ______________
2. ______________ 5. ______________
3. ______________ 6. ______________

7. ______________________ 9. ______________________

8. ______________________ 10. ______________________

Editing Exercise 3 Punctuation, Word Choice, and Mechanics

Correct the following errors in punctuation, word choice, and mechanics.

2 capital letter errors
3 apostrophe errors
2 underlining errors
1 error in use of quotation marks

[1]Our local bookstore, Templeton's books, is a comfortable place to shop. [2]Opening the heavy wooden door that leads to the shop, a customer is greeted by a blast of air conditioning and the aroma of Starbuck's Coffee. [3]Inside the store, soft classical music plays in the background, and comfortable overstuffed chairs invite customer's to sit and read. [4]Templetons Books has paperback books, hardback books, and a small collection of books on tape. [5]Along the back wall, magazines such as Psychology Today, Vogue, and Newsweek are displayed in neat rows. [6]Templeton's also sells a wide variety of newspapers, from the New York Times to sleazy tabloids with headlines such as Mom Abducted by Two-Headed Alien. [7]At Templeton's customers are welcome to browse, so it is not unusual to see people chatting in the coffee shop over cups of cappuccino or sitting in the comfortable chairs reading a copy of USA Today or People. [8]With such an inviting atmosphere, its no wonder Templeton's is the most popular bookstore in town.

1. ______________________ 5. ______________________

2. ______________________ 6. ______________________

3. ______________________ 7. ______________________

4. ______________________ 8. ______________________

Part 3
Readings

Complaining

Maya Angelou

Sometimes—if we are lucky—someone will catch us at just the right time in our lives and teach us a lesson we will carry throughout life. Maya Angelou writes about such a lesson, learned from a wise grandmother.

When my grandmother was raising me in Stamps, Arkansas, she had a particular routine when people who were known to be whiners entered her store. Whenever she saw a known complainer coming, she would call me from whatever I was doing and say conspiratorially, "Sister, come inside. Come." Of course I would obey. 1

My grandmother would ask the customer, "How are you doing today, Brother Thomas?" And the person would reply, "Not so good." There would be a distinct whine in the voice. "Not so good today, Sister Henderson. You see, it's this summer. It's this summer heat. I just hate it. Oh, I hate it so much. It just frazzles me up and frazzles me down. I just hate the heat. It's almost killing me." Then my grandmother would stand stoically, her arms folded, and mumble, "Uh-huh, uh-huh." And she would cut her eyes at me to make certain that I had heard the lamentation. 2

At another time a whiner would mewl, "I hate plowing. That packed-down dirt ain't got no reasoning, and mules ain't got good sense. . . . Sure ain't. It's killing me. I can't ever seem to get done. My feet and my hands stay sore, and I get dirt in my eyes and up my nose. I just can't stand it." And my grandmother, again stoically with her arms folded, would say, "Uh-huh, uh-huh," and then look at me and nod. 3

As soon as the complainer was out of the store, my grandmother would call me to stand in front of her. And then she would say the same thing she had said at least a thousand times, it seemed to me. "Sister, did you hear what Brother So-and-So or Sister Much to Do complained about? You heard that?" And I would nod. Mamma would continue, "Sister, there are people who went to sleep all over the world last night, poor and rich and white and black, but they will never wake again. Sister, those who expected to rise did not, their beds became their cooling boards, and their blankets became their winding sheets. And those dead folks would give anything, anything at all for just five minutes of this weather or ten minutes of that plowing that person was grumbling about. So you watch yourself about complaining, Sister. What you're supposed to do when you don't like a thing is change it. If you can't change it, change the way you think about it. Don't complain." 4

It is said that persons have few teachable moments in their lives. Mamma 5
seemed to have caught me at each one I had between the age of three and thirteen. Whining is not only graceless, but can be dangerous. It can alert a brute that a victim is in the neighborhood.

Building Vocabulary

For each question, use your dictionary and context clues to choose the meaning that most closely defines the underlined word or phrase as it is used in the essay.

1. The word particular most nearly means
   a. special.
   b. picky.
   c. tiresome.
   d. thorough.
2. The word conspiratorially most nearly means
   a. with an air of secrecy.
   b. complainingly.
   c. in a bored manner.
   d. unhappily.
3. The word distinct most nearly means
   a. distant.
   b. distinguished.
   c. clear.
   d. vague.
4. The word frazzles most nearly means
   a. heats.
   b. dazzles.
   c. energizes.
   d. tires.
5. The word stoically most nearly means
   a. carelessly.
   b. excitedly.
   c. sympathetically.
   d. unemotionally
6. The word lamentation most nearly means
   a. lesson.
   b. speech.

c. complaint.
d. praise.

7. The word mewl most nearly means
   a. whine.
   b. say.
   c. shout.
   d. assert.
8. The phrase winding sheets most nearly means
   a. bed sheets.
   b. shrouds.
   c. blankets.
   d. covers.
9. The phrase teachable moments most nearly means
   a. times when people are ready to learn.
   b. times when people are reluctant to learn.
   c. times when someone tries to teach a lesson.
   d. the last five minutes of class on Friday.
10. The word graceless most nearly means
   a. appealing.
   b. effective.
   c. unsafe.
   d. unattractive.

Understanding the Essay

1. A good alternative title for this essay would be
   a. "My Life in Stamps, Arkansas."
   b. "My Grandmother's Store."
   c. "The Art of Complaining."
   d. "The Uselessness of Complaining."
2. Sister Henderson was
   a. Angelou's grandmother.
   b. Angelou herself.
   c. one of the complainers.
   d. Sister Much to Do.
3. The people who came into the store and complained were people who
   a. worked hard and had every right to complain.
   b. complained about things that could not be changed.

c. spent little money in the store.
d. were role models for Angelou.

4. It is implied that one reason Sister Henderson objected to complaining was that
   a. she had no time to listen.
   b. complaining attracts brutes.
   c. she thought people were fortunate just to be alive.
   d. complaining was unattractive in children.
5. Which of the following is *not* mentioned as a cause for complaint among Sister Henderson's customers?
   a. the heat
   b. a bad back
   c. mules
   d. plowing
6. Sister Henderson believed that if a situation could not be changed, the way to handle it was to
   a. complain only to a close friend or family member.
   b. keep resentment bottled up inside.
   c. change one's way of thinking about the situation.
   d. learn a lesson from it.
7. Which of the following bumper stickers would Sister Henderson be most likely to put on her car?
   a. Life is Unfair
   b. If You Can't Say Something Nice, Come Sit Beside Me
   c. Whine Connoisseur
   d. Celebrate Life!

Looking at Language

8. Find and list at least two words from the essay that mean the same as *complain* or *complaint*.

   ____

9. Sister Henderson's remarks ("Uh-huh, uh-huh") to the complainers say little, but her body language speaks volumes. What does her body language say to the complainers and to her granddaughter?

   ____

   ____

   ____

10. Readers can often pick up clues about the way to view a character by the way that character speaks. Compare the whiners' complaints with Sister Henderson's lecture about not complaining. Whose words are stronger and more poetic? Give an example that seems to reveal a whiner's attitude and an example that reveals Sister Henderson's attitude.

____

____

____

____

____

____

____

____

____

Discussing the Essay

Prepare to discuss the following questions in class by thinking about them or writing about them in your journal.

1. Are there times when complaining is useful and even productive, or does complaining simply waste time?
2. Sister Henderson took every available opportunity to warn the young Maya Angelou against complaining. What behaviors do you remember being strongly urged to avoid when you were a child?

Topics for Writing

Assignment 1: It Takes All Kinds

Essay or Journal Entry

Angelou wrote about one type of person she observed while helping her grandmother in a store. Write an essay or journal entry about one or more types of people that you have observed in a particular situation and would not want to be like. These may be types of people you have observed at work, at school, or in a social situation.

If you are writing about more than one type of person, be sure to keep the context the same. For example, write about types of workers or types of classmates, but don't mix the two. Keeping the situation or setting constant throughout the essay will lend continuity and unity to your essay.

Assignment 2: Complaint Department

Essay

Write an essay about a complaint you have. Take one of the following approaches:

Describe the problem and write about what you could do to change it.

Analyze the causes of the problem and/or its effects on you.

Describe the problem and, if it is something you cannot change, describe how you can alter your attitude toward it.

Assignment 3: A Teachable Moment

Essay

Write a narrative essay describing a time when someone caught you at a "teachable moment." Before you write, reread Angelou's narrative. Notice how vividly she describes her grandmother and the complainers who came into the store. Try to present the characters in your narrative, as well as the lesson you learned, in a vivid and memorable way.

Assignment 4: A Strong Influence

Essay

Angelou's grandmother was obviously a strong influence in her life. Write an essay describing an adult who influenced you when you were a child. Focus on the traits of character and personality in your role model that helped to make you the person you are today.

Two Ways of Seeing a River

Mark Twain

The river stays the same, but as Mark Twain gains experience in navigating it, he realizes that the way he sees the river has changed forever.

Now when I had mastered the language of this water and had come to know every trifling feature that bordered the great river as familiarly as I knew the letters of the alphabet, I had made a valuable acquisition. But I had lost something, too. I had lost something which could never be restored to me while I lived. All the grace, the beauty, the poetry, had gone out of the majestic river! I still kept in mind a certain wonderful sunset which I witnessed when steamboating was new to me. A broad expanse of the river was turned to blood; in the middle distance the red hue brightened into gold, through which a solitary log came floating, black and conspicuous; in one place a long, slanting mark lay sparkling upon the water; in another the surface was broken by boiling, tumbling rings that were as many-tinted as an opal; where the ruddy flush was faintest was a smooth spot that was covered with graceful circles and radiating lines, ever so delicately traced; the shore on our left was densely wooded, and the somber shadow that fell from this forest was broken in one place by a long, ruffled trail that shone like silver; and high above the forest wall a clean-stemmed dead tree waved a single leafy bough that glowed like a flame in the unobstructed splendor that was flowing from the sun. There were graceful curves, reflected images, woody heights, soft distances, and over the whole scene, far and near, the dissolving lights drifted steadily, enriching it every passing moment with new marvels of coloring. 1

I stood like one bewitched. I drank it in, in a speechless rapture. The world was new to me and I had never seen anything like this at home. But as I have said, a day came when I began to cease from noting the glories and the charms which the moon and the sun and the twilight wrought upon the river's face; another day came when I ceased altogether to note them. Then, if that sunset scene had been repeated, I should have looked upon it without rapture and should have commented upon it inwardly after this fashion: "This sun means that we are going to have wind tomorrow; that floating log means that the river is rising, small thanks to it; that slanting mark on the water refers to a bluff reef which is going to kill somebody's steamboat one of these nights, if it keeps on stretching out like that; those tumbling 'boils' show a dissolving bar and a changing channel there; the lines and circles in the slick water over yonder are a warning that that troublesome place is shoaling up dangerously; that silver 2 streak in the shadow of the forest is the 'break' from a new snag and he has located himself in the very best place he could have found to fish for steamboats; that tall dead tree, with a single living branch, is not going to last long, and then how is a body ever going to get through this blind place at night without the friendly old landmark?"

No, the romance and beauty were all gone from the river. All the value any 3
feature of it had for me now was the amount of usefulness it could furnish toward compassing the safe piloting of a steamboat. Since those days, I have pitied doctors from my heart. What does the lovely flush in a beauty's cheek mean to a doctor but a "break" that ripples above some deadly disease? Are not all her visible charms sown thick with what are to him the signs and symbols of hidden decay? Does he ever see her beauty at all, or doesn't he simply view her professionally and comment upon her unwholesome condition all to himself? And doesn't he sometimes wonder whether he has gained most or lost most by learning his trade?

Building Vocabulary

For each question, use your dictionary and context clues to choose the meaning that most nearly defines the underlined word or phrase as it is used in the essay.

1. The word trifling most nearly means
   a. small.
   b. important.
   c. ecological.
   d. lovely.
2. The word acquisition most nearly means
   a. question.
   b. object of greed.
   c. something learned or gained.
   d. something that is not needed.
3. The word witnessed most nearly means
   a. swore.
   b. testified.
   c. saw.
   d. interrogated.
4. The word ruddy most nearly means
   a. rudder.
   b. smooth.
   c. rude.
   d. red.

5. The word densely most nearly means
   a. thickly.
   b. sparsely.
   c. stupidly.
   d. barely.
6. The phrase cease from noting most nearly means
   a. look at more closely.
   b. stop taking notes on.
   c. stop noticing.
   d. see anew.
7. The word wrought most nearly means
   a. sought out.
   b. brought about.
   c. erased.
   d. surfaced.
8. The phrase shoaling up most nearly means
   a. becoming shallow and dangerous to navigate.
   b. becoming deep and easy to navigate.
   c. infested with sharks.
   d. rolling up.
9. The phrase sown thick with most nearly means
   a. filled with.
   b. decaying from.
   c. missing.
   d. rejecting.
10. The word unwholesome most nearly means
   a. physical.
   b. beautiful.
   c. partial.
   d. unhealthy.

Understanding the Essay

1. Which statement most nearly expresses the main idea of the essay?
   a. There is hidden beauty in everything.
   b. Having to navigate the river as part of his job made the author grow to dislike the river.

c. Thorough knowledge of steamboating made the author the less able to see the river's beauty.

d. Physicians, who see only sickness, are likely to have a difficult time appreciating the physical beauty of the human body.

2. The statement that a broad part of the river "was turned to blood" suggests that
   a. the setting sun turned it red.
   b. predatory fish were having a feeding frenzy.
   c. the author felt he was pouring his lifeblood into a job he did not enjoy.
   d. red algae had taken over the river.

3. The author's reaction to the river as he saw it in paragraph 1 is
   a. indifference.
   b. boredom.
   c. rapture.
   d. mild appreciation.

4. As an experienced steamboat pilot, Twain tended to notice
   a. sunsets, trees, and other elements that enhanced the natural beauty of the river.
   b. only the dangers.
   c. the slightest variations in the amount of steam produced in the boiler and the resulting effect on the speed of the boat.
   d. any conditions that might affect the passage of a steamboat through the waters.

5. Which of the following statements is *not* true about the second way that the author sees the river?
   a. It is a method that did not come naturally; he had to learn it.
   b. The author feels that he has lost something in gaining the new way of seeing the river.
   c. It is necessary for his job.
   d. He can give it up and go back to the old method any time.

6. Mark Twain develops his essay mainly through
   a. description and contrast.
   b. narration and comparison.
   c. process and cause-effect.
   d. argument and narration.

7. The author's pity for doctors suggests that
   a. he would not make a good physician.
   b. he believes that learning a thing too thoroughly can destroy some of the pleasure one might take in its beauty.
   c. he feels sorry for doctors because they have to witness so much sickness and death.
   d. piloting a steamboat gives him too much free time to worry about things that are none of his business.

Looking at Language

8. Notice the extreme variation in sentence length in this essay. Underline one extremely short sentence and one extremely long sentence. What is the main advantage of varying sentence length?

____

____

____

____

9. Twain's essay is filled with descriptive language that allows the reader to see the river as he saw it. Below, list three descriptive phrases that you find particularly vivid.

____

____

____

10. Twain's essay ends with several questions about doctors. How do those questions relate to Twain's experience on the river?

____

____

____

____

____

Discussing the Essay

Prepare to discuss the following questions in class by thinking about them or writing about them in your journal.

1. Does thorough knowledge of a place, person, or activity take away the magic? If so, are there any compensations?
2. Thinking beyond rivers, what are some of the advantages and/or disadvantages to viewing issues and situations in more than one way? Can you think of a specific example?

Topics for Writing

Assignment 1: A River Runs Through It

Journal Entry

Rivers, lakes, and oceans have fascinated humans for eons. Write about a memory involving water.

Assignment 2: An Insider's View

Essay

Twain writes about how his work as a steamboat pilot gave him a different view of the river. Often, a job can change the way a person sees things. A day-care worker who begins the job thinking of children as sweet, innocent cherubs may see them differently after a few weeks on the job. An actor may never watch a movie or a play with the same simple enjoyment that most people experience. And many fast-food workers have cut down on trips to the drive-through after working behind the scenes. Write an essay describing how a job changed your view of the job itself or of something that the job involves.

Assignment 3: A Child's View, An Adult's View

Essay

As people mature, they begin to see the world through adult eyes. Like Twain's first view of the river, our childhood way of seeing is innocent and unspoiled, and once we have left it behind, we can remember it but can never go back. Think of something or someone—Santa Claus, a relative, a teacher, a place you have lived—that you see differently now that you are an adult. Write an essay about your two ways—the child's way and the adult's way—of seeing that person, place, or thing.

Assignment 4: Not What You Expected

Essay

Maybe it was a marriage or some other significant relationship. It could have been a job, a friendship, a business arrangement, a recreational activity, an organization, or a class. Whatever it was, you had expectations. But six days, six weeks, six months, or six years later, there you were, shaking your head in amazement. It had not worked out the way you expected. It was much worse, much better, or somewhere in between. Write an essay about a job, relationship, or experience that was not what you expected.

Growing Up Bilingual

Sara Gonzalez

Does a parent have a duty to teach a child English and to speak English in the home, no matter what the parent's native language? Sara Gonzalez, who wanted her child to speak two languages, found herself at odds with a teacher and principal at her child's school.

About 30 years ago, I arrived in the United States as a refugee, accompanied by my two small children. I had been forced to abandon our beautiful island of Cuba. 1

A few months after getting settled (more or less) in Brunswick, N.J., I enrolled my son in kindergarten. Several weeks later, I received a letter from the principal asking me to come to school and meet with him and my son's teacher. I accepted the invitation and strolled into what was to become my first unpleasant experience in the United States: a lesson in cultural prejudice and exposure to a very unsophisticated American educational system. 2

All my life I had looked up to the education system, believing it to be filled with sophisticated, smart role models. I soon would learn differently. 3

As I entered the principal's office, greetings were exchanged. Then, without wasting any time, the principal and teacher confronted me with very blunt questions: "Is your son mentally retarded? Does he suffer from any kind of mental disability?" 4

My young heart grew 100 years old. The blood seemed to drain from my body and tears swelled in my eyes. Were they talking about my wonderful Luis? No, no, it can't be. What a helpless, lonely moment! I told them that Luis was not mentally disabled, that he was a quiet, sweet little boy. 5

To this they said, "Well, maybe he witnessed too many atrocities in your war-torn country and that has affected him?" No, I said again. We never witnessed any fighting or killings. I asked them why they were asking me all these questions. 6

My son was incapable of following the teacher's directions, they told me, and thus, he was disrupting the class. Lo and behold! Didn't they know my son did not speak English yet? 7

They were outraged: "Why hasn't your son been taught to speak English? Don't you speak English at home?" 8

No, I didn't speak English at home, I replied. I was sure my son would learn English in a couple of months, and I didn't want him to forget his native language. Well, wrong answer! What kind of person would not speak in English to her son at home and at all times? "Are you one of those people who come to 9 this country to save dollars and send them back to their country, never wanting to be a part of this society?"

Needless to say, I tried to tell them I was not one of "those people." Then 10
they told me the meeting was over, and I left.

As I had anticipated, my son learned to speak English fluently before the 11
school year was over. He went on to graduate from college and become a part of corporate America, earning close to six figures. He travels extensively and leads a well-adjusted, content life. And he has benefited from being bilingual.

Speaking more than one language allows people to communicate with oth- 12
ers; it teaches people about other cultures and other places—something very basic and obviously lacking in the two "educators" I encountered in New Jersey.

■ Building Vocabulary

For each question, use your dictionary and context clues to choose the meaning that most nearly defines the underlined word or phrase as it is used in the essay.

1. The phrase cultural prejudice most nearly means
   a. intolerance of the ways of other societies.
   b. fear and dislike of operas and art galleries.
   c. genocide.
   d. favoring other cultures over one's own.
2. The word unsophisticated most nearly means
   a. complex.
   b. elite.
   c. excellent.
   d. primitive.
3. The word atrocities most nearly means
   a. horrors.
   b. acrostics.
   c. soldiers.
   d. crimes.
4. The word disrupting most nearly means
   a. failing.
   b. not understanding.
   c. corrupting.
   d. disturbing.
5. The word outraged most nearly means
   a. understanding.
   b. angry.

c. curious.
d. sympathetic.

6. The word anticipated most nearly means
   a. precipitated.
   b. expected.
   c. taught.
   d. planned.
7. The word fluently most nearly means
   a. haltingly.
   b. smoothly.
   c. reluctantly.
   d. temporarily.
8. The phrase a part of corporate America most nearly means
   a. a salaried employee in a large corporation.
   b. a part-time worker.
   c. a union member.
   d. a company such as IBM.
9. The word extensively most nearly means
   a. at great cost.
   b. widely.
   c. briefly.
   d. luxuriously.
10. The word bilingual most nearly means
    a. biological.
    b. educated.
    c. able to speak fluently.
    d. able to speak two languages.

Understanding the Essay

1. Which statement most nearly expresses the main idea of the essay?
   a. Coming to a school in a country where one does not speak the language can be a frightening experience.
   b. The American education system is in need of reform and greater cultural awareness.
   c. The author encountered cultural prejudice when she enrolled her son in school.
   d. Living in a war-torn country can damage a child's ability to learn.

2. The author implies that on leaving her native land, she felt
   a. regretful.
   b. thankful to escape.
   c. glad for the opportunity to build a new life.
   d. frightened.
3. The author did not speak English to her child because
   a. she had not yet learned the English language.
   b. she thought it was the school's job to teach her son English.
   c. she wanted her child to have the benefit of two languages.
   d. she was afraid she would not teach her child properly.
4. When her son started school, the author was summoned by the principal
   a. immediately.
   b. after a few days.
   c. after a few weeks.
   d. after a few months.
5. Which of the following was *not* a stated result of the meeting between the author and school personnel?
   a. The author became disillusioned with the school system.
   b. School officials implied that the author did not want to contribute to American society.
   c. The author began speaking English at home.
   d. The author discovered that school officials were not aware her child did not speak English.
6. The essay is mainly developed by
   a. process.
   b. cause-effect.
   c. definition.
   d. narration.
7. With which statement would the author most likely agree?
   a. Parents owe it to their children to speak whatever language the child uses in school.
   b. Children of immigrants to the United States have a right to be educated in their native language.
   c. Culture and language taught in a child's home are not the business of school officials.
   d. School officials have a responsibility to call any problems to a parent's attention before the situation becomes serious.

Looking at Language

8. What specific words and phrases tell you how the author felt about the education system before and after the meeting with her son's teacher and principal?

____

____

____

____

____

9. What words show the emotional impact the school meeting had on the author?

____

____

10. Why do you think the author chooses to use dialogue in describing the incident in the principal's office? What effect does hearing the characters' exact words have on the reader?

____

____

Discussing the Essay

Prepare to discuss the following questions in class by thinking about them or writing about them in your journal.

1. In what ways did school officials handle their concerns about the author's son in an appropriate manner? In what ways did they handle the situation inappropriately? If you were a school principal, how would you handle a situation such as this?
2. Gonzales was confident that her son would learn English once he was enrolled in school. Some parts of the country have tried bilingual education programs in which teachers speak English along with the native language of the students they teach. Do you believe such programs are a good idea?
3. Gonzales says that speaking another language "teaches people about other cultures and other places." In many countries, children are

routinely taught to speak a language other than their own. In the United States, learning a second language is the exception rather than the rule. Should children in the United States routinely be taught a second language?

Topics for Writing

Assignment 1: A Different Country

Journal Entry

Imagine that you are forced to leave your country and move to a country where a different language is spoken. You have a school-age child. Discuss in a journal entry whether you would speak the language of the new country at home or speak your first language. How important would it be to you to preserve your native language and culture? Why?

Assignment 2: Ancestral Journey

Essay

Because the United States is a fairly young country, most of its residents can look back just a few generations and find ancestors who began life in another country. In an essay, discuss the events that brought your family to this country, including some of the challenges they faced.

Assignment 3: Problems in Communication

Essay

Few people make it through twelve years of schooling without suffering setbacks and traumas. Have you (or your child, if you are a parent) ever had problems in school that stemmed from language or communication difficulties? How did you overcome these problems?

Assignment 4: Melting Pot or Patchwork Quilt?

Essay

The United States used to be termed a "melting pot" because it was a land in which many cultures blended into one and in which people celebrated their similarities. Recently, however, the idea of cultural diversity has challenged that of the melting pot. In this view, the United States is more like a patchwork quilt, with all the pieces joined yet with each possessing its own pattern. In a culturally diverse society, people celebrate their differences. Write an essay in which you discuss the advantages and/or disadvantages of one or both of these views.

The Game of My Life

Jeff Obafemi Carr

To succeed in unfamiliar arenas, it sometimes helps to have the support of a special person. Jeff Obafemi Carr, always more comfortable with books than with basketballs, searches the stands for one special face.

The atmosphere was tense. We were the top-rated team in the league, on a two-game losing streak. It was late in the season. Fatigue had settled in, and our top players were losing their touch. 1

I looked around in anticipation, scanning the sparse crowd for his face. No show. Maybe telling him about the game just three hours earlier had been too short a notice. Maybe he was busy at home. Maybe it just wasn't important enough to come to. 2

Of course it wasn't the intercity high-school marquee game or the NBA. It was only the Tuesday night winter league at the downtown YMCA. Yet for the past seven weeks, this aging gymnasium had been my field of dreams. 3

You see, I hadn't been an athlete while I was growing up. Sure, I ran in the neighborhood and climbed trees, threw rocks and shot bottle-cap guns. But except for a short stint on the seventh-grade track team and a horrific summer in Little League baseball, I stuck with the choir and the stage. I didn't know how to play basketball. My father hadn't taught me the game, probably because he had grown up in the hills of east Tennessee and had had me late in life, when he was in his mid-forties. Whatever the reason, I wasn't on the court Saturday mornings hooping. In childhood pickup games, I was a liability to the team. I didn't even look athletic—I wasn't very tall, I had no bulging biceps or explosive calves, and my round, slightly chubby face struck no fear in an opponent. After so many jokes about my deficiencies, I figured out the way to conquer them all: quit. But somehow quitting never stopped the desire within. It just made me dream harder and higher, all the while fearing the serious thought of picking up that ball or hitting that track. 4

So I grew up with my self-esteem coming from my intellect rather than my physical prowess. Then I went to college and met some brothers and sisters who put some funk into my soul. They helped me discover that my ancestors founded civilizations and were kings and queens and architects and doctors. After a few months of study, I began to believe I could do anything. Anything? 5

I hit the track one day, or should I say the track hit me? I sputtered along, covering a little more ground each day, until I was running a mile, then two, then three. (Now I run four miles without a problem and work out every day.) 6

For a year before the night of the big game, I had been playing basketball with a passion. My growth spurt at age 19 had helped me develop my slender six-foot two-inch frame, and I would work my legs extra hard. I had finally developed enough confidence to sign up for the league at the local YMCA. 7

It was also the place where I, at 29 years old, found a chance to live my dream. I might not ever be the lead scorer, but I figured that if I could just score a few points and snatch a few rebounds, I would be satisfied. I had already surpassed this goal, averaging ten points going into that night's game. 8

I was hanging around the perimeter practicing my now potentially deadly three-pointer. When I finally saw him come through the gym door, my heart leapt. There he was, just as he'd been there for me so many times before—at the choir concert, the play I was starring in or the speech I was giving. But this time my pops was coming to see his boy play ball. I ushered him to a seat in the bleachers as the ref blew the whistle for the opening tip. 9

I was in the starting lineup, and I found myself playing harder than I had ever played before. We lost the game by more than 30 points. But I had fun in a strange, boyish sort of way. I scored 13 points, a career high—9 of them from behind the arc. The last minute of the game I got a steal and passed it downcourt to our big man. He passed it back to me on the break. I went up hard and, you guessed it, made a slam dunk! My very first in a game, and my pops was a witness. 10

As I headed to the locker room in defeat, yet carrying an odd air of victory, I heard a voice in my ear. It was the voice that the latent athlete in me had longed to hear since I was young, uttering the words of empowerment, love and pride. 11

"You played a good game, son." 12

Better than you may ever know, Pops. 13

Building Vocabulary

For each question, use your dictionary and context clues to choose the meaning that most nearly defines the underlined word or phrase as it is used in the essay.

1. The word sparse most nearly means
   a. thin.
   b. cheering.
   c. unenthusiastic.
   d. large.
2. The word stint most nearly means
   a. limitation.
   b. coach.
   c. period of service.
   d. year.

3. The word horrific most nearly means
   a. dreadful.
   b. fun-filled
   c. hot.
   d. playful.
4. The word liability most nearly means
   a. help.
   b. person of ability.
   c. key player.
   d. burden.
5. The word deficiencies most nearly means
   a. shortcomings.
   b. proficiencies.
   c. defeats.
   d. physical traits.
6. The word prowess most nearly means
   a. size.
   b. physique.
   c. body.
   d. skill.
7. The word sputtered most nearly means
   a. stammered.
   b. moved gracefully.
   c. sped.
   d. toiled.
8. The word surpassed most nearly means
   a. surprised.
   b. moved beyond.
   c. given up.
   d. set.
9. The word potentially most nearly means
   a. possibly.
   b. unquestionably.
   c. lethally.
   d. immediately.

10. The word latent most nearly means
    a. potent.
    b. talking.
    c. hidden.
    d. late.

Understanding the Essay

1. When he played the game he writes about, Carr was
    a. twelve.
    b. nineteen.
    c. twenty-nine.
    d. forty.
2. Which method of introduction does the author use?
    a. anecdote
    b. broad to narrow
    c. quotation
    d. contrast
3. Before he went to college, Carr's method of overcoming his problems with athletics was to
    a. believe in himself.
    b. practice occasionally, but not often enough.
    c. read books about sports.
    d. give up.
4. The author states that his father
    a. was an older parent and therefore too busy to give time to a young son.
    b. was always there to cheer his intellectual and artistic accomplishments.
    c. was habitually late.
    d. was disappointed that he had never made it as an athlete.
5. The author implies that he was spurred on to athletic achievement by
    a. the taunts of schoolmates who pointed out his deficiencies.
    b. his sense of athletic inadequacy.
    c. hearing about the accomplishments of his ancestors.
    d. his father's patient coaching.

6. The author implies that athletic prowess
   a. still eludes him.
   b. developed overnight.
   c. came slowly but surely.
   d. required too much work.
7. Which of the following is *not* a reason that the game was special to the author?
   a. He played the best game ever.
   b. It was an important intercity championship game.
   c. His father was there to watch him.
   d. He was competing in a field in which he had never excelled.

Looking at Language

8. Often, writers are advised to explain any technical or specialized language that they use in an essay, yet Carr uses basketball terminology without explaining it. Find four examples of basketball terminology and write them on the lines below. Do you believe that a person unfamiliar with basketball would have a hard time understanding the essay as a whole? Why or why not?

____

____

____

____

____

____

9. The author uses transitions of time to guide the reader through his essay. Find and list five.

____

____

____

____

____

10. Carr's father says, "You played a good game, son." But Carr hears much more than casual congratulations. What do the words mean to Carr?

Discussing the Essay

Prepare to discuss the following questions in class by thinking about them or writing about them in your journal.

1. Though Carr was an adult when he played the basketball game he writes about, he describes himself anxiously scanning the crowd for his father. Do you think people outgrow the need for parental attention and approval?
2. Explain what Carr means when he says that he walked off the court "in defeat, yet carrying an odd air of victory."

Topics for Writing

Assignment 1: The Game of Your Life

Journal Entry or an Essay

Write a journal entry or a process essay describing your participation in a sport or athletic pastime that you enjoy. You might include such things as how you became interested in the game and how you improved your skills, or you might focus on your performance in a single game.

Assignment 2: Inspiration from the Past

Essay

Carr writes of drawing inspiration from studying the accomplishments of his ancestors. Are you inspired or otherwise affected by what your ancestors have done? Write a cause-effect essay showing how you are affected by those who have gone before. Alternatively, choose up to three of your older relatives or ancestors you have heard stories about and show how their example affects your life today.

Assignment 3: Struggle

Essay

Mastering skills we find difficult is sometimes more meaningful than doing well at skills that come easily to us. Discuss an accomplishment that you value because it was a struggle.

Assignment 4: Support

Essay

Carr writes of his father's support and how much it has meant to him. Write an essay about a person who has supported your efforts. In each body paragraph, give a different example showing how that person has supported you. Alternatively, write about three people who have supported you at various times in your life. Again, each paragraph should be supported by specific examples.

Rebel with a Dye Job

Sono Motoyama

Have you ever thought of dyeing your hair a neon shade? Such bold acts appeal to the rebel in all of us, says essayist Sono Motoyama.

For two weeks, I was a glorious mutant with fuchsia hair. It started when I quit my job and had too much time on my hands. Then there was my friend Jason, a stylist in training at a local Baltimore salon, who was practicing on all his friends for free on Tuesdays. 1

As an Asian woman with a semirespectable job, Day-Glo hair coloring was never an option. Asians with semirespectable jobs do not come with cotton-candy hair. But when I didn't have to appear in an office, I figured it was time to play. Fuchsia was not my color of choice—I dreamed of Marilyn Monroe-style platinum blond—but after three bleaching processes and a stinging scalp, I called a halt to the torture. That's when Jason pulled out a bottle of the hot-pink stuff. 2

Jason and the other stylists in the salon that day oohed over the result. But what can you expect from hairdressers? They're itching to try something new. When I looked in the mirror, I laughed. My hair was a glow-in-the-dark color that doesn't occur in nature. But in a strange way it suited me. Its brightness complemented my tawny complexion. Still, I was nervous about how people would react. Would I get catcalls? Would adolescents sneer at me? Would blue-haired ladies cross to the other side of the street? 3

Quite the contrary. 4

But first you have to understand something about Baltimore: Baltimore is full of eccentrics. And as the Baltimore native John Waters has made famous in his movie, *Hairspray,* Baltimore is the hairdo capital of the world, populated by what in the early 60's were called hair hoppers, women with elaborate coifs. There are still women in beehives and young girls in Farrah Fawcett dos, and the black women here are known up and down the East Coast for their hair sculptures. People in this city know what it means to use hair to make a personal statement. 5

Women stopped me in the street to ask where I'd had my hair done. Some homeboys on the streetcar started a friendly bantering session with me: "Do you like Nine Inch Nails?" "Uh, not really." "She listen to Megadeth," one concluded, smiling at me. As I passed a couple of construction workers on the street, one said, "Pretty, senorita, pretty." (Was it because I looked so "other" 6 that he slipped into a foreign language?) A rotund man in a subcompact car said to me while I was standing on a corner, "I like your hair." "Thanks," I said. As he rounded the corner, he emphasized his point: "I really mean it." Well, *O.K.*

7 At a hospice where I volunteer, I was feeding an AIDS patient, a man so sick he could barely speak. After watching me in silence for a good long while, he finally said to me in a soft, strained voice, "Hair."

8 "My hair?" I asked him, and told him the story of how I had come to have pink hair. He smiled, and as I was leaving his room, I looked around twice and he was still smiling at me.

9 The hair elicited positive reactions, I think, because most of us spend our time trying to conform. We get a vicarious thrill from someone who rebels, even in the smallest way. A subversive act can be embraced by even the timid if it doesn't rock their world too violently. Unlike wearing a Mohawk or piercing your cheek, pink hair is not an aggressive gesture. It subverts people's expectations in a basically nonthreatening way. (Drag queens mine some of the same territory.) After all, maybe my intense hair recalled Bozo the Clown. Or, as one guy called me, Ronica McDonald.

10 After two weeks, though, my hair color began fading. (It had already started to leave its mark on my clothes, towels, and pillow cases.) I went to see Jason for a touch-up—I thought I might go for a richer, cranberry-red color. But somehow Jason and I misunderstood each other and I wound up with my more or less natural hair color. And now I guess the owners of Jason's salon consider him "trained," because they're no longer letting him give freebies to his friends.

11 I must admit, having Technicolor hair was sometimes a bit tiring—unlike a funny hat, you can't take it off. Yet the outgoing, exhibitionist side of my personality mourns my return to the ordinary human race. Generally, I was enjoying the interaction with my fellow Baltimoreans. But given the mélange of oddballs in the city and the mischievous child in all of us, I probably shouldn't have been surprised by their welcome.

Building Vocabulary

For each question, use your dictionary and context clues to choose the meaning that most nearly defines the underlined word or phrase as it is used in the essay.

1. The word catcalls most nearly means
   a. compliments.
   b. noises of ridicule.
   c. wolf whistles.
   d. meows.

2. The word eccentrics is a synonym for what word or phrase in the last paragraph?
   a. exhibitionist.
   b. human race.
   c. Baltimoreans.
   d. oddballs.
3. The word coifs most nearly means
   a. hairdos.
   b. women.
   c. sculptures.
   d. statements.
4. The word beehives most nearly means
   a. home for bees.
   b. behaves.
   c. kind of hairstyle.
   d. source of honey.
5. The word elicited most nearly means
   a. brought out.
   b. prevented.
   c. illicit.
   d. lost.
6. The word vicarious most nearly means
   a. visionary.
   b. immediate.
   c. secondhand.
   d. dangerous.
7. The word subversive most nearly means
   a. secret.
   b. poetic.
   c. rebellious.
   d. timid.
8. The word intense most nearly means
   a. colorful.
   b. strained.
   c. funny.
   d. ugly.

9. The word exhibitionist most nearly means
   a. timid.
   b. introverted.
   c. talkative.
   d. expressive.
10. The word mélange most nearly means
   a. assortment.
   b. lack.
   c. unfriendliness.
   d. contrast.

Understanding the Essay

1. What led the author to dye her hair pink?
   a. Her friend Jason, an inexperienced hairdresser, dyed it pink by mistake.
   b. Going blond proved too difficult, so she settled for pink.
   c. She wanted to rebel because she had been fired from her job.
   d. As an Asian with a semirespectable job, she felt people stereotyped her, so she wanted to subvert their expectations.
2. Which best describes the author's attitude immediately after her hair was dyed pink?
   a. She was not unhappy with it but feared people's reactions.
   b. She was unhappy and afraid to face people.
   c. She liked it and did not care what others thought.
   d. She worried that people would not see her as respectable.
3. Choose the way in which people did *not* react to the author's pink hair.
   a. People noticed her.
   b. Strangers commented favorably on her hair.
   c. Blue-haired ladies crossed the street to avoid her.
   d. People smiled at her.
4. True or false? The author implies that some hairstyles can be aggressive.
   a. true
   b. false

5. Along with narration, which pattern of development is used predominantly in the essay?
   a. comparison-contrast
   b. cause-effect
   c. argument
   d. process
6. The author implies that because most people conform most of the time,
   a. they believe others should conform too.
   b. they are pleased by small acts of rebellion.
   c. they lead unhappy lives.
   d. they welcome any chance to be unconventional.
7. Why did the author go back to her natural hair color?
   a. Her friend Jason misunderstood what she wanted.
   b. She was tired of having unconventional hair.
   c. She was tired of being stared at.
   d. Jason, now a trained hairdresser, refused to dye her hair pink.

Looking at Language

8. The author uses colorful metaphors and descriptive language to describe her hair. List at least three of these colorful words and phrases.

____

____

____

____

9. In paragraph 3, the author writes, "Its brightness complemented my tawny complexion." Use a dictionary to look up the words *complement* and *compliment*. What is the difference? Write a sentence using each.

____

____

____

10. Note the author's references to popular culture: music, movies, hairstyles, and people. List five references to popular culture in the spaces

below. What is their effect on today's audience? How might readers react fifty years from now?

___

___

___

___

___

___

___

Discussing the Essay

Prepare to discuss the following questions in class by thinking about them or writing about them in your journal.

1. Are small acts of rebellion a positive or negative force in society? In the lives of individuals?
2. Why do some people react negatively to other people's hairstyles, clothing, language, or jewelry? Do certain types of hairstyles or clothing tend to draw more widespread disapproval? If so, which ones?

Topics for Writing

Assignment 1: The Change in You

Journal Entry

Write a journal entry telling about a change in appearance that you have made. Discuss how it affected the way people reacted to you.

Assignment 2: Outrageous

Essay

If you dared to make one outrageous change in your appearance, what would it be? Write an essay about how the change would affect the way you see yourself, the way people who know you well would see you, and the way strangers would see you. Alternatively, if you have ever changed your appearance in a bold way—by dyeing your hair, shaving your head, or getting a tattoo, for instance—write about the effect the change had on you and on others.

Assignment 3: Harmless Rebellion

Essay

The author says that "most of us spend our time trying to conform. We get a vicarious thrill from someone who rebels, even in the smallest way." Brainstorm on some of the small and harmless ways people rebel. Then see if you can classify them. For example, a person who rebelled by dyeing her hair pink would be rebelling through appearance, while a person who rebelled by writing poetry would be rebelling through art. Write a division and classification essay describing three types of harmless rebellion. Support each paragraph with a specific example.

Assignment 4: Hometown

Essay

Motoyama describes her hometown, Baltimore, as "the hairdo capital of the world," filled with eccentrics who are likely to accept her fuchsia hair. Write an essay describing your hometown. You may describe it as the _________ capital of the world, or you may simply think of a single word that describes it: conservative, sleepy, bustling, energized, diverse, laid-back, historic. That single word will be your dominant impression, and every paragraph will show how the town's various aspects reflect that dominant impression. You may choose to describe your town in terms of its people, its appearance, its attitudes, its opportunities for education, work, or recreation, or in terms of some other aspect that you feel is important.

When Words Get in the Way

Athlone G. Clarke

Athlone G. Clarke finds that English is used differently in the United States than in his native Jamaica.

Coming from Jamaica, I have discovered that even among people who speak the same language, there can be artificial barriers. 1

In my island home, greetings are usually informal and taken at face value. I assumed it to be the same here, but I soon discovered there are deep historical wounds hidden behind everyday words. 2

One evening, as I passed my elderly neighbor Mr. Gabinsky on the stairs, he greeted me with his usual thick accent: "Hey there, young boy, how is the family doing today?" We exchanged a few pleasantries and went our separate ways. 3

That same evening, another neighbor who lived in the apartment upstairs dropped by. "You shouldn't let that man from across the hall get away with calling you 'boy,'" Al said. "He is disrespecting you in a big way." 4

This was news to me. Back home it was commonplace for elderly people to refer to younger adults as "boy" or "girl." Al, who is African American, explained that it was different here, that the "b" word has its roots in slavery and was to be deemed derogatory when used by my white neighbor. 5

So, the next time Mr. Gabinsky greeted me in such a manner, I quickly put a stop to it. He apologized profusely. As it turned out, he was from Hungary and, like myself, was not yet accustomed to choosing his words according to historical context. 6

And then there was the day I got lost trying to find a "shop" that sold milk. Many of us who grew up in the islands know what a vital link the "shop" is in the food chain. My journey would have been less complicated had I been looking for a "store" that sold milk. It is interesting to note that if my mission had been to buy clothes instead of milk, then that would mean I was out "shopping." 7

Here I am, an English-speaking man living in an English-speaking country, but with the feeling of looking in a mirror where everything appears the same, except it's reversed. 8

One of the most complex words I have had to work into my vocabulary is "minority." I had to learn what a "minority contract" was, and why someone like Mr. Gabinsky, who is white, could not qualify. The word is almost always used in the context of racial classification. It hardly matters that there may be 9 fewer Hungarian Americans living here than African Americans or Asian Americans or Hispanic Americans.

Sports is a subject dear to my heart, and my hopes were cruelly dashed 10
when I discovered there would be no African, European or Asian nations competing in the "World Series." One of my favorite athletes is now an unrestricted free agent. The words "unrestricted" and "free" at first seemed a little superfluous, until I learned there is no such thing as excess in American sports when it comes to words and salaries.

At least the language of business appears to be universal. The first time I 11
passed a certain Persian rug establishment in Atlanta, there was a big sign out front that said: "Going out of business sale. Fifty percent off." Ten years later, the sign is still there, touched up with a fresh coat of paint.

Building Vocabulary

For each question, use your dictionary and context clues to choose the meaning that most nearly defines the underlined word or phrase as it is used in the essay.

1. The word face most nearly means
   a. confrontational.
   b. surface.
   c. countenance.
   d. little.
2. The word pleasantries most nearly means
   a. serious insights.
   b. insults.
   c. Jamaican or Hungarian coins.
   d. friendly remarks.
3. The word commonplace most nearly means
   a. crude.
   b. communal.
   c. ordinary.
   d. unfair.
4. The word deemed most nearly means
   a. regarded.
   b. suppressed.
   c. dreamed.
   d. screened.

5. The word derogatory most nearly means
   a. forced.
   b. flattery.
   c. democratic.
   d. belittling.
6. The word context most nearly means
   a. custom.
   b. background.
   c. history book.
   d. fantasy.
7. The word unrestricted most nearly means
   a. casual.
   b. obsessive.
   c. free.
   d. signed.
8. The word superfluous most nearly means
   a. more than is necessary.
   b. perfect.
   c. less than is necessary.
   d. fluent.
9. The word excess most nearly means
   a. overabundance.
   b. success.
   c. lack.
   d. enough.
10. The word universal most nearly means
   a. changeable.
   b. widespread.
   c. subject to historical interpretations.
   d. on sale.

Understanding the Essay

1. A good alternative title for the essay would be
   a. "English and You."
   b. "Longing for Jamaica."

c. "Language Barrier."
d. "The Language of Business."

2. The thesis of the essay is
   a. implied.
   b. stated in the first paragraph.
   c. stated in the second paragraph.
   d. stated in the last paragraph.
3. The author implies that his neighbor, Mr. Gabinsky, is
   a. insensitive.
   b. malicious.
   c. well-meaning.
   d. racist.
4. The method of development primarily used in the essay is
   a. description.
   b. definition.
   c. cause-effect.
   d. example.
5. The author's tone would best be described as
   a. objective.
   b. critical.
   c. humorous.
   d. bitter.
6. With which of the following statements would the author probably *not* agree?
   a. Whether a word causes offense may depend on who uses it.
   b. Storekeepers' use of language often is motivated by desire for profit.
   c. The government should make an effort to standardize English usage.
   d. Athletes in the United States are often overpaid.
7. Which statement best expresses the main idea of the essay?
   a. Only business English is consistent and predictable.
   b. A person from another country may not understand the historical context of American English usage.
   c. Even an English-speaking person can be tripped up by the idiosyncrasies of American English.
   d. Speaking a common language ensures that people will understand one another.

Looking at Language

8. Long before Clarke specifically tells us that his neighbor is Hungarian, he hints that his neighbor may not be a native of the United States. What specific phrase provides the clue?

____

9. One of Clarke's points of confusion was the difference between the word *shop* and the word *store.* How would you explain the difference?

____

____

____

____

____

____

____

10. Choose and define two unfamiliar words from the essay that are not included in "Understanding Vocabulary."

____

____

____

____

Discussing the Essay

Prepare to discuss the following questions in class by thinking about them or writing about them in your journal.

1. The title of the essay suggests that words sometimes hinder communication instead of enhancing it. Do you agree? Can you think of examples other than those given in the essay?
2. Clarke attributes his confusion over language to being from Jamaica. Do you think linguistic confusion also exists among people born in the United States? Can you think of examples?

Topics for Writing

Assignment 1: An Unintentional Offense

Journal Entry

Have you ever unintentionally offended someone through your use of language, or has someone offended you without meaning to? Discuss in a journal entry.

Assignment 2: Generation Gap

Essay

Write an essay contrasting the way members of two different generations use language. You may write about generations as a whole or choose a representative of each generation (for example, your grandmother and your younger brother) to contrast. In either case, include specific illustrations of the types of language used.

Assignment 3: Pet Language Peeves

Essay

Write an essay discussing your pet peeves about the way people use language. Explain why you react as you do.

Assignment 4: The Language of Advertising

Essay

Write an essay analyzing how the language of three specific commercials or advertisements appeals to the particular needs and characteristics of its target audience. For example, an ad for a luxury car might use words associated with wealth, such as "rich leather," "a wise investment," or "platinum service guarantee," to appeal to a wealthy audience. If you use a radio or television commercial as one of your examples, record it or take notes so that you can discuss exact words used.

Letting in Light

Patricia Raybon

For author Patricia Raybon, washing windows is more than a chore; it is a link to the past and a bridge to the future.

1 The windows were a gift or maybe a bribe—or maybe a bonus—for falling in love with such a dotty old house. The place was a wreck. A showoff, too. So it tried real hard to be more. But it lacked so much—good heat, stable floors, solid walls, enough space. A low interest rate.

2 But it had windows. More glass and bays and bows than people on a budget had a right to expect. And in unlikely places—like the window inside a bedroom closet, its only view a strawberry patch planted by the children next door.

3 None of it made sense. So we bought the place. We saved up and put some money down, then toasted the original builder—no doubt some brave and gentle carpenter, blessed with a flair for the grand gesture. A romantic with a T-square.

4 We were young then and struggling. Also, we are black. We looked with irony and awe at the task now before us. But we did not faint.

5 The time had come to wash windows.

6 Yes, I do windows. Like an amateur and a dabbler, perhaps, but the old-fashioned way—one pane at a time. It is the best way to pay back something so plain for its clear and silent gifts—the light of day, the glow of moon, hard rain, soft snow, dawn's early light.

7 The Romans called them *specularia*. They glazed their windows with translucent marble and shells. And thus the ancients let some light into their world.

8 In my own family, my maternal grandmother washed windows—and floors and laundry and dishes and a lot of other things that needed cleaning—while doing day work for a rich, stylish redhead in her Southern hometown.

9 To feed her five children and keep them clothed and happy, to help them walk proudly and go to church and sing hymns and have some change in their pockets—and to warm and furnish the house her dead husband had built and added onto with his own hands—my grandmother went to work.

10 She and her third daughter, my mother, put on maids' uniforms and cooked and sewed and served a family that employed my grandmother until she was nearly 80. She called them Mister and Missus—yes, ma'am and yes, sir—although she was by many years their elder. They called her Laura. Her surname never crossed their lips.

11 But her daughter, my mother, took her earnings from the cooking and serving and window washing and clothes ironing and went to college, forging a life with a young husband—my father—that granted me, their daughter, a lifetime of relative comfort.

12 I owe these women everything.

13 They taught me hope and kindness and how to say thank you.

14 They taught me how to brew tea and pour it. They taught me how to iron creases and whiten linen and cut hair ribbon on the bias so it doesn't unravel. They taught me to carve fowl, make butter molds and cook a good cream sauce. They taught me "women's work"—secrets of home, they said, that now are looked on mostly with disdain: how to sweep, dust, polish and wax. How to mow, prune, scrub, scour and purify.

15 They taught me how to wash windows.

16 Not many women do anymore, of course. There's no time. Life has us all on the run. It's easier to call a "window man," quicker to pay and, in the bargain, forget about the secret that my mother and her mother learned many years before they finally taught me.

17 Washing windows clears the cobwebs from the corners. It's plain people's therapy, good for troubles and muddles and other consternations. It's real work, I venture—honest work—and it's a sound thing to pass on. Mother to daughter. Daughter to child. Woman to woman.

18 This is heresy, of course. Teaching a child to wash windows is now an act of bravery—or else defiance. If she's black, it's an act of denial, a gesture that dares history and heritage to make something of it.

19 But when my youngest was 5 or 6, I tempted fate and ancestry and I handed her a wooden bucket. Together we would wash the outdoor panes. The moment sits in my mind:

20 She works a low row. I work the top. Silently we toil, soaping and polishing, each at her own pace—the only sounds the squeak of glass, some noisy birds, our own breathing.

21 Then, quietly at first, this little girl begins to hum. It's a nonsense melody, created for the moment. Soft at first, soon it gets louder. And louder. Then a recognizable tune emerges. Then she is really singing. With every swish of the towel, she croons louder and higher in her little-girl voice with her little-girl song. "This little light of mine—I'm gonna let it shine! Oh, this little light of mine—I'm gonna let it shine!" So, of course, I join in. And the two of us serenade the glass and the sparrows and mostly each other. And too soon our work is done.

22 "That was fun," she says. She is innocent, of course, and does this work by choice, not by necessity. But she's not too young to look at truth and understand it. And her heart, if not her arm, is resolute and strong.

23 Those years have passed. And other houses and newer windows—and other "women's jobs"—have moved through my life. I have chopped and pureed and polished and glazed. Bleached and folded and stirred. I have sung lullabies.

I have also marched and fought and prayed and taught and testified. Women's work covers many bases. 24

But the tradition of one simple chore remains. I do it without apology. 25

Last week, I dipped the sponge into the pail and began the gentle bath—easing off the trace of wintry snows, of dust storms and dead, brown leaves, of too much sticky tape used to steady paper pumpkins and Christmas lights and crepe-paper bows from holidays now past. 26

While I worked, the little girl—now 12—found her way to the bucket, proving that her will and her voice are still up to the task, but mostly, I believe, to have some fun. 27

We are out of step, the two of us. She may not even know it. But we can carry a tune. The work is never done. The song is two-part harmony. 28

Building Vocabulary

For each question, use your dictionary and context clues to choose the meaning that most nearly defines the underlined word or phrase as it is used in the essay.

1. The word dotty most nearly means
   a. eccentric.
   b. charming.
   c. beautiful.
   d. polka-dotted.
2. The word romantic most nearly means
   a. exhibitionist.
   b. lover of the opposite sex.
   c. lover of beauty.
   d. poet.
3. The word translucent most nearly means
   a. sheer.
   b. thick.
   c. transmitted.
   d. opaque.
4. The word forging most nearly means
   a. building through hard work.
   b. living.
   c. falsifying.
   d. working in metal.

5. The word disdain most nearly means
   a. approval.
   b. fear.
   c. cheer.
   d. contempt.
6. The word sound most nearly means
   a. noisy.
   b. worthy.
   c. secondhand.
   d. dangerous.
7. The word heresy most nearly means
   a. against religious beliefs.
   b. in tune with what everyone else thinks.
   c. against popular wisdom.
   d. against the writer's beliefs.
8. The word croons most nearly means
   a. cries.
   b. sings.
   c. talks.
   d. shouts.
9. The word resolute most nearly means
   a. timid and withdrawn.
   b. lively and active.
   c. determined and purposeful.
   d. expressive and emotional.
10. The word testified most nearly means
    a. made a will.
    b. spoken out.
    c. sworn in court.
    d. taken a test.

Understanding the Essay

1. The house that the author buys is
   a. small but new and filled with windows.
   b. odd and windowless.

c. old, rundown, and small but with many windows.
d. large, open, and filled with light.

2. Which of the following is *not* mentioned as one of the "clear and silent gifts" of a window?
   a. letting in sunlight
   b. affording a view of the snow
   c. keeping out rain
   d. letting in moonlight
3. The author's attitude toward window washing is
   a. mostly positive.
   b. mostly negative.
   c. neutral.
   d. inconsistent.
4. The author says that women today do not do windows because
   a. it is demeaning work.
   b. they are poor housekeepers.
   c. they are too busy.
   d. they consider it "men's work."
5. Along with narration, which pattern of development is used predominantly in the essay?
   a. comparison-contrast
   b. cause-effect
   c. argument
   d. process
6. According to the author, which of the following is "women's work"?
   a. fighting
   b. teaching
   c. cooking
   d. all of the above
7. In teaching her daughter to do windows, the author believes all of the following *except*
   a. She is passing on something important.
   b. She is doing something unconventional.
   c. She is out of step with the times.
   d. She is teaching her daughter that housework is strictly a woman's role.

Looking at Language

8. Look at the use of parallel structure in paragraph 9. Write the parallel phrases on the lines below.

____

____

____

____

____

9. Look at the way Raybon describes the first time she and her daughter wash windows together. Which of the five senses does Raybon emphasize in her description? Write down four phrases from the description that convey a sense impression.

____

____

____

10. Look at the following sentence from paragraph 27: "Last week, I dipped the sponge into the pail and began the gentle bath—easing off the trace of wintry snows, of dust storms and dead, brown leaves, of too much sticky tape used to steady paper pumpkins and Christmas lights and crepe-paper bows from holidays now past." How does Raybon feel about the task she is describing? Specifically, which words and phrases serve to tell you how she feels?

____

____

____

Discussing the Essay

Prepare to discuss the following questions in class by thinking about them or writing about them in your journal.

1. How does Raybon feel about the work her mother and grandmother did?

2. Why does Raybon attach significance to the fact that her grandmother's employers called her "Laura" and never used her surname? Think about the relationships you have with others. Who addresses you by your first name? By your surname? How do you address them? Does it make a difference to you? Why or why not?
3. Look at the tasks mentioned by Raybon as "women's work." Are all of them "women's work" in the stereotypical sense? Are any of them normally stereotyped as "men's work"?

Topics for Writing

Assignment 1: "Wash Me"

Journal Entry

You are a window in a house or a car. You are so dirty that some prankster has written "Wash Me" in the grime that covers you. In a journal entry, convince the owner of the house or car to wash you. Include the advantages to the washer as well as the advantages to you.

Assignment 2: An Enjoyable Chore

Essay

Write a process essay telling your reader how you go about doing some chore that you enjoy. Perhaps you enjoy doing laundry, shopping for groceries, cleaning a closet, washing your car, or mowing the lawn. Make sure the essay conveys your enjoyment as well as the steps involved in the chore.

Assignment 3: Handed Down

Essay

In an essay, describe a special tradition, knowledge, or way of doing something that has been passed to you by older members of your family.

Assignment 4: What's in a Name?

Essay

Write an essay discussing the different messages people send through the way they use others' names. There are a couple of different approaches you might take. One is to write a process essay telling what rules should apply in using others' names. You might consider such matters as whether the other person is a stranger or an acquaintance, whether the person is older or younger, and whether the relationship is business or personal. Another is to write an example essay discussing the names various people call you and what those names convey to you.

Coping with Procrastination

Roberta Moore, Barbara Baker, and Arnold H. Packer

Procrastination—why do people put things off, and what should they do about the problem? The authors have some suggestions.

Any discussion of time management would not be complete without an examination of the most well-intentioned person's worst enemy—procrastination. The dictionary *(Webster's New Collegiate)* defines procrastination as "the act of putting off intentionally and habitually the doing of something that should be done." Interestingly, most procrastinators do not feel that they are acting intentionally. On the contrary, they feel that they fully *intend* to do whatever it is, but they simply cannot, will not, or—bottom line—they *do not* do it. Procrastinators usually have good reasons for their procrastination (some would call them excuses): "didn't have time," "didn't feel well," "couldn't figure out what to do," "couldn't find what I needed," "the weather was too bad"—the list is never-ending. 1

Even procrastinators themselves know that the surface reasons for their procrastination are, for the most part, not valid. When procrastination becomes extreme, it is a self-destructive course and yet, people feel that they are powerless to stop it. This perception can become reality if the underlying cause is not uncovered. Experts have identified some of the serious underlying causes of procrastination. Think about them the next time you find yourself struck by this problem. 2

Often procrastination stems from a real or imagined fear or worry that is focused not so much on the thing you are avoiding but its potential consequences. For instance, your procrastination over preparing for an oral presentation could be based on your fear that no matter how well prepared you are, you will be overcome by nerves and forget whatever you are prepared to say. Every time you think about working on the speech, you become so worried about doing "a bad job" that you have to put the whole thing out of your mind to calm down. You decide that you will feel calmer about it tomorrow and will be in a much better frame of mind to tackle it. Tomorrow the scenario gets repeated. The best way to relieve your anxiety would be to dig in and prepare so well that you can't possibly do poorly. 3

Being a perfectionist is one of the main traits that spawns fear and anxiety. Whose expectations are we afraid of not meeting? Often it is our own harsh judgment of ourselves that creates the problem. We set standards that are too 4 high and then judge ourselves too critically. When you picture yourself speaking before a group, are you thinking about how nervous the other students will be as well, or are you comparing your speaking abilities to the anchorperson on the six o'clock news? A more calming thought is to recall how athletes measure improvements in their performances by tracking and trying to improve on their own "personal best." Champions have to work on beating themselves in order to become capable of competing against their opponents. Concentrating on improving your own past performance, and thinking of specific ways to do so, relieves performance anxiety.

On the surface this would seem to be the reason for all procrastination, and the obvious answer is for the procrastinator to find a way to "get motivated." There are situations where lack of motivation is an indicator that you have taken a wrong turn. When you seriously do not want to do the things you need to do, you may need to reevaluate your situation. Did you decide to get a degree in Information Systems because everyone says that's where the high paying jobs are going to be, when you really want to be a social worker or a travel agent? If so, when you find yourself shooting hoops or watching television when you should be putting in time at the computer lab, it may be time to reexamine your decision. Setting out to accomplish something difficult when your heart isn't in it, is often the root cause of self-destructive behavior. 5

Often procrastination is due to an inability to concentrate or a feeling of being overwhelmed and indecisive. While everyone experiences these feelings during a particular stressful day or week, a continuation of these feelings could indicate that you are in a state of burnout. Burnout is a serious problem that occurs when you have overextended yourself for too long a period of time. It is especially likely to occur if you are pushing yourself both physically and mentally. By failing to pace yourself, you will "hit the wall," like the long distance runner who runs too fast at the beginning of the race. Overworking yourself for too long without mental and physical relaxation is a sure way to run out of steam. Learning to balance your time and set realistic expectations for yourself will prevent burnout. 6

Sometimes you put off doing something because you literally don't know how to do it. This may be hard to admit to yourself, so you may make other excuses. When you can't get started on something, consider the possibility that you need help. For example, if you get approval from your favorite instructor for a term paper topic that requires collecting data and creating graphics, you can be stymied if you don't have the necessary skills and tools to do the work and do it well. Does the collection and analysis of the data require the use of a software program that you don't have and cannot afford to buy? Sometimes it is difficult to ask for help and sometimes it is even hard to recognize that you need help. When you feel stymied, ask yourself, "Do I need help?" Do you need information but haven't a clue as to where to go to get it? Have you committed to doing something that is really beyond your level of skills? Being able to own up to personal limitations and seek out support and resources where needed is a skill used every day by highly successful people. 7

Building Vocabulary

For each question, use your dictionary and context clues to choose the meaning that most nearly defines the underlined word or phrase as it is used in the essay.

1. The word well-intentioned most nearly means
   a. well-meaning.
   b. well-rounded.
   c. well-spoken.
   d. well-dressed.
2. The word procrastination most nearly means
   a. perfectionism.
   b. putting things off.
   c. predicting the future.
   d. time management.
3. The word intentionally most nearly means
   a. creatively.
   b. conventionally.
   c. carelessly.
   d. deliberately.
4. The word valid most nearly means
   a. false.
   b. valiant.
   c. genuine.
   d. reasons.
5. The word perception most nearly means
   a. reception.
   b. belief.
   c. condition.
   d. power.
6. The word underlying most nearly means
   a. false.
   b. surface.
   c. root.
   d. mild.

7. The word potential most nearly means
   a. potent.
   b. possible.
   c. confidential.
   d. favorable.
8. The word spawns most nearly means
   a. prevents.
   b. relieves.
   c. produces.
   d. spurns.
9. The word burnout most likely means
   a. fire.
   b. energy.
   c. productivity.
   d. exhaustion.
10. The word stymied most likely means
    a. helped.
    b. hindered.
    c. stylish.
    d. successful.

Understanding the Essay

1. Which of the following most closely expresses the main idea of the essay?
   a. People who procrastinate need to get motivated.
   b. Procrastination is unintentional.
   c. Procrastination can be understood and controlled.
   d. Some of the world's most famous people have been procrastinators.
2. Procrastinators tend to be
   a. lazy.
   b. male.
   c. perfectionists.
   d. low achievers.
3. Which of the following is *not* mentioned as a cause of procrastination?
   a. not being sure how to do something
   b. expecting too much of oneself

c. not being sure when a project is due
d. not being motivated

4. According to the authors, inability to concentrate or feeling overwhelmed and indecisive could be a sign of
   a. procrastination.
   b. physical illness.
   c. burnout.
   d. mental instability.
5. Which of the following methods of development is *not* used in the essay?
   a. narration
   b. example
   c. definition
   d. process
6. The authors imply that a tendency to procrastinate
   a. is always a problem for college students.
   b. can be controlled with several simple steps.
   c. is something the individual can at least partly control.
   d. is a sign of more serious problems.
7. To overcome procrastination, the authors suggest all but which of the following?
   a. Set realistic expectations.
   b. Do only the things you enjoy.
   c. Seek out support.
   d. Recognize your limitations.

■ Looking at Language

8. The authors' tone can best be described as
   a. helpful.
   b. stern.
   c. humorous.
   d. apologetic.
9. How do the authors define *burnout?* How can it be prevented?

____

____

____

10. The essay is written primarily from a second-person point of view, with the authors addressing the readers as "you." Why do you think the authors chose second-person point of view for this essay?

____

____

____

Discussing the Essay

Prepare to discuss the following questions in class by thinking about them or writing about them in your journal.

1. Who is the intended audience for this essay? How do you know?
2. Does the essay change your views of procrastination? If so, how?

Topics for Writing

Assignment 1: Consequences of Procrastination

Journal Entry

Write a journal entry about a time when you procrastinated on something important. What were the consequences of your procrastination?

Assignment 2: Overcoming Procrastination

Essay

Write a process essay giving advice on how to overcome procrastination. Include specific examples as you write.

Assignment 3: Your Worst Habit

Essay

Procrastination is a real problem for some people. Others have different habits that they would like to break. Write an essay answering one or more of the following questions: What is your worst habit, and why do you want to break it? Alternatively, why don't you want to break it? What does it do for you that makes you want to keep it?

Migraine Blues

Candace Dyer

For people with migraines, there is often little relief and, worse yet, no sympathy. Writer Candance Dyer offers a view from inside the head of a migraine sufferer.

My new friend at the bar was clutching her temples and looking mad enough to kick a puppy if it stumbled into her path. 1

"I have a migraine," she announced. 2

"Oh, man, I have those, too," I commiserated. "Aren't they the worst?" 3

"Mine last for days," she said. 4

"So do mine." 5

"Well, mine are so bad I've had to have an I.V. of Demerol." 6

"Well, so have I." 7

Thus began one of those ridiculous games of swaggering one-upmanship that define modern culture. Whose headaches were worse? She's had a few more CAT scans than I have, but I've undergone the dreaded spinal tap. 8

Ultimately she won. She once had a migraine attack that lasted 31 days—*she said*. 9

That settled, we bonded like a couple of war veterans. There is an instant rapport among migraine sufferers, similar to that of Trekkies, mimes, square dancers and other misunderstood groups. When we meet, we discuss our throbbing craniums with the same detail and absorption of mothers talking about their pregnancies at a baby shower. 10

Why this obsessive camaraderie? Only those who have felt a nuclear holocaust raging within their skulls know what it's like, and the rest of the world sniffs at us as if we're football players sitting on the bench because of a hangnail. 11

A migraine attack is a blinding headache that often is accompanied by nausea, vomiting, vision blurred with pulsating circles of light and overwhelming sensitivity to all stimuli. Imagine all of the dark phantoms and demons in your mind kicking and howling at once. 12

It is a hereditary, organic illness related to blood flow and biochemicals, and it often coexists, but is not necessarily linked, with anxiety. Specific causes aren't known, and treatments are trial and error; but researchers have found a way to give a pig a migraine, poor creature. (Scientists say they can't be certain that the animal is replicating the human headache, but its facial expression looks unquestionably ticked off.) 13

Because of its association with neurosis, migraine is viewed as just another symptom of being uptight, the deserved affliction of the anal-retentive. "It's all in your mind," is among the kinder diagnoses people have made while sizing me up as a Camille swooning with the vapors. "Just relax a little. Shake it off. Don't let things bother you so much." 14

In her 1968 essay "Sojourn in Bed," Joan Didion wrote, "That in fact I spent one or two days a week almost unconscious with pain seemed a shameful secret, evidence not merely of some chemical inferiority but of all my bad attitudes, unpleasant tempers, wrongthink . . . all of us who have migraine suffer not only from the attacks themselves but from this common conviction that we are perversely refusing to cure ourselves by taking a couple of aspirin, that we are making ourselves sick, that we 'bring it on ourselves.' " 15

I've consumed so many painkillers that my body should be able to absorb several rounds of artillery and keep on partying, and my savings account gurgles with a cavernous sinkhole forced by dozens of trips to the E.R.; two respected neurologists; two chiropractors; and a spooky, pompadour-coiffed faith healer who studied my eyes and feet for clues. I've given myself injections; put peppermint oil on my temples as an earthy friend suggested; and I've worn a head-shaped *milagro,* a Latin-American charm designed to flag down divine intervention. 16

Yet I've had pals, supervisors and even doctors question my commitment to getting better. Migraine is a tut-tut offense in workplaces that wouldn't dream of chiding employees for diabetes or allergies, and many unfeeling health-care workers treat migraine patients like junkies jonesing for a narcotic fix. 17

But enough of that. If migraine is the worst medical problem I ever suffer, I'll be truly lucky. 18

It is primarily an illness of the young, usually affecting people under thirty-five, most of them women. Its survivors—it may not be fatal, but it feels like the prick of mortality—say they eventually outgrew or outlasted it. Time healed their heads as it did their broken hearts, my grandmothers say. Migraine is often described as a circuit breaker for an overloaded system, one doozie of a growing pain that allows its victims to marvel at their own endurance. 19

Didion goes on to describe the heightened awareness and euphoric, cleansed feeling she enjoys when the pain subsides. She explains that over the years she has made peace with her migraine, that it has become something of a friend. 20

While I have friends who can be pains, the converse doesn't hold true right now. But I know I can count on the woman at the bar, the one with the Job-like, thirty-one-day tribulation, to take me to the E.R. 21

Building Vocabulary

For each question, use your dictionary and context clues to choose the meaning that most nearly defines the underlined word or phrase as it is used in the essay.

1. The word rapport most nearly means
   a. dislike.
   b. pain.
   c. bond.
   d. report.
2. The word stimuli most nearly means
   a. comments.
   b. headaches.
   c. irritants.
   d. experimental environments.
3. The word organic most nearly means
   a. mental.
   b. physical.
   c. false.
   d. imaginary.
4. The word affliction most nearly means
   a. anxiety.
   b. affiliation.
   c. reward.
   d. ailment.
5. The word perversely most nearly means
   a. stubbornly.
   b. pervasively.
   c. all.
   d. happily.
6. The phrase a tut-tut offense most nearly means
   a. stealing artifacts.
   b. a misdemeanor.
   c. an act that is frowned on.
   d. a firing offense.
7. The word chiding most nearly means
   a. scolding.
   b. docking employees' pay.
   c. praising.
   d. paying.

8. The phrase jonesing for a narcotic fix most nearly means
   a. saying "no" to drugs.
   b. requesting a prescription medication for an illness.
   c. craving a drug one is addicted to.
   d. keeping up with the Joneses.
9. The word mortality most nearly means
   a. life.
   b. death.
   c. illness.
   d. totality.
10. The word tribulation most nearly means
    a. month.
    b. tribute.
    c. ordeal.
    d. hangover.

Understanding the Essay

1. Which statement most nearly expresses the main idea of the essay?
   a. Migraine is a hereditary, organic illness related to blood flow and biochemicals.
   b. Though medicine or a *milagro* may work occasionally, no real cure for migraine exists.
   c. Joan Didion's essay, "Sojourn in Bed," shows how a person can learn to live with migraine.
   d. Migraine is a painful and often misunderstood condition.
2. Which method of introduction does the author use?
   a. anecdote
   b. broad to narrow
   c. quotation
   d. contrast
3. The main reason that the author quotes Joan Didion is
   a. to show that she has researched the subject.
   b. to give an opinion from a medical doctor who is an expert on headaches.
   c. to lend support to her own thesis.
   d. to show a contrasting point of view.

4. According to the author, migraine most often affects
   a. people who are anxious.
   b. creative, temperamental people.
   c. men and women under forty.
   d. women under thirty-five.
5. Which pattern of development is used predominantly in the essay?
   a. comparison-contrast
   b. definition
   c. argument
   d. process
6. Which of the following does the author *not* imply about people's attitudes toward migraine sufferers?
   a. People often believe migraine sufferers are neurotics whose affliction is more mental than physical.
   b. Bosses sometimes frown on employees who miss work because of migraines.
   c. People always look down on migraine sufferers and have no sympathy for them.
   d. Those who understand the problem best are other migraine sufferers.
7. Which technique does the author use to conclude her essay?
   a. prediction
   b. recommendation
   c. quotation
   d. full circle

Looking at Language

8. An *allusion* is an indirect reference to a work of literature that is familiar to most members of a culture. Allusions often refer to a work of mythology or religious literature. Look in the last paragraph and find the allusion. To what does it refer? Explain how the allusion relates to the essay.

____

____

____

9. Dyer's essay is enriched by visually descriptive language. Find and list three examples of visual description from the essay.

10. When the author says in paragraph 21, "While I have friends who can be pains, the converse doesn't hold true right now," what does she mean? (If you are not sure, look at paragraph 20 for a hint.)

Discussing the Essay

Prepare to discuss the following questions in class by thinking about them or writing about them in your journal.

1. Dyer's conversation with the woman in the bar begins with "one of those ridiculous games of swaggering one-upmanship that define modern culture." Do you agree that people often try to outdo one another, even on such matters as illnesses? Can you think of an example from your own experience?
2. Dyer quotes Joan Didion as saying that her migraine has become a friend. How can a pain or affliction be a friend? Have you ever experienced such a feeling? Is it good to accept pain, or does acceptance signify giving in?

Topics for Writing

Assignment 1: Becoming a Pain

Journal Entry

You are a migraine headache, just entering a victim's head and spreading your painful tentacles. Write a narrative journal entry describing how you affect your victim.

Assignment 2: Serious Business

Essay

Do you have, or have you ever experienced, an illness or a condition that people viewed lightly even though it was serious to you? In an essay, contrast your view of the condition with others' view of it.

Assignment 3: A Misunderstood Group

Essay

Dyer describes the feeling of comradeship among migraine sufferers, whom she portrays as members of a misunderstood group. Write an essay that defines a particular misunderstood group. It may be a group that you belong to, or it may be one you have observed sympathetically because you know someone who belongs to it. Your definition should be mainly subjective—that is, it should reveal your feelings—but you may also want to include objective details. (See Chapter 9 for a detailed explanation of subjective and objective definitions.) The group you choose may suffer from a particular disease, as did the one in "Migraine Blues," or it may share a different common bond. Some possibilities are listed below.

fans of a particular type of music
gays and lesbians
members of a particular ethnic group
overweight people
people with disabilities
police officers
senior citizens
shy people
single parents
teenagers

Assignment 4: The You-Name-It Blues

Essay

Dyer's essay describes the migraine blues. Write an essay about a type of blues that you have experienced. What was the cause? How did you feel? What was the cure? To start you off, a list of possibilities appears below.

the homesick blues
the lost-love blues
the penniless blues
the transportation blues
the working blues

The Right to Die

Norman Cousins

Suicide is traditionally considered a tragedy, even a sin. Under certain circumstances, can it be considered a triumph over a slow and painful death?

1 The world of religion and philosophy was shocked recently when Henry P. Van Dusen and his wife ended their lives by their own hands. Dr. Van Dusen had been president of Union Theological Seminary; for more than a quarter-century he had been one of the luminous names in Protestant theology. He enjoyed world status as a spiritual leader. News of the self-inflicted death of the Van Dusens, therefore, was profoundly disturbing to all those who attach a moral stigma to suicide and regard it as a violation of God's laws.

2 Dr. Van Dusen had anticipated this reaction. He and his wife left behind a letter that may have historic significance. It was very brief, but the essential point it made is now being widely discussed by theologians and could represent the beginning of a reconsideration of traditional religious attitudes toward self-inflicted death. The letter raised a moral issue: does an individual have the obligation to go on living even when the beauty and meaning and power of life are gone?

3 Henry and Elizabeth Van Dusen had lived full lives. In recent years, they had become increasingly ill, requiring almost continual medical care. Their infirmities were worsening, and they realized they would soon become completely dependent for even the most elementary needs and functions. Under these circumstances, little dignity would have been left in life. They didn't like the idea of taking up space in a world with too many mouths and too little food. They believed it was a misuse of medical science to keep them technically alive.

4 They therefore believed they had the right to decide when to die. In making that decision, they weren't turning against life as the highest value; what they were turning against was the notion that there were no circumstances under which life should be discontinued.

5 An important aspect of human uniqueness is the power of free will. In his books and lectures, Dr. Van Dusen frequently spoke about the exercise of this uniqueness. The fact that he used his free will to prevent life from becoming a caricature of itself was completely in character. In their letter, the Van Dusens sought to convince family and friends that they were not acting solely out of despair or pain.

6 The use of free will to put an end to one's life finds no sanction in the theology to which Pitney Van Dusen was committed. Suicide symbolizes discontinuity; religion symbolizes continuity, represented at its quintessence by the concept of the immortal soul. Human logic finds it almost impossible to come to terms

with the concept of nonexistence. In religion, the human mind finds a larger dimension and is relieved of the ordeal of a confrontation with non-existence.

Even without respect to religion, the idea of suicide has been abhorrent 7 throughout history. Some societies have imposed severe penalties on the families of suicides in the hope that the individual who sees no reason to continue his existence may be deterred by the stigma his self-destruction would inflict on loved ones. Other societies have enacted laws prohibiting suicide on the grounds that it is murder. The enforcement of such laws, of course, has been an exercise in futility.

Customs and attitudes, like individuals themselves, are largely shaped by 8 the surrounding environment. In today's world, life can be prolonged by science far beyond meaning or sensibility. Under these circumstances, individuals who feel they have nothing more to give to life, or to receive from it, need not be applauded, but they can be spared our condemnation.

The general reaction to suicide is bound to change as people come to un- 9 derstand that it may be a denial, not an assertion, of moral or religious ethics to allow life to be extended without regard to decency or pride. What moral or religious purpose is celebrated by the annihilation of the human spirit in the triumphant act of keeping the body alive? Why are so many people more readily appalled by an unnatural form of dying than by an unnatural form of living?

"Nowadays," the Van Dusens wrote in their last letter, "it is difficult to die. 10 We feel that this way we are taking will become more usual and acceptable as the years pass.

"Of course, the thought of our children and our grandchildren makes us sad, 11 but we still feel that this is the best way and the right way to go. We are both increasingly weak and unwell and who would want to die in a nursing home?

"We are not afraid to die. . . ." 12

Pitney Van Dusen was admired and respected in life. He can be admired 13 and respected in death. "Suicide," said Goethe, "is an incident in human life which, however much disputed and discussed, demands the sympathy of every man, and in every age must be dealt with anew."

Death is not the greatest loss in life. The greatest loss is what dies inside us 14 while we live. The unbearable tragedy is to live without dignity or sensitivity.

Building Vocabulary

For each question, use your dictionary and context clues to choose the meaning that most nearly defines the underlined word or phrase as it is used in the essay.

1. The word theology most nearly means
   a. study of death and dying.
   b. study of God and religion.
   c. general education.
   d. thanatology.

2. The word stigma most nearly means
   a. shame.
   b. thought.
   c. approval.
   d. need.
3. The word infirmities most nearly means
   a. certainties.
   b. finances.
   c. inequities.
   d. disabilities.
4. The word sanction most nearly means
   a. sanctity.
   b. approval.
   c. mention.
   d. disapproval.
5. The word quintessence most nearly means
   a. worst.
   b. essence.
   c. sidelines.
   d. most believable.
6. The word ordeal most nearly means
   a. imbalance.
   b. pleasure.
   c. ordinance.
   d. difficulty.
7. The word abhorrent most nearly means
   a. repulsive.
   b. desirable.
   c. accepted.
   d. thought-provoking.
8. The word condemnation most nearly means
   a. applause.
   b. pity.
   c. disapproval.
   d. consecration.
9. The word assertion most nearly means
   a. confirmation.
   b. suggestion.

c. withdrawal.
d. rejection.

10. The word annihilation most nearly means
    a. affiliation.
    b. impression.
    c. destruction.
    d. exhilaration.

Understanding the Essay

1. Which statement best expresses the main idea of the essay?
   a. Suicide should be considered legal and ethical under any circumstances.
   b. Even without respect to religion, the idea of suicide has been abhorrent throughout history.
   c. When death is close at hand, people should be able to choose suicide as an alternative to a lingering death in a hospital or nursing home.
   d. Suicide is not the answer, no matter what the circumstances.
2. Which of the following statements about Henry P. Van Dusen is *not* made in the essay?
   a. He was a former president of Union Theological Seminary.
   b. He required almost continual medical care.
   c. He was profoundly depressed.
   d. He believed in exercising free will.
3. The author states that opposition to suicide
   a. has traditionally come from both religion and culture.
   b. has been traditionally prohibited for religious reasons only.
   c. is a cultural tradition of fairly recent origin.
   d. comes mainly from Protestants.
4. Which of the following was *not* a reason that the Van Dusens gave for their choice to commit suicide?
   a. They would have little dignity left.
   b. Hospital and nursing home care is too expensive.
   c. The world's food and resources are scarce.
   d. Medical resources are best used on someone else.
5. From paragraph 8, it can be inferred that the author reluctantly accepts the idea of suicide because
   a. medical science can now prolong life artificially, beyond reason or dignity.

b. like Dr. Pitney Van Dusen, he believes in the exercise of free will.
c. customs and attitudes change, and society is constantly changing.
d. he is convinced that the Van Dusens believed that they were doing the right thing.

6. Which of the following would the author likely consider most important factor in a decision to commit suicide?
   a. religious beliefs
   b. the law
   c. hospitalization or the necessity of going into a nursing home
   d. the person's quality of life

7. Norman Cousins develops his essay mainly through
   a. description
   b. comparison
   c. process
   d. argument

■ Looking at Language

8. The essay contains many transitional words and expressions, particularly time transitions and cause-effect transitions. Write three of them on the lines provided.

   ____

   ____

9. In writing, plain language and short, simple words often carry greater emotional impact, while elevated language and long words often create emotional distance. In this essay, Cousins uses elevated language. Why would he want to put his audience at an emotional distance?

   ____

   ____

   ____

10. Choose three unfamiliar words from the essay that are not among the vocabulary questions. Define each.

   ____

   ____

   ____

Discussing the Essay

Prepare to discuss the following questions in class by thinking about them or writing about them in your journal.

1. List some of the reasons that a culture might have for opposing suicide.
2. Cousins says that the Van Dusens' deaths raise this moral question: does an individual have the obligation to go on living even when the beauty and meaning and power of life are gone? What is your answer to that question?

Topics for Writing

Assignment 1: Something to Live For

Journal Entry

Working late in your high-rise office, you look out the window and see a person standing on a ledge, ready to jump. You pick up the phone to call 911, but all the phone lines are out and the battery in your cell phone is dead. If this person is to be saved, it is up to you. What do you say to convince the person that life is worth living?

Assignment 2: The Right to Die

Essay

Should people who are terminally ill and/or old and infirm have the legal right to commit suicide? Why or why not?

Assignment 3: Nursing Homes

Essay

Before their deaths by suicide, Pitney and Elizabeth Van Dusen wrote, "We are both increasingly weak and unwell, and who would want to die in a nursing home?" Few people want to die (or live) in a nursing home. Write an essay that answers *one* of the following questions about nursing homes.

1. What are the main reasons that people are reluctant to live in nursing homes?
2. What changes could be made to make nursing homes desirable places for elderly people to live?
3. Have you ever had an elderly relative who had to make the transition from living in his or her own home to living in a nursing home? Describe your relative's experience.

Assignment 4: Fear of Old Age

Essay

Aside from a fear of death, what are some of the reasons people fear getting old? Write an essay describing some of the major reasons.

The Brutal Business of Boxing

John Head

Supporters of boxing say it is legitimate sport and good entertainment. Opponents say it is a cruel bloodletting. John Head weighs the evidence.

1 Long ago, I thought I was a fight fan. I was fooling myself. It wasn't boxing that fascinated me. It was Muhammad Ali.

2 The brash young man who entered the world's consciousness as Cassius Clay had the same effect on millions of people. The force of his personality made them sit up and take notice of his sport. He was confident, articulate and charismatic. He spouted poetry and predicted knockout rounds.

3 Ali performed with a grace and athleticism previously unseen in heavyweight boxers. He said he was too pretty to be hit, and he fought that way. His speed and fancy footwork befuddled many an opponent. He really did "float like a butterfly and sting like a bee," delivering lightning-quick jabs that individually did little damage but in their aggregate wore the other fighter down. His matches seemed more like ballet than boxing.

4 But looking back now, as someone who knows better, I can see that it was the dirty business of boxing after all. Ali's prefight taunting and ridiculing of opponents wasn't always just hype. At times he stepped into the ring intending to hurt the other guy as much as possible, and he did. From time to time he refused to finish off adversaries, delighting in prolonging their humiliation and punishment.

5 And Ali paid a price. Even as he appeared to duck most punches, he took lots of blows. Long after the skills that protected him had diminished, he still fought. He continued to win, but he took terrible beatings doing it.

6 The results can be seen in what Muhammad Ali has become compared to what he once was. He suffers from symptoms of Parkinson's disease, but it would better be called punching disease, the result of all those blows to the head. The man whose movements were so fast they seemed acts of sorcery now has trouble with a slow shuffle. The voice whose words once flowed like a mighty river has been reduced to a hesitant whisper.

7 My mind has been on Ali—and what he made me think boxing was so long ago—because the sport recently showed once again what it really is. Jimmy Garcia, a 23-year-old super featherweight from Colombia, was pummeled in Las Vegas, much to the delight of fans who paid big bucks to see the fight. He was taken to a hospital, where he was in a coma for nearly two weeks before life support was disconnected.

He was the latest boxer to suffer fatal injuries in the ring, the latest proof 8
that boxing isn't a sport. It's legalized barbarity.

Garcia had barely breathed his last breath before defenders of boxing deliv- 9
ered preemptive strikes against its critics. Boxing is the most elemental sport there is, they said, a contest of courage and skill between two individuals. People are killed in all kinds of sports, from football to auto racing, they said. Why do people who aren't fans, who know little about boxing, single it out as dangerous?

What sets boxing apart is that it is the one sport in which one scores by in- 10
juring the opponent. One can, in fact, win by injuring the other guy to the point that he is unable to continue. Two men step into the ring intending to do as much damage to each other as possible, and people pay to see it happen.

A magician named Muhammad Ali once upon a time created an illusion 11
that this was sport. But it was an illusion.

Boxing is no sport, and it has no place in civilized society. Ban it. Ban it now. 12

Building Vocabulary

For each question, use your dictionary and context clues to choose the meaning that most nearly defines the underlined word or phrase as it is used in the essay.

1. The word befuddled most nearly means
   a. pleased.
   b. confused.
   c. angered.
   d. bespattered.
2. The word aggregate most nearly means
   a. totality.
   b. strength.
   c. aggravation.
   d. power.
3. The word taunting most nearly means
   a. complimenting.
   b. punching.
   c. disliking.
   d. mocking.
4. The word hype most nearly means
   a. confidence.
   b. agitation.
   c. exaggeration.
   d. greeting.

5. The expression finish off most nearly means
   a. defeat.
   b. fight.
   c. give in to.
   d. shake hands with.
6. The word sorcery most nearly means
   a. quickness.
   b. magic.
   c. brutality.
   d. speed.
7. The word pummeled most nearly means
   a. headquartered.
   b. living.
   c. killed.
   d. beaten.
8. The word barbarity most nearly means
   a. offensiveness.
   b. civility.
   c. savagery.
   d. sarcasm.
9. The expression preemptive strikes most nearly means
   a. defense.
   b. criticism.
   c. proof.
   d. threats.
10. The word elemental most nearly means
    a. brutal.
    b. elementary.
    c. basic.
    d. purely mental.

Understanding the Essay

1. Of the choices below, the best alternative title would be
   a. "Muhammad Ali: A True Champion."
   b. "Float Like a Butterfly, Sting Like a Bee."
   c. "The Sport of Boxing."
   d. "Why Boxing Should Be Banned."

2. In paragraph 7, the primary purpose of the example of Jimmy Garcia is
   a. to show that boxing is a brutal sport.
   b. to show that the physical harm done to Muhammad Ali by the sport of boxing is not an isolated case.
   c. to show that Muhammad Ali is fortunate not to have died in the boxing ring.
   d. to show that boxing fans are callous and bloodthirsty.
3. The writer's attitude toward Muhammad Ali can best be described as
   a. neutral.
   b. unsympathetic.
   c. condescending.
   d. admiring.
4. In paragraph 9, the writer presents the case of those who support boxing because
   a. he wants to present a balanced view.
   b. he believes the supporters of boxing make some good points.
   c. he wants to answer and argue against their views.
   d. he is not sure how he feels about boxing.
5. With which statement would the author most likely agree?
   a. Boxers are sometimes victimized by the cruel sport of boxing.
   b. Boxers go into the sport knowing the risks and thus deserve little sympathy if they are killed or injured.
   c. Boxing should be banned along with all other dangerous sports.
   d. Boxing is a contest of courage and skill between two individuals.
6. Which statement best describes the author's attitude toward boxing?
   a. He hates boxing and everything associated with it.
   b. He enjoys watching boxing, but hates what it does to athletes.
   c. He used to dislike boxing, but is now convinced that it is a legitimate sport.
   d. He was once fooled by Ali's artistry but now sees that boxing is not a sport.
7. The author's primary purpose in writing the essay is to
   a. inform.
   b. persuade.
   c. compare and contrast.
   d. describe.

Looking at Language

8. Look at this sentence from paragraph 6: "The voice whose words once flowed like a mighty river has been reduced to a hesitant whisper." What do the words *like a mighty river* suggest about Ali's words? What does the entire sentence suggest about Ali himself?

9. Look at the first sentence of paragraph 9 and consider the words "Garcia had barely breathed his last breath" in the first sentence. How does this opening make a reader feel about defenders of boxing?

10. Look at the last two sentences of the essay: "Ban it. Ban it now." What effect do the short, repetitive sentences have? Imagine that the author had ended instead with this sentence: "Therefore, if we are to call ourselves a civilized society, we must seriously consider banning the brutal business of boxing." Would the change make the ending weaker or stronger? Why?

Discussing the Essay

Prepare to discuss the following questions in class by thinking about them or writing about them in your journal.

1. Do you agree or disagree that boxing should be banned? Why?
2. The United States has laws to protect people against their own actions. Some examples include the prohibition of alcoholic beverages in the

1920s and mandatory seatbelt and motorcycle helmet laws. Some believe that these laws are necessary, while others argue that people should have the freedom to control their own actions. What is your view?

Topics for Writing

Assignment 1: Banning Boxing

Journal Entry

Do you believe boxing should be banned? Discuss your reasons in a journal entry.

Assignment 2: Off the Books

Essay

If a law banning boxing went into effect, supporters of boxing would call for its repeal. If you had the power to take any current law off the books, what law would you choose? Explain why in an essay.

Assignment 3: Take It Away!

Essay

If you could ban anything in the world, what would it be? The choice is yours, from nuclear weapons to pink plastic lawn flamingos, from violent television programs to using cellular phones while driving. Discuss your choice in an essay.

Assignment 4: Not the Same

Essay

Look at paragraph 6, which contrasts the Ali of today with Ali in his heyday. Write a descriptive essay showing how someone you know has changed. The change you write about may be one of appearance, ability, behavior, or outlook. Describe the change specifically, and if the change is within the person, show the reader outward actions that reflect the change.

Date Rape: Exposing Dangerous Myths

John J. Macionis

Rape is almost always committed by a stranger . . . isn't it? Sociologist John J. Macionis sheds light on the dark subject of date rape and exposes the myths that surround it.

Completing a day of work during a business trip to the courthouse in Tampa, Florida, thirty-two-year-old Sandra Abbott pondered how she would return to her hotel. An attorney with whom she had been working—a pleasant enough man—made the kind offer of a lift. As his car threaded its way through the late afternoon traffic, their conversation was animated. "He was saying all the right things," Abbott recalled, "so I started to trust him." 1

He asked if she would join him for dinner; she happily accepted. After lingering over an enjoyable meal, they walked together to the door of her hotel room. The new acquaintance angled for an invitation to come in and talk, but Abbott hesitated, sensing that he might have something more on his mind. She explained that she was old-fashioned about relationships but would allow him to come in for a little while with the understanding that talk was all they would do. 2

Sitting on the couch in the room, soon Abbott was overcome with drowsiness. Feeling comfortable in the presence of her new friend, she let her head fall gently onto his shoulder, and, before she knew it, she fell asleep. That's when the attack began. Abbott was startled back to consciousness as the man thrust himself upon her sexually. She shouted: "No!" but he paid no heed. Abbott describes what happened next: 3

> I didn't scream or run. All I could think of was my business contacts and what if they saw me run out of my room screaming rape. I thought it was my fault. I felt so filthy, I washed myself over and over in hot water. Did he rape me? I kept asking myself. I didn't consent. But who's gonna believe me? I had a man in my hotel room after midnight.

Abbott knew that she had said "No!" and thus had been raped. She notified the police, who conducted an investigation and turned their findings over to the state attorney's office. But the authorities backed away. In the absence of evidence like bruises, a medical examination, and torn clothes, they noted, there was little point in prosecuting. 4

The case of Sandra Abbott is all too typical. Even today, in most incidences of sexual attack, a victim makes no report to police, and no offender is arrested. 5

The reason for such inaction is that many people have a misguided understanding of rape. Three false notions about rape are so common in the United States that they might be called "rape myths."

A first rape myth is that rape involves strangers. A sexual attack brings to mind young men lurking in the shadows who suddenly spring on their unsuspecting victims. But this pattern is the exception rather than the rule: Four out of five rapes are committed by offenders known to their victims. For this reason, people have begun to speak more realistically about *acquaintance rape* or, more simply, *date rape*. 6

A second myth about rape holds that women provoke their attackers. Surely, many people think, a woman claiming to have been raped must have done *something* to encourage the man, to lead him on, to make him think that she really wanted to have sex. 7

In the case described above, didn't Sandra Abbott agree to have dinner with the man? Didn't she invite him into her room? Such self-doubt often paralyzes victims. But having dinner with a man—or even inviting him into her hotel room—is hardly a woman's statement of consent to have sex with him any more than she has agreed to have him beat her with a club. 8

A third myth is the notion that rape is simply sex. If there is no knife held to a woman's throat, or if she is not bound and gagged, then how can sex be a crime? The answer is simply that *forcing a woman to have sex without her consent is a violent crime*. To accept the idea that rape is sex one would also have to see no difference between brutal combat and playful wrestling. "Having sex" implies intimacy, caring, communication, and, most important of all, consent—none of which is present in cases of rape. Beyond the brutality of being physically violated, date rape also undermines the victim's sense of trust. This psychological burden is especially serious among rape victims under eighteen—half of the total—about one-fourth of whom are attacked by their own fathers. 9

The more people believe these myths about rape, the more women will fall victim to sexual violence. The ancient Babylonians stoned married women who became victims of rape, convinced that the women had committed adultery. Ideas about rape have changed little over thousands of years, which helps to explain why, even today, only about one in twenty rapes results in an offender being sent to jail. 10

Nowhere has the issue of date rape been more widely discussed than on the college campus. The collegiate environment promotes easy friendships and a sense of trust. At the same time, many students have a great deal to learn about relationships and about themselves. So while college life encourages communication, it also invites sexual violence. 11

To counter this problem, colleges have been facing—and debunking—myths about rape. In addition, attention has centered on the prevalence of alcohol in campus life and the effect of cultural patterns that define sex as a sport. To address the crisis of date rape, everyone needs to understand two simple truths: Forcing sex without a woman's consent is rape, and when a woman says "no," she means just that. 12

Building Vocabulary

For each question, use your dictionary and context clues to choose the meaning that most nearly defines the underlined word or phrase as it is used in the essay.

1. The word pondered most nearly means
   a. perused.
   b. reserved.
   c. wondered.
   d. plotted.
2. The word animated most nearly means
   a. meaningless.
   b. animalistic.
   c. dull.
   d. lively.
3. The word lingering most nearly means
   a. spending time.
   b. salivating.
   c. spending money.
   d. kissing.
4. The word angled most nearly means
   a. turned.
   b. longed.
   c. became eligible.
   d. hinted.
5. The word contacts most nearly means
   a. contracts.
   b. associates.
   c. conduct.
   d. corrective lenses.
6. The word myth most nearly means
   a. legend.
   b. lie.
   c. false belief.
   d. theory.

7. The word violated most nearly means
   a. threatened.
   b. sexually active.
   c. touched.
   d. assaulted.
8. The word undermines most nearly means
   a. weakens.
   b. reinforces.
   c. precludes.
   d. determines.
9. The word debunking most nearly means
   a. discrediting.
   b. hiding.
   c. proving.
   d. debasing.
10. The word prevalence most nearly means
   a. enjoyment.
   b. widespread existence.
   c. condemnation.
   d. sale.

Understanding the Essay

1. Which statement most nearly expresses the main idea of the essay?
   a. Date rape is a common occurrence on college campuses.
   b. False ideas about rape can encourage sexual crime against women.
   c. To prevent rape, women should "just say no."
   d. Increasing penalties for rape and decreasing campus alcohol use are the solutions to the problem of date rape.
2. Which method of introduction does the author use?
   a. anecdote
   b. broad to narrow
   c. quotation
   d. contrast
3. The author implies that Sandra Abbott did not run or physically resist the man who raped her because
   a. she was afraid her attacker would kill her if she resisted.
   b. she felt inviting him in was the same thing as inviting him to have sex.

c. she was afraid of looking foolish in front of her colleagues.
d. she was asleep at the time of the attack.

4. According to the author, which of the following is *not* a myth about rape?
   a. Most rapes do not result in the rapist being sent to jail.
   b. Victims are often guilty of behavior that implies an invitation to sex.
   c. Most rape victims do not know their attackers.
   d. If no weapon is used, then what some call rape is simply sex.
5. Which pattern(s) of development does the author use most predominantly?
   a. comparison-contrast
   b. definition and classification
   c. cause-effect
   d. narration and description
6. Which is *not* mentioned as a reason date rape is prevalent on college campuses?
   a. Alcohol use is relatively common.
   b. Students are naive and too trusting.
   c. Morals are more lax than in previous years.
   d. Some students have much to learn about relationships.
7. With which statement would the author most likely agree?
   a. Blaming women for rape began with the rise of feminism when women were no longer seen as under the protection of husbands and fathers.
   b. All instances of rape involve alcohol use.
   c. When a woman says "no," sometimes she means "yes" or "maybe."
   d. Not much progress has been made in the way people think about rape.

■ Looking at Language

8. Look at the language that Macionis uses to describe date rape, rapists, and rape victims. What specific word choices emphasize the seriousness of this crime?

____

____

9. Reread Sandra Abbott's statement in paragraph 3. The answer to her question, "Did he rape me?" ultimately requires Abbott to define the word *rape.* How do you define rape? Based on your definition, how would Abbott's question be answered?

____

____

10. The author writes, "'Having sex' implies intimacy, caring, communication, and, most important of all, consent." In your opinion, which of the four listed items is implied most strongly by the words *having sex?* Why? Which is implied least strongly? Why?

____

____

____

____

■ Discussing the Essay

Prepare to discuss the following questions in class by thinking about them or writing about them in your journal.

1. According to the author, how did the ancient Babylonians define rape? How did this definition affect women? What does your answer suggest about the power of language? About the power of those who define?
2. Is date rape a problem on your campus? What can be done to eliminate it on your campus or at other colleges?

Topics for Writing

Assignment 1: A Definition

Journal Entry

Write a journal entry giving your definition of rape.

Assignment 2: Police Business

Journal Entry

You are a police officer taking the statement of John L., a suspect arrested in a crime against his neighbor Kristen G. The suspect, John, uses the following excuses: "She invited me in." "She was always flaunting it." "What else was I supposed to do, with temptation right there in front of me?" John's crime, however, is not rape. Instead, he locked Kristen in a closet and stole her new Sony high-definition television. Use your imagination and write up John's statement in a journal entry.

Putting the traditional excuses for rape in the mouth of a television thief presents them in a new light and exposes their absurdity. This form of writing, called satire, uses humor to expose the faults of humanity or society.

Assignment 3: Causes of Date Rape

Essay

What factors do you believe account for the prevalence of date rape? Write an essay discussing them.

Assignment 4: Reluctance to Report

Essay

Write an essay discussing some reasons women might be reluctant to report date rape.

Assignment 5: Solving the Problem of Date Rape

Essay

What can be done to solve the problem of date rape on college campuses? Write an essay proposing your solutions to the problem, including why you think your solutions would work.

Assignment 6: Advice for a College Student

Essay

Macionis suggests that while a college atmosphere promotes trust, many students may be vulnerable because they "have a great deal to learn about relationships and about themselves."

Imagine that you have been asked to give advice to a student just beginning college. What are the three most valuable things that student needs to know before entering college? Your essay may be addressed to male students, female students, or both. It may touch on the subject of date rape or it may deal with other things entirely. It is simply your best advice to a beginning college student.

Education Unplugged

Floyd Allen

Does American society—and its education system—rely too heavily on technology? Writer Floyd Allen says it does.

1 My friend Mike was shaking his head in disbelief, and I could see the consternation on his face. I asked him what was wrong.

2 "You know the girl who just waited on me?" he asked, motioning to a fast-food employee with a nod of his head. "She just had to call someone over to help her make change from the drawer. The register told her I needed 99 cents, but she couldn't figure out how to count it out for me."

3 I understood Mike's concern, and, as an educator, I felt it myself. What we have done, albeit unintentionally, is to create several generations of individuals who no longer know how to think; how to research; how to be creative; and, in the worst-case scenario, how to survive.

4 The reason for these problems: pseudo-intelligence.

5 People no longer know how to think, how to do simple math, how to be creative. The reason for these problems: pseudo-intelligence. The perpetrators: digital watches, calculators, computers, video games, and VCRs.

6 It is time that we made a reality check regarding an educational system—and parents—that only teach our children how to operate an "on" button. The damage we are doing is irrevocable.

7 Our kids can't tell time if the clock/watch has hands. They cannot add, subtract, divide, and multiply. And they opt not to read because their imagination cannot create enough excitement to sustain interest. This creates not only a sad situation, but a dangerous one.

8 Extending this even further, society itself is endangered by its reliance on pseudo-intelligence. While visiting the library recently, I was informed that the computer, which houses the card catalog, was inoperable and I could not look up the books I needed to complete my research. When I asked to use the "old" system (you remember that one—it actually had cards), I was advised that it no longer existed.

9 If the computer in the grocery store goes down, we can't buy groceries.

10 When the system at the bank goes down, tellers can't perform certain transactions, or everything has to be done by hand, which slows things down immensely because so many of the employees don't know how to proceed without "the system."

It is not enough to recognize that a problem exists. What society needs is a solution. The one I offer is simple to suggest, but may be impossible to implement: We must unplug our children. 11

Instead of classrooms being inundated with electronic wizardry, let's get back to the basics of reading, writing, and arithmetic. Instead of teaching computer literacy, teachers should concentrate on teaching students to be literate. The students should be instructed and encouraged not to rely on electronic "brains," but to think and figure for themselves. 12

This process must begin in the home, not the classroom. 13

My children were not to have digital watches until they could tell time on a standard clock. Reading is not merely suggested or encouraged in my house—it is mandated. Video games, TV and movie videos are a welcome treat, not daily sustenance. 14

Unless the majority of parents take similar stands, and demand that our educators do the same, pseudo-intelligence will run rampant in our society, until eventually any foe can simply unplug us and grind society to a halt. 15

Building Vocabulary

For each question, use your dictionary and context clues to choose the meaning that most nearly defines the underlined word or phrase as it is used in the essay.

1. The word consternation most nearly means
   a. joy.
   b. confusion.
   c. concern.
   d. smile.
2. The word albeit most nearly means
   a. intentionally.
   b. not.
   c. such.
   d. although.
3. The word scenario most nearly means
   a. situation.
   b. ambiance.
   c. fast-food place.
   d. scenery.

4. The word pseudo-intelligence most nearly means
   a. high intelligence.
   b. low intelligence.
   c. false intelligence.
   d. true intelligence.
5. The word perpetrators most nearly means
   a. participants.
   b. offenders.
   c. machines.
   d. controls.
6. The word irrevocable most nearly means
   a. recommended.
   b. not damaging.
   c. negligible.
   d. irreversible.
7. The word inoperable most nearly means
   a. irreparable.
   b. not working.
   c. high-tech.
   d. not state of the art.
8. The word implement most nearly means
   a. act on.
   b. prevent.
   c. talk about.
   d. pay for.
9. The word mandated most nearly means
   a. recommended.
   b. required.
   c. forbidden.
   d. enjoyed.
10. The word rampant most nearly means
    a. overtly.
    b. clandestinely.
    c. intelligently.
    d. uncontrolled.

Understanding the Essay

1. Another title that would fit the essay is
   a. "Technology: A New Frontier"
   b. "Computers in the Classroom"
   c. "Ban Technology Now"
   d. "Technology: Undermining Education"
2. Which method of introduction does the author use?
   a. anecdote
   b. broad to narrow
   c. quotation
   d. contrast
3. Which of the following does the author *not* mention as a form of pseudo-intelligence?
   a. calculators
   b. computers
   c. robots
   d. VCRs
4. According to the author, reliance on technology affects three of the following skills. Which skill is *not* mentioned in the essay?
   a. reading
   b. writing
   c. researching
   d. telling time
5. The example of the library catalog is used to illustrate
   a. overreliance on technology.
   b. kids who lack basic skills.
   c. the author's lack of research skills.
   d. the wisdom of banning computers from classrooms.
6. Which of the following bumper stickers would the author most likely display?
   a. "Video Maniac"
   b. "Online and Loving It"
   c. "I'd Rather Be Net Surfing"
   d. "If You Think Education Is Expensive, Try Ignorance"

7. The technique used in the concluding paragraph is mainly
   a. recommendation.
   b. summary and closing thought.
   c. full circle.
   d. prediction.

Looking at Language

8. The author sees technology as a threat, and the language he uses reflects that view. Below write five words or phrases the author uses to suggest the danger of technology or its effects.

   ____

   ____

   ____

9. Which of the following transitional expressions would work best after the second sentence in paragraph 8?
   a. However
   b. Instead
   c. For example
   d. Although
10. In paragraph 12, the author begins two sentences with the words *instead of.* What is the most likely reason for the repetition?
   a. It shows the possible alternatives.
   b. Repetition adds coherence by emphasizing the similarity of the ideas.
   c. It makes the paragraph redundant.
   d. There are no synonyms for *instead of.*

Discussing the Essay

Prepare to discuss the following questions in class by thinking about them or writing about them in your journal.

1. Do you agree with Allen that we depend too much on machines? If so, should we "pull the plug" as he suggests?
2. Discuss Allen's "worst-case scenario"—that of not knowing how to survive. What kind of disaster might make ours a society with no

technology? What skills would be most important in that kind of world?

Topics for Writing

Assignment 1: Essential Machinery

Journal Entry

What one machine would you find it hard to live without? Why? Answer in a journal entry.

Assignment 2: Technology in the Classroom

Essay

Write an essay in which you argue for or against the use of computers, word processors, or calculators in schools.

Assignment 3: The Effects of Television

Essay

Write an essay discussing the effects of television on a specific audience. For example, you could discuss the effect of soap operas on a child's view of money, sex, and use of drugs and alcohol. Or you could discuss the effects of commercials aimed at older Americans (for instance, commercials for nutritional supplements, various drugs, or adult diapers) on a young adult's expectations about old age. Below are lists of possible audiences and types of programming. Mix and match as you wish, or come up with your own categories.

Possible Audiences	Possible Programming
children	soap operas
teenagers	talk shows
people over 65	music television
people whose second language is English	true crime shows
males	public television
females	cooking shows
poor people	at-home shopping shows
lonely people	home and garden shows
people with credit problems	news programs
dieters	financial advice shows

Assignment 4: A Post-Technological Society

Essay

Write an essay in which you imagine that depletion of oil and other fuels has made us a post-technological society, that is, one that has no technology because no fuel remains to run it. We cannot use our air conditioners, computers, cars, televisions, or riding lawnmowers. Your CD player is silent, and you are using your CD collection as a coaster set. Write an essay discussing three important changes in this post-technological society. To better visualize the new society, consider the following prewriting questions: What kinds of jobs would be available? Who would be highest paid? What formerly high-paying jobs would now be unimportant? Who would our heroes be?

Should College Athletes Be Paid?

Steve Wulf

College teams often bring in enormous revenue for the school. Is it time for athletes to receive a piece of the pie? Steve Wulf considers the question.

They are required to put in long hours of work for next to nothing, often in hostile conditions, always under the intense scrutiny of their bosses. They are imported from faraway places, isolated from the rest of the population and ultimately exploited for their sweat. Migrant farm workers? Child seamstresses for Kathie Lee? No, we're talking here about major college-football players. 1

Hard as it is for some of us to admit, the Dink-Stover-at-Yale days are over. 2 The ideal notion that a lad should just be grateful for the education he receives in exchange for a few hours of practice and the glory of Saturday afternoon is as dead as the dropkick. Who knows what the time of death was? It might have been when the shoe companies began dropping unmarked bills on coaches to wear their swooshes and stripes. It might have been when NBC decided to pay holier-than-thou Notre Dame $38 million for the exclusive rights to five football seasons. It might have been the day—true story—that a student-athlete was asked to get rid of his soda at a press conference sponsored by a different soft-drink company. How is it that Tennessee quarterback Peyton Manning gets nothing when a Peyton Manning jersey sold for $70 in Knoxville? According to Walter Byers, the executive director of the NCAA from 1952 to 1987, "The coaches own the athlete's feet, the colleges own the athlete's bodies, and the supervisors retain the large rewards. That reflects a neoplantation mentality on the campus that is not appropriate at this time of high dollars."

For Byers to admit that is somewhat akin to Pope John Paul II recanting his 3 stance on women in the priesthood. Byers' recent change of heart, set forth in his book, *Unsportsmanlike Conduct: Exploiting College Athletes* (University of Michigan Press), came with his realization that "the wheel of fortune is badly unbalanced in favor of the overseers and against the players." His call has been taken up by coaches, administrators, journalists and the athletes themselves. Some of the more radical proponents of change wonder openly about the possibility of a strike on, say, the eve of the championship in basketball's Final Four.

Student athletes would probably never go that far; they have been pro- 4 grammed to obey, not rebel. The elite ones also have the option of abandoning school before their eligibility expires and signing a pro contract, something they are doing in ever increasing numbers after ever decreasing course hours. That's one of the reasons the NCAA is finally looking into granting intercollegiate athletes, many of whom come from disadvantaged backgrounds, some financial relief. Other reasons are their susceptibility to glad-handing agents and boosters, the alarming number of incidents of petty theft and hostility involving jocks—just check today's sports section—and the isolation of athletes from the rest of the campus. "I would love to see college athletes have a little spending money," says Archie Manning, Peyton's father and a quarterback legend at Ole Miss a quarter-century ago. "I've been outside college dressing rooms, and I'm ready to go to dinner with my family, and I see kids going back to the dorm who can't afford to do anything."

Back when Archie played, football players were given a modest "laundry stipend" of fifteen dollars. Nowadays they don't even get that, though television-rights fees have increased exponentially, and shoe money has pushed the income of some coaches into seven figures. According to NCAA rules, a player can't hold a part-time job during the school year, lest he neglect his studies, or worse, be given a no-show, easy-money position. The current executive director of the NCAA, Cedric Dempsey, has appointed a special committee to explore ways to help the welfare of student athletes. 5

Yes, yes, student athletes should be grateful for the educational opportunities afforded them, not to mention the cost of tuition, books, room and board (worth about $12,000 at a large state university like Tennessee). But who can blame them if they feel resentful at the millions of dollars being made off their talents? No wonder so many turn pro so early; no wonder so many succumb to Faustian handshakes with agents. University of Maryland president William E. Kirwan, who is heading the NCAA special committee, says, "We realize we underestimated the magnitude of the problem. We estimate that 90% of those who would be picked in the first round of a pro draft have had some form of contact with agents and perhaps received improper gifts. I don't think there's anyone who would look at the system as it is and say this is how it should be." 6

Here's a modest math problem for presidents and student athletes alike: Multiply $100 a month times nine months times the 130,000 Division I men and women who juggle sports and academics. The answer is $117 million, or peanuts compared with what major college sports generate in TV revenue, gate receipts and apparel sales, not to mention the untold bounty from endowments and name recognition so dependent on football and basketball. In fact $117 million is about what a network would pay to televise the oft-discussed college Super Bowl. 7

Building Vocabulary

For each question, use your dictionary and context clues to choose the meaning that most closely defines the underlined word or phrase as it is used in the essay.

1. The word scrutiny most nearly means
   a. scruples.
   b. relationship.
   c. encouragement.
   d. supervision.
2. The word akin most nearly means
   a. alien.
   b. related.
   c. different.
   d. dubious.
3. The word recanting most nearly means
   a. refusing.
   b. recounting.
   c. taking back.
   d. repeating again.
4. The word proponents most nearly means
   a. opponents.
   b. supporters.
   c. strikers.
   d. officials.
5. The word susceptibility most nearly means
   a. resistance.
   b. support.
   c. payments.
   d. vulnerability.
6. The word stipend most nearly means
   a. stipulation.
   b. allowance.
   c. detergent.
   d. loan.
7. The word exponentially most nearly means
   a. at a fast-growing rate.
   b. modestly.
   c. in the same manner.
   d. slowly.

8. The word afforded most nearly means
   a. spent.
   b. able to buy.
   c. given.
   d. educated.
9. The phrase succumb to most nearly means
   a. give in to.
   b. support.
   c. ignore.
   d. reject.
10. The word magnitude most nearly means
    a. size.
    b. solution.
    c. exaggeration.
    d. attitude.

Understanding the Essay

1. Which statement most nearly expresses the main idea of the essay?
   a. College football players are required to work long hours under the scrutiny of their bosses.
   b. College athletes do not get the recognition or appreciation they deserve.
   c. Because college athletics brings in so much money for schools, athletes should be paid.
   d. College athletes should be paid because many are disadvantaged and cannot afford to go out to dinner.
2. The phrase "Dink-Stover-at-Yale days" probably refers to
   a. a winning season for Yale.
   b. a time when players were content to play for love of the game.
   c. a scandal involving a shoe company representative and a Yale football coach.
   d. the years from 1952 to 1987.
3. The author implies that Walter Byers, former executive director of the NCAA,
   a. has recently changed his mind about paying college athletes.
   b. has always favored paying college athletes.
   c. has a neoplantation mentality.

   d. admits in his book that he has been guilty of unsportsmanlike conduct and exploitation.

4. According to the author, a strike by college athletes on the eve of an important tournament is
   a. a certainty if treatment of college athletes does not improve.
   b. reason to dismiss every member of the team.
   c. of little consequence to the average American.
   d. not likely.

5. Which of the following is *not* cited as a reason that the NCAA is looking into paying college athletes?
   a. Too many good athletes are signing pro contracts rather than remaining on the school team.
   b. The NCAA views payment to athletes as the fair thing to do.
   c. Many athletes come from disadvantaged backgrounds.
   d. Many players are involved in incidents of hostility and petty theft.

6. Which of the following is not implied by the author?
   a. College athletes should avoid dealing with agents while on a college team.
   b. College athletes should focus on the game and on education, not on money.
   c. It is not good for a college athlete to sign a pro contract before his or her eligibility expires.
   d. Coaches and college administrators would probably not object to paying athletes.

7. The purpose of the "modest math problem" in the last paragraph is
   a. to show that the amount it might take to pay college athletes is relatively small.
   b. to show that although paying college athletes is a good idea, it would be far too costly.
   c. to test the reader's mathematical ability.
   d. to show how many athletes would be affected.

Looking at Language

8. Wulf begins his essay with the word *they.* Where in the paragraph does the reader find out who "they" are? Why do you think Wulf uses this technique?

9. Walter Byers, the author of the book quoted in Wulf's essay, speaks of the "*neoplantation mentality*" of colleges and of their *ownership* of athlete's bodies. He says "the wheel of fortune is badly unbalanced in favor of the *overseers*." What associations do the italicized words bring to mind? Do you think Byers's word choice is deliberate?

10. The opening sentence of paragraph 6 begins "Yes, yes, student athletes should be thankful for the educational opportunities afforded them." Imagine the sentence without the first two words, "Yes, yes." What difference do those words make in the tone and meaning of the sentence? Why does the author use them?

Discussing the Essay

Prepare to discuss the following questions in class by thinking about them or writing about them in your journal.

1. According to the author, who favors paying college athletes? Can you think of anyone who might not favor it?
2. List some of the arguments Wulf uses to support the idea of paying college athletes. Are they sound? Why or why not?

Topics for Writing

Assignment 1: Two Viewpoints

Journal Entry

Write two paragraphs or journal entries, one from Viewpoint 1 and one from Viewpoint 2.

> Viewpoint 1: You are a college athlete, barred by NCAA rules from holding a part-time job. Your family is not wealthy. You have a full scholarship with room and board but have little extra money to spend. Should you be paid?
>
> Viewpoint 2: You are a single parent. You work all day at a dead-end job and attend evening classes, struggling to maintain your high B average and support your child. Do you think college athletes should be paid?

Assignment 2: Benefits of Being a Sports Fan

Essay

Sports fascinate Americans, who watch anything from T-ball to professional ice skating. In an essay, discuss the benefits that watching sports provides.

Assignment 3: Spotlight on Sports

Essay

Is too much emphasis placed on college athletics? Include in your essay your reasons for believing the way you do.

Assignment 4: Benefits of Playing a Sport

Essay

Are organized sports such as Little League good for children? If you believe they are, give specific examples of the benefits children derive from sports. If you believe organized sports are bad for children, give examples of the harm organized sports can do.

Assignment 5: Sports and You

Essay

Write an essay describing your relationship to sports. As a prewriting exercise, consider the following questions: Are you athletic? Do you enjoy playing competitive team sports, competitive one-on-one sports, or sports in which you compete only against your own best performance? If you are a spectator, what sports do you enjoy watching? Do you also read about sports and sports figures, collect memorabilia, or memorize statistics?

Reading, Writing, and . . . Ethics?

Larry Fennelly

While the tug-of-war over school prayer continues, violence and apathy in schools continue to grow. Larry Fennelly prescribes a dose of philosophy.

In propounding his now-famous "categorical imperative," the 18th-century German philosopher Immanuel Kant set up a hypothetical situation: He's in a difficult predicament, and he knows that telling a lie would extricate him. Yet, he says, "while I can will the lie, I can by no means will that lying should be a universal law. For with such a law there would be no promises at all." 1

Kant's "categorical imperative" sounds to our modern ears a lot like the Golden Rule, itself an idea which most of us would like to see more demonstrations of in daily life. Kant, of course, is but one of dozens, even hundreds, who have tried to come to grips with ethical philosophy and moral living. I mention Kant and others like him because they have a direct bearing on a dilemma that confronts us today. 2

Salvo after salvo has been fired in the editorial page war over prayer in the nation's public schools. No end is in sight; if anything, the partisans grow further apart. As violence, sexual activity and academic indifference creep steadily down the scale of age and school grade, the cry will only increase for some moral component to be included in the school curriculum. 3

But at the same time, as "diversity" continues to replace the notion of "melting pot" as the dominant descriptive concept of American life, it seems increasingly unlikely that any one moral, religious or spiritual doctrine will be found that is acceptable to all—Protestants, Catholics, Jews, Muslims, Taoists and others. 4

The problem is compounded by the lack of unanimity among the various branches of each of the major religions. While to an outsider, all members of the same faith may look the same, somebody's law says that the closer two denominations are, the fiercer their differences. And when there actually are significant differences, the misunderstandings can increase exponentially. I recently received a pamphlet raising the question, "Are Catholics Christians?" 5

If not prayer, then what? It seems madness to keep building more prisons or mandate stiffer sentences for young offenders. These measures are not working, either as prevention or cure: The recidivism rate is enormous. 6

So it is that, as a non-controversial alternative, I propose that a unit on ethics be included in the school curriculum at appropriate levels. A study of the 7 historical development of various ethical systems by the world's philosophers—not to be confused with a course of comparative religion, which might again cause tempers to flare—could not help but focus attention on correct behavior and the consequences of human action.

Skeptics, especially those who have studied ethics or some other form of philosophy themselves, will hoot at this proposal, not because they themselves did not benefit from such instruction but because they will recall the difficult reading level of much philosophical writing. It is true that the original writings of the likes of Aristotle, Boethius, Descartes, Epicurus, Hegel, Kant, Mill, Rousseau, Voltaire and Wittgenstein can be tough going, even for an honor student. 8

But the argument that many students wouldn't be capable of reading the assignments won't hold water. Ethics can be discussed intelligently at any reading level; it's not necessary for students to read the original texts. Furthermore, in reading as in physical fitness training, it is only through continued challenge that we see improvement. In fact, teaching school children about contrasting ethical theories would undoubtedly, as a bonus, raise reading levels, improve vocabulary and lead to higher SAT scores. Indeed, one branch of philosophy that was taught frequently in high school is logic—a study which would definitely pay at SAT time. 9

We live in an age which—be it true or not—is widely regarded as a time of spiritual, moral and philosophical decline. The study of philosophy would address two of those issues, and perhaps even the third, and do so in a way not likely to offend any segment of our diverse society. 10

In the 1950s, Will Durant's *The Story of Philosophy* sold more than 1,250,000 copies. This best seller was then regarded as a "must" for every intelligent person's library. But that was before our philosophers and ethicists had names like Donahue, Raphael and Winfrey. 11

Building Vocabulary

For each question, use your dictionary and context clues to choose the meaning that most nearly defines the underlined word or phrase as it is used in the essay.

1. The word propounding most nearly means
   a. disproving.
   b. owning up to.
   c. presenting.
   d. impounding.
2. The phrase a hypothetical situation most nearly means
   a. a real instance.
   b. an imaginary instance.
   c. a scientific maxim.
   d. an experimental environment or a laboratory.

3. The word extricate most nearly means
   a. blame.
   b. free.
   c. distinguish.
   d. incriminate.
4. The phrase a universal law probably refers to
   a. a law of physics, such as the law of gravity.
   b. speculation about the origin of the universe.
   c. a rule that everyone should follow.
   d. a rule that involves lying.
5. The phrase ethical philosophy most nearly means
   a. customs of various cultures.
   b. philosophy that is hard to understand.
   c. an act that people frown on.
   d. beliefs about right and wrong.
6. The word dilemma most nearly means
   a. problem.
   b. solution.
   c. rule.
   d. mediation.
7. The word unanimity most nearly means
   a. agreement.
   b. animation.
   c. religious feeling.
   d. argument.
8. The word mandate most nearly means
   a. prohibit.
   b. soften.
   c. lengthen.
   d. require.
9. The phrase recidivism rate most nearly means
   a. rate of crime committed by adult offenders.
   b. the rate at which a number is redivided.
   c. the rate at which offenders are rehabilitated.
   d. the rate at which offenders return to prison.

10. The word segment most nearly means
    a. part.
    b. social agency.
    c. leader.
    d. class.

Understanding the Essay

1. According to the author, Kant's categorical imperative is
    a. a rule that helped Kant lie his way out of a tough situation.
    b. a law that governs situations not covered by religion.
    c. a lot like the Golden Rule.
    d. a law that applied in the eighteenth century but is not relevant to modern life.
2. Based on information in the first paragraph, which of the following most exactly states Kant's categorical imperative?
    a. Telling a lie is acceptable if it is the only way to get yourself out of trouble, but a person who lies must be willing to accept the consequences.
    b. Before acting, you should decide if your actions would work as a universal law; that is, decide if it would be acceptable for everyone else to act in that way.
    c. Make no promises and tell no lies.
    d. Do unto others before they do unto you.
3. All of the following ideas are mentioned in the essay. Which is *not* an argument against school prayer?
    a. The idea of diversity is replacing the notion of the "melting pot."
    b. It is unlikely that one doctrine would be acceptable to all faiths.
    c. "The closer two denominations are, the fiercer their differences."
    d. The recidivism rate of youthful offenders is on the rise.
4. According to the author, what would be the main benefit of ethics as a part of the school curriculum?
    a. It would allow students to compare different ethical systems throughout history.
    b. It would put a focus on correct behavior.
    c. It would ensure a reduction in the crime rate.
    d. It would promote a rise in vocabulary and SAT scores.

5. Which method of development is used predominantly in the essay?
   a. comparison-contrast
   b. definition
   c. argument
   d. process
6. What criticism does the author believe skeptics might raise toward his proposal?
   a. Teaching ethics is too controversial and would cause needless friction among different religious groups.
   b. Ancient ethical beliefs are irrelevant to modern society.
   c. Ethics leaves God out of the classroom.
   d. Students would have a hard time understanding philosophical readings.
7. Which statement most nearly expresses the main idea of the essay?
   a. Teaching ethics in schools is a categorical imperative.
   b. Teaching ethics in schools is a possible solution to a social problem and a good alternative to school prayer.
   c. Prayer in schools would cause too much divisiveness among different religious groups.
   d. Teaching ethics in school is not the same thing as teaching religion in school.

■ Looking at Language

8. What is the level of vocabulary in the essay? What assumption do you think the author makes about his audience?

   ____

   ____

9. Explain what the author means by this comparison: "in reading as in physical fitness training, it is only through continued challenge that we see improvement."

   ____

   ____

   ____

   ____

10. In paragraph 10, the author writes, "We live in an age which—be it true or not—is widely regarded as a time of spiritual, moral and philosophical decline. The study of philosophy would address two of those issues, and perhaps even the third, and do so in a way not likely to offend any segment of our diverse society." Which issues are the two that philosophy would address? Which is the third that philosophy might address?

Discussing the Essay

Prepare to discuss the following questions in class by thinking about them or writing about them in your journal.

1. What is the difference between seeing American life as culturally diverse and seeing it as a "melting pot"? What are the benefits and drawbacks of each view?
2. What does Fennelly mean when he says "that was before our philosophers and ethicists had names like Donahue, Raphael and Winfrey"? How do you think he feels about these new ethicists? How do you feel about them?
3. Immanuel Kant decided against lying after considering whether he could recommend it as a general principle. That is, he considered what would happen if everyone else in his situation lied. What do you think Kant would say to a person about to try drugs for the first time, to a person about to cheat on a test, to a person about to rob someone else, or to a person about to have unprotected sex? What ideas might he ask them to consider?

Topics for Writing

Assignment 1: Bumper Sticker Philosophy

Journal Entry

If you had to boil down your philosophy of life to fit onto a bumper sticker, what would that bumper sticker say? Why? Discuss in a journal entry.

Assignment 2: Your Ethical Principles

Essay

In an essay, describe the principles you use in trying to live an ethical life. Give specific examples showing how you put these principles into action.

Assignment 3: Causes and Cures

Essay

Fennelly observes that violence, sexual activity, and academic indifference are occurring at younger and younger ages. Write an essay discussing the reasons for this trend. Alternatively, write an essay proposing solutions to violence, sexual activity, and/or academic indifference in today's youth.

Assignment 4: Making Ethical Decisions

Essay

What is the most difficult moral decision you have ever faced? How did you solve it?

Acknowledgments

Maya Angelou, "Complaining" from *Wouldn't Take Nothing for My Journey Now* by Maya Angelou. Copyright © 1993 by Maya Angelou. Reprinted by permission of Random House, Inc.

Mark Twain, "Two Ways of Seeing a River" from *Life on the Mississippi* by Mark Twain (1883).

Sara J. Gonzalez, "Growing Up Bilingual" from *The Atlanta Journal/Constitution* (September 18, 1995). Copyright © 1995 by Sara J. Gonzalez. Reprinted with the permission of the author.

Jeff Obafemi Carr, "The Game of My Life" from *Essence* (March 1997). Copyright © 1997 by Jeff Obafemi Carr. Reprinted with the permission of the author.

Sono Motoyama, "Rebel with a Dye Job" from *The New York Times Magazine* (August 4, 1996). Copyright © 1996 by The New York Times Company. Reprinted by permission of Sono Motoyama.

Athlone G. Clarke, "When Words Get in the Way" from *The Atlanta Journal/Constitution* (January 30, 1995). Reprinted with the permission of *The Atlanta Journal* and *The Atlanta Constitution.*

Patricia Raybon, "Letting in Light" from *The New York Times Magazine* (February 21, 1993), "Hers" column. Copyright © 1993 by The New York Times Co. Reprinted with permission.

Roberta Moore, Barbara Baker, and Arnold H. Packer, "Coping with Procrastination" by Roberta Moore, Barbara Baker, and Arnold H. Packer, from *College Success.* Copyright © 1997 by Prentice-Hall, Inc. Reprinted by permission.

Candace Dyer, "Migraine Blues" (editor's title, originally titled "A Big Headache") from *The Macon Telegraph* (September 9, 1996). Reprinted with the permission of the publishers.

Norman Cousins, "The Right to Die" by Norman Cousins, from *Writing for Love or Money: Thirty-Five Essays Reprinted from the Saturday Review of Literature* (Essay Index Reprint Series) by Norman Cousins (Editor), (North Stratford, NH: Ayer Publishing, 1980). ISBN: 0836915348. Used with the permission of the Eleanor Cousins Trust.

John Head, "The Brutal Business of Boxing" from *The Atlanta Journal/Constitution* (June 12, 1995). Reprinted with the permission of *The Atlanta Journal* and *The Atlanta Constitution.*

John J. Macionis, "Date Rape: Exposing Dangerous Myths" from *Sociology,* Sixth Edition, by John J. Macionis. Copyright © 1997 by John J. Macionis. Reprinted by permission of Pearson Education, Inc., Upper Saddle River, NJ.

Floyd Allen, "Education Unplugged" (editor's title, originally titled "Pull the Plug") from *The Atlanta Journal/Constitution* (September 14, 1995). Copyright © 1995 by Floyd Allen. Reprinted with the permission of the author.

Steve Wulf, "Should College Athletes Be Paid?" (editor's title, originally titled "Tote That Ball, Lift That Revenue") from *Time* (October 21, 1996). Copyright © 1996 TIME Inc., reprinted by permission.

Larry Fennelly, "Reading, Writing, and . . . Ethics?" (editor's title, originally titled "Ethics Unit Would be a Good Alternative to School Prayer") from *The Macon Telegraph* (January 9, 1995). Reprinted with the permission of the publishers.

Index

Texas Academic Skills Program Objectives

Florida Exit Test Competencies